I TATTI STUDIES IN
ITALIAN RENAISSANCE HISTORY

Published in collaboration with I Tatti
The Harvard University Center for Italian Renaissance Studies
Florence, Italy

GENERAL EDITOR
Kate Lowe

BEING A JESUIT IN RENAISSANCE ITALY

Biographical Writing in the Early Global Age

CAMILLA RUSSELL

Harvard University Press
Cambridge, Massachusetts
London, England
2022

Copyright © 2022 by the President and Fellows of Harvard College
All rights reserved
Printed in the United States of America

First printing

Library of Congress Cataloging-in-Publication Data

Names: Russell, Camilla, author.
Title: Being a Jesuit in Renaissance Italy : biographical writing in the early
   global age / Camilla Russell.
Other titles: I Tatti studies in Italian Renaissance history.
Description: Cambridge, Massachusetts : Harvard University Press, 2022. |
   Series: I Tatti studies in Italian Renaissance history | Includes bibliographical
   references and index.
Identifiers: LCCN 2021016803 | ISBN 9780674261129 (cloth)
Subjects: LCSH: Jesuits—Italy—History—17th century—Sources. | Jesuits—
   Biography—Sources. | Jesuits—Historiography.
Classification: LCC BX3737 .R87 2021 | DDC 271/.53045—dc23
LC record available at https://lccn.loc.gov/2021016803

For Mario

CONTENTS

Introduction: A New Society and Its Jesuits, 1540–1640   1
1   Vocation and Entry   18
2   Candidates for Overseas Missions   52
3   Being a Jesuit in the "Indies"   86
4   On the Italian Home Front   115
5   Deaths and Departures   146
     Afterword: Writing Jesuit Lives   173

NOTES   179

ACKNOWLEDGMENTS   255

INDEX   259

Introduction

A New Society and Its Jesuits, 1540–1640

In 1637, just under a century after the founding of the Society of Jesus, Giovanni Raffaele de Ferraris sought entry to the Jesuit novitiate in Rome. At fifty-one years old, widowed with two children, his was an unusual vocation to the Society. A lawyer by profession, he was from Piedmont, where he had also served in public life. We know this from a detailed questionnaire that he completed early in his probation. We also know from a separate document the exact number and type of goods that he brought with him at the time of entering. It was a long list of items, mainly clothing and some objects that display a relatively high degree of wealth, including "a hat, a silk mantle from Milan . . . a pair of hose . . . six shirts . . . two pairs of shoes," and, perhaps most surprising of all, "a fire arm." However, the traces of this Jesuit's life do not end there. Not long after, we hear from de Ferraris again, as a novice, on April 30, 1639, in a letter seeking appointment to the overseas missions, and addressed to the superior general of the whole Society. In his petition, he wrote of his burning desire to travel to the "Indies" despite his self-professed "demerits," including his "poverty of spirit, age, and physical weaknesses." His son, a Jesuit, was already there, and he wanted to join him, as well as serve the enterprise of evangelization to non-Christian peoples. In that same year, the catalogues that were produced regularly about every member of the Society confirmed that his health was poor, that he was gifted with high intelligence, and that he showed talent for governance. Despite his abilities, presumably due to his age and ill health, he died not in the Indies but in Italy, as recorded in Rome in 1642.[1]

The Jesuit de Ferraris and others who, like him, lived in the Society's first century, are the protagonists of this book. The biographical documents that underpin the study are all located in the Archivum Romanum Societatis Iesu (ARSI). These documents were produced to aid the organization and governance of the Society, but they also recorded the spiritual and communal life envisaged by its founding leader, Ignatius of Loyola (1491–1556) and the first companions, while in some cases they were written with an eye to posterity. There are scores of these documents in the Roman archive, including letters, petitions, personnel catalogues, confidential reports, and life narratives. They are the primary focus of this book, which enlists them to follow the earliest generations of Jesuits in their own words.[2]

Using the image of a genealogical tree, the book views the documents as though they were branches in a tree, tracing a number of common features to their roots—the Society's foundational texts. The result is not the idealized portrait, the so-called Ignatian Tree presented to Jesuits and the wider world as securely grounded, seamlessly encompassing the world, and harmonious, with all of its roots and branches in place (see Figure 1). While this image certainly reflected the aims of the Society, the fruits of Jesuit efforts were not always the intended ones, nor did they necessarily meet with success. The triumphalist celebrations of the first century in 1640 gave way in the following century to a gradual unraveling that culminated in the ignominy of a worldwide papal suppression between 1773 and 1814, represented in one satirical report as a felled tree (see Figure 2). The "tree" in the portrait that follows is constituted of myriad textual elements recorded about dozens of members, often exchanged across great distances. Laying bare both individual and organizational experience in Italian lands and beyond, the study's documents will be used to garner a sense of not only what it was like to be a member of the Society of Jesus, but also what the Society itself was like.[3]

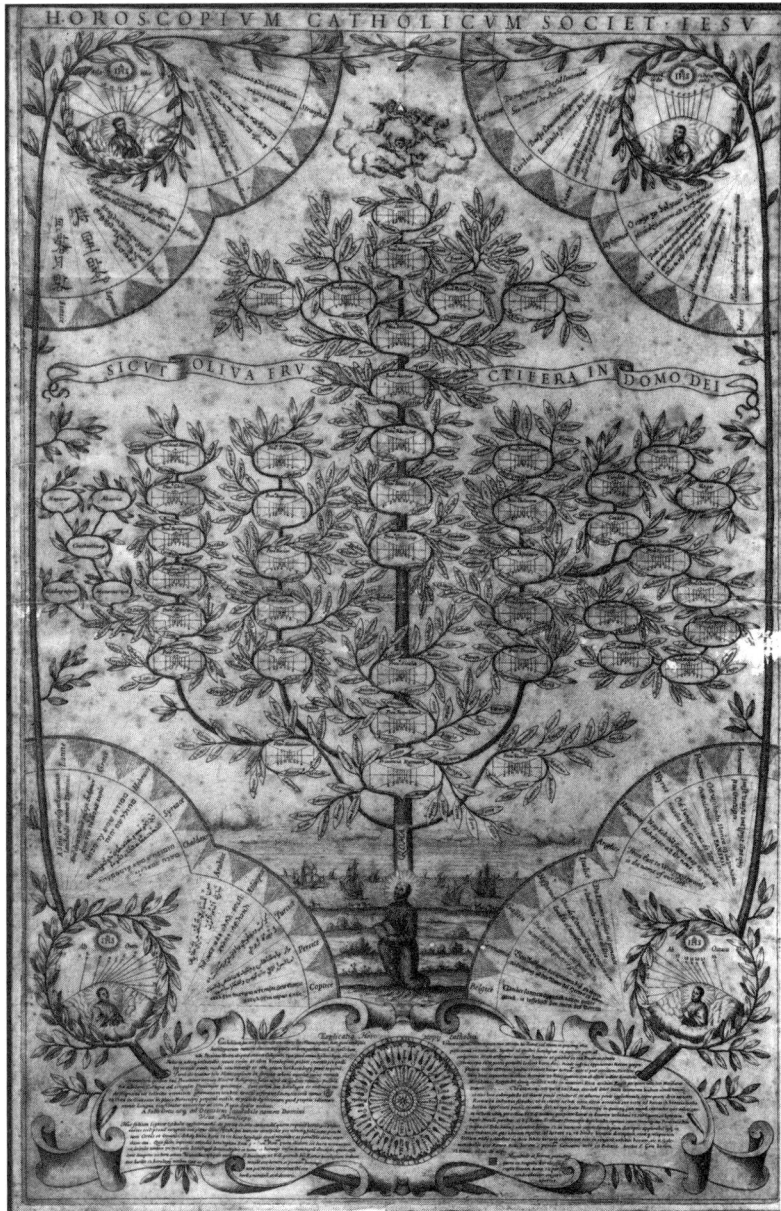

Figure 1. Ignatian Tree, or "Horoscopium catholicum." Athanasius Kircher, *Ars magna lucis et umbrae* (2nd ed., 1671). Reproduction © Archivum Romanum Societatis Iesu.

Figure 2. The Suppression of the Society of Jesus. Published satirical engraving from 1773, Fototeca, fondo 1, 10. Reproduction © Archivum Romanum Societatis Iesu.

I argue that the biographical records, grounded in Jesuit foundational texts, contained three core characteristics: they were relational, factual, and spiritual. These features provide the interpretive lens for analyzing the sources in this book. They also provide a key, I argue, to understanding the Society of Jesus: how it worked, its appeal to the documents' authors who joined it, as well as the influence it exercised—in Renaissance Italy where it was forged, and in the early global age that it sought to shape.

Jesuit biographical documents naturally have been used in previous studies to furnish evidence about numerous themes, single members, and the Society's institutional history more broadly.[4] This book does something different by identifying them as a specific genre, and placing them at the center of the study—and not in the background. The documents drive the analysis in a number of distinct ways. By following the grain of their contents and taking account of the contexts and motivations for their production, as much as possible, individuals are allowed to speak for themselves. The result is a new view of the early Jesuits, derived from perspectives that came from "within" rather than from "above" or "outside" the Society, as with institutional histories. Its biographical focus is not limited to a single life story, like traditional biographies, nor does it attempt a comprehensive analysis of the many Jesuit lives that it surveys, in the vein of prosopographical research.[5] Instead, it seeks to recreate qualitatively through the texts and from multiple perspectives the broad outlines of life in the Society.

The sources have also informed the book's geographical focus. The largest number of biographical documents from 1540 to 1640 were generated and preserved from the Italian Assistancy, one of the administrative groups (with oversight of five provinces, Rome, Naples, Sicily, Venice, and Lombardy) into which the Society was organized. Italy in many ways was center stage: this was where the distinctively hierarchical and centralized worldwide Society established itself, in Rome, the place of the Society's ratification and where the *Constitutions* (from 1547; printed 1558–1559) stipulated its governance and the residence of the superiors general. The *Constitutions* stated, "That the location may be favorable for communication between the head and his members, it can be a great help for the general to reside for the most part in Rome, where communications with all regions can more easily be maintained."[6] In the "Ignatian Tree" in Figure 1, the word "Rome" is placed just above Ignatius, in the lower center of the trunk, the most stable and broadest part of the tree. This was the hub through which records pertaining to the Society's worldwide operations flowed and where they were carefully preserved.

Large numbers of vocations came from the Italian peninsula and its islands: at the Society's most important novitiate, S. Andrea al Quirinale, in Rome, over 3,340 men and boys are registered as having entered between 1556 (when records began) and 1640, an average of thirty-nine per year, with the highest average of entrants in the first thirteen years of records (an average of forty-six per year between 1556 and 1569). In Italy, a catalogue of Jesuits compiled for the first twenty-five years (1540–1565) counted 1,750 members. These Jesuits were part of a Society whose membership increased dramatically over its first century: in 1556 there were 1,500 members; in 1600 there were just over 8,500; in 1615 there were 13,000 members in thirty-two provinces; in 1626 there were over 15,000 Jesuits; that expanded further to over 17,000 in 1679 (before the 1773 papal suppression, there were over 22,000 Jesuits, recorded in 1749).[7]

Instructive as these numbers are, the purpose of this study is to give more meaning to them, through the documents, by situating members back into their lived experiences and environments. The Jesuits' vast documentary production often obscures from sight the settings in which their authors wrote; physcial environments remain relatively unseen, like a head without a body. This is understandable. In some senses, their letters *were* the Society. Other religious orders had their monastic houses and chapter meetings; bishops had their sees and parishes; but the Jesuits had their letters, which made up the edifice of the Society itself, overseen by its most prolific letter-writer, the superior general.[8] Figure 3 illustrates this point. It shows a Jesuit and his pen apparently having merged into one, the index finger of this elegantly cuffed manicule depicted rather humorously as having transformed into a quill pen.

Yet the Society was more than its textual records; it was conceived of as a *body,* made up of the members themselves, which were movable parts of a whole. Jesuit documentary production serviced this body and kept it united. It was the connecting point for the Society's many constituent elements, underpinned by the foundational texts. Especially important were the Ignatian *Spiritual Exercises* (begun 1521; first published 1548), the pro-

Figure 3. Manicule, with index finger depicted as a quill pen. *Hist. Soc.* 43 ("Defunti 1595–1642"), fol. 1r (detail). Reproduction © Archivum Romanum Societatis Iesu.

gram of meditation that every member took upon entry and generally annually ever after.[9] The *Exercises* pointed the way for Jesuits in their prayer, place, and action—what came to be termed as their "way of proceeding." The biographical documents functioned as the *Exercises'* continuation and application: with their multiple purposes and meanings—from the bureaucratic, to the intimate and personal, to the spiritual—they carried these roots within them and reveal a kind of genetic code of what made a Jesuit a Jesuit. The origins of these texts belong to the earliest years, when Ignatius insisted on regular correspondence with the first companions, as they progressed under his leadership from a loosely formed group to a papally ratified new religious institute of clerks regular in 1540. The Society's centralized structure meant that, from the beginning, correspondence was an essential tool in its dispersive operations. Mostly in the vernacular, it replaced verbal communication for those who could not meet in person and rapidly gained normative status in Jesuit practice, evolving into the many different types of biographical documents studied in this book.

Correspondence, further, became enshrined in the *Constitutions* as an organ of the Society's government, as one of the "aids toward the union of hearts," whereby "a very special help will be found in the exchange of letters." The first purpose of the documents thus was practical: to assist the Society's operations. Their second purpose related to method, as facilitator of multilateral communication. The *Constitutions* stated: "Some of the helpful means lie on the side of the subjects, others on the side of the superiors, and others on both sides." Communication was to take place both vertically—"between the subjects and the superiors"—and horizontally—such that "each region can learn from the others." The third purpose of the documents was concerned with their meaning, which was spiritual, providing "mutual consolation and edification in our Lord." Their contents perpetuated the view that in spiritual terms the whole world was a vineyard whose soil Jesuit laborers had the task to till (see the book's front cover). In sum, the Society's biographical documents were factual, dialogic, and edifying.[10]

The relational features that underpin the *Constitutions*' "union of hearts" are present also in the *Spiritual Exercises*. The fourth and final week of the meditation program describes the role of "love" in human activity as "a mutual communication between the two persons.... Each shares with the other."[11] This idea was translated organizationally into Jesuit epistolary practice. Juan Alfonso de Polanco (1517-1576) set the example in his role as Ignatius's secretary. Comparatively few letters survive from Ignatius before 1547, the year when Polanco became secretary to him and to the whole Society. After this time, the correspondence ballooned to several thousand letters—making Ignatius/Polanco probably the most prolific of all early modern letter writers.[12]

Polanco was responsible, too, for developing the Society's writing manual, the *Formula scribendi*, which went through a number of revisions and name changes between 1547 and its definitive version in 1578.[13] The spiritual meaning of these texts was not lost on him either: in 1547 (before the publication of the *Constitutions* and even of the *Spiritual Exercises*), Polanco devised a small text of "Instructions," consisting of "twenty spiritual considerations, to promote and maintain the regular practice of epistolary writing addressed to the Father [or superior] General." The instructions aimed to ensure "the unity of the Society, which, because of its vocation is dispersed in various parts, and much more than any other [religious order] necessitates communication to keep it together as one, and that is by way of continuous letters."[14]

This "apostolic" self-understanding and attendant communication practice made the Society midwife to the new global age. Many members did not stay in their hometowns or lands; they traveled near and far in their lifetimes, and this study follows the textual traces they generated (see map). At the same time, the book's focus on the Italian Jesuit provinces seeks to provide a geographical anchor to the Society's early history, which can tend to appear in a vacuum. In part, this is because of its self-understanding as being universal, rather than local, and as missionary, rather than grounded in any one particular place. The reality was more complex. It was a Society that attempted organizationally to override territorial and regional boundaries and at the same time governed through its assistancies and provinces, carefully identifying the point of entry or provenance of each member in its catalogues: "Parma," "Venezia," "Chieti," "Messina."[15] At the individual level, these place names marked the local parameters for many Jesuits' own worldviews and experiences. Members tended to identify themselves as inhabitants of a particular town, region, college, or novitiate, and perspectives tended to stay local, regardless of where the Jesuits were. With its starting point in the Italian provinces, the study seeks to reflect the many local contours of a Jesuit life, and take account of its universal ones, in its aim to see the Jesuits as they themselves did.[16]

The archival holdings on which this book is based reflect the hierarchical and centralized structure of the Society. Compared with other Jesuit archives, ARSI possesses a much higher number and better quality of documents, sent in from the "spokes" and converging on the "hub." In its narrowest sense, the Roman archive functions to preserve documents relating to the Society's governance, and this is the tenor of its holdings. In reality documents, books, and artifacts relating to almost any conceivable topic (and not just concerned with governance) converged on the Jesuit headquarters, making its archive a treasure trove of information and insight. It has its limits, however: individual provinces maintain their own archives and still do not transfer their internal documents to Rome. These have tended to fare less well than the Roman archive due to damage suffered through periods of war, suppression, expulsions, and other strife (or simple lack of funds), somewhat diminishing a precious window onto the horizontal dynamics that animated the Society along with its more vertical ones. There are of course notable exceptions, and further research using multiple Jesuit archives will shed more light on these connections between regional operations. While following the magnetic pull that Jesuit Rome exerts, my analyis attempts also to follow the multidirectional dynamics that appear in these sources.

The documents shape the study in other precise ways. The many constraints of the surviving documentation prompt a flexible approach:

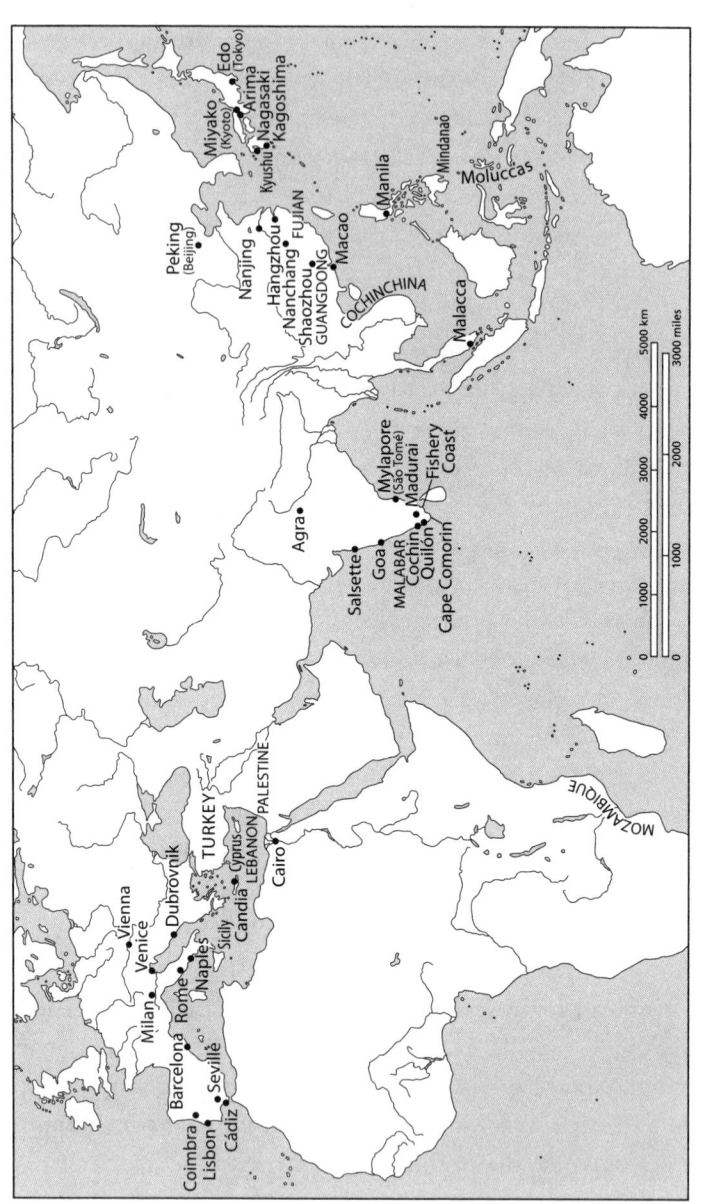

Map. Main places mentioned in the book.

several sources from the Italian provinces are restricted to certain arcs of time in the course of the century under consideration (for example, vocation questionnaires cover a later period, 1636–1644, while collated petitions for the Indies are extant from the late 1580s). Rather than analyzing the sources in the chronological order in which they were produced, or focusing on only one or a few individuals for their whole time in the Society, the book is ordered following key phases in a Jesuit life, from entry to departure or death. Dozens of individuals provide the focus, across several generations and time frames, not always presented in chronological order, with single Jesuits coming in and out of view.

The fact that the sources for each life phase are not available in chronological order—from Italy or indeed any province—means that the broader historical shifts, convulsions, and continuities of the Society's first century will come into focus in unexpected ways. A possible limitation of this approach is that developments, regressions, and changes over time may not be as visible as they need to be, and indeed were, while the documents treated out of chronological order may not reveal sufficiently the changing fortunes of the Society in its broader context. For this reason, the book should be read alongside the general histories of the Society. Despite their limitations, the sources provide a view of the Society that cannot be gleaned from an institutional or chronologically organized history.

The choice of documents is necessarily selective and is by no means exhaustive of the genre; there are many more biographical documents at ARSI than the study's scope permits for inclusion.[17] This means that the Society's many spheres of activity are represented to different degrees: the overseas missions receive focused analysis, while a sidelight is thrown on the equally important field of education. One of the aims of the study thus is to provide a framework for further research, including of a quantitative nature. Documents have been selected for the information they provide about single Jesuits, especially if that individual appears alongside his peers in similar documents, such as petitions, vocation statements, or questionnaires. They were ususally produced at a turning point, helping provide insight into not just the individual and his peers at key moments in a Jesuit life, but also how the Society worked from the contemporary perspective of those involved.[18]

The book is structured to follow a Jesuit life span. Chapter 1 looks at vocation and entry to the Society of Jesus; Chapter 2 turns to the allure of the Indies for many Jesuits. The relatively few Jesuits from the Italian provinces selected and sent to the overseas missions are the focus of Chapter 3, while Chapter 4 returns to the home front: What work did Jesuits in Italy do? How did they use their correspondence, catalogues, and self-narrative documents as they proceeded through the Society? Finally, Chapter 5 completes the Jesuit life cycle through departure, dismissal, or death, but not before pausing in our analysis over the memoirs that many Jesuits wrote toward the end of their lives at the behest of their superiors. These accounts ensured that the biographical document entered into the history-making of the Society of Jesus, pointing to its central place in Jesuit practice, spirituality, and identity; they also provide the compass for embarking on our exploration of the first century of the Jesuits in Italy.

Having thus presented the book's main aims, sources, and overall structure, before proceeding, I will outline the main historical, historiographical, and methodological approaches that underpin the analysis.

The Society's archival riches, and the Jesuit cultural impact more broadly, help explain the substantial scholarly interest of recent decades in Jesuit history, especially concerning the Old Society but increasingly also the New Society—that is, the period after its papal restoration in 1814.[19] The measured historiographical treatments in recent decades— written mostly by non-Jesuits but also by several members of the Society— have left behind partisan interpretations of the past. These lurched from hagiographic celebration (often written from within the Society) to demented attack (by critics who saw "wily Jesuits" around every corner pulling the strings of political power, or as the black-cassocked "shock troops" of the Counter-Reformation).[20] Even the famous injunction in the *Constitutions* about obedience resembling a lifeless corpse (*perinde ac cadaver*)—has been contextualized and given nuance, although rightly still cause for much debate. Scholars for some time now have embraced the call, first made by Luce Giard, and taken up by Antonella Romano and Pierre-Antoine Fabre, to a *désenclavement,* or "opening up" of Jesuit history from the religious history that once provided its frame of reference.[21]

Simon Ditchfield and others have asked: Should we consider the Jesuits to be a distinct, corporate entity, or a Society that was as diffuse as its individual members? By methodological consequence, should we investigate the Society as a product and reflection of the world in which it operated, or as a remarkable premodern anomaly?[22] Another question posed by current scholarship is how Jesuits navigated between conformity and conscience, between obedience and free will. These questions as well as possible answers help to steer the analysis that follows.[23]

One theme that has received relatively little attention outside the Society itself is the intersection between Jesuit spirituality and Jesuit history. This is despite the centrality of spirituality to understanding Jesuit identity and indeed the documents that underpin this study. Its significance lies in the specifically Ignatian understanding of "spirituality in action." At the beginning of the fourth week in the *Spiritual Exercises,* the following direction is given: "Love ought to manifest itself more by deeds than words." A Jesuit is to be grounded in prayer, to be sure—only a few paragraphs later, detailed instructions include one of three methods of praying by saying a single word, "Father," and "continue to consider the word as long as meanings, comparisons, relish, and consolations connected with it are found"—yet action is also required, as is work in the world, where "God dwells." This particular type of love-in-service is also relational: "If the one has knowledge, one gives it to the other who does not; and similarly, in regard to honors and riches. Each shares with the other."[24]

This approach characterized the missionary work that Jesuits engaged in and the method they used for it, but it also informed the "dialogic" relationships of Jesuits with each other, traceable in the texts analyzed here. In the Trinitarian view that Ignatius had of the Society, members operated not singly but in constant communion, animated by filial obedience and familiar exchange. The inspiration for applying this approach, unsurprisingly, was scriptural: Ignatius drew on Paul's epistles to the early Christian communities as his guide for how to turn religious insight into apostolic practice.[25]

The apostolic aims of the Society naturally were conditioned by the maleness of its protagonists, and the study takes account of scholarship in early modern masculinities to discern how gender, identity, and the articulation of both come into relief in the lives of these men.[26] Relatively little has been written about Jesuits and gender, although this is changing.[27] The history of Jesuits and women—after a few early experiments, female membership was permanently excluded—shaped the Society's history in distinct ways.[28] On the one hand, all-male membership made the Society more obviously masculine than other orders with both male and female arms. On the other hand, the *Spiritual Exercises* and *Constitutions* opened up opportunities for engagement with the female sphere: in the former case, the *Exercises* were available to women and, in the latter case, in more modern times, many female religious congregations adapted the *Constitutions* for the governance of their institutes. Jesuits famously served women as confessors, too.[29]

The Society itself, however, remained the preserve of men that precluded formal or close ties with women. This was a homosocial world, defined by its gendered organizational structure. Yet this study shows just how porous the Society was. For the Jesuit hierarchy, female patrons and donors were ever present in the records; so too were family members, especially if they were female and needed help (mothers, sisters, cousins).[30] More than that, the *Spiritual Exercises* did not distinguish between men and women: all could follow them, and the many women who wished to join the Jesuits in the early years, before Ignatius made his definitive decision to exclude them, may help explain why he did so. Perhaps the Society was *too* successful with women to be viewed as productive to its aim to go to the aid of "souls" wherever they were. Whatever the reason, identity in this context was tied up with questions of early modern masculinity, which these sources help to illuminate.

Another related theme concerns the lack of evidence of forced vocations in these texts; on the contrary, many were turned away. Vocation, thus, was closely linked to individual male agency in the context of the Society of Jesus, and both are key themes in the texts under discussion. Yet even in this selective religious institute, the records of voluntary entry to religious life should be seen in terms of the period's preoccupation with confessionalization. The role of organized religion as an agent of social control in the religious landscape of post-Reformation Europe is present in high relief in many of the lives and documents of these men, and it was accepted as how things should be.[31] Confessionalization, as these generations of men might have conceived of it, represented one of the legitimate frames for an ordered life. Unguided individual choice was relatively suspect both inside and outside religious life, for autonomy in a modern sense tended to be associated in this period with all kinds of dangers. This did not mean that Jesuits always conformed—my study shows that they did not on numerous occasions—but they navigated their roles as individual members, many with strong wills, within a clearly defined collective framework, based on obedience.

For this reason, I am not concerned with trying to locate in the writings of these Jesuits evidence of freestanding individuals, or even of their direct unmediated relationship with God.[32] While this was possible in prayer, it was not foreseen in the Society's textual records, which were carefully circumscribed, like their authors' environments. The documents were inspired by the *Spiritual Exercises,* and in some senses were like them: for those who came after the mystic Ignatius, spiritual insight and mystical inspiration were accompanied processes. Following the example of the *Exercises,* Jesuit thought and action did not evolve in isolation: the presence of a mediating entity was important and assumed several possible forms, acting as a kind of guarantor. Depending on the context, this third party might be the guide of the *Exercises,* a superior, or the ultimate mediator, the Church with its entire Catholic cosmology, explained in the famous final chapter of the *Spiritual Exercises,* "Rules for Thinking, Judging, and Feeling with the Church" [352–370]. The system branched out to include the sacraments, saints, martyrs, doctors of the Church, the pope and ecclesiastical hierarchy, other founders of the religious orders and their religious teachings, indeed, history itself—all markedly present in the Society's early texts, Ignatian thought, and Jesuit identity more broadly.

This guided structure established in the *Spiritual Exercises* was the preferable model for the biographical documents, more than other Ignatian writings, such as his *Spiritual Diary* (1544-1545), which recorded events as they were happening and were spontaneous jottings of Ignatius's intensely personal experience in prayer. The diary was not intended for circulation or publication. A closer model is Ignatius's *Autobiography* (dictated 1553-1555). Even in this case, the informal style of this dictated account, which included frank self-appraisals of Ignatius's weaknesses prior to his conversion, came to be seen by his successors as unsuitable for circulation in the Society, let alone outside it. Neither the diary nor the autobiography was published in the period under discussion, and, while they were drawn on for other works, most of the Jesuits mentioned here would not have seen them.[33]

Since novelty, further, tended to be viewed with suspicion in this period because of its association with heresy and heterodoxy, the study does not treat the Society as an innovator. Nor does the book interrogate the Society's relationship to modernity, even if it leaves open the possibility that it was indeed original in many aspects and had multiple points of contact with new religious, organizational, and cultural forms, as well as with the coming of modernity—as participant, promoter, but also detractor.[34]

Modern or not, the "first-person Jesuit" features among the book's sources, sometimes called "ego documents." Coined by Jacob Presser in connection to first-person accounts by Holocaust survivors, and given wider circulation through the works of Winfried Schulze, this term has come to signify a document type. It also refers to a set of theoretical approaches and methodologies in relation to nonliterary texts written in the first person (and distinct from the modern autobiographical genre, for example). It has been used fruitfully also in premodern studies, such as in analyses of diary accounts from the Thirty Years' War and, more recently, in the early modern Catholic sphere among female religious. There are problems with the term, however—particularly for premodern sources—including the anachronistic psychoanalytic connotations of the word "ego." As Miriam Turrini observed, drawing on Eva Kormann's work, "The question of an '*io*' . . . in the early modern period is defined in perennial relationship with an alterity, with networks and with received models of the realization of the self."[35]

The biographical documents in this study belonged more to the "textual communities" of Brian Stock's classic study and to the "imagined communities" of Benedict Anderson's research.[36] They carried spiritual elements derived from the *Exercises*, but they were also grounded in reality. For the Jesuits, their contents were used to assess suitability for a particular role, to register a vocation, or to make any number of decisions based on unique information provided about individual members. Such a practice came naturally to the social elites and the well educated who joined and took up leadership positions within the Society: this was how these men managed their affairs and got things done, whether inside or outside religious life. The use to which the documents were put also meant that while they were formulaic in much of their content, with spiritual and rhetorical underpinnings, a key function was to reveal the individual, as distinct from the group. Both features of the sources—the collective-formulaic and the individual-unique—reveal that the single Jesuit was at the heart of operational procedures. The biographical documents facilitated the process of identifying each member's talent, character, and inclinations at the service of the institution.

This system, I argue, helps explain the Society's remarkable ability to attract vocations and be responsive, flexible, and agile in its operations across the known world. For our purposes, it encourages us not to dismiss these biographical documents as constructs whose factual details remain elusive. While they were partially this, their administrative function meant that their authors were also concerned with how things worked, what they saw, and what happened. Such a rich informational vein informs one of the study's aims to mine the texts for "how things worked" in the Society's first century. At the same time, the documents' focus on individual Jesuits, each one of whom was considered to constitute a unique element in the body of the Society, provides an access point into Jesuit worlds and worldviews, as well as a key, I argue, for understanding the Society's distinctiveness, appeal, and influence in Renaissance Italy and the new global age.

In turning now to the rest of this study, it is possible that an echo from the sixteenth century may be heard. The echo comes from Polanco's *Chronicon Societatis Iesu*. Penned by the Society's first general secretary, it singled out individual Jesuits (and the documents about them) to construct a portrait of the larger whole.[37] Polanco's chosen method for history writing (unusual for the time) points to the Jesuit self-understanding that this book seeks to record, where individual elements are brought together into a single corpus.

In its own way, this work attempts to operate like a Polanco, with numerous individual segments of text and multiple records of single Jesuit voices. It brings them to light and through them provides new insights into the origins, development, and structure of the early Society—as well as the individuals who joined it—for current and new generations of scholars working in the vast and deep waters of early Jesuit history.

1

Vocation and Entry

*F*or Jesuits, the phases of vocation and entry to religious life were located at crossroads, where individuals left one path, *il secolo* (the world), and entered another one as consecrated members of a religious institute. The documents that describe this phase open onto a rich world of people and physical environments, as well as recorded inner lives that are of particular interest to this study. They include especially the meeting of individual will, conscience, and agency with obedience, communal life, and conformity, and the constellations of people that made up these (mainly young) men's lives on entry. These included relatives, Jesuit teachers, confessors, friends, mentors, and many others who appear in the documents as either having helped or hindered this momentous crossing point—and the first step to becoming a Jesuit.

Two main types of documents guide the analysis. The first are entrance records of the Roman novitiate ("Ingressus Novitiorum") and the second relate to individual vocations, also generated for the Roman novitiate ("Vocationi").[1] Together the extant documents about those who joined the Society in Rome during its first century constitute a unique set of records for the first phase in a Jesuit life. The most important novitiate, S. Andrea al Quirinale, attracted candidates from throughout the Italian lands and Europe, such as Spaniards, Portuguese, Flemish, French, German, English, and Scottish, although the majority were from Italy. For example, in the early years (1540-1565), out of 1,750 Jesuits in Italy, between just over one-half and two-thirds were from Italy. The largest number of those from outside Italy, 193, were from Spain; 162 were from France, 111 from Belgium, and 108 from Germany; almost 40 were from different parts of the British Isles; a few were from Czech lands, Hungary, and Greece, respectively; and, reflecting the extremely precocious impact of the overseas missions, one was from Japan (Bernardo of Kagoshima (d. 1557), who entered the Society in Portugal and came to Rome in 1554).[2] This cosmopolitan environment, together with the extensive available documentation from S. Andrea (unmatched with respect to other Jesuit provinces), provide the backdrop for this chapter.

The documents underpinning the analysis have received relatively little scholarly attention to date: the "Ingressus Novitiorum" are practically unknown, while the autobiographical narratives of the "Vocationi" are the subject of important analyses by Miriam Turrini. These studies have done much to explain the context for their production, the major themes they contain, and some key characteristics underpinning a Jesuit vocation from a number of measurable viewpoints.[3]

The subject of vocations more broadly, also treated by Turrini, has fared better in the historical scholarship of the Society: Adriano Prosperi produced a thematic study based mainly on retrospective vocation narratives written by individual Jesuits toward the end of their lives, in the genre of the spiritual memoir. Prior to these Italian studies, the work of Thomas V. Cohen remains a beacon for this subject, as does that of A. Lynn Martin and John O'Malley; the latter provided essential overviews of procedures in relation to individual Jesuit vocations, formation, and retention, while Aliocha Maldavsky applied the question of the religious vocation to the Jesuit overseas missions, specifically, the Peru province.[4]

Two key objectives underpin this chapter: the first is to shed light on the organizational structures that these sources touch on; the second is to interrogate the dynamics at play between the individual and collective worlds of these would-be Jesuits on the cusp of entry to religious life. The aim is to tease out how the applicant, through his vocation, became a hub among the many spokes in the turning wheel of the Society as he stepped away from the life that he knew before; for a short time, at least, he was the meeting point between the past, present, and future of the Jesuits. This special value given to the single individual—revealed in these documents through the Jesuits' own written accounts of their life stories and life choices—provide important clues for this book's aim to understand the appeal of this new Society.

Approaching a Jesuit Life

In Rome, in the early years after the Society's foundation, the novitiate was not separate but was located in the professed house, and novices lived as part of the regular community there, alongside those who were already fully incorporated members. Gradually, however, Jesuit novices were being housed in buildings or quarters separate from those who had completed their training. This was already taking place in 1559. Nevertheless, in Rome, novices continued to live in the *casa professa* until 1564, after which they lived separately from professed members but still remained in the same building. The professed house then became the primary residence of Jesuits who had completed all training, while, numerically, colleges remained the place of residence for the largest number of Jesuits. Following the example of older religious orders, and as the Society continued to grow and become more settled, it was decided that a separate house would be provided for all novices in the Society. The first novitiate was established in 1550 in Messina. In Rome, the novitiate of S. Andrea, located on the Quirinal Hill, was established in September 1565, although novices continued to share the building with the professed members there.[5]

For most seeking entry to the Society, the novitiate did not constitute the first point of contact because more than 50 percent of novices were drawn from Jesuit schools. Nevertheless, these records represent the earliest moment in the initial phase of a long period of training and preparation to become a Jesuit, which lasted around ten years (and even longer for some, depending on the grade). Membership in the Society was conferred according to four possible grades, each with distinct formation and training. They were temporal coadjutors (the equivalent of lay brothers); spiritual coadjutors with two possibilities—a nonprofessed member of the Society (not an ordained priest) or ordained priests (professed with three vows); and the fourth grade of membership, which entailed the fullest possible integration into the Society as professed with four vows. The fourth vow included the promise to obey the pope "concerning missions" to go anywhere that was deemed necessary and it provided a core impetus for the Society's works. This grade was reserved for Jesuits with the most learning and promise for governance, and the Society's senior positions, such as provincials, were conferred only on them. Of 1,750 members in Italy between 1540 and 1565, 1,314 were priests and scholastics; the remaining number, a minority, were temporal coadjutors or unprofessed spiritual coadjutors.[6]

In general, the phases of training to become a Jesuit priest took the following path: the novitiate lasted for about two years, after which time he took simple vows and became an approved scholastic whose activities involved a period of studies and other tests. This was followed by his regency, when he taught in Jesuit schools and colleges. After his regency he commenced his theology training of about four years. Toward the end of this phase he was ordained to the priesthood, after which the ordained scholastic completed his fourth year of theology. Then he set aside his academic studies and other works to become a tertian in preparation for final vows. The whole process toward full incorporation into the Society took between ten and fifteen years to complete.[7]

The admission and vocation records for S. Andrea are the product of a series of stipulations contained in the *Constitutions*. Developed between 1547 and 1558/1559 (when they were published), and attributed to Ignatius of Loyola with substantial assistance from his secretary Juan Alfonso de Polanco, this document defined the government and outlook of the Society. It provided practical and conceptual elaborations of its briefer predecessor, the *Formula of the Institute of the Society of Jesus* (written for the 1540 papal ratification of the Society and revised in 1550).

The *Constitutions* provide guidelines for the Jesuit life path and selection to appointments, from entry to the highest positions in the Society. With the active apostolate in mind, they are structured on developmental principles, on the idea that the Jesuit would grow spiritually and that different tasks would become appropriate, according to the stage of the individual in the Society.[8] They are also very complex, even unwieldy, and notoriously difficult to follow. They consist of not one but several separate documents, each with distinct parts—the *Formula of the Institute,* the *General Examen* (and their accompanying *Declarations on the Examen*), and the *Constitutions of the Society of Jesus* (with their *Declarations on the Constitutions*)—collectively named after the longest core part of the work, the *Constitutions* (here, where the cited text refers to the *Formula* or *Examen,* this is indicated). On the one hand, they are filled with minute detail about how things must be organized; on the other hand, they contain surprising latitude for applying their prescriptions flexibly, or not at all, depending on the circumstances. It is difficult to gauge how much they were apprehended and implemented, even by those in the Society whose task it was to do so. They were not so much slavishly followed—the document itself advises against this—as much as used to provide the outlines for how to be a Jesuit.

Conditions for entry were defined in the chapter "The candidates who should be admitted." It stipulated that "the greater the number of natural and infused gifts someone has from God our Lord which are useful for what the Society aims at in his divine service, and the more experience the candidate has in the use of these gifts, the more suitable will he be for reception into the Society." It then follows the attributes ideally sought for each grade—such as, for temporal coadjutors, to be "content with the lot of Martha," the woman in the Gospel account who served Jesus and other guests in her home while her sister, Mary, chose to sit and learn. For all applicants, the following direction was given: "In regard to their exterior these candidates ought to have a good appearance, health, and age as well as the strength for the bodily tasks which occur in the Society." It added that "to admit persons who are difficult or unserviceable to the congregation is not conducive to His [God's] greater service and praise, even though their admission would be useful to themselves."[9]

Those pertaining to grades other than that of temporal coadjutor, that is, those "who are admitted to serve in spiritual matters," should "have sound doctrine, or ability to acquire it." Indeed, theological training before or after entrance rose sharply and quickly in the Society, held by just over 50 percent between 1540 and 1556, then 70 percent in 1600, and over 90 percent between 1650 and 1750. The *Constitutions* advised that those destined for spiritual work in the Society should possess "a pleasing manner of speech, so necessary for communication with one's fellowmen," "a good appearance," "health and strength," plus a suitable age: "more than fourteen for admission to probation and more than twenty-five years for profession."[10]

From the just over 1,700 members in Italy during the period from 1540 to 1565, Ladislaus Lukás ascertained the age groups of 748 Jesuits at the time of their entry to the Society. The most numerous were between the ages of sixteen and twenty (289, or 39 percent); the next most numerous were between the ages of twenty-one and twenty-five (192, or 26 percent). The lowest number (10) joined between the ages of forty-one and fifty-three, while a considerable group (107, or 14 percent) entered before the suggested age of fourteen stipulated in the *Constitutions* (of these youths, 44 percent eventually left).[11]

Social standing was also mentioned in the *Constitutions:* While "nobility, wealth, reputation, and the like, are not necessary when the others [attributes discussed above] are present . . . the more an applicant is distinguished by those qualifications the more suitable will he be . . . and the less he is distinguished by them, the less suitable."[12] It is in these words that a complicated and ambiguous relationship comes into view between the Society of Jesus and the elites that it tended to attract, and in some senses sought, especially in light of the broad meaning of nobility—analyzed very effectively by Patrick Goujon. The ultimate aim was to do God's work, with the ambition that the best possible talent be applied to that work; of secondary importance for Ignatius was the fact that much of that talent was identified among the elites, whether through birth or education, or both.[13]

On the social-cultural level, of course, the elite weighting of vocations to the Society was significant, while its very codes were written by several members of the nobility (and therefore in some sense also *for* the nobility). Because those codes were not only about prayer life and spirituality, but also concerned the specific mission of the Society to work in the world, they by necessity and perhaps more than those of equivalent religious orders dealt with the elevated social values and well-educated worldviews of the original companions. The Society of Jesus—apart from the ecclesiastical hierarchy around the papacy, the college of cardinals, bishoprics, and other such high Church offices—was more successful than most at harnessing worldly status and talent and using them in the world for its purposes of conversion. This is a key to understanding the Jesuits' success, and ability to attract fellow elites and talented males to their mission: those from privileged backgrounds could see in the Society the opportunity to influence their world in a way that was already familiar; those without privilege who could show their ability had the chance to *aspire* to such influence. The appeal of such prospects for both groups, elite and not, is unmistakable.

The stipulations in the *Constitutions*, further, reflect long-standing attitudes and theories found in conduct books, and other literature, such as Francesco de Barberino's *Documenti d'Amore* from the early fourteenth century. These drew on commonplaces found in Augustine, Cicero, Seneca, and others and that included treatment of the intimate relationship between exterior and interior life. As Shelly MacLaren observed, "Appearance and behaviour could be accurate indicators of interior qualities. As the age, clothing and attributes of the virtues can be read to indicate an essential quality or characteristic of that virtue, so too can the appearance of people in the world be read to indicate something essential about them."[14]

While it was understood that this view was a guide, not a rule, and that looks could be deceiving, it was an attitude that, as Dilwyn Knox observed, was "a staple to medieval and Renaissance Christian doctrine,"[15] and is amply present in the *Constitutions*. Several physical characteristics and external circumstances potentially rendered an applicant unsuitable for entry to the Society. "Notable ugliness," "debts and civil obligations," and "notable disfigurements or defects" tended to render these persons as "unsuitable except when . . . outstanding virtues and gifts of God are present."[16]

The main impediments to entry, which were treated in part 1, chapter 3 of the *Constitutions*, were more serious. They included: having separated oneself from unity with the Church or causing others to fall away from it; having received a public sentence; serious crimes or being "infamous because of enormous sins" (homicide is mentioned); belonging to another religious order, being married, or in legitimate slavery; finally, being mentally ill to the point of having impaired judgment.[17]

Peter Togni's study of novices in northern Italy provides a reminder that, more prosaically, sometimes there were simply no funds to accept new novices. In Venice the rector Antonio Micheli wrote in 1570, "For the present it is not possible to accept more [novices] because those that are here are very confined, taking up not only the normal rooms but even rooms used for other purposes such as the library.... Some are even in the infirmary." Of those who were accepted, the novice master wrote the following report eight years after the founding of the Novellara novitiate (in Reggio Emilia): "Many good persons have come to the novitiate, such as Venetian gentlemen, and vicars of Genoa, Ferrara, and others of quality from Genoa and Brescia... who tried themselves in the house with mortifications and self-denial." Around the same time, Sebastião Morais, who had the role of visitor to the Lombard province, reported of the novitiate at Arona: "The discipline of the house as far as the novices are concerned seems to be going well enough.... The quality of the novices for now is satisfactory... and they are excited about our Institute and particularly about prayer."[18]

According to these reports, the problems sometimes lay in those who were training the novices, which in turn negatively impacted their charges. In 1570, Nicolás Bobadilla (1511–1590), one of the original companions, wrote a small "Booklet of Consolation" on the subject of Jesuits abandoning their vocation, addressed to the provincial in Sicily, Jerónimo Doménech (1516–1592): "Since the Society of Jesus was a new religious order, and it did not have members experienced in government, they would overexert those who entered... the superiors being inexperienced and the subjects, weak—it would take but a slight temptation to blow them away, as they say."[19]

The novitiate's function for ensuring suitable candidates for the Society was taken seriously, and departures from it were common. In Italy between 1540 and 1565, 35 percent of entries resulted in voluntary departures or dismissals; 22 percent who left were novices (within two years); 46 percent left in the course of the following seven years; and 29 percent left ten years or more after entry.[20] In the case of one prominent dismissal, that of Cosimo Puccio (who had left Cardinal Ippolito II d'Este's service to become a Jesuit), the novice master reported in 1577 about Puccio's "great liveliness" and "his inordinate desire for study which he brought with him from the beginning." The result was that he "clearly still has not been able to acquire indifference." He continued: "I indicated [to Puccio] that either he resolves his indifference or he is not for the Society and with this he seemed ready to leave but with tears and pangs of conscience. God help him."[21]

As already noted, each of the distinct sections that collectively made up the *Constitutions* (the main part that carried this name was further divided into ten parts) pertain in different ways to the selection, instruction, and appraisal of members of the Society. A remarkable feature of them is that the first part in particular (the *General Examen*) was intended to provide an overview of the Society specifically for reading and reflection by those considering entering it. Drawing on the *Spiritual Exercises* in aspects of style and approach, the two-way nature of this guide to assist both the candidate and examiner in the process of entry and selection is the most original of the Society's foundational documents, and no other order possesses such a detailed text for this purpose.[22]

The largest section, the *Constitutions,* contains details about the process by which a candidate should be admitted. This was added to later by Ignatius's trusted confrere, Jerónimo Nadal (1507–1580) in a series of instructions on admissions as part of his Society-wide efforts to establish the institutional framework of the congregation and apply the Ignatian vision for it based on the *Exercises* and the other early documents that grew out of them. The instructions advise superiors to ensure that the candidate familiarize himself with the Society by reading the *General Examen* or having the relevant parts explained to him and that he show himself ready to renounce personal property. The assessors should get to know the candidate as much as possible and establish whether there are any impediments to his entry (such as being married); if none are found, he may enter wearing his own attire, after which a more detailed examination should be undertaken.[23]

It was during the initial phase of entry to the Society that the admissions information was recorded. The *Constitutions* stated, "During this time of the first probation the candidates will also manifest their consciences to the superior or the one he assigns.... They will make a general confession.... In a book provided for this purpose, they write down and sign with their own hand what they have brought to the house, and also their agreement to observe everything that has been proposed to them."[24]

As we will see in the following discussion, the form, content, and intent of the *Constitutions* provided the framework for Jesuit biographical documents. The practice began with entry to the Society. The individual and his vocation was of intense interest to those whose task it was to decide who would enter; many did not make it through the evaluation process before being dismissed, no doubt raising even more the already high desirability and somewhat exclusive reputation of this new religious institute.

Through the first step of vocation, and aided by the *Spiritual Exercises* and *Constitutions,* a program was established whose aim was that each individual be guided to identify and further develop his unique contribution to the world "for the greater glory of God." Judging by the numbers that sought entry to the Society, and the many that stayed, this was an appealing prospect for many males in Italy between the mid-sixteenth- and mid-seventeenth centuries. In the next section, we shall observe the first recorded steps of the individuals who chose this path.

Admission to the Roman Novitiate

In ARSI, four separate folders dating between 1556 and 1675 are extant concerning several thousand individuals admitted to the Society as novices in Rome.[25] The very first extant entries are recorded in the year of Ignatius's death, in 1556. It was in this year, too, after some early experimentation with the probation process, that the 1556 text of the *Examen* and *Constitutions* set the norms for the Society. In this text, the first probation lasted around two weeks, during which time the candidate became familiar with the Society and was himself examined for his suitability to it.[26] Into this early Jesuit context, where the system of recruitment and entry was becoming codified, the first candidate from these documents appears. He was a Spanish painter, "Giovanni di Moraga" (whose entry was crossed out, presumably because the vocation did not go ahead, although no reason is given). The opening sentence reads, "He entered the house on 8 June 1556; he was examined for temporal coadjutor, and not having any impediments, he demonstrated that he was ready to perform all that was shown to him in the *examen*."[27]

All entries list the names of the candidates and in some cases their provenance. Only at the third admissions book (ARSI, *Rom.* 172, 1594–1630) are the ages of candidates gradually introduced. Several were very young, such as the Genoese Giovanni Luigi Saluzzo, who presented himself in 1637 at the age of fifteen, and Nicolò Mascardi of Sarzana (1624–1674) near La Spezia, who arrived in 1638 and had just turned fourteen;

he studied under Athanasius Kircher (1602–1680) at the Collegio Romano and went on to become a missionary in Chile and Patagonia, where he met a violent death.

Toward the end of the 1640s, a figure with an interesting future in the natural sciences arrived at S. Andrea: Francesco Lana Terzi (1631–1687). After the novitiate, he went on to study at the Collegio Romano, where he worked as an assistant in the famous museum curated by Kircher (see Figure 1 in the introduction, depicting the "Ignatian Tree" printed in one of Kircher's many books, the *Ars magna lucis et umbrae,* first published in 1646). Lana made his profession with four vows in 1665 and acquired a high level of intellectual liberty at Brescia as director of the Academy of Nobles, the school for the laity of the college, where he wrote and experimented in a field later known as aeronautical engineering, and included plans for a "flying ship." He worked in many other scientific areas as well, such as mechanics, magnetism, acoustics, and mineralogy. In his lifetime he attracted enemies, both inside and outside the Society, especially while teaching at Ferrara. Eventually the Jesuit hierarchy in Rome removed him from teaching and sent him back to his native Brescia, where he was assigned to hearing confessions for the last eight years of his life, although he continued to experiment and publish. He enters the scene in our story, instead, as a sixteen-year-old patrician from the north of Italy, trying his luck in the city of Rome as a would-be Jesuit. His entry record states:

> Francesco Lana Bresciano came to S. Andrea on 10 November 1647; he brought with him a hat, a fine coat of black cloth, a pair of breeches, a coat and mantel of Spanish cloth, two pairs of silk tights, one fawn and the other black, five shirts, four pairs of socks, four pairs of fine shoes, ten handkerchiefs, one pair of sheets and one towel, five collars, five pairs of cuffs, one pair of slippers, one pair of shoes, a small hair brush, a comb, a small black satin biretta, a trunk.

He signed his name: "I, Francesco Lana, affirm everything above." It is unclear how many Jesuit scholars and scientists like Lana would have pursued their fields had they remained outside the Society.[28]

At the other end of the age spectrum, some were older entrants, and a small but significant number who entered were already priests:

Francesco Maria Gonzaga, for example, arrived in 1649 at the age of forty already an ordained priest.[29] Men who had been ordained to the priesthood prior to joining the Society accounted for many of the more mature candidates. They were a minority, however: out of over 1,500 entrants between 1594 and 1630, 140 (or almost 10 percent) were listed as "Padre."[30]

Most admission records were written by the Jesuit conducting the interview and signed by the candidate, in some cases with an additional note confirming the accuracy of the information provided. Several were marked with a cross, made by the entrant, next to which the Jesuit interviewer wrote, "Not knowing how to write." These candidates were entering as future temporal coadjutors, the equivalent of brothers in the religious orders; this grade carried the title *fratello*.[31] That some could not write did not mean that they could not read: it was common for this to be the case in an early modern world that had more use for reading than it did for being able to write.

A number of entries are written by the novice himself, and in the first person. Indeed, the *Constitutions* stipulate that candidates should write their own statements; only when they are unable to write should the information be recorded for them, followed by their signature in their own hand, or, if that is not possible, a mark indicating consent.[32] The majority of the Roman candidates provided just their signature; a single secretarial hand wrote most of the entries. There were some exceptions—for example, Giovanni Francesco Stefanoni, who was sent to Japan in 1567. He wrote his own statement, with very poor handwriting: "I came to the house on 6 January 1560. I was examined for temporal coadjutor." Among his very few items, he recorded that "I brought with me a black tabard."[33] Another entrant who wrote in the first person, but with a far superior hand, was Robert Bellarmine (1542–1621), the nephew of Marcello Cervini (Pope Marcellus II, r. 1555). He arrived at the house declaring, "I, Roberto, came to the house on 20 September 1560. I was examined to be indifferent, and not finding any impediment, I offered myself to be ready to do anything that my superiors command me to do. I brought with me a black tabard, four shirts, ten handkerchiefs, three towels, three pairs of socks, and three caps."[34]

Robert Bellarmine's clear statement of vocation is rare. In the early records, the theme instead is treated more perfunctorily: many indicate whether the candidate is intended for the role of temporal coadjutor. Typically these were sons of artisans, land-owning peasants, or small-goods merchants working within the Society on manual and practical tasks; in other cases, candidates are listed as being "indifferent" to the grade of membership that they would later take.[35] Even these brief details relating to vocation were dropped in 1589, with an explicit acknowledgment of the change noted thus: "This inventory of 4 June 1579 is the last to note the formula, 'he was examined for coadjutor,' or the other, 'he was examined as indifferent.'"[36]

The main subject from this point on was the material possessions of those who had been accepted to enter the novitiate. The array of belongings listed was myriad: a black cap; socks; shoes (specifying if they were used, new, and how many there were); weapons (including swords and a firearm); paintings and devotional objects; books (number in the vernacular and in the ancient languages); furniture, such as chests and cupboards; precious gems; and money. One entrant brought a horse, in 1558, which was sold and the proceeds used for essential items.[37]

Assessors were advised in the *Examen* that an appropriately designated person "will put into a copybook all that each one brings, in case it may be necessary on some occasion to have this knowledge." Why was this information recorded in such detail? On a practical level, these lists had two main purposes: first, in case the goods needed to be returned should the novice leave for any reason, and, second, as a guide to their renunciation and distribution at the end of his novitiate. Goods remained in the novices' possession (although cash or income derived from property was not permitted for personal use); this lasted until they had taken their first vows at the end of the probation period, usually lasting two years. Upon first vows—taken on conclusion of the novitiate—Jesuits were obliged to renounce all revenue derived from any goods or property and to divert it to some good purpose. On final vows, they had to renounce ownership and dispose of goods or properties. They were free to make the disposal as they judged fit but were reminded of the scriptural injunction to give to the poor. As in the mendicant orders and in Benedict's rule, personal property or inheritance was forbidden; unlike some religious, however, the Society could not inherit "through those individual members" or on their behalf. Echoing the *Examen*, the admissions records state for the years 1594–1630: "In this same book it is advisable to leave space to list the belongings when, upon anyone's departure, they may be returned, or when, at the conclusion of two years or after having taken vows, with the will of their owners, they be distributed elsewhere."[38]

If a candidate were dismissed, then his belongings were returned to him, including those he had given to the Society. Some candidates either left or were sent away: in 1583, Valentin Dubuisson of Savoy "was let go with all of his possessions and money." Similarly, in August 1585, Domenico Pinardi, who had arrived seven months previously, in January, "was sent home and took all of his belongings with him." In the winter of the same year, Francesco Galletti "took his things and was *licenziato*."[39] Some names and their relevant entries are crossed out without explanation, presumably to indicate their departure (such as that of Giovanni di Moraga, mentioned above); some died, with the note *discessit* and the date of death written next to their entry.

A distinctive feature of becoming a Jesuit was that it did not require a dowry, as was the case for other orders, so goods actually were intended to be distributed elsewhere and were not to be used by the Society. The renunciation of cash or income derived from property, inheritance, or other means was a particularly important topic for Ignatius, and the *Constitutions* mention it several times and in great detail. A significant part of chapter 4 in the *Examen* is devoted to the question of the renunciation of the world:

> The intention of the first men who bound themselves together in this Society should be explained to the candidates. Those founders' mind was that those received into it should be persons already detached from the world ... and further ..., all those who seek admission into the Society should, before they begin to live under obedience in any house or college belonging to it, distribute all the temporal goods they might have and renounce and dispose of those they might expect to receive.[40]

In practice, this renunciation was deferred until after studies had been completed. Ignatius established that it should take place one year after entrance, or on the direction of the superior. In the early days, members would help other poor members with their own goods, but by the time of the *Constitutions*, it was stipulated that goods should be given to the poor, in imitation of St. Jerome; if appropriate, goods could also be given to a member's family in cases of need. Such possessions included all property that was owned already or that subsequently might come into a member's possession through inheritance; early admission records include the explicit question of whether candidates were willing to renounce their right to such property. Crucially and quite unusually for this period, it encompassed any Church benefices that might already be possessed; these and their incomes had to be renounced at the end of probation.[41]

Indeed, unlike some members of religious life, ecclesiastical benefices were forbidden to Jesuits and had to be resigned on entry to the Society.[42] This rule was a leading cause of protest from families who may have looked more kindly (than many did on sons wishing to become Jesuits) on ecclesiastical roles for their sons that included benefices and ecclesiastical offices. These often brought wealth, privilege, and influence not only to the individual in question but also to entire families and subsequent generations.[43] For this reason, families were almost as relevant to Jesuit vocations as were the individual circumstances of the would-be Jesuit about which these documents were produced. Both themes contained in them—the vocation that prompted the entry of the individual into the novitiate, and the material assets linked to that individual—had important consequences for the financial and other interests of the candidates' relatives.

Given the gravity for many families of a vocation to the Society of one or more of their male relatives (many Jesuits were related as brothers or by other means, such as cousins), the admission statements provided crucial documentary transparency—signed by the candidate as proof of his consent—in the Society's aim for correct management of the goods that a candidate brought with him. The economic ramifications were all the more pronounced, including at a societal level and not just for the individuals involved, given the elite status of many who joined. Seismic disruptions to the patrilineal dynastic system on which European society rested were the consequence of many vocations to the Society. The fact that to some extent Jesuit efforts were co-opted back into the same elite social system through their work as confessors, educators, and eminent cultural figures somewhat mitigated the "revolutions" that many set off on entry. However, the impact on the secular social system that they left behind was keenly felt by some relatives not least because, on entering the Society, like all religious, Jesuits would not be able to perpetuate family lines through offspring and direct heirs. In contrast to many in consecrated religious life, further, the renunciation of all ties to personal wealth and ecclesiastical benefices meant that Jesuits had even fewer openings to assist with the affairs and interests of their relatives, both in the present and future.

Proof of a vocation freely entered into thus was important in the Society's dealings with some families and other interested parties. Evidence of the veracity of the vocation, further, was intended to show the absence of any suspicion of coercion on the part of the Society. None of the biographical documents contain traces of forced vocations, a phenomenon in this period for other religious institutes; instead, suspicion around the possibility of incomplete vocations to the Society came from families.[44]

While several candidates came from the nobility and upper to middling social ranks, many new arrivals evidently were very poor. A typical entry was that of the impoverished Antonio Poretta, who was listed as having been accepted into the novitiate in 1556. Among his items were "a black cassock of thick Sicilian cloth, old, without sleeves...two large white coats with holes in the sleeves...two old shirts, a very old felt hat, an old office of the Madonna and an image of St. James." In this entry statement, we already learn what position he is expected to hold: "He was accepted as a cook and domestic help."[45]

Several new arrivals were very rich. The future visitor to the Indies, Alessandro Valignano (1539–1606)—who, in 1573, would be entrusted with the assessment and reform of the entire Jesuit mission operations in Asia on behalf of the superior general—arrived at the novitiate at twenty-seven years old on May 29, 1566; he wrote his own entrance statement, which included a large amount of gems and money and a small box containing some objects of pure gold, including a "rosary." The individual contents of the "four (further) chests of goods" he brought with him were listed separately at the back of the book (presumably they were too numerous to list in the brief entry).[46] Frustratingly, this list with further details of entrants' belongings no longer exists. One of those mentioned on this extra list was key collaborator and future superior general of the Society, Claudio Acquaviva (1543-1615; elected 1581), who arrived just over a year after Valignano, on July 22, 1567.[47] In between these two arrivals was another entrant, from Rome, Fabio de Fabii (1542-1615). On February 17, 1567, he came simply with "a good black cape, a pair of gloves, a pair of shoes."[48] All three of these arrivals were from the nobility, and all three would play crucial roles in planning, governing, and selecting Jesuits for the overseas missions in Asia: Valignano as visitor to the Indies, Acquaviva as superior general, and de Fabii through his personal hand in guiding, teaching, and selecting several missionaries from his various leadership roles across Italy.[49]

Acquaviva's successor, Muzio Vitelleschi (1563-1645; elected 1615) arrived on August 15, 1583, with a modest collection of clothes, such as breeches, socks, a "simple" white coat, a biretta, and a pair of handkerchiefs; his entry concluded with the following comment: "Everything is second-hand."[50] Interestingly, secondhand items disappear from the records—or are no longer identified as such—from about 1630. At about the same time, the number of personal effects listed goes up considerably, which may be a sign of a trend of increased wealth among candidates; many more could write their own names by this time, too.

The list of books that the novices brought with them is provided in intriguing detail, although this information gradually stops being listed in the seventeenth century. In the sixteenth-century entries there is some evidence of the pan-European Renaissance culture in which these boys and men lived, as well as of the pious literature that was so prevalent in the period and accompanied them into the novitiate. The Spanish painter mentioned above, Giovanni di Moraga, apart from having arrived in 1566 with paintings and models for sculptures in plaster [*gesso*], also possessed many books, including a "book on Architecture ... an office of the Madonna ... in Spanish, another small office also of the Madonna in the Italian language, a Bible in Italian, together with the Testament [or Gospels]." Giovanni di Polo da Villa, who was a builder, could only sign his name with a cross on his arrival in 1556 but brought with him a "small office, and a rosary of the Madonna." Camillo Vannuzo came to S. Andrea on March 15, 1557; a little later, on June 14, he brought several possessions and an extensive personal library, including Greek and Latin classics and works of theology, grammar, rhetoric, logic, philosophy, history, medicine, and natural science. The collection contained numerous devotional works, as well as commentaries on religious themes and controversies of the day, including the trial of Girolamo Savonarola, and titles such as Erasmus's *Enchiridion militis Christiani* and Johann Eck's *Enchiridion locorum communium adversus Lutteranos*.[51]

Another novice, an Englishman, was entering as a temporal coadjutor; he was accepted into S. Andrea in the summer of 1557 with a number of possessions, including a book about pilgrimage to Jerusalem and a book of *Lettere toscane*. On September 21, 1558, Gioan Maria Gratiani, from Rome, brought "two new shirts, three handkerchiefs, a cloth-lined coat, new, one pair of old tights, a pair of used shoes, a tunic and a new black cape, a used black biretta." His book collection was impressive: "Plato's *Letters*, Greek. Clenardus Greek [Cleynaerts's *Institutiones ac meditationes in Graecam linguam*]. The first book of Homer's *Iliad*, Greek. Dionysius Cartusianus [Denis the Carthusian] *De quatuor Novissimis* Latin. Jean Gerson [one of his works], Latin, bound together with [a work by] Pope Innocent [probably III], Girolamo Sirino's *Libro de gratia*, in the vernacular. A small office of the Madonna. An inkwell. The whole of Homer's *Odyssey*, Greek."[52]

On May 1, 1561, Joseph de Mazancourt brought with him a large collection of books, including Mathieu Ory's treatise against heretics (*Alexipharmacon*); Johann Gropper's *Catholic Institute*; Rabby Samuel's *Treatise against the Jews*; Ludolph the Carthusian's commentary on the Book of Psalms; and the *Treatise on the Mysteries of the Mass* (by Franz Titelman).[53] The reconversion of the Protestant lands, and the conversion to Catholicism by Jews, thus appeared as themes within some aspiring Jesuits' book collections, especially the ultramontane candidates.

Even though from about 1630 most candidates were able to sign their own names, many entrants after this date continued to arrive with very few possessions. "Francesco Sulyok" of Transylvania arrived at S. Andrea in 1584 with a pair of boots; others arrived with nothing at all. In 1562, an entrant named "Giovanni Bruneo de Senas" "arrived from Loreto ... where he was sent from Naples on pilgrimage, and he brought nothing." Others came from further afield: "Guglielmo Scharp" (William Sharp), born in London, was admitted in December 1637 with little more than a pair each of shoes and gloves, while another non-Italian, the "very rich" Swiss "Francesco [Franz] Wisenbach," arrived in 1641 with a large number of possessions, including a sword with a gorget embroidered with gold. Goods, especially those of the elite, were listed according to their provenance: Francesco Maria Gonzaga of Mantua brought in

December 1649, among many other possessions, "a hat, a mantle of Spanish cloth; a robe of light twill from Milan, a belt of silk . . . breeches of dark fawn twill from England."[54]

The most regularly occurring item provided in detail throughout the period covered by these documents, 1556–1640, is clothing.[55] The details of other information become briefer over time—such as books and furniture—while later entries continue to focus on clothing and footwear. In chapter 1 of the *General Examen*, the following directive regarding Jesuit attire is given:

> Although there is no specified habit, it will be left to the discretion [prudence] of the one in charge of the house to decide whether he will allow novices to go about in the same clothes [apparel] which they brought from the world or [if unsuitable] have them wear others; or again, when the garments become worn, whether he will give to the novices others more suitable.[56]

The apparent novelty of this freedom of attire for members of the Society was mitigated by the fact that many entrants already possessed the cassock or soutane and other accoutrement (black socks, caps, capes) of clerks regular for which the Jesuits became known in their dress. One reason for the interest in clothes in these lists, then, must have been to establish what the novice needed and what he could retain for use from among his own possessions. Mario Squadrini entered the novitiate in 1600 with, among other things, a cassock, a felt hat, an overcoat, a shirt, and shoes. Many others had soutanes and cassocks. Much clothing not suited to religious life, however, no doubt would have been stored like other items, to be renounced upon definitive entry into the Society, such as in the case of one entry describing a candidate arriving with a lined fur coat from Naples.[57]

These lists are revealing of their functional meanings, but they also have deeper significance. As Elisabeth Salter argued in her study of wills in sixteenth-century Greenwich, making wills envisaged transitions of great moment—the passing of the subject from life to death—and the decision of what to leave behind to whom was imbued with a series of practical and sentimental meanings ascribed to each object. Jesuits were passing from one life to the next, too, and these lists of personal goods bore for them a mix of characteristics similar to those items listed in a will. As Salter observed about willed items: "The goods and property bequeathed carry with them significant aspects of an individual's identity; the individual description given to an object confers on it a 'biographical status.'"[58]

The functionality of the goods that we have observed in these documents should not be separated from their symbolic and other meanings. For the Jesuits, renunciation required discipline as part of entering religious life; for those making their wills, it was part of a gift-giving practice, an aspect of which, however, was also present in the Jesuit act of renunciation. Having clothing described, with the contemporaneous permission to continue wearing it, is particularly interesting in the Jesuit context, for, as Catherine Richardson observed in her analysis of clothing culture, "Clothing is tied up with identity and recognition because it is such a fundamental part of the visual image of the individual within the community—one of the essential tools of social recognition, and more easily quantifiable and demonstrable than, for instance, their gait."[59]

Similar to Richardson's observations about the significance of clothes used in court cases involving marriage or engagement disputes, the Jesuit records of individual items of those entering the novitiate had a legalistic purpose, but they reveal to the scholar deeper cultural meanings about these objects and their relationship to their owner. Like the subjects in Richardson's study, the Jesuits arrived with certain social characteristics encoded into their belongings. Some Jesuits arrived with little more than the clothes on their backs; others came with gems and large sums of money. What they arrived with, then, was another point of porosity rather than separation between the Society and the social world from which they came. They kept some possessions, including the clothes they brought with them.

Yet their entry marked a separation, too. The lists detail dramatic breaks from past lives that were left behind; their contents previously had contributed to making the men who they were. On renouncing these objects, they disappeared to the previous life and reappeared as members of the Society. We might ask: Did they lose their individuality as they donned their black robes, or did the Ignatian stipulation of nonspecific garb for Jesuits as well as retaining birth names rather than acquiring new religious ones point to something else? Did these departures from the practices of other religious orders leave some room for maneuver, pointing to a space for the individual would-be Jesuit, who, according to the Ignatian vision, had the chance to become more truly himself than any other man of the "world" upon joining the Jesuits? To the extent that it is possible to answer such questions, the entry lists reveal an awareness of the uniqueness of the individual and his circumstances that suggest the seriousness with which the subject was treated: the fact that this uniqueness was not altogether left behind but was brought into the Society to serve its aims may explain why so many wished to enter.

A quantitative study of the items in these lists would do much to highlight the socioeconomic panorama of the Society at this time, but we can still establish some qualitative points from them here. Socioeconomically, the candidates that presented themselves for consideration by the Society as prospective Jesuits appeared to have come from a wide variety of backgrounds, from the very poor to the very rich, and many in between. Some appear to have renounced all worldly possessions already, so their arrival with nothing does not necessarily mean that they had poor backgrounds. Some might have been very rich before entry—like Ignatius himself, who, after his conversion, chose the clothes of a beggar-pilgrim (and the new name of Ignacio; he was born Iñigo Lopez de Loyola), and Francis Borgia (1510-1572), the Spanish nobleman and third superior general (from 1565), who also chose the garb of a beggar when he traveled to Rome on foot to present himself for entry to the Society.

In terms of their contents, the fact that the lists originally recorded both the vocational intent and property in the possession of each candidate on entry clearly reflects the directives of the *Constitutions,* which understood these two matters to be inseparable and the essential first step toward joining the Society. In its early version, this document understood that the vocation, offered by the will of the candidate, was akin to his goods and property, since the vocation required the individual to renounce both what he possessed on entry and also what he might earn in the future were he to remain a layman.

Both matters—the vocation itself and the material assets linked to the individual—had important consequences for more than just the individual Jesuit, and these entry lists recognize the wider societal and familial implications of a vocation to enter the Society. They hint at how radical this vocation was in the lives of many—in specific ways, for the duty-bound elite, but also for those whose families' vulnerable economic circumstances were put at risk by the vocation of their male and ablebodied relative. The allusion in these documents to the many obligations already in place or yet to be fulfilled in the lives of these candidates also helps explain why the Society and its different set of obligations might have provided a wider and even potentially more diverse canvas on which to paint one's life story than that offered by remaining a layman.

Even though the practice of stating the will of the candidate—to offer himself freely to the Society with no impediments—was dropped from the entry lists to the Roman novitiate in the course of time, the continued practice of listing personal possessions implied that the vocational requirements had been met. What was left was these details of personal effects, produced about thousands of entrants to S. Andrea. In these lists, individual information could not be generalized, omitted, or standardized, since the data was required to be accurate for future reference. They remain the first valuable record of the individuality of these entrants taking their first steps inside the Society of Jesus.

Recording a Jesuit Vocation

Thus far, I have shown how the personal effects of generations of males accepted into the Roman novitiate not only provide access to the material world they inhabited on entry to the Society—and which they renounced—but also reveal that these records functioned on multiple levels, including the metaphorical and spiritual meanings implicit in the recording of such details. The second set of documents, the "Vocationi" from the Roman novitiate, permits an even richer insight into accounting for the origin, nature, and path of Jesuit vocations in the first century of the Society of Jesus.

As already noted, the *Constitutions* stipulated that as part of establishing a candidate's suitability to be confirmed in the novitiate, an examination was to be conducted concerning his background and the nature of his vocation. The intention behind these interviews, and all of the steps preceding them, was to gain familiarity with the candidate. Part 1, chapter 4 of the *Constitutions*—titled "The manner of dealing with those admitted"—opens with the following statement: "We are convinced in our Lord that what follows is of great importance.... The persons who are accepted into [the Society] should be not only long tested before incorporation into it but also well known before they are admitted to the probation." The initial phase, known as the first probation, usually consisted of a few weeks prior to being accepted into the novitiate proper, or second probation. During this time, the chapter continues, "candidates may inform themselves better about the concerns of the Society and the Society may come to know them better."[60] In order to do this, the *General Examen* stated that the aspiring Jesuit was expected to "ponder the bulls of the Institute of the Society, and the Constitutions and rules which he must observe in it."[61] The *Constitutions* then explains what would happen next: "When two or three days have passed after he entered the probation, he will begin to be examined more in detail according to the method explained in the Office of the Examiner." If candidates are deemed suitable to enter the second probation, they will "manifest their consciences to their superior" and "make a general confession." After this, they "enter the house of common living where the second probation is made during a longer time."[62] The "Vocationi" from S. Andrea pertain to this period of discernment and assessment for confirmation into the novitiate.[63]

As with most documents in the Society, the origins of the "Vocationi" and instructions for producing them can be found in the foundational texts. In this case, the *General Examen* lists thirteen questions to be put to a candidate before being admitted; these were grouped around three themes: background and family, the candidate himself, and the nature of his vocation. The candidate was asked about the circumstances of his birth: Was it legitimate or not? "Has he come from a family long Christian or one recently converted," or one whose correct faith has been questioned at any time? Are his parents alive, and what are their names, financial circumstances, occupations, and manner of living? Are they in need in any way?[64] In the event of difficulties, such as debts or family hardship, is the candidate prepared to "relinquish his personal judgment and opinion and leave the matter to the conscience or judgment of the Society or of his superior to decide upon what he thinks to be just?"[65] How many brothers and sisters does he have, and are they still living? What is their occupation or manner of living? Has he been promised in marriage, and does he have any children? Does he have any debts or civil obligations? Does he have a manual trade? Does he know how to read and write (he should be tested on this, if unknown)? What is the nature of any present or past illnesses? Has he received any sacred orders, or any similar obligation? What are his habits and inclinations in matters of conscience, attendance at religious worship and personal spiritual practice? Does he digress in any way from Church teachings? If there were any spiritual difficulties or uncertainties to be overcome would he submit to the guidance of superiors? Was he prepared to abandon the world, and since he made that decision, has he wavered in it? Is he prepared to "live and die in the Lord with and in this Society of Jesus? . . . Where and through whom was he first moved to this?"[66]

Jesuit administrative records relating to this phase in the probation reveal that there was a great variety across the different provinces in how the *Constitutions* were applied in practice; considerations about how to apply them sometimes even flared into disagreements, and some directives lapsed into disuse.[67] Some administrative practices were not introduced in some areas; others possibly were but left no documentary trace of them. In 1561-1562, at the request of the new superior general, Diego Laínez (1512-1565; elected 1558), Jerónimo Nadal conducted questionnaires, or surveys, of Jesuits in Spain and Portugal (which then were adapted to include the other destinations in his wide-ranging visitations across Europe, such as Leuven, Vienna, Olmutz, and Moravia—but not Italy, or the distant missions, or a number of French lands troubled by war). They were intended for every member of the Society, not just novices, as part of Nadal's visitation of the provinces. Circulated prior to his arrival, they were expected to be completed and presented to him to better inform him of the situation in each community that he visited.[68]

Particularly interesting are those of 1561-1562 (Portugal, Castile, Andalucía, Aragon) studied by Cohen, especially for what they reveal about the social backgrounds of the Jesuits as well as the motivations for their vocations. Consisting of thirty questions, these surveys were longer than others and included introspective questions about vocation and motivation for entry to the Society. Despite being administered to all Jesuits at every stage, they are extremely similar to the questions listed in the *Constitutions* intended for the novitiate. Cohen warns against confusing the myriad motivations that underpinned vocation and the statements presented in the questionnaires; many statements reveal the desire to fulfill certain expectations concerning a vocation to the Society, which included enlisting various established tropes to build a case: "Yet when, as often happens with the Jesuit documents, one can begin to trace in detail the evolution of individual decisions, the psychological context emerges; one can detect the mood of the young man's deliberations, the imagery with which he clothed his options, the feelings with which he greeted the resolution of an often painful crisis."[69]

The "Vocationi" of S. Andrea reveal a similar blending of formulaic responses with insights unique to their authors. That the candidates tended to tell the truth may be gleaned from the seriousness with which the directive in the *General Examen* and *Constitutions* treated the subject: "Certain things ought to be asked that the candidates may become better known," and that "in reply to these questions they ought with sincerity to tell the whole truth." More importantly, entrants were held to the honesty of their answers under pain of sin: "It is good to advise the confessor to oblige him in conscience if he did not reply truthfully."[70] Expectations were high, however, and so were the stakes. No doubt candidates aimed to satisfy these expectations as best they could, given the penalty for not doing so within the limits of the truth.

The 179 Roman surveys from 1636 to 1644 contain twenty-two brief questions and answers; eighty of these questionnaires are followed by a personal statement, in fluent prose much like a letter, outlining the nature of the vocation.[71] There was quite a lot of variety in their production, but questionnaires do not exist for everyone who entered the novitiate at this time; those who entered marking their names with a cross in the absence of writing ability are not found here. The accompanying index contains information about candidates' geographical origins: forty-seven in total were not Italians (26 percent of those interviewed in this period). The largest number came from the British Isles (twelve), and then there were six from Dubrovnik, slightly fewer from the German-speaking lands and Poland, and single entrants from Moravia, Corsica, and other European locations. These surveys include fascinating details about conflict with disapproving families and, with some, reconciliation. They contain information about brothers, sisters, chance meetings, misfortunes, and educational achievements, as well as self-appraisals and criticisms.

The "Vocationi," in their two parts, focus a lot more on the spiritual side of the vocation than do the more rudimentary lists of the "Ingressus Novitiorum," and they provide a great deal more biographical information as well. Above all, they illustrate the principles and guidelines set out in the *Examen* and applied in practice through these questionnaires. The aims of the *Examen* and its framework become animated in the replies through the individual life stories, circumstances, and religious declarations they contain.[72]

On the question-and-answer side of the page, information was sought of each candidate, such as age, health, family background ("whether his father and mother are alive"), and the family's financial status ("if they are rich or poor," with responses ranging from poor, to average, to rich). The questionnaire asks if any debts are owed, whether the candidate has ever been married or betrothed, and whether he has brothers or sisters. Also sought were details of his occupation on entry, if any; of his educational background; of any significant illnesses he had experienced. Missing from this section were the first three questions of the *Examen:* about his legitimacy or otherwise, about the possibility of a New Christian family background (that is, being descended from Jewish converts to the Christian faith), and whether he had ever held beliefs contrary to Church teachings. No doubt this reflects a different outlook concerning matters of family origin compared with the Iberian one of the Jesuit founders, especially concerning the question of Jewish family backgrounds, as well as a lack of relevance for most Italian candidates in dealing with the question of possible Protestant connections.

From question eleven onward—at precisely halfway through the questionnaire—the themes revolve around the nature of the vocation itself: "What inclination do you have toward matters of the spirit?" "With what inspiration did you enter the Society, and by whom were you received, where, and in what place or time?" The survey sought details concerning the origins and motivations of the vocation, and the final question asked, "What do you feel more inclined towards, assuming indifference, to the Indies, or to Germany, or to any other mission, or a difficult ministry to the greater service of God, his help, and that of others?"[73] Many specified the "Indies" in their responses; one nineteen-year-old declared, "Also as a child I have always felt inclined ... to go to India."[74] Others are more neutral; a twenty-two-year-old from Flanders, named as Antonio della Ferra, states in his 1638 vocation responses,

"I have an inclination to go to England or Holland because of the language and because of my familiarity with how they live."[75] Entrant "Domenico Weibel" was born in Constance to German parents but had no geographical preference for his work in the Society, except for a particular "zeal to help souls, especially to instruct the youth and simple people."[76]

The questionnaires provide a window into many details of individual lives. Some were widowed; many were students or secular priests or had taken simple vows; others had been lawyers or had worked in trade; others still had worked as teachers to support their family before finally being free to enter. Like many, the first candidate with a record of this nature, Pietro Conti, had "always studied."[77] Most were young, from fourteen to early twenties; eighteen was a particularly common age. Those with past careers or formerly married lives were few.[78]

They describe family circumstances: Giovanni Luigi Saluzzo was only fifteen years old when he completed his questionnaire: "I have two brothers and a sister who are still living as children of the family [that is, unmarried]." The twenty-three-year-old Giovanni Battista Cattani was an orphan when he was interviewed in 1639. He had "younger brothers [he does not mention how many] all moderately well off"; in the past he had debts, but they had been paid. The Genoese Uberto Spinola, at seventeen years, described his family as "rather poor": "I have four brothers in religious life and one *secolare* with a wife; I have three sisters who are nuns and one married sister in average circumstances, although rather poor." By contrast, thirty-year-old Paolo Ottolini of Lucca (who entered on December 12, 1638), had he remained "in the world" working with his mercantile family, would have expected to receive a "good inheritance," which instead "will pass to my brother Lelio."[79]

These vocation statements reveal something about individual self-awareness. For example, nineteen-year-old Costanzo Gubernali from the Marche described his family's wealth as "average rather than poor." But they also reveal a lack of it: the fifteen-year-old Giovanni Luigi Saluzzo, mentioned above, in response to the question of whether his family's financial status was rich, poor or average, replied simply, "I really do not know." Saluzzo was much more forthright about his vocation in his longer statement, however; initially, he had wanted to join the secular clergy rather than the Jesuits, but when he saw the "integrità grande" of the Society, the "modestà" of the Jesuit novices, and by comparison the "troppa austerità" of other orders, he decided to become a Jesuit. However, subsequently a woman in his household spoke badly of the Jesuits, so he stayed away. Then he saw them with his own eyes at the school he attended in Savona, upon which he confided his vocation to his (Jesuit) confessor, who made him wait on account of his young age. After this, the confessor told the Roman provincial about the boy, who had him examined by no less than five of the provincial's assistants (possibly because of his young age) before he was allowed to be received into the Society.[80]

The question of a candidate's role within his family clearly was significant. The eighteen-year-old Ludovico Lazarini from Ancona entered S. Andrea on October 31, 1637; he stated that "I have absolutely no role as 'son of the family,' and [was] born last, out of all my brothers."[81] Some candidates were held back from their vocation because of pressure from their relatives, many because they were very rich and were expected to continue their roles as sons of the family; others were very poor and weighed down by their sense of obligation to their relatives. One applicant, named as Guglielmo Euskirchen, had been a poor orphan with three sisters, originally from Cologne and a student at the Collegio Germanico. Already a priest, he relayed how "I have had various temptations, such as feeling I could be more fruitful *nel secolo* [in the world], [and] not being able to help my relatives." These statements reveal how radical a religious vocation could be, going against the grain of family expectations and responsibilities, and other interests.[82]

Uberto Spinola had only one brother and one married sister; the rest were in religious life, and his family supported his vocation. As he recounted, he entered "with permission from relatives who made little difficulty over my coming here." The forty-two-year-old Giacomo Antonio Scaravellini was not so free. With both parents having been poor and at the time deceased, Scaravellini was responsible for his sisters, one of whom was yet to marry. In relation to his debts, he observed, "I had to give dowries to my brothers-in-law, which I have already provided from my fortune in its entirety." In response to the question of what kind of life he had before entry, he replied, "I had a school of grammar and of music, and of the cymbal for many years; I have not studied anything else, except for the compendiums of the canonists." In relation to his vows, he reported, "I have the vow of chastity on account of being a priest." He was received into the Society by Superior General Vitelleschi. As he wrote in his vocation statement, he could not follow his vocation as he had wished until that time, "for the burden of my sisters." However, when he saw himself almost free of that burden, he wondered if his age and health might yet stop him. He had considered the Capuchins, but their habit, "which I had desired and procured in my youth," was "no longer for me." When he turned for advice to the fathers in the Society, they all said that his sisters presented an impediment. Nevertheless, he secured permission from Vitelleschi to enter and came to Rome after receiving help from the rector of his college. He was received into the Society "without heeding so many opinions," which apparently clamored for attention around him and sought to stop him.[83]

Family considerations constituted one of the most important factors in establishing the suitability of a vocation. This is no surprise, given the very young age of many who were still living under the tutelage of their parents when they entered. It helps explain why the Society was at pains to have the candidate's family's approval.[84] Tommaso Rustici, who was twenty and from Lucca, stated that his inspiration for becoming a Jesuit was a desire "to escape from sin." In response to the question of whether he had "temptations, or impediments, or delays on account of relatives, friends, the world, or from the Devil," he responded, "I had some delays on account of my relatives, and some loitering followed, caused by my laziness."[85]

The questionnaires contained a great deal of autobiographical information, spiritual reflections, and personal insight. For example, a novice described the inspiration behind his vocation: "I often read the life of our Father Ignatius and of St. Francis Xavier, and of Blessed Stanislaus [Kostka], and when in my city [Subiaco], I happened to see a Jesuit, it seemed always as if I had seen an angel."[86] Another gave a sense of how life itself might be understood; the sixteen-year-old Innocenzo Innocenzii declared his readiness to obey his superiors until the last: "As long as I breathe, I will be completely obedient, since I see that this Life is fleeting like the Wind."[87] The seventeen-year-old Ludovico Lazarini from Ancona entered S. Andrea on October 31, 1637, and was very explicit about his vocation. In his questionnaire, he stated, "I have the inclination to wish to imitate St. F[rancis] Xavier." In reply to the question of whether he wanted to suffer injury and calumny for Christ's sake, he replied, "For this reason especially I entered the Society because they [the Jesuits] are often subject to insults and calumnies." The battles that he experienced, he reported, very often were spiritual, not reputational, and "temptations from the Demon" had come to him "in great number." Prior to entering the novitiate, for three years he was a member of the lay "Congregation of Padre Pietro Caravita" attached to the Collegio Romano in central Rome.[88]

The Society, for many, offered safety from worldly dangers and a better chance of reaching salvation than if they remained in the world: "Giovanni Battista De Schuldthaus" from Tyrol reported, "I chose for myself the Society of Jesus, not doubting in the least that for me it would be the safest ship for arriving to the port of perfection." Temptations sometimes came in the form of other states of religious life. Guglielmo Euskirchen, a poor orphan from Cologne who was twenty-six years old, stated in 1636, "I am a priest." However, he wanted to join the Society and avoid the secular clergy "considering the dangers and the many opportunities to sin that assail secular Ecclesiastics in the function of their offices, and the little assistance they have to resist continuous temptations." Another, named as Francesco Eschinardi (presumably of Jewish origin), whose family was rich, sought a structured life as well as freedom from the social pressures of the world: "having always desired an ordered life, and where it is not necessary to conform to human conventions."[89]

Opposite the questionnaire was the extended personal statement of vocation, usually the length of one page in continuous prose, sometimes longer. There is no precedent for this type of account, either in the *Examen* and *Constitutions* or in Nadal's survey.[90] This statement seems to have been used as the basis for the answers to the questionnaire, which evidently was supplemented by further information provided in the interview. One survey notes, "To these questions each one is to respond in his own hand."[91] At the top of the following page, where the prose vocation statement commences, written indeed in the hand of the candidate, notes are provided about what should be included, from "name, surname, age and place of origin" to "the origins and motivations of the vocation to Religious life in community and to the Society in particular."

At the top of the folio of one questionnaire is the following heading: "Points for writing the Vocation."[92]

All of these points are present in the vocation statements, revealing the preordained shape of them but also providing glimpses into individual circumstances—if embellished and carefully molded in the telling—as well as the overarching objective for candidates to plot the path to arriving at the establishment of the divine calling that must underpin each vocation to the Society.[93] There were exemplars in circulation as well: Girolamo Pichi referred to them when he described how his vocation was inspired "by the lessons of certain vocations written by the hand of some fathers of the Society," which he read at roughly fourteen years of age.[94] These influences were interwoven with specific and individual details. The fifteen-year-old Antonio Maria Galletti from Perugia wrote in his own hand how, once secure in his vocation, he found himself "in Rome for a while." In Rome, he was "prevented [from entering] and threatened with letters from my [relatives], and held by friends here in person; my uncle also came here to stop me; since no one was able to stop the grace that God wished to give me, I was received by the *consulta* (assistant) of Provincial Father Piccolomini [Francesco (1582-1651), future superior general, 1649-1651]." He entered on December 20, 1638: "Now I am extremely content in the Society."[95]

Another applicant described the impediments to his vocation: Paolo Ottolini, already mentioned, was thirty years old and from Lucca. There he had "attended to his business affairs," maintaining at the same time his contact with his studies in the humanities: "From the age of twenty-four until now I looked after the administration of a business in Messina." In his vocation statement opposite the questionnaire, he told of how "while I was in Lucca in the year 1631 and I survived the plague, during those sufferings, some considerations came to me about leaving the worldly life," especially on account of the terror for his own soul instilled in him by the preachers there.[96] However, he recounted that he went back to his business; then in Messina while on business, he came into contact with the Society, from which grew his vocation to enter.

Niccolò Mascardi's initial obstacle to joining the Society was another religious order. He had arrived at the novitiate at only fourteen years of age with a hat, a pair of hose, and shoes (we have his entrance lists). On November 20, 1638, he described how he had always wanted to join the religious life but had thought that he would join the Capuchins. Then his Jesuit schoolteacher in the humanities spoke with him about how he might better use his "God-given talents" by entering the Society instead. After joining the Jesuits, he was sent to Chile, where his activities lived up to the "missionary-explorer-scientist" model and were characterized by extensive work among indigenous peoples. He was killed in Argentina in 1674.[97]

Domenico Weibel, despite his early vocation to the religious life, became distracted by "certain vanities of the world." Further obstacles included "the war and troubles in Germany"; moreover, he was "accompanied by temptations, being very bowed down and doubtful about entering one of the other Religions," and he wrote of "the dangers not only of losing my Vocation but also my life." The Fleming Antonio della Ferra, mentioned above, was twenty-two years old on entry. He wrote that he came to his vocation after "having travelled around the greater part of Europe for three or four years, and many times in danger, not only in body, but also in soul." Finally, he was given "the light to know such a great danger, and I spent two or three days without being able to eat on account of those thoughts."[98]

The documents analyzed in this chapter were produced above all to assist the individual and his interviewer to discover the candidate's unique path within a context of prospective communal religious life, framed by obedience to superiors and the Church. If this was the documents' function, their value resided in their status as textual continuators of the *Spiritual Exercises* and the *Constitutions,* since they bore the hallmarks of conceptual unity found in all of the Society's texts. Their focus on the individual is remarkable, albeit within clear parameters (particularly the call to obedience in religious life). They were also relational, produced in the context of an interview. As Turrini observes, "The accounts ... might be located at the confluence of two points of view, on the one hand the process of the candidate seeking a common thread through his own life story, and on the other hand the Society's exam that scrutinizes the soundness of a choice in the reconstruction of a subjective journey. A two-sided exchange, therefore."[99]

These biographical documents, further, come into view as being situated between two readings of religious vocation in this period: as a reflection of social and institutional obedience (that is, as something conformed to), and as a thing that was freely chosen (that is, vocation as an expression of individual will, of conscience and agency). Both dynamics were at play here—sometimes separately and at other times concurrently—as candidates entered the life of the novitiate.[100]

In this period, everyone owed obedience—with serious consequences for not doing so—to a family, town, region, parish, diocese, civic ruler—all with a vast apparatus, both physical and mental, to support the imperative of fulfilling one's duty. Indeed, the special agency that the Society's system of selection reveals—and that it afforded to its members, encoded into the *Constitutions* with mechanisms for securing the best person for the job through a combination of vocation, indifference, and consultation—may help explain the appeal to males wishing to join. It may even go some of the way toward highlighting the threat the Society was seen to pose, present here in the responses of candidates' families but evident in other spheres as well. With such aims for individual and collective excellence in carrying out the Society's aims, devised by some of European society's brightest and noblest, the potential to influence the wider world and its interests and systems of operation was high.

Returning to the individual level, the contents of the "Ingressus Novitiorum" and "Vocationi" are a reminder of intensely lived experiences, not just textually constructed ones. Pietro Conti, already mentioned, held back from his vocation because he knew it would upset his mother. However, on going to Rome to study rhetoric (it was not available to him in his small town in Serra, near Ancona), and having studied with the Jesuits, his vocation was reignited, and he was accepted into the Society after an interview with the provincial. He described how he even was able to gain his mother's approval eventually, "through the particular grace of God."[101] His path was not an easy one; while its telling fits a recognizable narrative structure, his mother likely really *did* object to him joining.

Two years later, at the age of nineteen and still undergoing his formation in the Society, Pietro Conti wrote another kind of letter: a petition to the superior general asking to be considered for a missionary appointment overseas. He wrote from the Collegio Romano that he wanted to go in particular to Japan and if necessary "to spill my blood . . . for the love of God."[102] He described his desire for the overseas missions as constituting "not a small part of my vocation to the Society." He outlined his reasons for wanting to go to the missions as being threefold: for the glory of God, the help of his neighbor, and the chance to imitate the crucified Christ. He wrote, "Since God has given me the desire, he can also provide me with the necessary ability." It is this vocation to the missions, and its documentary record, that is the subject of Chapter 2.

2

Candidates for Overseas Missions

As soon as Jesuit hopefuls approached the Society seeking entry, they were presented with its missionary identity, exemplified in the S. Andrea questionnaires, about whether they had an inclination "to the Indies, or to Germany, or to any other mission." After joining the Society, thousands of Jesuits revisited this question by writing *Litterae indipetae,* that is, petitions to the superior general for an overseas appointment. These missionary candidates, whom the superior general called *indiani,* are the subject of the analysis that follows.[1]

The Jesuit overseas missions were integral to Jesuit identity from very early in the Society's history. Everyone was touched by them in some way. Jesuit foundational texts reflected this. The *General Examen* stipulated that candidates must confirm that they had understood and accepted the Society's missionary imperative. The Ignatian aim to "help souls" and "see God in all things" was at the core of this apostolate—that is, the requirement to go where help was needed, including where God was believed to be present but not accepted, such as among "pagan" peoples.[2]

Mission was the reason for the perpetual movement that the *Constitutions* envisaged for the Society's members. Already in Paris, where the first companions joined together in 1534 at Montmartre, a (never realized) mission to the Holy City was planned. By the time of the Society's 1540 papal ratification, its missionary path had been set, with papal requests that resulted in Jesuits arriving in the Holy Roman Empire (1540), Ireland (1542), and India (1542); they landed in Brazil and Florida in 1565, and in England in 1580. Before fifty years had elapsed, the most famous chapter in Jesuit history—its worldwide missions—had mushroomed into a large-scale global undertaking.[3]

The people most engaged with this enterprise were the Jesuits themselves. This was the case whether they departed or not, and is the perspective that sets the frame for my exploration of the vast material at ARSI relating to the *indiani* from the Italian provinces during the Society's first century. The biographical documents that guide the analysis cover each stage in the application process, from petitions to the superior general, to their responses from him, as well as separate provincial assessments of candidates. The geographical focus of this analysis is Asia, where most Italians sought appointments and were subsequently sent.[4]

The aim is to understand how the early Society assimilated its missionary priority, both in theory and practice. The documents help explore not only "how things worked" in relation to this phase in a Jesuit life, but also how the Society's missionary intentions were apprehended by its members, and what they meant for those involved. As one of the cornerstones of Jesuit identity, the overseas missions as they come into view in these documents provide yet more means for understanding the mechanisms of this far-flung enterprise of dispersed Jesuits straining to unite into a single body of the Society of Jesus. The limits and opportunities that resulted from such a vision are nowhere more evident than in the texts about the overseas missions. The recorded experiences of single Jesuits reveal the mechanics for this dynamic, which drew on individual vocations to animate the Society's operations in the world's "vineyard."

Manning the Missions in Asia

In the Indies of the East, the Portuguese crown had assumed oversight of religious life by papal delegation, an arrangement known as the *Padroado*, and it was to the newly established Jesuits that this task primarily was entrusted. In the period covered by this volume, 1540–1640, almost 900 Jesuits were sent east. By 1550, India was one of the three separate provinces operating in the Society; Portugal and Spain were the other two, while the Italian lands and Northern Europe were still under the superior general's direct oversight in the first decade. The arrival of the Jesuits in the Spanish Americas and the Philippines came later, in the mid-1560s; other religious orders and the secular clergy were more prevalent in those areas than were the Jesuits.[5]

In 1548, six years after his arrival in the East, Francis Xavier (1506–1552) wrote the following instructions for selecting suitable candidates to join the overseas enterprise: "Those of our Society whom you send here for the conversion of infidels should be so reliable that any one of them could be sent either alone or with a companion to any region where there is hope of the greater service of God our Lord."[6] As we have seen, this emphasis on personal character and the voluntary nature of vocation was common to all roles in the Society, from entry level to the highest rank, including missionary appointments, but in the overseas missionary context it acquired even more gravity. It meant that in practice the process of selecting and sending individuals from Europe to the overseas missions was a complex and on occasion contested part of Jesuit operations.

Free from the institutional structures and routines of the monastic house, and separated from familiar European surroundings, a Jesuit in Asia was expected to be an exemplary representative of the Christian religion and the Society of Jesus. He was to operate without the support props familiar to consecrated religious life, of institutional heritage, rules, or walls, and without the cultural familiarity enjoyed by fellow Jesuits in Europe.[7] Ignatius of Loyola and his immediate successors originally had conceived of the overseas operations as constituting a small core of European missionaries, whose communities gradually would gain permanence through training secular clergy drawn from the local European and converted indigenous populations, along the lines of the Society's expansion patterns in Europe. Yet there were many hurdles in achieving this aim. Apart from the difficulty in converting the local populations and retaining their religious conviction, many Jesuit leaders both in Europe and abroad believed that admission to local candidates of either European or indigenous extraction was harmful to the enterprise; such candidates were eventually barred from entry in the late sixteenth century, along with descendants of converts from Judaism and

Islam, although exceptions did exist to this rule. Consequently, the Jesuit missions in Asia required a steady stream of reinforcements sent from Europe.[8]

Portugal was the natural recruiting ground for the enterprise and in line with appointment practices throughout the Society it provided the majority of the missions' personnel. This was because although the Society theoretically was structured according to supraregional principles, administratively its organization into roughly geopolitical regions meant that the eastern missions operated under the aegis of the Portuguese Assistancy.[9] However, Portuguese Jesuits could not single-handedly man the missions; at the same time, mission fields overseas had a special place in the universal self-understanding of the Society, and the makeup of missionaries was expected to reflect this fact as well as the superior general's ultimate oversight of the whole Society and all of its members.

In the course of Claudio Acquaviva's thirty-four-year generalate (1581–1615), the geographical scope of the enterprise in Asia reached its broadest dimensions in the Society's pre-suppression period, fanning out from the capital of Portugal's *Estado da Índia* at Goa to locations that included Cochin, Macao, Colombo, Malacca, Japan, and China. The overseas enterprise was for Acquaviva an important plank in his authority over the Society, which underwent intense pressure at numerous stages in his long generalate, most notably from dissenting members from Spain. The missionary expansion, already underway in the time of his predecessor, Everard Mercurian (1514–1580; elected 1572), entailed a significant increase in the number of Jesuits in the region: in 1582, 167 Jesuits were operating in Asia; by 1607, this number had risen to 559.[10]

Originally, Francis Xavier had wanted European recruits to be sent from Northern Europe (it was thought that they were physically stronger and better suited to the cold weather in Japan and China).[11] However, members from these regions remained relatively low in the early years of the Society, and they tended to work in their own religiously contested lands. In the early years, instead, Spaniards were sent to bolster the Portuguese-administered enterprise. However, the Spanish Assistancy had overseas territories of its own to attend to, and the unification of the Spanish and Portuguese crowns in 1580 resulted in so much animosity between the two groups of Jesuits that Spaniards ceased to be sent. They were almost entirely replaced by Italians, and prior to the 1773 Suppression they were the largest cohort to travel to the East, after the Portuguese.[12]

One of the most important appointments from Italy was that of Alessandro Valignano, in 1573, as visitor to the Indies. The role of visitor in the Society was occasional rather than permanent and involved direct representation of the super general and his authority in a given region, to identify, coordinate, and direct any required reforms. In the Asian missions, keeping up with demand for manpower was only one of the challenges that Valignano faced; another was the search for quality recruits.[13] The impression that inferior or troublesome candidates were being chosen was not helped by attitudes among the early Jesuit leadership, such as Jerónimo Nadal's suggestion in 1561 that the Germans, whom he considered to be less bright, could be sent overseas. Xavier, too, was famously dismissive of many local populations that he encountered, especially the Indians, prompting him to advise that for certain remote settings "in these pagan lands, there is no need for learning beyond what is required for the teaching of prayers. . . . Therefore send those who are not for the Society." In the same letter, however, he had this recommendation: "You should also send those who have talent for hearing confessions and giving the Exercises. . . . They will remain in Goa or Cochin, where they will do great service for God."[14]

By the time of Valignano's appointment as visitor almost thirty years later, the overseas enterprise had come of age and had emerged as a clear priority for the Society's leadership. In his role, Valignano sought talented and quality recruits for the East, regardless of where they were to be sent. He made no secret of the fact that he refused to countenance the kinds of recruits that Xavier in the early years had mentioned. Of the poor recruits he encountered, he blamed their lack of suitable attributes on provincials for their "little zeal" for the conversion of India, and by failing to release their capable members. Another problem that Valignano saw was misguided perceptions among the recruits themselves, which Valignano believed came from the unreliable travel literature and "news" literature arriving from Asia. From 1552, the Jesuits became prolific producers of such published accounts, with their rather haphazardly compiled, and not always reliable *Nuovi avisi* and *Avisi particolari*. In 1575, Valignano wrote from

Goa, "In Europe, on the basis of the letters that are sent from here, very different impressions are formed from what is then found here [in Goa], so that, on arrival in these parts, their vocation goes cold."[15]

In 1574, Valignano had to make do with the resources in hand. For his outward journey, he chose a majority of Spaniards (twenty-four, compared with only ten Portuguese), but this preference did not last, as recruits from Spain had ceased by the end of the decade. The next largest group in his company, a total of seven, was the Italians. From this starting point, he made plans for improving the system. From Lisbon, writing before his departure, Valignano sent Superior General Mercurian a detailed list of recommendations for the organization of the missions.[16] Among these, two were prominent: to bring the Asian enterprise more explicitly under the control of the superior general, and to draw personnel from a mix of regions. "If Your Paternity wishes truly to be lord of the Society in India, and to govern it your way, there must be a good mix between nations, and not in small number." However, they were to be of the best kind, like the few candidates whom Mercurian recently had sent to join him; they were Italian, and considered much better than the ones already in Lisbon whom he chose not to take with him. "Our Italians are few in number, but they are good and I remain greatly consoled.... Out of the whole cohort, these are the most welcome: if Your Paternity wishes really to help India, send some good Italian candidates, but be sure that they are good, such that they can be like cornerstones between these two nations [Portugal and Spain]."[17]

Valignano singled out the Italians with three main objectives. First, the provision of more labor by drawing on the large pool of Jesuits in the Italian provinces, with the aim of assisting the Portuguese in whose assistancy the expanding missions fell. Second, the close scrutiny and oversight of Italian candidates as part of a concerted effort to ensure quality candidates, not below-par ones. Third, to secure for Rome and the office of the superior general more direct oversight of the whole enterprise and its direction in terms of missionary practice, governance, and method.

On this last point, Valignano was especially critical of the Portuguese. On January 12, 1574, he wrote a ciphered letter to Mercurian from Lisbon (the decoded words were later noted above the ciphers, provided in square brackets): "Here, there is nothing but the 90 [spirit] of 94 [servitude] and 227 [fear], and the poor fathers 69 [Padri] and 71 [brothers] come to 306 [suffer] almost a miserable b.o.d. [servitude]." In another letter sent at the end of the same month, Valignano wrote that the Portuguese Jesuits were "aiming to catechize and indoctrinate me in their way, in order that India be governed with this spirit to which they hold here [in Portugal]." His January 12 letter described to Mercurian how the Roman way of governing with "b.m.o [love]," in Portugal, was seen as "contrary to the spirit of Father Ignatius."[18] It was in the "good Italian candidates," mentioned above, that Valignano placed his hope for bringing the Roman (and for him, Ignatian) method to the Indies.[19]

Valignano's advice seems to have been followed, both by Mercurian and by his successor, Claudio Acquaviva: as the sixteenth century drew to a close, the number of Jesuits sent from Italian provinces increased. In the years from the beginning of the mission until 1581, Spaniards were the largest group to travel east (28.3 percent) after the Portuguese; in the following decades that quota was filled by Italians (26.8 percent). This development did not take place without occasional hurdles. On the one hand, the Portuguese provinces sought reinforcements from other provinces from the earliest years and in 1603 even declared their intention to curb what they saw as the relentless flow of talented individuals from Portugal. On the other hand, in 1601, interventions were required from Superior General Acquaviva to allow Italians to continue to sail to India, after some Portuguese Jesuits and the crown (now held by Spain) tried to stop Italians from being sent. Later that decade, the papacy had to intervene once more to reverse a Spanish directive for all foreign missionaries to return to Europe. The Italians managed to sail: in 1609, a slightly higher number than usual, nine, left Europe for Asia. A ban finally did arrive between 1611 and 1614, when all but a few missionaries in these years were Portuguese, while Italians resumed sailing again in 1615, with five onboard; previously intermittent, a small number of other European Jesuits also began sailing regularly from this time.[20]

The Italian applicants to the overseas missions about whom by far the largest documentation exists at ARSI, as appointees remained a minority, if a significant one; they became a byword for quality and the preferred choice for augmenting the much larger but stretched Portuguese cohort in Asia. In the first sixty years of the Society (from 1540 to the end of the sixteenth century), roughly eighty Jesuits traveled east from the Italian provinces (out of a total of 401, or 20 percent). Most of these came from the south, seven from Naples alone, compared with three originally from Rome and two from Milan.

Why were the Italians chosen for the Asian missions? During the Mercurian and Acquaviva generalates, when the missions expanded, there were sufficiently plentiful vocations to the Society in Italy to allow some members from there eventually to be assigned to Asia. A large number of these came from the Italian lands ruled by Spain, where recorded vocations for the missions were particularly high. In those territories in the 1540s, letters from the eastern missions reached the hands of Jesuit leaders, who in turn had them read to their young charges in colleges and novitiates—leaders such as the Sicily provincial Jerónimo Doménech and the Naples provincial (and first companion) Alfonso Salmerón (1515–1585), both Spaniards. Later, when the Iberian crowns united under Spain in 1580, subjects from the Italian territories were chosen for the Asian missions over Spanish ones, no doubt helping ease the well-known animosities among Iberian confreres. Acquaviva was having problems of his own with the Spanish arm of the Society, while the call for manpower in its overseas territories mainly in the Spanish Americas ensured that the majority of Spaniards were sent there.[21]

More generally, there was a pivot in the Asian missions' operations toward Rome. The superior general and the visitor could have a direct hand in selection through the administrative system that they set up, and the scale of documents suggests this was most assiduously practiced in the Italian provinces; they could choose the type of missionaries they wanted. Quite apart from considerations of numbers and politics, talented individuals from the Italian provinces were singled out for this apostolate, which in Asia was identified with a distinct style of formation, suited to accommodating rather than intimidating locals. This suited the style of conversion developed by Ignatius, and it was practical, as Jesuit missionaries increasingly moved out beyond the slim coverage offered by the Portuguese Empire in Asia. Such a qualitative choice was most recognizable in (although by no means exclusive to) the cohort from the

Italian provinces; it shaped in a determinative way the foundations of European-Asian contact at the dawn of the modern era.

The biographical documents about overseas missionary appointments permit access to the mechanisms of this system. They reveal that the starting point for selecting candidates was the vocation of the individual Jesuit. They also record that, in between the two pillars of vocation and selection, there was a process of negotiation and consultation. It is to these multilateral textual exchanges that we turn for the rest of this analysis.

Petitions for a Place

Letters of petition for the overseas missions, the *Litterae indipetae,* made their first appearance as a permanent administrative tool in the Jesuit missions' appointment system toward the end of the sixteenth century. Approximately 16,000 petitions were addressed to the superior general from all over the Old Society, prior to its 1773 suppression; the practice resumed in the New Society, that is, after the 1814 worldwide papal restoration, and continued well into the twentieth century.[22] Most candidates wrote their letters in their early twenties at some point in their long training while still in the novitiate or during a period of teaching during regency; several applied more than once for an overseas appointment. The majority of applicants specified the Indies of the East as their preferred destination; in theory, however, these documents were conceived as applying to the Indies in their broadest sense, including the Americas or even territories closer to home, such as the lands under Ottoman rule and Protestant Europe.[23]

While such letters were written sporadically from the earliest years of the Society—several thousand are estimated to be dispersed throughout the Roman Jesuit archive—it was not until Acquaviva's generalate that they were systematically brought together into a single collection. For the Italian provinces, where by far the highest number of petitions was sent, this process began in the late 1580s: nineteen large folders contain letters from Italy, with many hundreds from Acquaviva's generalate and even more from that of his successor, Muzio Vitelleschi; this compares with two folders each from Flanders-Belgium and Spain for the entire period up to the 1773 suppression. Very few petitions survive from Portugal, probably because there was less Roman involvement in Portuguese appointments than for elsewhere; even though the superior general in theory had ultimate say over the departure lists, Portuguese appointments were treated as internal to their assistancy.[24]

In terms of their function, technically, they were part of an administrative process of members crossing from one assistancy to another, a move that was reserved for the superior general's express permission. The *indipetae* are much more, however; numerically, there is no other type of posting in the Society with this scale and type of documentation dedicated to it, nor with its continuity. Consequently, the *Litterae indipetae* have generated substantial scholarly interest: for the history of psychology, their administrative function, spiritual features, and specific literary-rhetorical features; as testaments to the appeal of evangelization and martyrdom in the Far East; and as evidence of the desire to leave familiar lives and environs.[25]

For our purposes, their mixture of formulaic and personal elements provide insights into collective yearning for the Indies as well as accounts of individual paths for arriving at the vocation. Belonging to the genre of the vocation statement, in some respects they resemble the written testimonies produced on entry to the Jesuit novitiate, discussed in Chapter 1, functioning as another recorded extension of the system of discernment set by the *Spiritual Exercises* and practiced in the daily examination of conscience. This frame affected the Society's view of the missions and that of its individual members, and the *Litterae indipetae* provide some important clues on this score.

For example, the successful candidate Francesco Corsi (1568-1635; he requested Japan and left for Goa in 1599) presented his vocation according to the threefold Jesuit values of discernment, indifference, and obedience: "The Lord gave me this desire" to go to the Indies, "calling me *interiormente*." He was careful to stress that he was "indifferent to obey everything that Your Paternity judges to be to [God's] greater glory."[26]

From the outset, the spiritual understanding of these regions is clear in petitions such as those by Corsi. One candidate wrote that he *saw* the Indies, as in a vision, rather than imagined them or read about them: "On seeing the multitudes in the Indies that, because of a dearth of laborers, so to speak, are almost cast out of Heaven into the darkness of Hell; I cannot fail do otherwise than be greatly moved, for which I need, then, to resolve everything in tears and sighs."[27] The Ignatian meditative practice of "compositions of place" found in the *Spiritual Exercises* is clear in this petition. Other applicants referred to the visual stimulus that led the way toward their vocation, again, reminiscent of the *Spiritual Exercises*. "One day," wrote Giuseppe di Maio, "upon seeing two paintings, one of our Blessed Father Ignatius and the other of Blessed Francis Xavier, the sight ... penetrated inside my heart and lit in me the desire to suffer and to die for Christ."[28]

The evident influence of affective mystical literature, most of all Ignatian, intersected in these petitions with news arriving from Asia. As we saw above, to Valignano's regret, these accounts had a strong impact on the young Jesuit minds listening to these and other news items circulated and read out during mealtime in refectories throughout the Society, on occasion producing unstable vocations. Giacomo Antonio Colacino wrote from Naples of the vast sea of souls in Japan waiting to be caught by fisherman-missionaries: "The cries of our companions that ask for help *in captura piscium* continuously intone in my ears." The successful candidate Francesco Buzomi wrote from Naples, "I was struck with a great deal of emotion on hearing the latest letters from Japan."[29]

Enough was known about the Indies—perhaps also thanks to the letters from the missions (such as those mentioned by Buzomi)—for Jesuits to understand the differences between the Indies to the east and to the west. The cultures of Asia tended to be viewed as sophisticated, and consequently the East became the favored destination. Giovanni Rho (1590–1662), writing from Como, exemplified this inclination toward Asia when he wrote in the first of many petitions that he was prepared equally "to go to the eastern, or western [Indies], as among the Turks," adding, however, that "it seems to me that I am called in particular to China, or else to Japan." In these lands, it was thought, and verified in the letters sent back to Europe from Xavier on, that potential converts were new "gentiles" and worthy successors to the Greeks and Romans of the ancient world to whom the first followers of Christ preached, making their salvation a higher prize than the salvation of the "Barbarian" peoples elsewhere.[30]

The attitudes in evidence here are what one might call a "spiritual Orientalism," a theme that requires more research and of which these documents certainly provide an illustration. Drawing in part on Edward W. Said's famous European conceptualizations of the Orient, there was a yearning among these Jesuits for contact, experience, and knowledge among the peoples of the East—underpinned by their conversionary ambitions. Theirs was a push-pull attitude, consisting of aversion to the "paganism" they encountered and, on account of that profound difference, attraction in the name of conversion. This mixed attitude produced a collective desire for proximity, but on the Jesuits' terms—that is, through the transformational project of conversion to Christianity.[31]

The yearning specifically for Japan, about which Valignano protested in his correspondence, included a further element: the prospect of martyrdom. It was in Japan that the greatest danger lay for missionaries to Asia, with the proscription of Christianity from 1587, followed by intermittent and intensifying executions of Christians, including Jesuits, then the final expulsions in the early seventeenth century, culminating by mid-century in Christianity's eradication as an openly practiced religion. This was a stimulus to the *indiani:* Vespasiano Bonamici, one of the relatively few selected to depart for Goa in 1602, wrote of his conviction that he must go to the missions and must die there too, if possible (*"Io devo morire"*). He wrote, "I have been in the Society for eleven years, and with ease, eating well and dressing well, and comfortable everywhere, and I will finish my life in a bed: is that possible? That my life ends in a bed while Christ died on the cross?"[32] The Indies thus were mystical for many applicants, while the conversion of what Jesuits saw as the sophisticated but spiritually imprisoned Eastern peoples was to be the prize. The petitioners' attitudes tended to be sympathetic, if patronizing: Asian pagan souls were referred to variously as "those poor little souls," and "those poor and abandoned people of the Indies."[33]

There was an element of pragmatism in many petitions, too. Candidates expressed their awareness of the enterprise's distinctive nature and demands, as well as the need to present their own skills in these terms. Applicant Francesco Pavone provides this kind of data in his petition of June 24, 1590. He starts with "my age, which is twenty," stating that "I still have time at this age to learn the language [he wanted to go to China] and afterwards to do something useful in the service of God." Unlike Pavone, another petitioner had his request met: Nicola Mastrilli (1568 or 1570–1653) sent his petition from Naples the day before Pavone; he described himself as "healthy," as "knowing the Spanish language," and more generally as "having some ability with foreign languages," proudly reporting that he learned Spanish very quickly with little assistance or method. Renouncing his family title and inheritance in favor of his brother (he was related to the famous Japan martyr Marcello Mastrilli (1603-1637), by 1593 he was in Lima, Peru, where he was ordained and assumed the name Durán; between 1623 and 1629, after holding a number of teaching roles, including college rector, he was provincial of Paraguay.[34]

Another contemporaneous petitioner from Naples was the artist Alonso di Cordova; he mentions the visit to Naples of the founding missionary to China, Michele Ruggieri (1543-1607), who advised of "the great need for painters and engravers in China." Cordova further reports that Ruggieri saw his work and commended him as an ideal missionary to China, prompting him to plead, "For the love of Jesus Christ, do not forget... or disparage... my application." Many were careful to display the virtue of humility, too. Again, Pavone wrote simply, "I know myself to be unworthy of this grace."[35]

A number of Jesuits with extant documentary records about their entry into the novitiate also appear among the *indiani*: the wealthy Mario Squadrini from Florence arrived at the S. Andrea novitiate in Rome at twenty-two years of age on May 7, 1600. "He brought with him a cassock, twill breeches draped with silk, felt hat, dark grey coarse wool coat, fawn woolen socks, a pair of worn tights, a handkerchief, a shirt, a pair of fine shoes, and a pair of shoes." He wrote with his own hand, "I, Mario Squadrini, confirm all that is written above." In his third year in the Society, he wrote an undated petition to the Indies in which he reminded the superior general how, in a previous letter, "I revealed to Your Paternity that the Lord God by His infinite mercy (in addition to having called me to this Holy Institute) deigned to call me to the Indies." He continued: "But because, for me, Your Paternity takes the place of Jesus Christ our Lord, it is from you that I wait to have my vocation fulfilled." By 1603, he was gone from Italy and listed in the Catalogues of Goa, about which phase in the missionary's journey Chapter 3 will shed more light.[36]

Pietro Lucari was not so fortunate. He died, not in China, as he had hoped, but in Aquileia, in 1656, at the age of thirty-seven. Originally from Ragusa (Dubrovnik), he entered the Roman novitiate with little more than a handkerchief and a pair of shoes on February 2, 1639. A few weeks later, on February 18, he gave answers to the vocation questionnaire: he was almost twenty years old, with two brothers (one *nel secolo* and the other in the Society) and two sisters; both parents were dead, and his family's financial situation was stable. Prior to entering the Society, the Jesuit administering the questionnaire reports how "he governed the household, and had responsibility for its affairs ... and he studied for the most part with the fathers of the Society." His lifelong inclination to the religious life (which included taking simple vows prior to entering the Society) almost came to a halt through a period of crisis, when, "after six months he again knew the will of God" to proceed on his path in religious life and to become a Jesuit. To the question about his preparedness to go to the Indies, his Jesuit interlocutor reported, "For now, if God does not want him elsewhere, he feels inclined, assuming indifference, to the Lands of the Turk, especially because he has the language with which he could serve God and help others in those lands." Another series of folios immediately after the vocation questionnaire contains *appunti per scrivere la vocatione* (points for writing a vocation), where Lucari describes under the category about graces received from God his survival from a near shipwreck while traveling to Italy and his prayers to St. Ignatius. He provided a generic response to the question about his inclination to serve his neighbor, without mention of distant India, or even of his own "Indies"—the Ottoman lands near those of his provenance.[37]

Over two years later, however, in August 1641, Lucari's original offer to go to the lands under Turkish rule had shifted to a vocation to China. He explained the reason: "All of those parts of the Indies ... for me are more meritorious than these of Europe." He added that now was the time to make the appointment because of the China procurator's presence in Rome (which he alluded to again in a second petition later that year, dated December 2, 1641), "an occasion which turns up extremely seldom.... Therefore I pray [you] that before he departs, you admit me among the number of other missionaries for China."[38]

Among the petitioners are two Jesuits whom I have already mentioned as entrants to the Society: one is typical and the other is quite peculiar. The youthful Pietro Conti arrived at the novitiate at seventeen years old in December 1635 with several items of clothing as well as twenty-eight books, a pair of scissors, a small broom, and a comb. In the following February, in response to the part in his survey about whether he was ready to go to India, he affirmed that he was ready to go "not only to India, and to Japan, but if beyond those parts there is a country, to open the road with my blood, where neither Fathers [priests], nor Others have ever been able to penetrate." In his petition, sent from the Collegio Romano the following year, in 1638, Conti felt called to the Indies, either to Japan or some other part where he could work among the *poverelli ignoranti*—but to no effect.[39] The widower, Giovanni Raffaele de Ferraris, mentioned at the opening of this book, sent a far more unusual petition in 1639. His son, also a Jesuit, was the China missionary Giovanni Francesco de Ferraris (1609–1671), who had departed Europe in 1635. At over fifty years, the Piedmontese sought a special "grace to follow my son to the Indies... and to give me a terrain to sacrifice to his divine majesty this my miserable life and those few days left to me." He wrote that he was painfully aware of his poverty of spirit, advanced age, limited strength, and "ignorance and inability above all to undertake such a great endeavor, only too well known to you."[40] Unsurprisingly, he was not chosen.

In these petitions, not only do individual *indiani* come into view, and the institutional, administrative, and spiritual frame within which they were written, but also another purpose for which the petitions were produced: to establish an unmediated avenue of contact between each petitioner and the superior general. This was intentional, and some candidates took the opportunity to complain that their superiors did not wish them to go. In his petition, Nicola Mastrilli wrote to the general that, after first having written seven years previously and having applied to his provincial by letter and in person, he decided to write in exasperation to the visitor to the Indies, in addition to his present petition. "I am suspicious towards my other superiors because, as far as I can see and understand, they love me with the kind of love that possibly could hold me back."[41] Clearly, in the minds of the applicants, as for Valignano, the petitions served to bypass jealous provincials trying to keep their best talent at home, while this direct line of communication appeared intent on the opposite aim: to open the path to the most suitable and committed candidates for the missions. It also permitted applicants to have a role in their own appointments, negotiating in written dialogue with the head of the worldwide Society, the superior general himself. In these petitions, they shared their views of the missions, imbuing them with spiritual meaning alongside—and on occasion more than—their geographical specificity. For Jesuits, the missions, no matter how distant or unfamiliar, were a constituent part of the world's "vineyard," reassuringly entrusted to the care of their Society.

From the date of the first petitions in 1590 until the end of Acquaviva's generalate in 1615, when over 600 requests were made, ninety-two Italians traveled east. Of these successful candidates, only twenty-three known petitions are extant. This shows two things: that more Jesuits than places were available for the overseas missions, and that a petition possibly was not a prerequisite for departure, since many Italians were sent overseas, apparently without having written one (although they may simply be lost).[42] Of those missionaries without a petition, a likely method of appointment was through the Jesuit procurators who served the overseas missions in numerous administrative tasks, and also recruited new missionaries for the Indies during their journeys back to Europe.

Some Jesuits were chosen from lists of potential candidates drawn up from petitions sent in to Rome: Andrea Simi left for the Indies in 1605, and an undated petition indicates not only that he had an inclination to go to Japan but also that his petition was marked on the address page as *cavato,* collated for a possible departure.[43] These candidates were expecting to cross from their own assistancy into another, and the vocation statements provided the procedural means for this to take place and for the requisite permission from Rome to be given. They aided the superior general and his assistants in Rome (who also probably consulted the Society's regular personnel catalogues and senior provincial members) to select candidates whom they did not know for missionary posts. They also provided proof to their correspondents in Rome—and to any protesting families—that the vocation was freely made and not imposed by superiors.[44]

The centrality of the individual vocation to the overseas missions in the textual record tells us something about how the Society saw itself: as a community of volunteers. The focus on individual discernment and the opportunity to give voice to it as the first step in making these highly desirable appointments must have been an appealing aspect of life in the Society; fulfilling individual potential, at least as an objective, if not always in reality, perhaps helps explain why so many joined. Numerous Jesuits were young men who expected the privilege of some measure of agency. It appears that they did not necessarily give this up on joining the Society as much as transfer it—even expanding their agency in certain circumstances, if we consider that some had the opportunity to travel to the farthest reaches of the known world and operate quite autonomously, something unthinkable for most people at the time. For some Jesuits, the prospect of realizing their potential by traveling afar and fulfilling the spiritual aims set by their times must have made this vocation—both as a Jesuit *and* a missionary—an attractive choice.

The Superiors General Reply

In 1607, Donato Sementi wrote to the superior general in tones that recall a child writing to his father, a reminder that many who wrote their petitions had barely left childhood: "*O Padre mio,*" he writes, "this is an affair of the utmost importance." "*O Padre, Padre mio,*" he intones a few lines later, begging to be considered to make reparation for the health of his own soul, and, invoking another father figure, he asks, "For the merits of Our Saint and Blessed Father Ignatius, please deign to write four lines of a letter in reply for my consolation." While it is unclear whether Sementi received an answer, many did. The tone was fatherly in return, even if replies sometimes were relayed through applicants' provincials. For example, Benedetto Turri, who eventually went to Asia, was begging to be sent to the Indies: in April 1599, the superior general wrote to Turri's provincial advising him to try to calm Turri down by asking "Your Reverence [the provincial] . . . to greet and console him."[45]

The somewhat unexpected existence of individual replies to mission applicants and their superiors written by the superior general—who after all oversaw thousands of members of the Society of Jesus—is a little-known chapter in the production of the *Litterae indipetae*. Several petitioners from the Italian provinces received letters from their superior general, no doubt assisted by secretaries who penned the letters. Evidence of these replies is preserved at ARSI among the *Epistulae Generalium* in the form of copy letters. Grouped according to province, the letters are abbreviated copies of the originals; they are difficult to read in places, with the ink letters and words bleeding, both into each other and from the folio beneath. Ordered chronologically rather than thematically alongside other letters sent out to the provinces on all manner of business, they are difficult to locate and apparently do not include all of the replies sent out to petitioners. (Some petitions refer to replies from the superior general for which there is no extant record.)[46]

The historiography concerning the *Litterae indipetae* until recently has shown little awareness that replies were sent. Yet the replies are significant, for they attest to the intimate connection between petitions and missionary appointments, both procedurally and in terms of their spiritual dimension. The petitions *and* their replies reveal the dialogic nature of the Society's operations and a shared set of values about the missions, from the most junior members of the Society to the most senior.[47]

In 1603, Giulio Orsino (1574–1640) received a letter in Naples from Superior General Acquaviva about "the offer, which you renew with so much affection, to go to Japan"; however, Acquaviva mentioned that Orsino's health problems made "such a long journey" prohibitive.[48] The letter was sent three years after Orsino's first petition for the Indies, followed by several subsequent ones spanning eight years. According to the first petition—written on May 23, 1600, from the Collegio Romano—his vocation for this "holy journey" was a long-standing one: "Since the first years of my life when I only just had perception, and the ability to reason, I felt these abundant rays ignite in my chest." What he wished for above all was "to go among infidel peoples especially to Japan, or else to China." Later in the same year, he wrote on the subject again. He described how "in Turkey many suffer the experience of most cruel torments for the faith of Christ," and he wrote about his fear that he would miss the opportunity to die for Christ (and die in his own bed instead) because of his recent poor health, and about how his recovering health inspired him to write another petition. Orsino wrote yet another petition almost two years later, from Naples, on November 27, 1602; this time he mentioned "my negotiations for going to Japan"—suggesting a possible understanding that he would be sent there—although he also complained that he still had not received his expected reply from the superior general.[49]

Eventually, Superior General Acquaviva sent four letters of reply to Orsino between 1603 and 1605. The main reason for his letters was to explain that Orsino could not be sent because of his fragile health. The informality of his letters revealed another reason for writing—to encourage the petitioner and to convey gratitude for Orsino's continued "desires for divine service." In his final letter, dated February 19, 1605, Acquaviva referred to Orsino's persistent desire to work in assistance of the Indians; yet as he had "replied other times," the Jesuit's "weak health and strength" continued to "render the matter a little difficult." Orsino never received his wished-for appointment; instead, in 1611 he was sent to head the first Jesuit college in Florence.[50]

Another candidate to whom the superior general replied was Pietro Cornaro. He had explained in his petition from Parma on March 31, 1611, that after discovering his vocation to the Indies, he had delayed sending his letter because he wanted to check if it came from God or was a temptation from the Devil. This was a clear reference to the method of discernment set out in the *Spiritual Exercises*—specifically, the meditation at the beginning of week two. On establishing the divine source of his vocation, Cornaro sought to proceed with it, following the example of Francis Xavier. However, one factor that gave him pause was that he was Italian: "I was born in Candia, even if my parents descend from Venice." He seemed to have been aware that Italians were not being sent to Asia in those years. Nevertheless, he wrote that "I find myself in very good health; I am twenty-four years old and I study physics." He added with a certain amount of frankness, "In spirit and virtue, however, which is the most important, I find myself very poor; but I feel some desire to acquire them." A few months later, on the feast of St. John the Baptist, June 24, 1611, Cornaro chose to write again, expressing some perplexity about not having received a reply to his earlier petition: "I am doubting that it has reached the hands of your Paternity." Undeterred, and "knowing that everything depends on you," he wrote his second letter, "despite the impediment that exists for Italians." He found the courage to write, even though he was painfully aware of his shortcomings in the face of such an important undertaking, "for which people of the highest virtue and doctrine are received." He resolved that he would come to Rome to discuss his vocation in person with the general.[51]

Acquaviva consequently decided to reply. On August 6, 1611, he advised Cornaro that he would "keep in mind" his vocation but that "for now, this cannot take place, there being—as I believe you know—some impediments for those parts." The following sentence explains the reason, already known to Cornaro, and crossed out in this copy letter: "The door is locked to Italians." Acquaviva adds, "But I hope that it will open . . . soon and at that time we will remember you. In the meantime persevere in your aim and in perfecting yourself increasingly in every virtue."[52]

Cornaro received another letter from the general on December 15, 1612, over a year after his previous one. Once more Acquaviva mentioned the ban on Italian candidates, although, again, this part was crossed out and replaced with a blander comment about the impossibility of sending Cornaro at that time (this apparent self-censorship attests to the sensitivity of the issue and probably points to Acquaviva's corrections of preprepared drafts). The superior general wrote one last time, on March 22, 1614; in this letter we learn that Cornaro's many relatives were in dire need, and that he was to be transferred.[53] Acquaviva expressed his sympathy at this disappointing outcome for his vocation to the Indies.

Much better news was delivered to the Neapolitan Francesco Buzomi, already mentioned. Over fifteen years after he wrote his first petition, he finally left for the Indies, in 1609, two years before the ban on Italians. He joined the Society in 1592 at the age of seventeen and, starting in 1595, wrote four petitions. He explained that while he was aware of the "great need in [God's] ancient Church" in Europe, his vocation to depart for the East had been ignited after hearing "the letters from Mogorr [Mughal lands]," as well as "the latest letters from Japan." Buzomi's petition was presented in terms of obedience, seeking the divine will, "in conformity with the advice of superiors, through prayers, fasts, and other mortifications." He wrote how "Father [Bartolomeo] Ricci, prefect of spiritual matters to whom I had confided all of the movements of my soul, also told me that the matter had progressed along a good path."[54] In 1599, Superior General Acquaviva sent acknowledgment of Buzomi's vocation (via the provincial, to whom the letter was addressed) by way of a salutation to him and several others, noted in the copy letter's margin as "Greetings—Indians." He wrote, "I ask Your Reverence to greet them most dearly . . . telling them how we embrace them . . . and we will keep in mind their desire that they do not fail to pray to God to inspire us."[55]

It would take a further ten years before Buzomi departed. His final dated petition was written in 1606. In an undated petition, probably chronologically his last, he wrote that he had a license to depart for "the Western Indies" with the following reminder: "My name is Francesco Buzomi, and I am the one about whom the Procurator of the Indies has spoken with Your Paternity." The arrangements changed, however, and he departed for the eastern, not western, Indies. He was professed with four vows in 1618 at Macao and from 1623 served as superior of the mission at Cochinchina for four years; he died in 1639.[56]

Like the *Litterae indipetae*, the replies sent by the superiors general provide insights into the organizational procedures for the missions. They tell us something more, too. They reveal the Jesuits in their relationship with their superior general. The process was rigorous and competitive, but it was also personal, and the general was directly involved. He emerges in this correspondence as a father figure for these young Jesuits who had left their own fathers behind in the secular world. The intimacy of these letters reveals a consciously nurtured familial closeness between members. These were the terms in which Jesuits preferred to write about themselves and their confreres. The fact that obedience was expected, and hierarchy maintained, with a solid vein of formality running through their exchanges, nevertheless made this dynamic not dissimilar to that of a real family, and it was consistent with the patriarchal structures of the time. Families, consisting of households (not necessarily related by blood) and other sometimes large configurations of *parenti*, constituted serious joint enterprises, not voluntary collections of individual members joined together primarily by affection and biology.[57] The more elite the person, as for so many Jesuits, the more complex and large-scale the family often was. In the Society of Jesus, even though the "father" made the final choice of who would sail and when, the impetus for the whole process began with the vocation. In this way, at least at the outset, the "son" of the Society moved to the center of the dynamic, guided as always by divine inspiration, together with his confessor and immediate superiors. The centrality of this vocation, however, was a key moment of individual agency, and one that must have been relished by those with the desire for the Indies.

On April 3, 1599, Acquaviva wrote to the college rector at Chieti: "We had written to Your Reverence that you were to send Father [Girolamo] Puerio to us in Rome as soon as possible, for the Philippines" ("India" was crossed out). However, since that original directive, Puerio had sent a letter to the general outlining a number of "difficulties," including "poor health and some decrease in his fervor." He went on to explain that Puerio subsequently "once more placed himself under obedience, he did not depart." Acquaviva concluded the matter by advising the rector to send his greetings to Puerio and to "tell him not to move and that we will put another in his place, not wanting to send anyone to such an important undertaking unless he feels absolute affection and desire towards it."[58]

The letters, then, were used to dissuade on some occasions, and encourage on others: in the margins of the general's copy letters to the Neapolitan province, the theme of one letter from 1599 was listed as "keep alive the vocation of the Indians." Provincial leaders thus were expected to collaborate in this aspect of the enterprise. In the letter itself, addressed to the rector, the general declared, "It gives us great joy regarding those that have the inspiration to go to the Indies, we are consoled, and may Your Reverence preserve them in this good spirit."[59] Alongside these rhetorical flourishes, the leadership in Rome clearly wished to have a ready supply of willing candidates who could be sent when needed.[60] Appointments were a difficult balance: Acquaviva wrote bluntly in one letter, dated April 30, 1599, "About Father Cicero [in Naples], I have already written to the Father Provincial . . . that it is difficult to satisfy everyone."[61]

The spiritual and organizational motivations for this correspondence are indistinguishable. As Acquaviva wrote in 1599 to the college rector at Naples about a repeated petitioner for the Indies, "Exhort him to nourish this holy desire and accompany it with the virtues that are necessary for it, such that we will keep him in mind."[62] The spiritual readiness of candidates was a precondition for departure, with the necessity of waiting patiently and demanding continual discipline to maintain fitness for the task. Another attitude comes into view in the correspondence: the Indies had come to stand for the continuation of a vocation within the Society itself; persisting with a vocation to the overseas missions was akin to persevering in the (often stationary) life of a Jesuit.

While the superior general had ultimate oversight of these appointments, his choice of candidate was not always guaranteed. In 1599, Acquaviva wrote to a Jesuit coadjutor brother, "The desire of Your Reverence to go to the Indies is dear to me: that you have proposed it, I will not fail to recommend to the Superior." In the same year, he wrote to Brother Giovanni Battista d'Orsi that it would not be possible to sail east:

"For now, the Father Provincial needs you in the province."[63] Clearly, among the most important figures in the appointment process were the provincials and provincial administrators who knew the candidates best. It is to their part in making missionaries for the Indies we now turn.

Assessing Candidates for the "Indies"

At the same time as the petitions became permanent features of the appointment system for the missions, with the lion's share generated from the Italian provinces, a second administrative document emerged from these provinces: reports addressed to the superior general in Rome with the purpose of appraising potential candidates for the overseas enterprise.[64] They were written at the request of the superior general, an example of which is in the *Epistulae Generalium* of 1599, addressed to the college rector in Naples on February 27. He wrote that his confrere would have been aware of the call for more manpower in the Indies: "I would like you to give some consideration to it and to propose a large number of those who in this holy inspiration you judge to be the most fervent and the most suitable. In this way, and in needing to call some to this effect, we can do so with more awareness and certainty." The provincial of Sicily, Giovanni Battista Carminata (1536–1619), received a similar request: he sent a list of suitable candidates to the superior general in 1600. Carminata writes of his purpose: "In fulfillment of the order that Your Paternity gave to me a few days ago, I am sending information about those people who applied for the Indies from this province."[65]

In these reports, the reader is privy to which candidates were deemed suited to an appointment, the basis for disqualification, and what attributes were thought to warrant selection. They also show that many people were involved in the appointment process. The Society's was a hierarchical system but also consultative; for these highly prized appointments, the search for quality Italian candidates for distant posts where the stakes were high, epistolary dialogue between members clearly was seen as the best way to proceed.

The largest concentration of extant reports from the Italian Assistancy is from a limited period between 1589 and 1603, although a small number from later periods also survive. For the period under consideration here, there are twenty-five separate reports in three folders concerning roughly 130 individual candidates from provincial officers in Palermo, Milan, Venice, Rome, and especially Naples, with the majority interspersed among the earliest Italian *Litterae indipetae*.[66]

These documents varied: some were produced annually, as a list of candidates from one particular novitiate or province; others were written as letters of recommendation about single candidates.[67] Most were written in a brief format of one or two paragraphs. Well-known missionaries appear among these reports: Roberto de' Nobili, Niccolò Longobardo, Giulio Aleni, and Francesco Sambiasi, as well as others who did not go to the Indies.[68] The provincial sent most, although some reports are without an author. In some cases, college rectors, teachers, and novice masters provided information to the provincials, often verbally.[69] In his 1593/1594 report from Milan, for example, Provincial Bernardo Rossignoli (1546–1613) took verbal advice from the college rector that the candidate Giovanni Medaglia was unsuitable. This was because of his advanced age and his stubborn and undisciplined character, whereas the same rector advised that Francesco Tezzoni, who had applied for Japan twice already, was enthusiastic, to be sure, but not yet sufficiently mature.[70]

The reports were consistent with regular Jesuit recruitment practices, which included the drawing up of discrete lists of possible candidates for specific missions. They also resembled the Society's personnel catalogues and likely drew on the information they contained.[71] These catalogues, discussed elsewhere in this study, provided information about age, stage of study, health, religious talents, character, esteem of peers and teachers, and spiritual fortitude. In his catalogue entry, Francesco Pavone, whose petition was discussed above, was "among the best in his class, and reflects every kind of virtue of the Neapolitan College."[72]

The technical skills of the temporal coadjutors (or lay brothers) were a particular focus of the reports. Temporal coadjutors tended to be requested by the missionaries in the East, who regularly complained that not enough were sent: there were six coadjutors for every ten Jesuit fathers in the Goa province (more than in the Portuguese province, which had a ratio of 5.5:10). However, the superiors in India also cautioned that their lack of theological training, and therefore their inability to help in the work of evangelization, meant that their numbers should be kept proportionate. The average of twelve Jesuit departures from Lisbon each year tended to be divided evenly between coadjutors, priests, and scholastics (who completed their formation in Asia, either as spiritual coadjutors or as professed members).[73]

Comments about scholarly strengths and limitations abounded in the reports: Sicily provincial Bartolomeo Ricci (c. 1545–1614; provincial 1590–1594) wrote that Father Barnaba d'Erma "possessed as little learning as he did fervor, so that he does not seem to me to be suitable." Coadjutors were assessed also for their literacy levels, since their social provenance meant that literacy could not be assumed. One candidate was praised for his delightful personality and for his skills as a cook, but "he knows neither how to read nor write, he has very little intelligence."[74]

While similar in some respects, the reports reveal a number of differences compared with other evaluative documents produced in the Society: they tended to be more detailed than the catalogues.[75] Also, health received special attention in the reports for overseas positions, particularly regarding the coadjutors. Beginning with the sea crossing, good physical condition was important for these roles. Xavier insisted on this point, especially for the coadjutors: "When you arrange for the sending of some of the Society who are not preachers . . . [ensure that] they be persons who have been well tried in the Society . . . and that they not be of poor health, since the labors in India require physical strength." Still, he insisted that "spiritual strength is more important."[76]

Xavier's advice was heeded. Many young men missed out on being recommended because of ill health, with several described as having had "pains in the chest, and sometimes spat blood." Priests were included in assessments about physical fortitude. The 1592 report from Sicily, sent in April by Provincial Bartolomeo Ricci, stated, "Father Benedetto Moleti would have been very good, because he is zealous, has the grace of preaching, and dealing fruitfully with others. . . . However, given that, when he was young, he suffered *il mal caduco* [epilepsy], and despite being well now (as I have noted elsewhere), it is feared that the initial stages of paralysis have set in." The talented Francesco Pavone (1568–1637) was destined to remain in Italy, perhaps because of his health, even though his assessor made light of the issue: "He has suffered on occasion with faint pains in the chest, but it was nothing remarkable." Pavone, originally from Calabria, went on to be a leading figure in popular missions, as well as author of theological works. In Naples, he taught literature, philosophy, Hebrew, and theology; he founded an academy for biblical exegesis for clergy, which transformed to include functioning also as a Marian congregation for priests, a model that was brought from Spain to Italy, and at the request of Acquaviva expanded throughout Italy and then India. (One of his students at the academy was the future missionary and martyr Marcello Mastrilli.) Other provincial reports comment on Pavone's health challenges, and this apparently was the reason why he was kept home. His contemporary, Nicola Mastrilli, who was chosen for Peru, had some health problems, but this did not stop him from being sent.[77]

The importance given to the maturity and experience of candidates is another feature of these reports. Xavier's advice to select only those who were "experienced in the Society" and Visitor Valignano's later request that candidates be "persons of great trustworthiness" appear to have been heeded by the report writers.[78] Experience and knowledge of the world were considered to be key attributes, in addition to skill. For example, despite being twenty-seven years old and having been in the Society for four or five years, according to his assessor, the tailor-novice Pietro Martini "does not seem mature for such a mission and it seems to me better if he were to try again at another time. This brother is in the novitiate and since his entrance he has never lived anywhere else, except perhaps for a few days." Experience and skills were highly prized: despite the disadvantage of his relatively advanced age, the 1592 report from Naples described the forty-year-old Father Francesco Albertino of Catanzaro as being "talented in teaching, and also preaching, and he's read the Christian doctrine in Church for a year now with much fruit."[79]

In many assessments, physical weakness and illness were treated as being connected to spiritual and character weakness. Similarly, the two themes of character and spiritual merits were closely linked. The Naples report, mentioned above, provided the following appraisal about the thirty-four-year-old Father Giovanni Palermo: "His devotion, humility and obedience are mediocre; he is very choleric, presumptuous and gives little edification and satisfaction." Similar weaknesses were listed in the 1592 report from Sicily about one Jesuit priest: "Father Antonio Cicala is not healthy enough for such a journey, its discomforts and demands; neither has he stability of the soul for such an enterprise; thus I would not send him."[80]

Manual skill also was valued by assessors: the forty-three-year-old coadjutor brother Francesco Laccio of Monaciglione was a gifted tailor—indeed, he had been promoted to the position of head tailor, and he had "a singular devotion and edification, and a great desire to suffer for the love of Christ." Another tailor, Brother Agostino Retava, a novice in the *casa professa* of Palermo and roughly twenty-five years old, was singled out in a solo report in December 1592: "He knows his art of cutting well and he demonstrates principles [strengths] of the spirit and of maturity."[81]

Like the petitions and the superior general's reports, spiritual values were by no means subordinated to pragmatic considerations. The Florentine Mario Squadrini, whose entry to the novitiate and petition are discussed above, also has an extant report about him. This report was produced in Rome as a stand-alone letter with no author and no date. It was written very soon after his entry to the novitiate, since both documents mention his age to be twenty-two. It also echoes his petition very closely and is distinctive for its highly rhetorical language. After describing his abandonment of legal studies in response to a divine call to enter the Society, the report outlines in spiritual terms the subsequent escalation of his vocation to an even higher calling: "His Divine Majesty, not content at having called him to religious life, has deigned to call him further to the highest perfection of saving others." The report states that after much prayer on the matter, he feels himself "to be called now with enormous love to the conversion of the infidels." He departed for the East in 1603.[82]

Quite surprisingly, these reports tell us about how porous the Society actually was in this period, between the religious life and the secular one, when relatives and family members vied for the attention, and duties and responsibilities, of these same men who technically had renounced any further connection with them. This is most evident in the importance given to the financial and family circumstances of candidates in the reports.[83] Many were deemed suitable partly by virtue of their financial status. For example, a very well regarded and experienced member of the Society, Stefano di Majo, in addition to a long list of impressive positions in the province of Naples, "has no poor relatives; he only has a brother who is a doctor, who has no need of him." In the same report, Father Francesco Albertino of Catanzaro, mentioned above, was described, in addition to being talented, as having "no relatives in need." The coadjutors were singled out for attention on this matter. For example, about the thirty-three-year-old tailor Pietro Antonio del Guasto, a stand-alone report just about him stated, "He does not seem to be burdened by any poor relations, so that he seems suited to such a mission."[84]

Coadjutors, by contrast, in many instances were identified as having poor relations, while poor health also seems to have been more common among them than among the professed members, whose social status tended to be higher. However, familial poverty was not restricted to the coadjutors, and it remained a serious impediment in the eyes of the assessors for all candidates. For example, the scholastic Giovanni Alfonso Sacco "has a mother and sister in some need; despite them having been extremely rich, they have now fallen into poverty."[85] Many such candidates with poor or needy relatives were deemed unsuitable, presumably because they might have been required to remain in Europe to assist their family, or even abandon the Society, if not fully incorporated into it, to help support dependent relatives. Being a Jesuit came first *only* if this did not cause harm to any members of the Jesuit's family. In a society where familial bonds were seen as the source for ensuring the necessities of life, even of survival, entering religious life and forming a new spiritual family and fellowship came second to such considerations.

Interestingly, none of the reports from Italy mention the unsuitability of a candidate on the grounds of protests from relatives, or a social standing that was deemed too *high* for such an undertaking. The records show, nevertheless, that many families protested and were even successful in keeping their sons at home, but these factors did not reach the reports here. Relatives were not the only ones reluctant to see these candidates depart for distant lands, for, like the *Litterae indipetae,* the reports reveal that provincials on occasion were loath to release their most talented candidates. On March 22, 1591, thirty-three-year-old Pietro Antonio del Guasto was identified as suitable for the missions, "even if this would be most inconvenient for this province [Naples]." In 1592, the Sicilian provincial Bartolomeo Ricci remarked of the extremely talented Father Gasparo Taraninfa—who preached with zeal and to great acclaim—"We had indeed thought to put him forward as the master of novices in Palermo."[86]

The reports provide a window onto the profile of an ideal missionary, but they also tell us about the enterprise's realities, including the process of working out which candidates were considered suitable and which were not. In terms of procedure and approach, recurring adjectives such as "virtuous," "humble," and "devout," and appraisals such as being "talented at dealing with others," or preaching with "much fruit," provide two important insights: first, assessors highlighted (if sometimes reluctantly) their most able members; second, these candidates were identified, not so much for their imposing style as for their all-around capabilities, and for their effectiveness among their peers and among those to whom they ministered. These traits were no different from qualities valued for European work. The *Spiritual Exercises* provided a guide on this score, too. One of the fruits of conversion was prayer, and in the fourth week, which discusses "Methods of Prayer," Ignatius is careful to highlight that prayer should be a positive experience, even joyful, and not an imposition: "This method of praying aims chiefly to give a manner of proceeding ... so that persons may become better able to profit from the exercises and to find their prayer a pleasing experience."[87] In theory, at least, this was the path to conversion for all, regardless of background or location.

In some senses, candidates appear to have been expected to be even better than they needed to be for Europe, at least in comparison with the equivalent stage of membership in the Society. This was because an overseas mission was seen as more difficult and, because of its spiritual weight, also more valuable. The list of candidates sent from Milan in the last decade of the sixteenth century (where missionaries Giulio Cesare Curione, Niccolò Levanto, Alfonso Vagnone, and future Japan martyr Carlo Spinola are also named) earmarks Giovanni Battista Laverna for "India or *some other difficult mission*" (emphasis added).[88]

This view of the missions' high value and intrinsic challenges came from the superior general himself. In 1595, Acquaviva wrote a confidential letter—these letters were known as *soli*—to Alberto Laerzio in Goa, where he was master of novices (and later Malabar provincial). It contains a valuable encapsulation of how the superior general understood the difficulty of securing quality workers for the Indies:

> I desire that Your Reverence attend with every effort and diligence to promoting the spirit in our brothers, since in large part the good progress of "ours" [Jesuits] in the colleges depends on that formation. While this is necessary in all places, it is particularly so in those parts where, having such a high undertaking in their hands as the help and conversion of so many nations, they need even greater spirit to be able to transfer it into others.[89]

The superior general appears to have been more committed to the vocation, assessment, and selection process for the Indies than were the provincials. For example, the 1600 provincial's report about candidates from Sicily states, "I did not know who they were, if not that I had their names extracted from the letters that Your Paternity wrote to me at the time of my government [previously provincial of Sicily in 1577–1581 and 1582–1586] when in your name I greeted one or another of these brothers who have this desire [for the Indies]. And they are the following, starting with the scholastics." This reveals a process in circular motion—from the petitioner, to the superior general, to the provincial, and back to the superior general, who made the final decision. It was hierarchical but also multilateral. Its source was the vocation; without it, nothing else advanced. The texts show how closely involved the office of the superior general was in communicating with petitioners—with the provincial acting as a somewhat disinterested go-between. One of the reasons for this emerges in the report from Sicily: "I cannot find any impediment in any of these [four scholastics], since they appear to be mature and spiritual, and, as far as one can tell, they are healthy, and desire to suffer. I only stress to Your Paternity the inconvenience to the province, since, in time, all of these candidates could serve the province well."[90]

One of these candidates, Antonio Zumbo, left for Goa in 1602. Zumbo is described in the 1600 report sent from Palermo in the following terms: "after having completed and defended his studies in philosophy, he undertook four years of school [teaching] and currently is in his first year of theology."[91] Clearly, in naming Zumbo, if reluctantly, as a potential candidate for the missions, the provincial leadership was unable to stop him from being selected to leave the province for overseas.

The assessors operated between competing demands: those of the missionaries (both those in the field and those back in Europe hoping to follow in their footsteps); those of their own provinces, which required talented men to take on all manner of leadership and other senior roles; and those of their superiors, who faced the inhibiting challenge of manning the missionary enterprise. It is possible that the superior general on occasion also kept back talented men whom he deemed more suited to roles back in Europe and perhaps who even were too talented in his estimation to be let go. This view, however, does not make it into the records.

The reporting system appears to have ceased in the Italian provinces early in the first decade of the seventeenth century, although it is possible that more reports were produced after that date and are no longer extant. Perhaps overworked provincials gradually stopped sending reports and may even have wished to avoid identifying their best members for work so far from their own provinces. Unlike these reports, the *Litterae indipetae* continued to be sent. The triennial catalogues, already used alongside the reports, probably replaced them as sources of information about mission candidates; the 1592 report from Milan, listing among others the future missionary to China Alfonso Vagnone, referred the superior general to the relevant triennial catalogue for further information.[92] A more likely explanation for the cessation of the reports is that this was the very decade when there were efforts from some in the Portuguese Assistancy and the Spanish-Portuguese crown to stop sending Italians. Acquaviva and the papacy successfully intervened so that the Italians managed to continue to sail—in 1602, the largest single contingent of Italians, thirty out of sixty Jesuits, sailed for India (destined for the Malabar coast)—but these reports do not reappear in any regular manner after 1603.

The personal meeting and the verbal evaluation remained important in making selections: the Sicily report from 1600 states that no information would be provided about Vincente Galletti, because he would soon be in Rome for his studies, when the superior general could make his own judgment. In the case of Benedetto Turri—whom the general had advised to remain calm about his vocation to the Indies—a report from Naples in 1589 reflects the process of personal negotiation in promoting certain appointments:

> Benedetto Turri desires to go to the Indies and has written about it to the Reverend Father General, and Father Pietro Antonio Spinello has spoken of him [Turri] to Reverend Father General in the month of June 1589. Our Father [the superior general] has ordered that they [including Ottavio Lombardo, mentioned in the same document, and who departed] be written in the book of those who want to go to the Indies.[93]

Other methods of appointment involved the provincial procurators. In the early years of the overseas enterprise, these Asia-based Jesuits (such as Alberto Laerzio, procurator for Goa) made the dangerous journey back to Rome, via Lisbon, where one of their tasks was to recruit new missionaries from Europe, many of whom were appointed on their recommendation. These procurators, along with the missions procurator in Lisbon and other senior missionaries who returned to Europe, such as Michele Ruggieri, were directly involved in recommending who should be sent. It appears that several appointments were made in this way, substituting the petition system, and without candidates having sent a letter to the superior general about their vocation.

In the case of Giulio Aleni, it was the provincial of Paraguay, rather than the procurator, who appears to have been involved in his selection for the missions, which, however, resulted in an appointment to the East and not the American missions. Also, the 1593/1594 report from Milan recorded that Niccolò Levanto (who set sail for India in 1593) was held in very high esteem by the provincial, and having requested to go to the Indies four times (although none of his petitions survive), Levanto "left finally... with the Father Procurator for the Portuguese Indies, Father Francesco Monclaro [Francisco de Monclaro]."[94]

From these texts, it is possible to gain a sense of the ideal missionary: most attempted to provide a positive portrait, either by describing themselves as candidates, sending replies and directives, or by providing evaluations. This imagined missionary can be neatly summarized in the assessment that was provided about the highly regarded but unsuccessful candidate Father Stefano di Majo. He was praised for his character ("humble"), his spiritual virtue ("devout"), the strength of his vocation ("he wants to suffer for the love of Christ"), his strong inclination toward missionary work to save souls, and his lack of poor relatives.[95] The basis for his suitability fluctuates between the pragmatic (such as family circumstances) and the purely religious (his desire to suffer for Christ), which together underpinned the approach, and the rhetoric, used by all involved—most with no experience—in trying to imagine, and then recommend, those best suited to little-known distant regions.

The documents about appointments from the Italian provinces reveal that the process was negotiated between candidates, provincial superiors, and the office of the superior general in Rome. Obedience was relevant here only for those disappointed not to be sent. For those who were sent, no one went only out of obedience. All asked for this mission. Here, at least, in the sphere of the overseas mission, is a potent example of individual agency within the Society of Jesus.

Single Jesuits come into view, too. Faced with the prospect of the Indies on entry to the Society through the questionnaires they were given, Jesuits still in the novitiate or else relatively early in their formation presented themselves for work overseas. The writing of a petition was almost like a rite of passage for them. Most appeared to be genuinely motivated, and for many it was a significant reason for seeking entry to the Society, or it was a vocation that had emerged in childhood.

How much can we take such declarations at face value? It is difficult to say; perhaps some petitioners in reality were reluctant to volunteer for the Indies. Yet the intensity of attention in the Italian lands given to the overseas missions, from the earliest entrant to the superior general, means that they were probably the most defining, sought-after, and high-profile of the Society's apostolates. For many, it seemed, this was what made its members true Jesuits.

The continued low numbers that were sent each year from their provinces further enhanced the enterprise's prestige among the Italians. From the over one hundred Italian candidates listed in the reports dated between 1589 and 1603, only a handful of those assessed actually departed for the East; similarly, a relatively small number of petitions are extant for these successful candidates in the same period, out of a total of sixty Italians who traveled east at the same time.[96] This was a selective posting, carefully negotiated, involving all parties, and leaving a paper trail the nature of which places the missions at the center of the Society's self-understanding and operations.

It is a paper trail that continues to give voice to those involved, in turn revealing a history of an enterprise that was remarkable for its diversity, made up not just of those who made the final decision or those who actually left, but also of those who provided assessments. By far the most numerically represented are the thousands of *indiani* who never left at all but earned themselves the name as if they had. This reveals the spiritual frameworks within which each participant operated in this process, bringing the physical Indies into the spiritual realm through the individual vocation. Everyone, in one way or another, could travel to the Indies. For each of the participants, these lands belonged in a special way to the Society of Jesus. In Chapter 3, we turn our attention to those missionaries who did depart on this extraordinary endeavor of the global age.

3

Being a Jesuit in the "Indies"

I have shown how a Jesuit did not necessarily need to travel to the Indies to earn the name *indiano* because the title was connected to his vocation, not to a place. In a similar vein, he became a *missionario* on his selection, well before his arrival at the destination. At the same time, the missions were actual places with real people, languages, and traditions that existed well before and beyond the Jesuit gaze. For the Jesuits, the missions represented a high point for the embodied spirituality that characterized the Society of Jesus; they were the meeting point for the saving of souls through bringing them for the first time to know the Christian God and, as a result, the hope for the salvation of one's own soul through the act of converting others. The "Indies" were both physical and spiritual. The analysis that follows further tests this idea and illustrates how it worked.[1]

Using the biographical documents of Jesuits from Italy sent to Asia, especially in the missions' first decades, this chapter aims to understand how the spiritual meaning of mission informed the ways that individual Jesuits and the Society operated in their overseas contexts. How did this spiritual perspective shape what was seen, experienced, and recorded?

Following the vein of the documents, the missionary path unfolds: our starting point is the crucial transition from *indiano* to *missionario,* by way of application, assessment, and selection of successful candidates. This phase is followed by their departure for the overseas missions. The next step is the journey, and then arrival, and, finally, staying there. A number of themes emerge from the documents that guide the analysis, from personal experiences—emotional, spiritual, cultural, political, and even climactic—to collective ones relating to Jesuit governance, mission policy, fellow Europeans, community life, religious identity, and, after arrival, host societies. Together the texts help paint a portrait of the overseas missions in the Jesuits' own words.

This is one of the most written-about subjects in Jesuit history. Numerous studies have carefully mined the relevant documents for what can be gleaned about global contacts and the many regions with otherwise few textual records from the period.[2] Here, such information remains in the background. What follows, instead, attempts to stay focused as much as possible on what it was like for a Jesuit to become a *missionario* in the early modern world.

The Selection

In this section, we shall focus on those Jesuits who were sent from Italy to Asia, especially to China (but not only) in the decades on either side of the turn of the seventeenth century.[3] From the start of the China mission in 1582 to the end of Claudio Acquaviva's generalate in 1615, fifteen Jesuits from the Italian provinces traveled to China.[4] Of these, there are eight surviving petitions and seven extant reports concerning five successful candidates: Giulio Aleni (1582-1649), Niccolò Longobardo (1559-1654), Francesco Sambiasi (1582-1649), Sabatino de Ursis (1575-1620), and Alfonso Vagnone (1568-1640).[5]

This was the second generation of missionaries that built on the foundations laid by Michele Ruggieri (1543-1607) and Matteo Ricci (1552-1610). All five, none of whom returned to Europe, engaged profoundly with Chinese culture and language and produced many writings to that end. Aleni was vice provincial for southern China (based in Fujian); he undertook important map work and several writings in Chinese. Longobardo was Ricci's successor as leader of the China mission from 1610. Sambiasi, whose older brother Giovanni Andrea Sambiasi (1578–1626) died violently in India, produced religious writings and a Chinese-language world map; he contributed to the reform of the Chinese calendar and was appointed "master of the people" and then a mandarin. De Ursis petitioned for Japan but was sent to China instead to assist Matteo Ricci in his work there. Vagnone produced many writings, including a Chinese-language catechism; he also became caught up in debates about the Chinese terms for God. In the course of 1616–1617, he and de Ursis were exiled to Macao from their missionary bases in Nanjing and Beijing, respectively. Vagnone returned in 1624, but de Ursis died in Macao in 1620.[6]

Textual traces of their selection process back in Italy can tell us something about each of these missionaries and about the enterprise more broadly. Vagnone has both extant petitions and reports; in 1602, he wrote to the superior general from Milan, asking to be sent to assist "those poor souls in China." His provincial supported the vocation, sending a "memorandum to the Most Reverend Father Visitor [Valignano], for Alfonso Vagnone, to recommend to Our Father [the superior general] his [Vagnone's] desire to go to the Oriental Indies."[7]

All three successful candidates with extant petitions—Aleni (three), Sambiasi (three), and Vagnone (two)—offered themselves in response to the need for more help overseas: Vagnone alludes to the shortage of laborers in the Indies; Aleni, who wished to go to Peru, sought to "offer life itself in assisting those poor souls." Sambiasi was already in Lisbon when he wrote in spiritual terms about the difficulties that he anticipated from such a mission "for the love of that cross." Imperialist themes are absent from these Italian petitions; instead, their authors present themselves somewhat patronizingly, as Aleni remarked, "to help those poor souls . . . who in many various parts of India are deprived of all spiritual help."[8]

The petitioners made their case for why they should be chosen in a number of ways: Vagnone focused on the theme of language, underlining that his knowledge of Greek and Hebrew made him well placed to learn new languages. Sambiasi focused on humility, characterizing himself as "a poor little one." Aleni also alluded to spiritual themes by drawing on the Ignatian method of humble discernment to identify his unworthiness due to his "sins, vices, and imperfections," and recognized that only God could provide "that grace and talent" necessary for the undertaking.[9]

In a subsequent letter four years later, Aleni added a discussion about his health and religious state: "Neither should you doubt my health and strength, since by the grace of God I have always felt well in religious life and outside it and I have not had any serious illnesses or indispositions." In his petition dated August 20, 1602, Vagnone was more anxious about this subject: he was the oldest of the applicants discussed here, and he shared his concerns with the superior general that deferring his departure meant fewer years for him to face the challenges and bear the fruits of mission.[10]

The petitioners enlisted a variety of rhetorical styles to articulate their vocations. Sambiasi wrote to Acquaviva from Naples in June 1608 that, on the question of his departure, his health and well-being were at stake; a few months earlier, in March, he had explained that his vocation had been kept secret for two years from everybody, except the superior general, "my Father Rector, and God." Vagnone wrote with a reminder that Acquaviva had promised that he would be appointed. In December 1607, Aleni wrote of the promise made to him by the Paraguayan province's procurator, Diego de Torres (1550–1638): on the occasion of the procurator's visit to Parma, the procurator "promised to remember me [for the missions] at the appropriate time, which seems to me to have arrived now."[11]

While these petitions help provide insights into how Jesuit missionaries in Asia viewed their vocation prior to departure, the extant reports can tell us something about the assessors, who themselves never departed but were instrumental in the enterprise through their selections. Extant reports concern Niccolò Longobardo (two), Sabatino de Ursis (two), and Alfonso Vagnone (three).

Longobardo was singled out as an individual of exceptional intellectual ability: a 1589 evaluation of missionary candidates from Sicily stated that Longobardo was "virtuous, zealous and prudent." In a report about him three years later, Bartolomeo Ricci, who became Sicily provincial in 1590, reported the following appraisal: "He seems excellent for his health, fervor and zeal. This is his first year of theological studies with the idea that a second year [out of the usual three] should suffice."[12]

A list of candidates for the Indies produced in Milan in the 1590s mentioned Vagnone as already having been put forward for the missions in 1588 on the recommendation of the provincial procurator, four years after Vagnone had entered the Society and almost ten years before he took his final vows, in 1597; he had to wait several more years before departing. Vagnone's scholarly skill and spiritual qualities were highlighted in the earliest of his three reports, from 1592: "Alfonso Vagnone is already an able and judicious philosopher; he has a virtuous and zealous spirit." The state of his health also received attention in another report from Milan, dated 1594: "Alfonso Vagnone has good strength, if he was not troubled by some catarrh; very spiritual." A further report a few years later, in 1597, is a reminder that twice previously, requests had been sent from Milan to have Vagnone's vocation considered. Along with updates about his studies and age—twenty-nine—the report adds that "he has talent in speaking [*conversare*] and helping others." His departure finally took place, in 1603, at the age of thirty-five.[13]

As always in these documents, family background was an important consideration in making overseas missionary appointments, mainly in terms of financial circumstances. On this score, Longobardo was described in the following terms: "Despite being born into a noble family, he nevertheless must support with very few means his mother, as well as a sister who is destined for the nunnery." The following sentence probably tipped the scales in his favor: "It is true that he has two other brothers at home, one of whom with his means can support everyone." Vagnone's circumstances were more difficult but not dire: "He has a mother and sister who are not comfortably off on account of a disgrace that befell the family; despite this, they manage without him, and it is hoped that they will not need his help in future."[14]

In the case of Sabatino de Ursis (originally from Lecce), the two reports about him—both dated in 1601, when he was twenty-six years-old—were written in letter form. The author of the first report, with a postscript signed by Naples provincial Fabio de Fabii, was as insistent as a petitioner might have been about de Ursis's desire to be sent to Japan: "For the love of God, and of Our Most Holy Lady, do not fail to help, and to console him in this, since he is unable to do anything in his current state, on account of his desire to go." The letter does not indicate an addressee, but it may have been sent to de Fabii to seek his assistance in securing the appointment from the superior general. It states that de Ursis is "hoping greatly to be helped by Your Reverence in this *negotio;* and still that you wish to help him now with Our Father General so that he is sent with these Procurators of Goa and of Japan." The procurators were the Italian Alberto Laerzio, based in India, and the Portuguese Francisco Vieira (1555-1619), named here as procurator for the Japan mission and later appointed visitor to the Japan and China missions. Both were in Europe to recruit for their missions. The postscript signed by de Fabii mentioned that, having recently completed his novitiate and made his vows, de Ursis was "very sound" in his ability to apply himself; he was praised for his "spirit and maturity." However, it was noted that he "has poor health."[15]

These few brief comments may well have carried a great deal of weight in what happened next. De Fabii knew de Ursis well: in Rome he had been novice master at S. Andrea, when de Ursis arrived there to begin his formation on November 11, 1598. De Fabii became provincial of Naples in 1600, the year when de Ursis transferred to that city's novitiate. As we will see, the correspondence between China and Rome testifies to an enduring bond between the two. More generally, de Fabii is a pivotal figure in the missionary enterprise because of the many leadership roles he held in Italy. Several Jesuits in this period nominated him and wrote letters and petitions to him; in addition, he was the author of several reports and short lists for the missions. His various positions meant that he probably knew more Jesuits in Italy than almost anyone else at the time. The last in a line of an ancient Roman family, de Fabii entered the Roman novitiate in 1567 and, as noted previously, was a contemporary there of Claudio Acquaviva and Alessandro Valignano. After leadership roles in Rome (including as novice master), he was appointed provincial (1584-1589) and later rector of the Collegio Romano (1602-1604); he was Neapolitan provincial (1600-1602) and visitor to all of the Italian provinces except Venice; he was assistant for Italy (1604-1608) to his former fellow novice, Superior General Acquaviva, and was also his admonitor (appointed to honestly advise the general, including offering criticisms). Together with his fellow former novices—Acquaviva and Valignano—de Fabii was one of three Italian architects of the missionary enterprise to Asia. He was their man on the ground, and his postscript about de Ursis illustrates how the system worked: he recommended de Ursis to Acquaviva, whose job it was to provide the license to leave; as we will see, once in Asia, authority passed to Valignano, who determined de Ursis's fate in the East.[16]

Back in Italy in 1601, only a few months after de Fabii added his postscript to the report from January, de Ursis was on his way to the overseas missions. On May 17, 1601, the day before he was to leave Rome for Lisbon, a letter was addressed to the superior general by an unknown author. In the letter, we learn that de Ursis would accompany the Goa procurator, Laerzio (later vice provincial and provincial of Malabar, between 1605 and 1611), together with a large number of new recruits. The letter's author was concerned that he would be sent to the Malabar Coast with Laerzio, for which reason de Ursis "reminds Your Paternity that he still wishes to go to Japan."[17] His final destination was neither Japan nor India, but China; he left Europe in 1602 and arrived on mainland China in 1606.

China was not the only destination for which we have extant petitions and reports for successful candidates. In the period of Acquaviva's long generalate (1581–1615), a total of twenty-three petitions and roughly half that number of reports are extant, out of ninety-two Jesuits who sailed east in those years. Details remain very brief about many of these, presumably functioning as short lists of those considered suitable. Many future missionaries were named in these brief lists, such as Roberto de Nobili (1577–1656, sent to India, and named in a list compiled by Fabio de Fabii), Francesco Eugenio (born c. 1573, sent to Japan and Macao), and Antonio Giannone (1577–1633, destinations included Macao, Cochinchina, and Japan).[18]

Of those who left for the Portuguese Indies in the same fleet as de Ursis in 1602, three have a report: Giovanni Vincenzo Cafiero, Giulio Cesare Curione, and Antonio Zumbo. Cafiero's is the briefest: his 1601 petition from Naples carries a note by de Fabii that he has made good progress in his studies in the humanities and that he "shows spirit." The 1594 reports, sent from Milan, list Curione (immediately after Alfonso Vagnone) as being "of good mind and spirit, and strength." Zumbo's progress in his studies and formation are the focus of the 1600 report from Palermo, mentioned in Chapter 2: he had completed the philosophy course, taught for four years, and was in his first year of theology.[19]

The future martyr Girolamo De Angelis (1567 or 1568–1623, died in Edo, Japan, and declared blessed by the Catholic Church) was described in Provincial Bartolomeo Ricci's report of 1592 from Sicily as having been free of dependent relatives except for a "rich married sister." The report further observes, "This year he has commenced his studies in logic, with great success." The future superior of the China mission, Longobardo, already discussed, appeared in the same report.[20] The Florentine Mario Squadrini, mentioned in Chapters 1 and 2, departed for the East in 1603; he has both a petition and a report. In his petition, he describes how several months previously he had made known to the superior general his vocation for the Indies (although it is not clear whether this was a written or a verbal petition—he was in Rome); he underlined that he was aware of his "unworthiness" but also requested to have his calling fulfilled. The undated report about Squadrini confirms in almost identical language to his petition that Squadrini felt "called to the conversion of the infidels."[21]

None of the reports recommended against the successful candidates' appointments; indeed, they almost certainly were crucial to the outcome. They confirm that the selection criteria for an overseas post tended to align with appointments for all roles in the Society: spiritual attributes such as interior discernment and obedience were highly prized, as well as practical factors, such as age, studies, health, moral rectitude, and overall suitability to the position were all important considerations. There were differences, however, since few were expected to return from this appointment. The seriousness of the decision about who to send can be seen in the attention to family circumstances, the state of the candidates' personal affairs, and overall fortitude for such an undertaking. Even the fact that the reports were written in the first place reflects the gravity of these appointments. Yet despite the high stakes, the reports were not so much prescriptive as indicative of a flexible approach, with room for variation in the types of candidates being considered. The possession of excellent health and exceptional intellectual capacities apparently was not present in all of the successful candidates: for example, de Ursis was described as sound in his studies and poor in health. Some provincials seemed to cooperate closely with the superior general in establishing the final choices, especially those from Sicily and Naples. De Fabii in particular was active in his role, and the tone of his reports reveals that he was close to the general. It is possible to trace a straight line between Acquaviva and his desire to make his mark on the overseas missions with the collaboration of Valignano in the Indies and leaders like de Fabii back in Italy. The result of these efforts was perhaps the most famous generation of missionaries in the history of the Christian missions, after that of their founders.

Both the petitions and the reports of these Jesuit missionaries to the Indies reveal that at the heart of the selection process were the candidates themselves, together with their superiors and provincials, all of whom on occasion (as we saw in Chapter 2) dialogued directly with the superior general. The Society's hierarchical appointment system actually was less vertically monodirectional than it was horizontal and multilateral in establishing who would travel to the Indies of the East. The Society's structure accommodated a process that was interactive, consultative, and included all parties, each with a certain degree of agency from the candidates themselves, to the pinnacle of this religious institute—the superior general. They shared a vision of Asia, too, that accompanied the missionaries there. This vision was underpinned by a spiritual understanding of the world and one's place in it, drawn from the *Spiritual Exercises,* recorded in these documents, embodied through membership in the Society, and applicable to any location, whether in the Italy of these applicants or beyond its borders. It was full of possibilities. As the *Spiritual Exercises* declared in the fourth week about the whole world and everything in it: "I will consider how God dwells in creatures; in the elements, giving them existence; in the plants, giving them life; in the animals, giving them sensation; in human beings, giving them intelligence; and finally, how in this way he also dwells in myself." This optimistic view of the world, including its peoples, and indeed the self (because God resided there) was the starting point for serving "his Divine Majesty" in the world. It also informed Jesuit ideas about mission. Following this thread, the next step after selection—the journey and arrival in the overseas missions—is the focus of the analysis that follows.

Departure, the Journey, and Arrival

Once chosen for a mission, a Jesuit faced a long journey to the East. All ships departed from Lisbon; Italians tended to spend time in Portugal, largely between Lisbon and Coimbra, the location of the Jesuit college, prior to the departure of the ships, and with a view to acquiring the Portuguese language and, for many, continuing their formation in the Society. Some Jesuits who had traveled to Portugal for departure never made it onto the ships. We have already seen how in the early years of the eastern mission enterprise, when the appointments system was still being established and when Alessandro Valignano was commencing his role as visitor to the Indies, some Italians, having reached Lisbon, were not so fortunate as to have their wish granted to proceed to Asia.

The result was a stream of letters of protest to the superior general in Rome on the part of these disappointed candidates. The petitions that were sent on occasion from Italians already in Lisbon also reveal anxiety around the uncertainty of departure. The Calabrian Francesco Sambiasi had written to the superior general several times from Italy requesting to be sent on the missions. In February 1609 he wrote once more from Lisbon on his way to China, apparently as a gentle reminder of his license to leave, expressed through gratitude: "I render infinite thanks first to God Our Lord who has moved Your Paternity to destine me for China, and then to you who has brought to effect this divine will."[22]

For the Jesuits, the missionary apostolate was considered to commence right away, through religious ministry to the ship's crew and the other passengers on board, as well as through continued study and especially learning the various languages required for work in the region, both European and local.[23] Ships usually departed annually in the spring. Visitor Valignano, who left Lisbon on March 21, 1574, is a valuable source of correspondence for the phase of travel between Lisbon and the East. His letters provide insight into individual protagonists: who was involved in the missionary enterprise and who found themselves excluded from it, even just before departure, and why. We first heard from him in his own words almost a decade earlier, when he entered the Jesuit novitiate in Rome in 1566 with "four chests of belongings . . . one small box with a rosary of gold," and other items, "also gold, weighing three-and-one-quarter ounces."[24]

On January 7, 1574, as he was preparing for his departure from Lisbon, Valignano wrote to Superior General Everard Mercurian, explaining his reasons for leaving so many Italians behind and complaining that they were not as good as the provincials claimed: he indicated that Francesco Vipera should stay behind because he suffered seasickness; further along in his letter he added that "he is judged unsuitable for the needs of India." Valignano and Vipera did not get along, and many letters were sent to Rome by both of them, the first seeking to depart without the other (and "console" him with the job of Lisbon-based procurator for the Indies instead), and the second trying to retain his mission appointment to the Indies. Vipera did eventually leave, only to return to Europe almost as soon as he had arrived.[25]

Vincenzo Lenoci was deemed unsuitable too. Valignano wrote:

> It has always been the view of everyone for it to be very dangerous and laborious if he were to go to India. This is because he has a trait that, as soon as he arrives in a city, he turns everything in it upside down; he does not leave anything decorous in his wake. He enters immediately into different friendships and receives visits from men and women; he embraces every sort of business without consideration.

Valignano got his way. Some months later, in June 1574, Lenoci was sent to Spain and from there on to a different assignment in New Spain: in Mexico, at the newly founded Colegio Máximo, he was assigned the task of introducing the Collegio Romano's system of study in the humanities; he taught rhetoric and was prefect of studies, but the difficult character observed by Valignano in Portugal was also in evidence here, and his grade was halted to that of spiritual coadjutor. In 1579 he obtained permission to return to Europe, settling back into his native Sicily until his death.[26]

Another would-be missionary receives an even clearer portrait of unsuitability in Valignano's estimation, at the same time revealing common (misguided) preconceptions about the appeal of the missions and the problem of discovering the truth about them:

> Bartolomeo Vallona [or Vallone] is a good person, but is not of stable character, and we are leaving him, since in the judgment of all, he does not have what is necessary in India. He came in great fear [to discuss his doubts] ... in the end ... he told me that he forgot to mention in Rome that he occasionally suffers great melancholy and breathlessness from his heart and that, thinking that he would be sent to Japan and undertaking different missions continuously, he thought he would always be cheerful. However, now that he has been told

that he would be in the colleges, a great melancholy came over him; and he told me many other childish things that were laughable.... He is a good person, certainly, but he is not for India.

Valignano's preference was not heeded. The Sicilian Vallone left in a different ship from the visitor but in the same fleet; he died in Goa in 1578 at the age of thirty-seven.[27]

For Valignano, the journey began on March 21, 1574. In his first letter from outside Europe, dated August 4, 1574, from Mozambique, the only reference to his physical environment was at the beginning of the letter. He described rather poignantly to Antonio Possevino (1533/1534–1611)—at the time the general secretary of the Society—"I wrote to you on several occasions from Lisbon and now I write to you more than 10,000 miles away, from this island of Mozambique." In this letter, apparently more important than his surroundings was the good fortune of the clement weather, a safe voyage, and the good health of everyone on board: "By the grace of God, we arrived on 14 July in two ships together, with propitious weather and more good health than we could have hoped for."[28]

The journey itself was a significant part of the missionary's path, and its spiritual importance was present in the accounts of those who wrote about it. Almost seventy years after Valignano's departure for India, an Italian Jesuit, Francesco Palliola (1612–1648), from Nola near Naples, left behind a rich corpus of letters from the 1640s about his journey east. The religious themes that run through these letters point to the spiritual worldview that enveloped these young men—and conditioned what they wrote about their surroundings and about themselves and the meaning of the missions for them.

In his letters, Palliola wrote explicitly to family and superiors alike about his vocation to martyrdom; he died violently in the Philippines in 1648 at the age of thirty-six. His extant correspondence (1640–1644) included evident trepidation and sadness at leaving family behind, with constant requests to greet, kiss, and embrace long lists of family members and friends, and signing his final letters as "most unworthy Indian son (*figlio indignissimo indiano*)." Palliola wrote that he was offering his hoped-for martyrdom for the salvation of his own soul and those of his loved ones, providing some insight into the appealing afterlife implications of a martyr's death for these young men, as well as their families. In one letter, Palliola explains to his fellow-Jesuit correspondent that he received in Rome the pope's blessing "with indulgence at the time of death . . . for all of our relatives in first and second grade." Death likely would come soon, he reasoned (both to his mother by natural causes and to him through martyrdom), thus speeding their reunion and ensuring its location (in Heaven). Not only is this a reminder of the short life expectancy for many, and how this reality shaped ideas about life and death in the premodern period; it also points to a "martyrological logic" that held for some young Jesuits the promise of future rewards in eternity that they otherwise could not be sure they would deserve without such a sacrifice. This prospect was a clear motivation for many to depart.[29]

Indeed, Palliola was terrified of an accidental death that would rob him of his desire for martyrdom. He narrowly escaped drowning before even leaving Europe, when those sailing in other ships with his fleet drowned after their ships sank. "The most glorious St. Felix [patron saint of Nola and reputed martyr, although he may have been persecuted for the faith and survived] will have to let me die by another means." Another time, still within Europe, writing from Cádiz, he described how "some days of the journey were appalling on account of the heat" so that "blood was running from my nose." He continued: "We are forty-two Jesuits in one boat: to each is given a little water, sufficient for necessity. The Holy God is keeping us so that we do not die . . . until that time when it is pleasing for His Divine Majesty to call us to that death which is pleasing to him, to that other life, where we shall see each other."[30] He left from Cádiz and traveled to the Philippines via Mexico. He arrived at his mission destination in July 1643.

In his final letter from the journey, Palliola recounted further dangers after his arrival in the Philippines. Between Manila and Mindanao, he and his party were in "a little boat" when they encountered "a great storm at sea" that nearly grounded them, "with a very great fear of other enemy peoples" in the area. This danger overcome, it was followed by yet more trials during another sea journey—"where there was a great deal of suffering one particular day that I thought that I would die from the blood that I vomited." In the same letter, Palliola begged for prayers from his mother, not because he was afraid of dying, but for fortitude in facing a good death if it should be violent. "In closing, please know how much I desire that you be holy, so much more in the understanding that you are praying to God for me, as you will do, above all when I am among infidels, not because I fear dying... as much that I hope that God will grant me this grace, to give my life for His Divine Majesty."[31] A bad death in the face of menacing violence was an ever-present fear for the would-be martyr. The prospect of the final painful and terrifying moments that must have accompanied many dying Jesuits also no doubt prompted a strong fear among those preparing for it that a bad death was a strong possibility.

Palliola's worst fears were never realized, and after almost five centuries the Catholic Church opened the cause for his beatification. For Jesuits like Palliola, physical security was not so much what kept these men safe. Instead, the *Spiritual Exercises* taught these Jesuits to remain grounded in the spiritual life, as roots in a tree; the branches were the places where these spirit-roots propelled them. In principle, life and death, the spiritual and the physical, near and far, the individual Jesuit and the whole Society, were all one. The lived experience, and threats like violence and fear, could cause considerable challenges, but these were things that could throw a Jesuit off course, or set him upon it, and were not the ultimate, single aim. They were secondary, and recorded as such. This is why it is often difficult to ascertain specific details about a given subject in the Jesuit documentation about the Indies. Yet in this single-minded vision, the individual pieces that made up the whole were held to be an essential part of the terrain, with each Jesuit life and its textual record constituting the worldwide Society to which Jesuits had bound their lives.

Not everyone was destined to die prematurely like Palliola. For those who survived their eastward journey, what did they find once they arrived in Goa (the Portuguese capital in the East, and the first destination for all missionaries to the region)? Valignano arrived there on September 6, 1574, almost six months after leaving Lisbon. On Christmas Day 1574 he wrote a long letter on the subject that in its modern published form runs for more than fifty pages. As with much of his correspondence, this was a report more than it was a letter. He describes reaching the college in Goa as part of a cohort of forty-four Jesuits: "There was so much merriment among those who were here, and those who arrived, that it is difficult to recount."[32]

In this missive, Valignano sees the replenishment of personnel, through his arrival with a large band of Jesuits, as a sign of God's grace and favor for the mission, and of the passing of time: "In coming here at a time when the Society in India was almost destroyed due to the death of many, and especially the principal ones [Jesuit leaders]." He continued: "And for this reason, this mission was recognized as much among 'ours' [the Jesuits] as among the foreigners as a grace and providence of our Lord towards this least Society, which is very loving and very distinct."[33]

Jesuit Letters from the Missions

As already discussed, if the Society was indeed distinct, a significant explanation for why can be found in its practice of writing letters—and the missions were no exception. Sending letters was a key requirement of the Society, outlined in its *Constitutions*, with particular attention to those who were most distant from their fellow Jesuits. The title of part 8 of the text explains this—"help toward uniting the distant members with their head and among themselves." This part observes, "The more difficult it is for the members of this congregation to be united with their head and among themselves, since they are so scattered among the faithful and among the unbelievers in diverse regions of the world, the more ought means to be sought for that union." The letters from the missions in fact embrace powerfully the requirements set out in the *Constitutions*—and explained in this book's Introduction—which underlined their need to be dialogic, factual, and edifying.[34] They are to be read within these multiple lenses, while the spiritual and cultural filters that permeated the letters lend themselves to being viewed more broadly as religious and self-narrative documents.

The prescriptions for letter-writing in the *Constitutions* were bolstered by the *Formula scribendi*. Alessandro Valignano applied the guidelines of the *Formula* in Asia, an arrangement described in a letter by Niccolò Longobardo from China concerning the requirement to provide an overview of the affairs of the mission and its government, something "that the Father Visitor ordered be done." He continued: "I send it now to our

Father Provincial in Japan, according to the order given in the *Formula scribendi.*"[35]

The system for sending letters was efficient in principle. In practice, often there were major delays in the exchange of information. As Valignano stated, "These letters will be sent in triplicate," via different routes, the famous *tre vie*.[36] It took over one year for correspondence to arrive in China from Rome. For example, Alfonso Vagnone began his letter, sent from Macao dated March 25, 1619, to Father Carlo Torniello in Milan, with the following: "The letter written to me by Your Reverence from Alessandria on 14 November 1617 arrived in my hands this summer of 1619." Sometimes the wait was even longer. In 1613, Longobardo began his letter to the superior general with a summary of the mission's state of affairs—including "what relates to the government of this China mission"; he did so for the previous three years "since it may be that the letters that I wrote to Your Paternity in the last three years did not reach you."[37]

The disjointed nature of Jesuit global communication is reflected in a letter written by Matteo Ricci in May 1605. Sent from Beijing, it was addressed to Italy Assistant Ludovico Maselli (c. 1539–1604), who had died the year before. The news clearly had not reached Ricci, who was Maselli's former student at the Collegio Romano. He concluded his long letter to Maselli with the following remark: "I do not know how to finish this letter, but the page has already turned and there is no more room." Ricci's strategy to finish the letter points to another challenge for the missionaries: the time it took to write them. In another letter, addressed to Superior General Acquaviva and dated August 15, 1606, Ricci set out to "provide an account to Your Paternity about persons and particular business," (Valignano, whose customary duty it was to send regular reports, had died in Macao on January 20, 1606, as Ricci wrote, leaving the Asia missionaries "orphans"); he had delegated the task to "Father Alfonso Vagnone as well as Father Niccolò Longobardo ... in the requested Italian language." The reason for not attending to the task himself was that "the affairs of this court [Beijing] are so many that I am continuously submerged and I cannot find the time to write."[38]

The letter-writing system depended on a consciously constructed network of correspondence, in which members sought to avoid having to write too much information in duplication. As Ricci wrote to Italy

Assistant Fabio de Fabii on May 9, 1605 (de Fabii had been appointed to the role the year before): "You will have heard the news of our affairs in letters from others that are closest to the ports of the sea, and from where letters for India and for Europe depart.... As for me, poor thing, being located close to the Tartars, very far not only from our European and Indian friends, but also from those companions who are in China, there would be nothing for it but to write if it weren't for the fact that I would not like to repeat the same things a year after they have been sent there by others."[39]

Another problem was the status that the correspondence carried, in some cases as organs of governance, not only from Rome but also within Asia. It was an imperfect system that, in a number of its applications, riled Ricci and made his own role more difficult (from 1597) as superior of the mission in China. He wrote about this to the superior general in 1606, in one of his *soli* (confidential letters about sensitive matters, for the eyes of the general only): "I was pained not a little by remaining with all of this on my shoulders [that is, responsibility for many areas of leadership]." He had "told the Father Visitor [Valignano]" of his concerns, "especially for staying so tied [to Macao] and not being allowed to govern without scruples the house and the people in it, by way of letters, without being able to see them in person." Indeed, he commented further along in his letter, he was not even in a position to report very effectively about those in mainland China. Appointments were at a glacial speed, because of the hierarchical, rather than regionally autonomous nature of the Society. Ricci wrote to the superior general that if recommendations for passing probation and granting full profession into the Society remained formally outside the purview of the China mission's leadership, "the process will be delayed by more than a year or two, if not more."[40]

The problem was not just distance and institutional frameworks but also internal politics, which seemed to run along roughly national lines. In his letter to Acquaviva, Ricci commented on the excellent work of several of his confreres, including Alfonso Vagnone and Niccolò Longobardo. Of the former, based in Beijing, he wrote, "He has been here two years with much diligence, studying Chinese language and letters with much fruit. In everything he has shown himself to be prudent and virtuous with great satisfaction of the superior of the house in Nanjing, where he was." Of Longobardo, he commented, "Three years ago, he made his vows of [spiritual] coadjutor by order of the Father Visitor, but always it has seemed to me that he deserved much more and that he should be made professed with four vows." He continued: "in other parts, some are embarrassed that we are here with profession [with four vows]; and if this enterprise were not in lands subject to the Portuguese—where it seems to me they do not easily create superiors who are foreign—it would seem to me that nobody in this residence would govern this enterprise better [than Longobardo] for the zeal and prudence and humility that he possesses." A year earlier, in his May 1605 letter to de Fabii in Rome, Ricci wrote how Longobardo was a "great worker in these parts, very devoted to Your Reverence and prolific in writing."[41] By contrast, Ricci wrote: "And here I have another companion, Diego Pantoja, who the Father Visitor sent here two years ago to make the profession of the fourth vow, who does not give much edification.... It appears to me that I would feel embarrassment at him being professed, and these other two coadjutors"—that is, the Italians Longobardo and Vagnone.[42]

He reported a similar problem that combined logistics of distance and the political ends to which they were put, in relation to securing the necessary permission to publish his writings: "Here, we do not have a license to print, neither from Your Paternity [Acquaviva] nor from the inquisitors of India.... It occurs to me that in this land Your Paternity should provide a license to the superior of the mission, to leave books to be printed that 'ours' [i.e., we Jesuits] produce, after being revised, and acquire the license from the inquisitors in India, as held by Japan." He added that the license should come from someone who knows Chinese, and, in any case, he writes, "The books that are written here are not new things, but we take from our books everything that can be relevant to China and we use our judgment only in selecting."[43] Ricci reports further that he is begged repeatedly to produce more than "these four or five books of mine," already written. He links these works with the stability of their position in China:

> Regarding things here, I think I can say that already our position here in China is almost secure, not because there was not much to fear with this Christianity—which already in four areas is growing, something that is dangerous for

suspicious people—but because, from what I understand about China, they would fear throwing us out of China more than they do keeping us inside it, since they think that we could do more harm outside, on account of how much we know about China.⁴⁴

It was because of this situation, according to Ricci, that books were so important: "One of the means with which to secure this position is with the books that I have written; and this is what 'ours' think, [both] our Christian and gentile friends; because in them [the books] they see clearly that we talk about peace and virtue and obedience to the princes, and not about war and rebellion." Further along he writes that the importance of books also is due to a special value placed on them in Chinese culture: "It is a particular trait of China, that all the sects work and spread their messages through books more than through sermons, and a high level of importance is given just for compositions, without saying a word."⁴⁵ In this way, into matters of Jesuit governance seep observations about local society in China, in this case, the premium put on the written rather than the spoken word.

Indeed, on occasion it was *only* the written word, specifically letters that could be brought into China. Ricci reported in one letter to the superior general: "This year, I can say that I received two [letters] from Your Reverence," even though Ricci had heard that "other items that you sent me are being kept there [in Macao] . . . because the courier was unable to bring anything other than letters." The value of these letters was left in no doubt by Ricci:

> Please know that, not only I, but all my companions that know you only by reputation, remain extremely edified by your charity; that being there in Europe and continually occupied in high offices in the Society, with all of that you remember with so much special affection a poor brother of yours, thrown here at the end of the world among infidels; and what I truly mean is that the causes for others to forget, including being far away and among strangers, to the true servants of God become the main and most efficacious reason to remember. With this and similar assistance, we live here happily in such sad places.⁴⁶

Even after taking into consideration the Renaissance rhetoric that required such expressions of humility and gratitude, as in this letter from Ricci, the fragile but vital thread of communication is visible here, in the Jesuit experience of the Indies. It was a thread along which news traveled in both directions and on which enormous value was placed, including for those at the very top of the hierarchy, for Acquaviva was well aware of the importance of this epistolary tie for his aims with respect to the Society that he governed.

Describing the "Indies"

What did the Jesuits write about their host societies? Niccolò Longobardo provided a number of details. Back in Italy, the Sicilian Longobardo had been described by his superiors, reporting about his suitability for the overseas enterprise, as "virtuous, zealous and prudent."[47] He had entered the Society in 1582, left Lisbon in 1596, and arrived in Goa the same year; in mid-1597 he was in Macao, and at the end of that year he was in mainland China, from where he signed his 1598 letter to the superior general, written during his first year in China and published in 1601. The letter runs for just over thirty pages. In it, like Sambiasi, mentioned above, Longobardo starts by thanking the superior general for selecting him for China, which "can be compared with the most illustrious [missions] that to date have been established in these parts of India, for the immensely rare qualities that this nation has over all the other gentiles." He goes on to describe some aspects of "this immensely vast kingdom of China": the kingdom is united and the Mandarin language can be understood throughout the kingdom. "And it is in fact like in Italy the courtly language of Rome, which is understood in all of the kingdoms of Italy." As Longobardo explains, this relative uniformity means that the Jesuits can learn Mandarin and easily teach Christian doctrine in that language and be understood. He recounts that the land is fertile and arable like in Europe, that "the people are very industrious and consequently wealthier, so that their standard of living is very comfortable." He reports, too, how happy he is to be there: "About myself, I can say that, with this air, studies, people, and similar things, I feel such familiarity and ease, that I feel myself to be in the middle of Italy."[48]

In a later letter, written in 1613, we discover that in the intervening period Longobardo had become Matteo Ricci's successor as leader of the

China mission. He recounts Ricci's death in 1510 and the mathematical assistance the Jesuits were providing at the court in Beijing. He describes the work they were doing for the reform of the Chinese calendar; this assistance must be carried out, he notes, on the understanding that it is done for the pleasure of it and not for any other reason, by which he means seeking conversions. He stresses that this is a necessary dissimulation, "even though the principal and primary aim we have placed in Conversion."[49]

In his letter, Longobardo provides insight into local life, especially among the Christians. He observes how the Chinese community of Christian converts in Macao are quite unlike the Japanese converts surrounded by gentiles: not only was the community well established and many were born Christians, but they were also exposed constantly to the Christian culture of the Portuguese, as if they were "in the middle of Christian Europe." He describes how "they are intelligent and learned, prudent and modest, capable and affectionate in matters of the spirit, they maintain a great deal of obedience and respect towards the Fathers, are very observant of the rules, zealous and committed to conversion." Longobardo wrote with admiration: "They take part in processions, go to sermons and sacraments just as if it were in the heart of Portugal." It is no coincidence that this letter was published, and clearly intended to be so, with its emphasis on the positive, harmonious experience of the mission in China, no doubt to attract benefactors and support among the Jesuit and political leadership back in Europe. Longobardo further reported that at the time of writing there were twenty Jesuits in China, thirteen of which were professed, and seven coadjutor brothers. He described in particular the arrival of three new members of the mission, two of whom we have encountered before, Giulio Aleni and Francesco Sambiasi (plus Pietro Spira). Aleni and Sambiasi left on the same boat in 1609, along with a number of other Italians. As already mentioned, Aleni had requested to be sent to Peru, but he traveled east instead, first to Goa, where he described an eclipse in Salsette, and then to China.[50]

Like Aleni, we know that Sabatino de Ursis also hoped for a different destination to China, and that he had requested Japan. He arrived in Macao in 1603, where he was possibly still expecting to be sent on to Japan, like several fellow Italians from his fleet, who followed the usual path from Goa to Macao, and then on to Japan. Instead de Ursis met

Alessandro Valignano, who identified his talents as being more suited to China. He was sent there in 1606 to assist Matteo Ricci.[51] He worked with Ricci as an astronomer, translator, and writer on hydraulics in Chinese, introducing European pharmaceutical knowledge to China and working on the early stages of the reform of the Chinese calendar. In 1608 he wrote a letter from Beijing to the superior general's Portugal assistant in Rome, João Álvares (1548–1623). We last heard about de Ursis in 1601, when his superiors reported about his suitability for the enterprise. After two years in China, de Ursis wrote to the assistant: "Knowing how much Your Reverence desires news from these parts . . . —and since until now I have found myself (we might say) on the move, not being in one definite place, [and therefore] I have not done it—now . . . I set about writing these two lines to give the latest news to Your Reverence."[52]

Like Longobardo, de Ursis praised the novices he encountered there—Chinese sons of Christian converts who helped "negotiate the entrance of our Fathers into China, and in their dealings with the Chinese." He also outlined the affairs of the mission, including disagreements and controversies about one of the Jesuit fathers, Lazzaro Cattaneo (1560–1640), who almost was barred by the Chinese from reentering China from Macao; about the Jesuits on the mainland, how many there were and how they were faring. De Ursis's letter includes a poignant reminder of the passing of time for the handful of Europeans clinging as outsiders to the fringes of China's powerful kingdom in his description of Father Matteo Ricci. He "is already a tired old man, already with many trials; he holds great credit and fame in the whole Kingdom."[53]

The intimacy of everyday life among the Chinese also is evident in de Ursis's letter when he describes how a Christian convert is teaching three Jesuits in his house, including Vagnone: "These three . . . Fathers are studying the Chinese letters and language with the Chinese Teacher who is already Christian, who comes to the house every day to teach the Fathers, from whom great service to Our Lord is expected, since all three have excellent ability."[54]

He described the mapping projects of the Jesuits, and the effect on their learned Chinese audience, when they saw China represented alongside other regions: "China was smaller than what they thought, since they imagined China to be the whole world." He described the ease with which violence could be carried out at the Beijing court and the entry given to the Jesuits, with their knowledge, maps, and clocks, and printing projects in the Chinese language. He narrated his own recent entry to the palace of the court: "We both went [with Diego Pantoja] into the palazzo, where we were received with great courtesy; they showed us the whole Palace, and other things, like gardens, bird houses, animals, lagoons, and ponds full of fish."[55]

After finishing his account of the Chinese court, de Ursis turns to linguistics: "In arriving in this house, I began to study Chinese language and letters with Father Matteo Ricci; the difficulty of the letters and language is not as great as I imagined, because the difficulty entirely consists in varying the voice (*voce*), since with one syllable, for example *pa*, they indicate more than two hundred completely different letters that signify different things.... All the difficulty consists in speaking." He added, however, that "our Fathers learn well."[56]

The linguistics lesson is accompanied by a hand-drawn diagram (see Figure 4), using European musical notation and Latin transcription to explain the many different possible pronunciations and meanings of the words resulting in Chinese from the single syllable *pa*. He provides examples to make his point, including: pá 霸 tiranno (tyrant); pă 捌 otto (eight); pā 肥 ponte di legno (wooden bridge); pá 怕 paura (fear). The musical notations served to indicate how the rise and fall of the tones should be for correct pronunciation.[57]

Of other matters at court, de Ursis commends Assistant Álvares to the letter that he understands will be written in Italian from Matteo Ricci to the superior general. He closes his letter by sending greetings to two friends, one of whom wrote the report recommending de Ursis for the mission: "I ask Your Reverence to do the same with Father Fabio de Fabii, my Novice Master, asking him to commend me to the Lord, because I hope that, just as he helped me many times in Rome, being in the midst of so many servants of the Lord at S. Andrea [at the Quirinale, Rome], now I will be helped even more in my greater needs and danger. I will not write now [to de Fabii], but on another occasion, I will do so."[58]

These letters were not studies in anthropology and linguistics to the extent that modern scholars would wish them to be. Nevertheless, the letter from de Ursis demonstrates that both themes were present in the

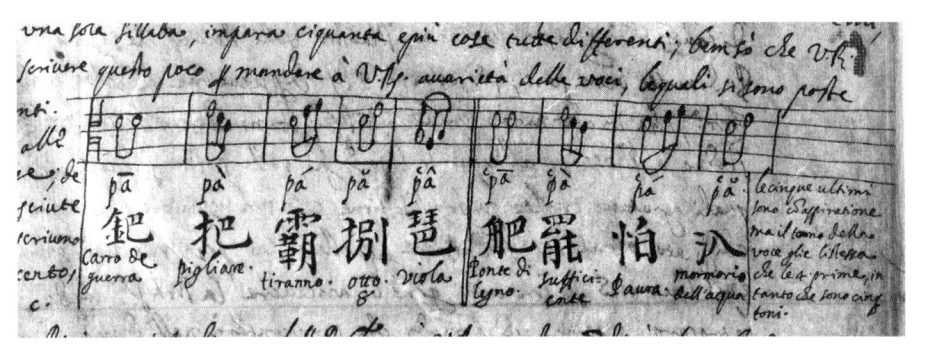

Figure 4. Letter of Sabatino de Ursis to Portugal Assistant João Álveres, Beijing, August 23, 1608. *Jap. Sin.* 14 II, fol. 316v (detail: diagram of musical notes to indicate pronunciation of certain Chinese words, with translations in Italian). Reproduction © Archivum Romanum Societatis Iesu.

letters from China; it reveals, too, the demand for exactly such information from superiors in Europe clamoring for news. The primary aim that these letters reported remained conversion, and the overriding framework was spiritual. Rome and China were united in spiritual terms, and the workers in the vineyards of both belonged to the same *corpus*. This had consequences for how both geographical realities were viewed by the Jesuits who wrote about them. If China and Rome belonged to the same spiritual frame, the needs of each in terms of the missionary apostolate clearly were different. Unlike in Rome, which certainly had its own problems, in the China mission, where Christianity constituted a negligible minority, the focus on those to be converted or on those who had already embraced Christianity had to be managed carefully. Conversions remained relatively few in the early years: in some senses this was acceptable news in the delicate environment of China, but less so for Rome.

Ricci's report sent to the Italy assistant, Ludovico Maselli, attempted to strike a balance: "It has been a long time since I have understood how much more help a few good Christians give us than would many imperfect ones; for this reason we make them [Christians] with much rigor [*essame*] and attractiveness, catechizing very well." Ricci was painfully aware of the low numbers of his mission's converts: "Many things happened during these years that could be written about these few Christians, but I do not know if it is correct to write so much, that it appears as if we are magnifying our affairs, even if I am certain that you will find out through the letters of others." He went on nevertheless to tell the story of one convert who understood a lesson about the Holy Trinity in an undecipherable dream whose meaning became clear only on his becoming a Christian.[59] Another Christian was saved from being wrongly accused in court when God appeared to the judge in human form in a dream, asking him to help the man in question, which he did. Another recounted the story of a sick man who had been healed by a vision of "the Madonna with Child in her arms, dressed in white."[60]

Material culture also appears in these exchanges. Ricci wrote, "This Christmas ... in the place of the image of the Savior ... a new image of the Madonna of St. Luke with the Child in her arms, painted very well by a young man who lives in the house [G. Niva], who learnt in Japan from our Father Giovanni Nicolò [Cola]. It was marvelous how happy everyone was with it."[61] The circularity of information and influence is also evident in these letters, not just in religious matters but also scientific ones. Ricci wrote to Portugal Assistant Álvares about the mathematical and scientific advances being made by some of the local Chinese through their instruction by the missionaries: "I ask Your Reverence to grant me this charity by communicating all of this to Father Clavio [Christopher Clavius (1538-1612)], and tell him that already many, many Chinese know the name of Father Clavio [the celebrated mathematician at the Collegio Romano, and Ricci's teacher]."[62]

In these small details and personal observations we can discern some of the features of the European response to Asia. But we can also trace the impact of Asia on the individual. As Filippo De Marini (1608-1682) observed in his letter from Tonkin (northern Vietnam), addressed to Giovanni Luigi Confalonieri: "He who does not depart already a saint from Europe deceives himself if he believes that upon arrival, he will become a saint." He goes on to describe the process not just of traveling through physical time and space but also of the transformation of the person that resulted from these sojourns and experiences. The Jesuits learned the risks only too well, and later in his letter to Confalonieri, De Marini wrote news about perhaps their most famous apostate, senior Japan missionary Cristóvão Ferreira (1580-1650), who was brutally tortured in 1633. He converted to Shinto, wrote anti-Christian tracts, and assisted with anti-Christian persecution in Japan. De Marini wrote, "Our Provincial Cristóvão Ferreira, who many years ago under torture repudiated [the Christian faith], after which he was left to go free, for two years now they say that he died a [re-converted Christian] martyr. Last year, we learnt this news, and we have endeavored to find out." Being barred themselves from Japan, the Jesuits tried to find out from Dutch merchants, who themselves ran into trouble and their reports on the matter did not reach De Marini.[63]

The personal, interior, and spiritual features of the letters from the missions are among the most important and also the most neglected by scholarship. For these Jesuits, the Indies were a spiritual theater as much as a physical one, and their letters—conceived as extensions of the *Spiritual Exercises*—were expressions of this spiritual path on which they traveled. This meant that in many ways they privileged what they considered as spiritual truths over factual ones. Such an attitude follows at least partly Edward W. Said's argument about Asia: the documents here suggest that it was not always so much understood by Europeans as much as constructed by them.[64] For the Jesuits, this was not accidental, since it was an explicit aim of their letters to report on what was seen, certainly, but also to edify, thereby imparting meanings on what they saw that originated in their own worldviews and clear objectives for the region. Spiritual truths were thought to be communicated by God through the natural world, so that the Indies served to glorify God through the Society's work. This work was the motivation for going there in the first place. The cultural information that resulted was of lesser importance in comparison and, for these Jesuits, of secondary importance to the spiritual meaning of what they were doing.

Personal elements appear, too, mixed with evidence of hardship. In 1619, Alfonso Vagnone wrote from China to his Jesuit friend Father Carlo Torniello in Milan. We last heard from Vagnone as a petitioner for the Indies in 1602, who emphasized that his particular abilities in Greek and Hebrew made him suited to acquiring the different languages of the Indies and that his superiors remarked on his intellectual skills, good character, and spiritual zeal. He arrived in China in 1605. With a reputation for having a difficult character, in 1616–1617 he went into temporary exile in Macao until 1624. He wrote his letter to Torniello from Macao on March 25, 1619, fifteen years after his departure from Europe and just over ten years after de Ursis wrote his 1608 account from Beijing. He wrote at length of the challenges and persecutions he had experienced "against this tender shoot, my Christianity"; at the same time, he wrote how recently "we have seen many portents of the heavens and earth, and especially two comets appeared of enormous size."[65]

Vagnone's letter contains other more personal information as well, including "the happiness caused by hearing news about those dearest Fathers and brothers, whom I have no hope of seeing again in this lifetime." Vagnone wistfully mentions how glad he was to receive news about their mutual friends. He greets affectionately Torniello's family, "who are imprinted on my memory, and are dearer to me even than my own family." He also gently chides Torniello's brother, through his correspondent, for not writing more often, and asking him to do so, and to share the letter with him as well. Letters, thus, were passed around, and goods were circulated, as we learn from Vagnone's letter: "When a convenient opportunity arises, I ask Your Reverence to send me a few miniature crystals from Milan; you may send them to the Father Assistant of Portugal, in Rome, who every year has the habit of sending us what he wants to Lisbon in time for the departure of the boats for India." He closes his letter with a nostalgic tone: "And with this I conclude embracing you with all my heart until we shall meet again in Heaven."[66]

The personal cost of this enterprise thus comes into view. In closing his letter, undated, from Vietnam, Filippo De Marini asks for greetings to be sent to his brother: "I will not write [now] to Father Giovanni Niccolò Marini, my brother, I pray Your Reverence to pass on my news. I also have another brother who entered into the Society in Messina in 1646.... He was weak [and] I do not know if he is alive... I wish them to have news of me." He sent greetings to many former friends and teachers from the Collegio Romano as well. He also mentions that he sent a separate letter to Giovanni Paolo Oliva (1600–1681), future superior general of the Society (1664–1681).[67]

The mix of the spiritual, personal, and factual in the letters from the missions is often difficult to untangle. This was intentional: the edifying and the mundane mutually reinforced each other. There was a shift underway, however. Gradually, the importance of faithful reporting of facts was understood in a Society that by necessity of distance depended on the written word for reliable information, rather than the face-to-face verbal account so valued in premodern societies. This value is clear in a letter from Valignano when he praises fellow Jesuit and traveler Juan Bautista de Ribera (1525–1594), whom he meets in Mozambique and will be discussed in more detail in Chapter 4: "He narrates of India things that are plausible and conform to that which others tell me and without showing passion."[68]

Factual reliability became a valuable commodity in this far-flung enterprise, and Valignano himself was acutely aware of this. As we saw in Chapter 2, in a letter describing the lamentable morale in Goa in 1575, he blamed the Jesuit letters arriving in Europe from the East for the unrealistic expectations they created. Valignano tried to improve on the published *Nuovi avisi* or *Avisi particolari* by insisting on the production of officially sanctioned, centrally compiled collections of reports from the East by reliable and qualified editors. These editions of "true" annual letters, the so-called *Litterae annuae,* first appeared in 1581 and were published on a semi-regular basis until 1619. Also, a decade earlier, in 1571, a new genre appeared, the histories and biographies, which consisted of accounts from and about the missions and their leaders, based largely on the letters. These produced more cohesive, if still flawed (and often much-criticized) accounts about Jesuit activities in the East.[69]

In his 1597 letter from Japan (published in 1599), Luís Fróis (1532–1597) reflected this new emphasis on detailed and accurate information. In his account about Japan, including the execution of twenty-six Christians in 1597, Fróis wrote: "In the following account, I only write that which I have heard from people . . . of good faith who, both verbally and by letter, have provided reliable and precise information about all that I will report here." Even in this account, however, the objective remains fixed, to describe the "great consolation and edification, which have resulted from this persecution."[70]

From the time they were written, the letters from the overseas missions were understood to be extremely important documents. The paper on which they were composed—with the multiple perspectives they contained—made up the walls of this missionary Society of Jesus. They testified to its existence in the four corners of the known world and provided the textual traces that would constitute its history. In some cases, they also provided precious information about the histories of the peoples to whom Jesuits ministered. Their concentration in the

Society's hub of Rome is a reminder of the organizational and spiritual ends for which they were used. These were not travel logs or journals, or geographies or ethnographies (even though many contained these elements); above all, they served to illustrate the application of the *Spiritual Exercises* across the spokes of the world, in real times and places, but grounded in a single entity, governed from Rome.

The letters from Asia were like a prism, intended to refract light in multiple directions. These myriad features are not a weakness but a reflection of the original intention in producing them, to inform, edify, and persuade. While they may not tell us as much as we would like to know about the lands and peoples encountered, whether published or unpublished, they do tell us something about the individuals who made the journey. They tell of the impact it had on them, and their own subjectivity. Their frame enables us to observe both the individual and his place within the wider group, as well as the world beyond. Let us leave the missions now and turn again to the documentary traces of the path for those many more Jesuits who stayed behind to work in the Italian provinces of the Society.

4

On the Italian Home Front

$\mathcal{U}$p to this point, I have used Jesuit biographical documents to reveal a particular feature of the Society of Jesus that envisaged each member as being rooted in a spiritual fixedness while moving about the physical world with the aim of securing the salvation of one's neighbor and oneself. The physical surroundings might have changed, but the spiritual frame, and core, in which everything took place, remained the same.

The spiritual meaning of indifference to place was connected to indifference to one's state more generally, mentioned in the *Spiritual Exercises* in the second week: "We shall . . . think about how we ought to dispose ourselves in order to come to perfection in whatsoever state of life God our Lord may grant us to elect." While the election was human, made by "us," it was granted by God. Its location was variable; all permanence was reserved for God and for human beings' only true home, God's kingdom. This framework was described in the fourth week: "Intense love, tears, or any other spiritual consolation . . . are a gift from God our Lord; and still further, they are granted to keep us from building our nest in a house which belongs to Another [that is, God]." As I have shown, this way of thinking had a consequence for how the Society viewed its overseas missions, as well as how they were organized. It also informed how Jesuits operated back home.[1]

Despite vast numbers of Jesuits in the Italian provinces expressing a vocation to the overseas missions, most stayed where they were. There was some movement of members between provinces, and to other European regions outside Italy, but most remained within the Italian lands. The textual records relating to some of these Jesuits—both those written about single members by their fellows and self-narrative documents—provide the focus of the analysis that follows.[2]

Sources of this kind from and about the home front are legion, and the scale of their preservation in the Roman Jesuit archive is impressive. The second half of the sixteenth century, from around 1555, is particularly rich with several thousand preserved documents of many different types. Their number drops off after 1600; Edmond Lamalle conjectured that Superior General Claudio Acquaviva wished to remove from the record the litigious material pertaining to the period of his generalate (1581–1615) and the threats to his leadership from a Spanish faction in the Society; overall increased caution toward the preservation of personal, sensitive, and potentially controversial materials seems to have informed the more conservative number of documents kept after that time. Despite this, the entire first century after the Society's ratification remains well represented by archival sources as well as published works.[3]

At ARSI, documents for the various Italian provinces are found under the broad grouping "Italiae." These sources, and the Jesuit members to whom they pertain, collectively came under the administrative responsibility of the Italian Assistancy. As would be expected, the majority of letters sent *to* Rome—their final resting place—are more numerous than those sent *from* there; fortunately, registers of outgoing letters were kept, containing abbreviated versions of the actual sent letters, with their essential contents and information. Secretaries drew these up as part of the administration of the Society, and as records of important directives, instructions, admonishments, or advice.[4]

As we have seen, correspondence networks were the mortar that held the Society's bricks together, replacing other religious orders' regular chapter meetings and voting processes. These networks enabled Jesuits to remain where they were for long periods without traveling back regularly to a "mother house." The texts themselves were imbued with both spiritual and practical features and functioned as essential working parts in the Society's system of "apostolic spirituality."[5] At the same time, the easy style, frankness, deep bonds, and open disagreements and battles of will evident in many of these documents—both those received and sent—are laid out and still visible.

If the walls of the Society were made of movable paper bricks, these documents' authors were the building itself, joined through their correspondence. Their records were part of a Jesuit's life, and their preservation, together with their multiple meanings, provide a valuable window onto what it was like to be a member of the Society of Jesus.

Organizing a Society of Individuals

The Society's corporate identity was described in its essential elements in the 1539 *Formula of the Institute*, with more shape given to Jesuit ministries in the expanded second version, presented for approval and then subsequently confirmed in 1550 by Pope Julius III (1487–1555; r. from 1550). While the *Constitutions* outlined details (for example, regarding the apostolate of education), it was the *Formula* that provided the foundation stone for the Society's various roles: "to strive especially for the defense and propagation of the faith and for the progress of souls in Christian life and doctrine, by means of public preaching, lectures, and any other ministration whatsoever of the word of God." Jesuits were to undertake the "education of children and unlettered persons in Christianity, and the spiritual consolation of Christ's faithful through hearing confessions and administering the other sacraments." Their tasks extended to reconciling "the estranged, compassionately," and "assisting and serving those in prisons or hospitals."[6]

In this highly centralized, yet dispersed and varied Society of individuals, biographical documents provided a record for "how things worked" as well as revealing a valuable vein that followed each Jesuit as he progressed from one role to another. Chapter 1 of this book outlined some aspects of the demanding process of becoming incorporated into the Society. Formation was a very serious undertaking for Jesuits: out of the many chapters that make up the ten parts of the *Constitutions,* the first five parts and their chapters are dedicated to the steps to be taken in order for full incorporation to take place, from admission, to probation and the novitiate, to the formation of scholastics, followed by a long section on the process of "admission or incorporation into the Society." The remaining five parts of the work are devoted to the following themes of membership: "the personal life of those already admitted or incorporated into the Society" (that is, the spiritual side of their vocation), and the "distribution of the incorporated members in Christ's vineyard"—the apostolic or missionary aspect of their vocation. These are followed by the sections concerned with governance: "the Society's head, and the government descending from him," and how the Society is to be "preserved" and "developed."[7]

Records had to be reliable and up to date if they were to reflect the perpetually itinerant, responsive, missionary ethos of the Society, envisaged by Ignatius of Loyola: in principle, members expected to be moved, reallocated, or promoted often, and the records had to keep up with the the organizational appetite for change. The *Constitutions* insisted on the importance of regular reviewing processes for members for this reason. They stated, "That more complete information may be had about all the persons ... there should be sent ... a brief list ... of all who are in that house ... with a brief account of the qualities of these persons."[8] These were to be sent regularly from each house to the provincial, and from the provincial to the superior general in Rome.

Yet the documents are much more than personnel records; they are also textual expressions of the multilateral process by which appointments were made: in the Jesuit system of government, the General Congregation was the primary governing body, with the responsibility of electing the superior general and entrusting to him the implementation of the decrees passed by it. Appointed for a lifetime term, he was at the head of the Society and was responsible for its oversight, including appointments. Below him were the persons in question—such as college teachers, university rectors, college janitors, or *casa professa* housekeepers; in the mediating role were the rectors, provincials, assistants, mission leaders, and others who relayed information back and forth between the top and bottom ranks of this vertically organized society. There were thus two driving forces behind the massive and unparalleled Jesuit documentary and epistolary production; these driving forces intentionally pulled in opposite directions—toward the hierarchy (according to its governance system) and away from it toward individual Jesuits (informed by the discernment enjoined on members through the *Spiritual Exercises*)— endowing these documents with their multiperspective richness.[9]

Much has been made of the Jesuit insistence on obedience, but equally important was the grave responsibility envisaged for the one who was to be obeyed. In this role, the risk associated with total obedience was allayed through a variety of measures, of which biographical documents are textual expression. Antonella Romano has termed this dynamic "negotiated obedience"; Silvia Mostaccio identified in the dynamic a perpetual, defining "tension" within the Society. For his part, Markus Friedrich observed in "Ignatius's attitude, which became a foundational principle of Jesuit organization . . . 'centralization with situational provisos.'" I have chosen to call this dynamic "dialogic."[10] The leadership's task of commanding obedience was ameliorated by careful listening and consulting and through the individual discernment of all members.

The dynamic was intensely relational and underpinned by the *Spiritual Exercises,* which stated: "Sometimes a good soul . . . wishes to say something which . . . contributes to the glory of God our Lord. But it gets a thought or temptation from without not to say or do it. We should reply as St. Bernard: I did not begin because of you, and neither will I desist for you." The invitation to individual initiative is unmistakable here: "If we see that it is for [God's] due service . . . we ought to act diametrically against the temptation [not to say or do it]."[11] Key in the Ignatian system, and consonant with his times, was that human initiative was always to be, as stated at [351], "in conformity with the Church or the minds of our superiors." Indeed, in the very next paragraph of the *Exercises* we find the final chapter [352-370] that takes up the theme of obedience, and gives this theme the last word in the *Spiritual Exercises:* "Rules for Thinking, Judging, and Feeling with the Church," and famously, at [365], "what I see as white, I will believe to be black if the hierarchical Church thus determines it."[12]

Or does it? The final paragraph of the entire work states: "It is granted that we should value above everything else the great service which is given to God because of pure love." This aim reflected the spiritual, mystical nature of the *Exercises*. While "servile fear" has its place, the true objective is "filial fear," that is, unequal but also relational loving exchange. The two attitudes described in succession—the individual inspiration of paragraph [351], quoted above, and the rule to be "obedient in everything to . . . the hierarchical Church" two paragraphs later, at [353]—were for Ignatius to be taken together as dual features that produced the "pure love" toward which humans aimed. One attitude could not be without the other; both must be present for the necessary balance to be struck.[13]

The *General Examen* contains both features of this dynamic. In its narrowest sense, this text concerned entry to the Society; however, it also functioned as a roadmap for how the Society worked and was intended as a model for how members and superiors might navigate roles throughout life in the Society, including the different grades of membership. For example, at chapter 6 of the *Examen* ("Another Examen, for coadjutors alone"), the following direction is given:

> If someone has been trained and examined to become a spiritual coadjutor, he ought to devote himself to the spiritual matters which are appropriate and suitable to his first vocation and not to seek, directly or indirectly, through himself or someone else, to inaugurate or attempt some change from his first vocation to another, namely, from that of a spiritual coadjutor to that of a professed or scholastic, or temporal coadjutor. Instead, he should with all humility and obedience proceed to make his way along the same path, which was shown to him by Him who knows no change [that is, God].[14]

However, there was a space in the *General Examen* for manifesting individual viewpoints as well. If chapter 6 was about knowing one's place, shortly after, in chapter 8 ("Another Examen, for those still indifferent"), the following provision appears: "However, when something occurs constantly to these candidates as being conducive to greater glory to God our Lord, they may, after prayer, propose the matter simply to the superior and leave it entirely to his judgment, without seeking anything more thereafter."[15] This is the last statement of the *Examen* text before the *Constitutions* proper commence, so it is intended as a final—and no doubt key—statement about those admitted into the Society.

The theme is taken up again in the *Constitutions*. For a Jesuit going through the process of incorporation into the Society, it was stipulated that "to represent his thoughts and what occurs to him is permissible," even though the superior had the final say. Further along in the *Constitutions,* concerning Jesuit missions "from the superior of the Society" (part 7, chapter 2), there was another clear provision, which allowed "for someone to propose the motions or thoughts which occur to him contrary to an order received."[16] The single voice, therefore, had a legitimate place in the Society, within limits.

Contemporary notions about the developmental character of human beings and the idea that people had different talents and capabilities lent weight to the value of individual agency in this period. The first century of the Society coincided with the appearance of Spanish *converso* Juan Huarte de San Juan's influential work *Examen de ingenios para las ciencias* (*Examination of Men's Wits,* 1575), which argued that such factors should be taken into consideration in the appointment of subjects to different tasks according to their ability. His theory about individual *ingegno* drew connections between human psychology and physiology, bringing together Spanish medical theories—themselves based on the theories of the humors derived from Hippocrates and Galen—the ancient Arabic medical tradition, Jewish culture, Italian and Spanish Platonism, and the Erasmian humanism that drew many of these confluences together.[17]

Huarte viewed *ingegno* as being divided into three tiers: those with theoretical-intellectual skill (theologians and philosophers), those gifted with memory (preachers and orators), and *ingegni inventivi* (those endowed with practical skills, which included merchants and military men but also artists, poets, and political men). He held that trying to be good at many things actually led to the suffering of the individual. He also argued that once the qualities of a person had been discovered by those qualified to find them out, then the suitable course of study should be assigned to him: "In order not to err in choosing the profession most suited to one's natural predispositions, it would be necessary to have in the state men of great prudence and doctrine who should discover each one's ability at a young age, obliging him to study the most suitable science without leaving it to his own choice."[18] Whether we are tempted to see here the beginning of the modern era—the specialist, rather than the "universal person," the power of merit over birth, and the codification and "scientization" of individual personality and potential—the success of Huarte's work was enormous and it was influential in some, although not all, Jesuit circles. For the Jesuits' part, they produced their own literary contributions on the human intellectual endeavor, with a work by Antonio Possevino (1533 / 1534–1611), *De cultura ingeniorum* (1593) (part 1 of his *Bibliotheca selecta,* a guide to orthodox Catholic books), outlining a system for classifying human knowledge, with theology unsurprisingly the head of the sciences; and Antonio Zara's *Anatomia ingegnorum* (1611), emphasizing the anatomical and natural frameworks for locating human intellectual ability. These texts point to a particular cultural moment, alongside Huarte's famous text, which we know was in Jesuit possession.[19]

They also reflect the male-only membership of the Society. Some degree of individual agency and individual prowess was considered a male preserve in this period, and therefore it is not surprising that provision was made for these values.[20] As discussed in Chapter 1, the opportunity outlined in the *Exercises* to discover and develop one's individual talents in the service of God and neighbor likely appealed to the upper and middle social strata that were drawn in large numbers to become Jesuits: this was exactly the type of male who expected to be a high-functioning person with substantial individual influence. His vocation gave him the chance potentially to wield even more influence than he might have done as head of a family or in service of its affairs, working instead as a Jesuit alongside likeminded men within a worldwide Society. According to Ulrike Strasser, the Society of Jesus participated in introducing a "novel gender form" to the early modern world. Seen in gender terms, it offered a powerful framework for the religious life that was all male, global, institutionally reinforced through rigorous training, legitimate in the eyes of the Church, and which might reasonably be expected to satisfy the goals of those who joined.[21]

Jesuit attitudes reflected broader social understandings of the correct order of things, also seen in gendered terms. The "woman question" was present in the *Spiritual Exercises,* if indirectly. In the section dedicated to what is known in the Ignatian tradition as the "discernment of spirits" ("the good motions that they may be received, and the bad that they may be rejected"), the Devil's conduct is compared to that of women: "The enemy conducts himself like a woman. He is weak against physical strength but strong when confronted by weakness." Commonplace misogyny thus provides Ignatius with one example of how the Devil behaves; he also compares the Devil to a "false lover" for his secrecy and to a "military commander" for attacking the weakest points of a soul's defense. Women, in this passage, thus had a natural and collective deficit, but they had the potential to be "strong" in areas other than physical prowess, such as those of the mind and spirit, which could be used for ill, as in this example; however, they were precisely the spheres that the *Spiritual Exercises* sought to develop: like the possibility of honest love or a virtuous military commander, the *Exercises'* method could assist women's strengths, as well as men's, to be developed and turned toward good.[22]

In terms of power—its limits, possibilities, and modes of exercising it—the male religious life carried certain similar traits that can be observed in early modern female experience. In a study of the famous "missionary martyr to England," Luisa de Carvajal y Mendoza (she was close to the Jesuits and inspired by their missionary charism), Anne J. Cruz observes parallels between women's desire and the power they exercised. She stated: "Power offers the means by and against which women's desire is formed and repressed." Something similar took place in the male religious life that was underpinned by obedience to superiors and their religious rule. The spaces afforded women such as Carvajal to attain a level of conscious subjectivity were fewer than those afforded men, and they took place in a context of "resistance" and by way of "multiple manoeuvres through which they seek to redeem their de-valued domain and conquer the territory reserved to men." The Jesuits, who, like women, had to negotiate a system of obedience, also, like them, achieved a certain subjectivity through negotiation—and sometimes resistance. Carvajal did so through subverting established norms. Interestingly, Cruz sees Carvajal's desire for martyrdom as an aspect of agency, seeking to control her destiny and justify it too by giving her unusual and transgressive missionary life a spiritual dimension. Jesuits professed a similar abandonment of their lives from earthly restraints (including the desire for martyrdom in many cases). In choosing spiritual liberty, they were perhaps also escaping from undesirable secular duties, authorities, and pressures.[23]

Yet the call to obedience threatened to be emasculating for Jesuits: they never married or became heads of households, the markers of male adulthood in premodern Europe. The religious male could be seen as ungendered, "emasculine," not fully adult. The Jesuit, however, was an active participant in the world, expected to be virile, strong, and authoritative in whatever ministry he performed. His was a Society without a female arm on the grounds that its missionary charism was not suited to women: this guaranteed him his share of masculinity—and possibly helps to explain the appeal of the Society to so many early modern males.[24]

Age was another characteristic that carried certain meanings and consequences for members. When sufficiently advanced, it was imbued with authority and surfaced as a relevant marker in Jesuit operations. Age nevertheless was a slippery concept and was less fixed than other factors in early modern culture, such as social and family background; even gender was somewhat subordinated to family identity and social rank, and so was age.[25] A young Jesuit, especially if he came from an elite family, might be expected to preach well—because he was a Jesuit—beyond what would be expected of him as a young man. For example, in 1564, the prominent Jesuit based in Bologna, Francesco Palmio (1518–1585), praised one such young Jesuit in the city. He wrote to the superior general in Rome of Giacomo Croce: "It seemed impossible that a youth like him was able to deliver an oration.... He demonstrated that, even if he does not have a beard on his face [that is, he is young], he does not lack it in his brain." On the other hand, his brother, Lombardy provincial Benedetto Palmio (1523–1598), recounted to Superior General Diego Laínez from Forlì in 1561 that a replacement was being sought for one of the teachers at the Jesuit college in Padua who had been removed; Palmio wrote that while the appointee should have suitable characteristics, "in goodness, and in mature manners, I know that in such cases . . . it would be very important if he [also] had a beard"—that is, presumably he should be old enough to hold down the role.[26] Aside from personnel challenges like this one, what the early Society lacked in experience—with few older men—may have represented an appealing choice for enterprising young men.

We saw earlier that the reputedly fractious original companion Nicolás Bobadilla reminded the provincial in Sicily that "the Society of Jesus was a new order" and that consequently the superiors were "inexperienced."[27] No doubt, this young religious institute presented problems of the kind that Bobadilla saw. However, with the appointment of young noblemen to senior positions, such as Alessandro Valignano as visitor to the entire East Indies at the age of thirty-four, and Claudio Acquaviva to the whole Society (as its superior general) at the age of thirty-seven, this must have appeared truly as a Society of opportunity. Assuming adult responsibilities or titles of governance at a young age was not unusual for members who had been born into the nobility; the Jesuits offered potentially wider horizons even than family titles, and for some a fast track to assuming broader authority. This prospect must have been of interest to some of them, or at least it must have seemed like a natural progression from the world to this new religious institute.

These are some of the themes that surface in the biographical documents—the gendered nature of being a Jesuit, the fluid concepts of age as it related to authority, and the opportunities and limits of agency that a Jesuit experienced in the Society. At the same time, underpinned by the *Spiritual Exercises* and endorsed by the *Constitutions,* the relational dynamic that they facilitated is also present. They functioned for the issuing of directives, to be sure, but they also worked as a kind of correcting safety valve, as a pressure release for individual members who felt the need to express themselves in any number of ways, including to protest. Whether through the personnel catalogues of the Society or in the words of the Jesuits themselves in letters and petitions, the distinctive individual-spiritual-collective framework within which these documents were produced means that each Jesuit is visible from different angles, emerging in intriguing ways. Let us turn, then, to consider these sources in order.

"He": Writings about Fellow Jesuits

The aim to identify suitable men for the myriad roles of the Society was the main reason for the generation of documents by Jesuits *about* Jesuits. The stakes were high: the most important senior positions that these documents refer to carried influence and authority, but also the lowlier ones carried weight, since each role was seen to affect the success or failure of entire communities, as well as the reputation of the Society.[28]

The most systematic and numerous appraisals of Jesuits reside among the catalogues. They were codified in the Third General Congregation of 1573, along with the regulation of correspondence that led to the 1584 *Formula scribendi*. They provide invaluable details about individuals, even if within a highly circumscribed framework of assessment. These voluminous and rich documents deserve some concentrated attention before we consider some of their contents. The two types of personnel catalogues were the annual catalogues—containing basic information about the current role of each member in the Society and sent to Rome from every province—and the triennial catalogues, which were more detailed. The provincial was responsible for sending the catalogues to the superior general; he was helped in his task by those with governance and administrative responsibilities in the province. The so-called *primus* section of the triennial catalogues contained brief assessments of the individual progress and status of each member (including age, state of health, time in the Society, and stage of studies). The *secundus* section (not always included, and not about every member for the Italian provinces in this period) resembled most closely the reports about mission candidates discussed in Chapter 2. Sometimes this was known as *secretus* because it did not include names but only numbers that corresponded to the lists provided in the first part of the catalogue; this section provided confidential personal appraisals (intelligence, judgment, prudence, experience, temperament). It was reserved for the use of provincials and superiors general and was consulted especially for appointing superiors. The *tertius* gave financial information about the relevant residence. Compared with the relative uniformity of the simpler annual catalogues, there was a great deal of variety in these triennial catalogues between provinces, which changed according to the style adopted by the superior. The 1573 triennial catalogue from Venice, for example, actually was given the title "Informationes" by the provincial who submitted it.[29]

Turning to the individuals that come into view in these documents, the earliest personnel information for Italy unsurprisingly relates to the first members located in Rome.[30] These listed names and grades, but little else. The first catalogues date from the Society's first decades. The most senior member, the superior general, was given first: for example, we have a one-page undated document from around 1555 listing thirty-eight members of the Roman Jesuit household, with, at its head, "Father *Illustrissimo* Ignatio," followed by "Father Polanco," "Father Bobadillia," and so on.[31] By later that decade, the name "Catalogue" was in use: for example, the 1559 "Cathalogus Collegialium Societatis Iesu in Urbe" named members, as well as their provenance (*"Italus," "Hispanus"*). They were grouped under their different roles, from the most senior faculty to temporal coadjutors, and according to the different areas of teaching for the relevant members (whether "*professores*" or "*auditores*," and for subjects such as "theology," "mathematics," and "logic").[32] In the following decade, the method of providing basic information about members continued: for example, the 1564 Rome catalogue described the occupations of the coadjutor brothers, including a tailor, baker, *scriptor,* nurse, painter, and builder. In the same year, in Loreto, one of the first personnel documents was drawn up in the form of a table—"information on the quality of the fathers and brothers of Loreto, 42 in number"—and set out according to name, age, provenance, time in the Society, study, office and occupation, complexion (health), and talent.[33]

By the 1570s, information that is more detailed begins to appear in these personnel records, some in the form of short paragraphs. The 1573 Roman triennial catalogue provides the basic biographical data, including stage of studies and grade of membership, plus state of health. The catalogue also tells about the provenance of members in the *Casa professa:* there were eleven Italians, seven from Spain, and one from Belgium. For example, Father Francesco Torres from Spain "is sixty-five years old—perhaps more—he entered [the Society] in Rome in 1567, is doctor of Theology, he was Professed with four vows two years after his entrance, is healthy and averagely robust for his years." Father Ludovico Corbinelli, on the other hand, "aged fifty-two, entered in Rome in 1566; he has three solemn vows, is a confessor, with poor health and very weak."[34]

In this catalogue, among the professed, assessments of character and ability are not provided; by contrast, in the case of coadjutors, skills are particularly appraised. One Jesuit was described as having served the superior general for eleven years: "He is a carpenter and has ability in any task, is healthy and robust." The twenty-six-year-old Englishman listed simply as "Tommaso Inglese" had been in the novitiate for eight months at the time of writing and "has not yet taken the vows of temporal coadjutor; he works in the dispensary [larder] and is good at all tasks, he is healthy and strong." Another temporal coadjutor, thirty-year-old Salvatore da Coldiscepoli entered the Society at Loreto: "He works in the kitchen... he has a good writing hand because he was a notary."[35]

These detailed records are an invaluable snapshot of individual Jesuits in Rome during the first decades of the Society's existence. In the early seventeenth century, such detail tends to be replaced by much briefer lists and tables of names with essential information. By 1639, the Roman catalogue is very succinct, as for the entry about Giovanni Raffaele de Ferraris, first encountered at the outset of this book as an applicant to the Society, listing the goods he arrived with, and then, in Chapter 2, as petitioner for the "Indies." De Ferraris appears several times in the catalogues for that year: in the *primus catalogus* of the Collegio Romano and the "Catalogus primus Domus Probationis Sancti Andreae," and the *secundus catalogus* of both institutions. Although referring to the same year (1639), the first mention seems to have been written chronologically earlier than the second one, since it lists his age as fifty-three and his health as average, while the second document lists him at S. Andrea as fifty-four and weak. The documents mention his legal training, and the second catalogues are predictably more detailed in every category, including judging de Ferraris to be highly intelligent, prudent, experienced, with talent in governance. He was also described as sanguine and choleric (see Figures 5 and 6, at number 57).[36]

Another sixteenth-century catalogue, produced in 1573 in the north of Italy, generated a wealth of information. It included individual appraisals in prose and fascinating accounts of the province's history, donations, and origins of various houses and colleges there. Of the "Fathers of the Province of Lombardy," for example, we discover that fifty-six-year-old Giovanni Battista Viola (c. 1517–1589), early member and correspondent of Ignatius, from Parma entered the Society in Rome thirty-two years previously—in 1541—and took his profession of four vows in Paris in 1550: "He is a master in the *Arti* [Arts], and studied Theology for some years. In France he was Rector of the College in Paris and in Bouillon, in Italy he had charge of a number of colleges. He is talented in governing and now he attends to confessions."[37]

Many clearly had illustrious lives as Jesuits, and these were recorded too, sometimes in simple detail. The 1573 document from Lombardy lists Father Francesco Palmio of Parma (mentioned above): "fifty-four years of age," who in Bologna "made the profession of three vows in the year 1568 on 1 January by the hand of the most Illustrious Cardinal [Gabriele] Paleotti; he governed the College of Bologna for twenty years with satisfaction; he preached, confessed, and assisted many Bishops of that city in many acts of reform in the city and diocese."[38]

The appraisals were varied—one member was described as talented in governing *"et conversare,"* and of another it was noted that "he is of a robust mind." Negative judgments were less frequent—such as the Perugian Flaminio Comitolo, who was thirty years old, with three vows (taken in 1560), about whom it was written, "He is not very healthy and has little talent." There were some unusual cases, too: twenty-seven-year-old Father Ottavio Cotta from Milan entered the Society in Rome at the age of twenty; we learn that subsequently "he spent three years outside the Society and became a priest; he was re-accepted by Father Leonetto." Another interesting case involved sixteen priests who originally belonged to a different religious congregation, in Brescia; six years earlier they sought permission and were accepted to enter the Society. One of them was Father Agostino Mutio, from Bergamo, doctor in philosophy and in law; in addition to his studies in theology, he is described as having an "acute intelligence, for preaching, teaching, but in [the ministry of] exhortation he needs to be restrained."[39]

Of the "teachers and scholastics" listed in the 1573 catalogue from Lombardy, the first entry is also the most famous. It describes Giovanni Botero, who went on to become a political theorist and writer (most notably of the 1589 treatise *Reason of State*) after he was dismissed from the Society in 1580 for his views, which he preached, about the papacy's claim to temporal power. The catalogue states, "Giovanni Botero from Bene in Piedmont . . . is twenty-nine and entered the Society in Rome fourteen years ago. He studied the course and taught rhetoric in France and in Italy in various colleges. He is a good poet, and has good intelligence; he is studying Theology, and is teaching the final course in rhetoric for teaching and preaching."[40]

Several assessments in this part of the catalogue dedicated to teachers and scholastics were harsh, and there were more negative appraisals than of the priests; these Jesuits were still in formation and still being assessed. According to the catalogue, one Jesuit has been "teaching

	Nomen et Cognomen	Patria	Aetas	Vires	Tempus Societatis	Tempus Studiorū	Ministeria quae exercuit	Gradus in Litteris	An Professus An Coadiutor
49	P. Jo: Bapta Floravantius	Pistoriensis	Ann. 46	Bona	26. Dec 1609	Rhet. 2 Phil. 3 Theol. 4	Docuit Hum. 3 Phil. 6 Cas. consc. 2 Rector		Prof. 4 vot. 25. Maij 1626
50	P. Jo: Bapta Giattinus	Panormitanus	Ann. 38	Bona	3. Octob. 1615	Rhet. 2 Phil. 3 Theol. 4	Docuit Gram. Hum. 2 Rhet. 2 Mathem. 2 Phil. 4		Prof. 4 vot. 31. Jul. 1634
51	P. Jo: Bapta Grassettus	Matiliensis	Ann. 30	Bona	20. Novemb. 1627	Phil. 3 Theol. 4	Docuit Gram. 4		
52	P. Jo: Bapta Rubeus	Mediolanensis	Ann. 64	Infirma	1593	Rhet. 2 Phil. 3 Theol. 4	Docuit Philo. Moral. 2 Theol. 12. Censor libro		Prof. 4 vot. 17. Dec. 1611
53	P. Jo: Bapta Joranus	Romanus	Ann. 45	Bona	4. Octob. 1613	Phil. 3 Theol. 1	Docuit Gram. 4 Procurat.		
54	P. Jo: Maria Vicecomes	Mediolanensis	Ann. 27	Bona	1. August. 1626	Rhet. 1 Phil. 3 Theol. 3	Docuit Hum. 4		
55	P. Jo: Paulus Farnesius	Romanus	Ann. 36	Mediocres	20. Jan. 1619	Phil. 3 Theol. 4	Docuit Phil. 3 Moral. 4 Theol.		Prof. 4 vot. 16. 7bris 1635
56	P. Jo: Petrus Caravadinus	Romanus	Ann. 51	Infirma	31. Octob. 1605	Phil. 3 Theol. 2	Docuit Gram. Hum. Minist. Subminist. Rector.		Prof. 4 vot. 3. Maij 1621
57	P. Jo: Raphael de Ferrarijs	Cunensis	Ann. 53	Mediocres	19. Decemb. 1637			J.V.D.	
58	P. Julius à Joli	Atinensis	Ann. 69	Mediocres	24. Mart. 1589	Rhet. 2 Phil. 3 Theol. 4	Docuit Hum. 3 Cas. consc. 4 Theol. 10. Rector. Instructor.		Prof. 4 vot. 7. Junij 1609

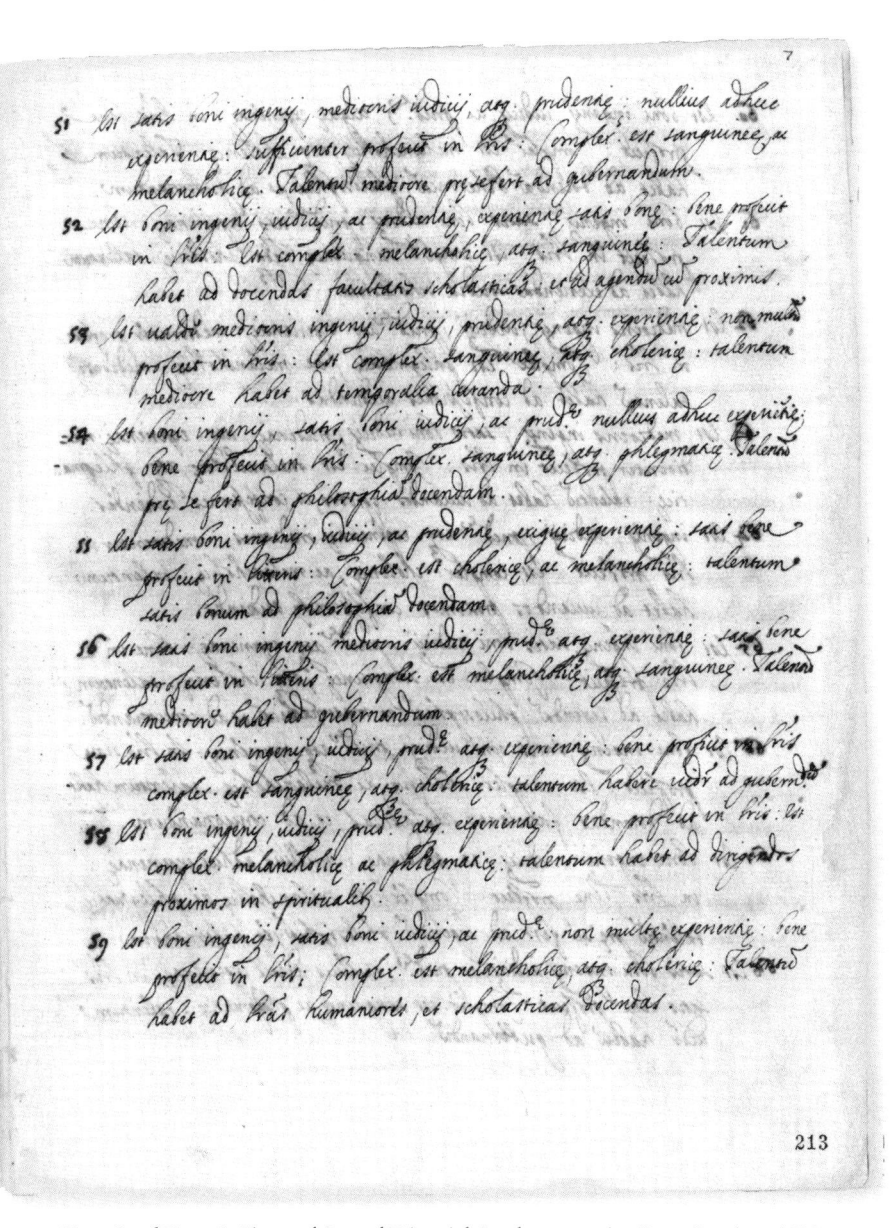

Figure 5 and Figure 6. First and Second Triennial Catalogue entries, Rome Province, 1639. *Rom.* 57 ("Catal. Triennal. 1636–1639"), fols. 155v, 213r (detail, see especially at number 57, Giovanni Raffaele de Ferraris). Reproduction © Archivum Romanum Societatis Iesu.

grammar for two years," at which he has "little talent, and his ability is elsewhere"; another "understands little in cases of conscience and confession." Lutio de' Lorenzi of Parma is listed as having been in the Society five years: "He is bright [*buon ingegno*] but on account of his shyness he is unable to teach," whereas Antonio Marzaro from Bassano "has a hard head and his vocation is in a state of inconstancy." Marcantonio del Bose, *Francese*, similarly, "is restless, and hard of head; in order to help him, he is given low offices." With such judgments reserved for some, other judgments identified potential future leaders, with one Jesuit described as having "good talent in preaching and governance."[41]

As to the coadjutors, one forty-seven-year-old who had been with the Society in Bologna for twenty-two years is described as having "poor health for any roles." Another thirty-four-year-old, "Alessio d'Argento, from Spoleto ... entered the Society eighteen years ago, [and] he suffers headaches and has melancholic humors," while forty-two-year-old Clemente Persico "is good for every kind of work."[42]

People were imperfect, of course, and so was the system. While the above data give the impression of a well-oiled machine, of a system of information exchange that facilitated the smooth running of a large enterprise, in reality there were limitations and problems. The system did not always work, and glimpses of the Jesuits' frustrations can be found among the Society's administrative and epistolary records. One *copialettera* reveals this very frustration from the superior general himself. In a letter sent from Rome, in February 1592, Superior General Acquaviva informs Father Cesare de Vico in Naples, "I have seen the letter of Your Reverence concerning the accounts"; the resulting confusion in attempting to decipher the information was such that he advised, "a good way of avoiding this inconvenience" would be to leave the task for one of their other confreres. This letter is part of the *Fondo Gesuitico* 268-299 ("Lettere 1585-1739"), sent from the superior general and mainly concerning finances. A large number are conserved from the early period of the Society, but they diminish over time, being the kinds of letters that Lamalle commented probably were eliminated by more cautious superiors general as time went on.[43]

With the impetus to produce records about the close details of the Society's administration, the problems that arose lay not just in the duplication of work but also in the enormous workload that this system demanded, not always with sufficient personnel. As Bobadilla conceded to Jerónimo Doménech, the lack of experienced leaders among the huge number of young entrants meant that the Society would "over-exert those who entered."[44] Not everyone who found himself in a leadership position was suited to it. In late 1558, the future Lombardy provincial (1559–1565), Benedetto Palmio, wrote from the Venice province to newly elected Superior General Laínez about the college rector in Padua, whom he described as *bonissimo*, "but not suited to this ... as much as to Provincial government."[45]

The demands for regular communication were onerous for leaders, and there were many potential hurdles in the supply of such regular information. The sick Ottavio Cesari explained to Ignatius in 1556 about his failure to write "as Your most Reverend Paternity ordered me to do ... having now got myself out of bed." He explained that the reason for not having written the previous week was that he was "very weak," and besides that, there was nothing to write. Benedetto Palmio's older brother, Francesco, who we have encountered in the Lombardy province catalogue of 1573, wrote to the Society's (and Ignatius's) secretary, Juan Alfonso de Polanco, over twenty years earlier, in 1551. Francesco was thirty-three years old at the time and he described the busy life of his community in Bologna at the end of a long letter: "For the rest, everyone at the house is well, and everyone attends to his study with diligence. We have the usual occupations, and many more besides, we hope with much fruit." He then adds in a postscript another telling remark about overwork: "I ask Your Reverence to forgive me if this is badly written. The reason is my [inferred: many] occupations."[46]

These letters provide insight into the human dimension of producing the paperwork that underpinned the Society's governance. It was time-consuming to be sure. Correspondents tried their best to be brief. In a letter dated January 11, 1551, addressed to Ignatius, the superior for South India (Fishery Coast, Travancore, São Tomé), Niccolò Lancillotto (died 1558), used the following strategy: "Last year, I wrote to Your Reverence how the Fathers of the Society were organized and divided in this vineyard of the Lord, and how everyone was producing much fruit. At present, there is no change, except that everyone is laboring in the same places as best they can." Toward the end of his letter, he returned to the subject of Paolo Battista da Camerino (died 1560), who he reported was substituting for Francis Xavier in his absence as superior of Goa; almost complaining, he wrote, "Entering into the particular details about him [Paolo Battista] and about the other Fathers would mean never finishing." In fact, he had just completed a rather detailed appraisal of Paolo Battista, Xavier's companion on the first Jesuit mission to India.[47]

Letters, by contrast, and despite complaints about the time they took, tended to be filled with key data about members. In the next section I will consider their features as self-narrative documents, but here I wish to focus briefly on the substantial attention paid in the Society's correspondence system to information about fellow Jesuits. Written between two individuals, letters tended to be more detailed and frank than the catalogues, which were for the eyes of many and were part of official records produced with a view to governance. The value and function of correspondence was set out in the *Constitutions*, which stated, "A very special help will be found in the exchange of letters between the subjects and the superiors." The aim was to find out "about one another frequently" and provide "an arrangement through which each region can learn from the others."[48] In practice, it meant that portraits of close friendships emerge in some letters, and a sense of real human connection can be seen in the quite surprising level of informality in many of them. Often, they contained a mix of styles.

When Visitor to the Indies Alessandro Valignano wrote to the superior general in Rome, the letter was also being composed for his former friend from the novitiate, the same Acquaviva. This connection gave Valignano license to report on things unreservedly. He was an exemplary practitioner of the candid and detailed epistolary report: he described at length those with whom he came into contact, and he did not hesitate to use his evaluations to advise Acquaviva about appointments. A native of Chieti (within the kingdom of Naples and near the Adriatic coast), his most remarkable time in the Society was spent outside of it, in the Portuguese "Indies," from where the following correspondence was sent back to the Italian home front. In August 1574, after Valignano had set sail for the East, he wrote a letter from Mozambique to an unspecified recipient, probably Antonio Possevino (who held the role of secretary to Superior General Everard Mercurian and the entire Society from 1572 to 1578); it contained a detailed character assessment of Juan Bautista de Ribera (called "Battista Rybera" in the letter), fourteen years his senior, with whom he crossed paths in Mozambique and who was due to travel back to Rome after ten years in Asia. It provides an excellent outline of the kinds of attributes that were highlighted for appraisal in this type of correspondence: "[De Ribera] seems good in essence and a son of the Society." The basis for this assessment, significantly, was "the plainness and ease with which he unveiled and offered an account of all of his life," which, Valignano added truthfully, included "some imprudences and indiscretions." Nevertheless, he outlined more examples of how well de Ribera acquitted himself and concluded that he was "a faithful son of the Society." In the same letter, and by way of contrast, Valignano commented on fellow Italian Alessandro Vallareggio [whom he names "Regio"], based in Lisbon, from where Valignano himself had departed shortly before for India. He explained to his correspondent that, in his view, Vallareggio gave little "satisfaction." He stated that, according to everyone, Vallareggio was very difficult and inadequate in his dealings. He concluded his observations by stating, "It seems to me that Father Ribera would be much more suitable for that office." The post was the Lisbon-based procurator for the Indies, to which Vallareggio eventually was appointed.[49]

Detailed letters sometimes were produced about single individuals for any number of reasons. For example, sixteen-year-old Pietr'Antonio Minadois, the son of a senior member of the government's administration in Naples, Giulio Minadois, was seeking entry to the Society. He was an important enough personage to warrant a report dedicated just to him. Dated 1611, the document is unsigned and incomplete, but the closewritten four folios provide another example of the intersection of the individual and his life outside the Society—especially his family affairs—with the corporate concerns and interests of the Jesuits. The letter opens with a description of the vocation of Minadois and his father's strenuous objections to it. The case is presented as a difficult one, on account of the father's high rank: he had only two sons, and while the other was married, he was childless, so the father's motivations to continue the family line are clear here. The situation is deemed still more complicated because no meaningful previous relationship could be established between the boy and the Jesuits as the basis for the Society's assessment of him: we learn that he had never attended a Jesuit school or sodality, nor had he sought confession with the Society as far as could be ascertained. Nevertheless, the report describes how the boy had applied to the Jesuits as the choice for his vocation to religious life. His father was very unhappy about it, insisting that his son did not have a vocation but that he was doing all of this because he did not want to study, that he was not in good health and, finally, that he was barely literate. Because of his father's objections, "this poor young man" was surrounded by guards and spies at his father's bidding to prevent him from pursuing his vocation. The Jesuits set about assessing him as best they could, based in part on what those who knew him said about him. However, the information they had was contradictory and of questionable reliability. The report appears to have been written with a view to providing a judgment on the matter, and to communicate the decision that his Jesuit interlocutors would test him some more as the basis for considering keeping him in the Society, despite the father's objections.[50] He is not mentioned in the Naples catalogues beyond this report and so probably did not proceed to full incorporation into the Society.

In the Society's correspondence, myriad different types of information were provided and stories recounted, often with a remarkable immediacy. For example, Francesco Palmio provided a portrait of the ideal preacher. In his August 1551 letter to Polanco, he gave a long description of a non-Jesuit, don Silvestro, who was preaching in Bologna at the time. His letter, written just before the feast of the Assumption of Mary, also tells of the amount of time that Jesuit letter-writing took and how the authors had to fit it around other tasks and try to be succinct: "Of Padre don Silvestro, it would be possible to provide a great deal of information on many things, but the confessions during this solemnity of the Madonna don't permit me to write of them. I will only tell you in brief." The account that follows provides a useful sense of what was considered to constitute a good and pious religious figure, as well as a successful preacher, and while don Silvestro was not a Jesuit, Palmio's description no doubt reflected his views about what made a good priest of the Society. He wrote of don Silvestro: "He speaks little, and eats less; he works so hard that I am amazed by it." Palmio then tells the amusing story about some confusion over a preaching schedule. He had thought that it was to be don Silvestro who would preach, whereas don Silvestro thought it should be him. The day arrived, "with the brothers of the house and a great many of the people, genuflecting and awaiting the sermon.... Finally, after I begged him, and without any preparation, he went to the pulpit and delivered a sermon that was so fruitful, and with such spirit and zeal, that many who saw and heard it were moved to tears. Several decided to serve God after hearing the preaching, and before leaving the church more than ten confessed."[51]

The mix of news, informality (even in writing to the secretary of Ignatius), "role modeling" (about what constituted a good priest), and promoting the good work being done through stories of spiritual edification reveals the administrative-literary nature of early Jesuit correspondence, as well as its spiritual underpinnings. These spiritual features are even more apparent in the first-person narratives to which we turn in the next part of the analysis.

"I": Writing in the First Person

Jesuit letters, aside from facilitating the business of the Society, and because of their particular nature tied to the Ignatian tradition of discernment, also contained much personal information by and about the author himself. In the vein of the *Spiritual Exercises,* they contained sometimes quite intimate exchanges between correspondents, like the interactive dynamic put in place by the *Exercises,* which was an accompanied process and never solitary. Ignatius of Loyola and his secretary, Polanco, set the example for this type of writing that so vividly occupies the folios of the Roman Jesuit archive, providing a matchless repository of such texts for the early modern period. Ignatius/Polanco wrote almost 7,000 letters alone from the time of Polanco's appointment as secretary, and with a level of pragmatic informality and candor that helped to set the tone for the Society's epistolary culture. In 1554, Ignatius wrote to the provincial of Vienna, Peter Canisius (1521–1597), with the following admonishment:

> Whoever might read the letter of Your Reverence and the way in which it complains about why those books have not been finished, may think that Your Reverence has forgotten that we have other things to do in Rome. I want you to know that Father Frussio (André des Freux [1515–1556], translator of the *Spiritual Exercises* into Latin) has been laboring on this work for the last few months, so that, despite being public lecturer at our College [that is, the Collegio Romano], he cannot

lecture [for lack of time], and you can think if our College will suffer or not.[52]

His tone is softer in a postscript about the affairs of the province:

> The plan of Your Reverence not to increase the number of colleges but to firmly establish those of Vienna, Prague, and Ingolstadt, seems to be very good. As for assuming oversight of the University, there is no doubt that it is necessary to proceed with dexterity and sweetly [*soavamente*], and by gradually acquiring oversight of all of the lectures of languages, philosophy, and theology, all of the others can also be attained easily.[53]

We can see from this letter that Ignatius received and responded to correspondence from all over the Society in these early years. The letters sent to him contained a surprising amount of details, from governance, to health and finances, to family affairs, and to news of mutual networks. In 1556, the Jesuit Ponce Cogordan wrote from Avignon to Ignatius in Rome, where the former also was about to return:

> For the great necessity that I had, I got thirty *scudi* of gold, which, by a letter that I wrote in my own hand to Your Paternity, I asked that you would be pleased to pay to the gentleman Melchior Valerio, agent of the most illustrious Mons. Farnese. If this seems correct, Your Paternity could have him paid. There are three gentlemen, who would like to pay him for me, two Florentines and one Bolognese, and they will pay in Rome, once I have arrived. We will proceed slowly. We are both well, even if I feel a large catarrh and I continue to feel some residual effects from my past illness.[54]

The next section of Cogordan's letter alludes to a subject that runs regularly through the individual correspondence of Jesuits: family members and their affairs (especially their difficulties). Cogordan tells of how he had to stay for longer than anticipated in order to assist his mother to recuperate the patrimony that rightfully was hers and that had been taken from her unfairly. As part of his efforts, he had threatened legal action, which brought the desired result of restitution of her goods: "The whole of Provence was edified to see that a poor old woman was restored her rightful goods."[55]

The level of detail about health and family affairs is striking in many letters to Ignatius. We have heard from Ottavio Cesari, who in his letter to Ignatius explained that he had been unable to write as required because he was too ill. In the same letter, he provided details about his improvement: "By the grace of the Lord, I am feeling better now, and the fever has gone, and because of this improvement, today I want to descend from the cross, where I have been for about a month—that is, I have been in my paternal home—and I will go with our Lord to the college, where I hope that I will get better."[56] The porosity between the Society and Jesuits' relatives is remarkable in these letters, and clearly accepted by all concerned, given the ease with which family affairs were remarked upon alongside the business of the Society. On the one hand, these Jesuits acquired a new "father" in the figure of Ignatius, evident in the filial-fatherly dynamic that emerges in the letters; on the other hand, earthly fathers, mothers, siblings, and homes still appeared in the lived experiences of these Jesuits—and in their affairs described in their letters.

Descriptions of acts of mercy were prevalent in Jesuit correspondence, and these unsurprisingly found their way into the published *quadrimestri* circulated throughout the Society and seen as valuable testimonies of the Jesuit imperative to "help souls" wherever assistance was needed. For example, in March 1558, Giorgio Passiu, the rector of the College at Cagliari, wrote to Diego Laínez a few months before the latter's election to the generalate in July 1558: "The enormous needs of this city are of the kind that, being called to hear the confession of a poor old woman, I found that she was dying of hunger; I thus was forced to go out and provide for her, and to visit her often." Another account from Cagliari, written by Father Pietro Spiga (the first Jesuit to arrive on Sardegna in 1557), described visiting prisoners, one of the core ministries of the Society. "I say mass to the detainees every Sunday, I hear their confessions, talk with them, and console them; I speak with the judges, and with others for their liberation [from jail]. . . . The prisoners, on seeing me, are overjoyed, as if they have seen their [guardian] angel, and they beg me not to abandon them. I would forget myself before I would them."[57]

Beyond the amplifications of the printing press, unpublished self-writings could be more frank. In 1607, Father Filippo Nappi reported about his mission with his *confratello* to Narni, within the Umbrian Papal States, and about the high-ranked youth of the town, "of whom there are many in this city without much to occupy them." He continued that in his view it would be futile to stay much longer, being "doubtful that we two can achieve very much" in such a small number. Difficult political encounters were recorded as well. In May 1607, Giuseppe Alamanni (c. 1556–1630) sent a long report from Turin, shortly after the lifting of the papal interdict of the city of Venice (which lasted from May 1606 to April 1607): "I went to visit the Most Illustrious Ambassador of Venice for the historic obligations that the Society has towards his most illustrious house, with the opportunity to give him a copy of the account of the six martyrs of Japan; and after our initial salutations, he issued forth—perhaps not speaking as a private individual, but as a public minister of that most Serene Republic—with a discourse full of complaints" directed against the Jesuits.[58] In fact, the role of several leading Jesuits in the crisis was such that the Society was not permitted back into the Venetian Republic until the mid-seventeenth century.

Many letters contained very personal responses to the workload. In 1616, Francesco Pavone, who sought so arduously to be included among the missionaries to India, complained to Muzio Vitelleschi about overwork in Naples, in much the same way as Ignatius had done on behalf of André des Freux over fifty years earlier: "To the task of teaching scripture, working as consultor, examiner, confessor . . . prefect of preaching, [and] father of the Congregation of Priests . . . holy obedience adds the task of teaching ethics; I leave to Your Paternity to consider whether I have time to take a breath." The strain of governance was felt by many too, and some wrote about it. The newly appointed provincial of Venice, Mario Beringucci, wrote in 1583, "I readily would have taken a break from governance, at least for some time, but then it seemed apposite to Your Most Illustrious Paternity to appoint me to the government of this house. I will embrace it as if it were a commandment from Our God."[59]

Sometimes the many deadlines that were placed on members were not kept. In 1607, Giovanni Dionisi wrote a letter to the superior general, acknowledging that the report that he was about to send was over a year late. The superior general had requested Jesuits in leadership roles throughout the Society to outline their views of the causes and remedies concerning the ills of religious life. Dionisi wrote: "Many months before now, I have wanted to write this letter to Your Paternity." He had intended to send his letter along with a *vita* that he was writing of one of his coreligionists, Brother Carlo Casario, known to the superior general, and whose loss he had felt deeply. However, he reported, "This task has taken and will take a lot longer than I would have believed, on account of various occupations, and obstacles."[60]

The trepidation felt by some Jesuits when embarking on new appointments remains palpable in the correspondence. Ignazio della Casa wrote to the superior general from Venice in 1583 on the night of his departure for the missions: "This evening after dinner we will be going to the ship, which will be leaving at around four or five in the night, I am going animated to suffer and greatly confident in the holy obedience and the great understanding that I have had and I have nothing else in this mission of mine except pure obedience." He continued that he was determined to persist in his aim to increase daily his faith and strength, "in the travails that will come, and which I believe will be many and various, and perhaps even life-threatening."[61]

Many self-narrative documents were petitions. One such petition was written (and preserved) in 1583 as a letter from Alessandro Petrucci, seeking entry to the Society. The psychological state of the writer, as well as the physical one, was described with particular intensity and detail. Petrucci wrote "of the constant melancholy" that he experienced and "of my long nights." "I have a fire in my breast," he wrote, and "there is no place, and no port, of quiet in the world for me." He described how he imagined himself at "a S. Andrea ... my house seems the college, my family the fathers." Then he revealed the possible reason for the obstacle to his entry to the Society: he was without a foot. "The lack of a foot has been given to me, I believe, in order to make me feel what the indisposition of the body is like." Nevertheless, he continued, he took heart in his infirmity, because "Ignatius limped a little," but God still allowed him to found his Society. He cited another example: "And how great is the figure of Father Girolamo Rubiola in the memory of the people of Siena, who was among the first to come here, and he too had a limp." He acknowledged the Society's stipulation that those entering must be in good health, and so he framed his request in the humblest terms: "I pray that you accept me for services in the house, not as coadjutor, but as servant of the least of the coadjutors."[62] The representations of loneliness, the desperate seeking of human company, a noble cause, a shared project, and, possibly too, simply a roof over one's head, are palpably present in this letter.

Many letters received and preserved in Rome are accompanied by brief, sometimes tiny, individual notes about the letters' contents, clearly written by secretaries on receipt at the Curia. Several of these letters received replies, toward which these secretarial notes likely served. Mario Scaduto's research revealed that the Society's first secretary, Polanco, replied to incoming letters almost immediately—either on the same day or a few days later.[63] For the period of Diego Laínez's generalate, between the years 1557 and 1559, letters were sent regularly to college rectors: in Bologna, sixty-seven; Florence, ninety-seven, Genoa, ninety; Loreto, 127; Naples, seventy; Perugia, ninety-seven; Forlì, thirty-five. Seventy letters were written to Benedetto Palmio as Lombardy provincial. Brevity and succinctness were highly prized; Polanco sent to the rector of Perugia an example of the kind of correspondence he required, based on the Spanish model: "so that from that [example] you may extract the kind of information that needs to be sent." This model, it was hoped, would help avoid "the multitude of wordy letters" being received, "which were giving [us] much to do, [both] in reading them, and, much more, in examining them."[64]

In certain circumstances confidentiality was required, and the administration of the Society created a distinct epistolary category to ensure this: the *soli*. These letters dealt with problems, about governance or about individuals, sometimes concerning sensitive topics, and on occasion functioning as a kind of appeals process by those further down the hierarchy against decisions made by the leadership. They were to be read only by the superior general, and only he could reply. Examples of both incoming and outgoing *soli* are extant from this period; some are preserved together and so named, grouped according to province or assistancy, while others are individually marked *soli* but interspersed among other correspondence, especially for the early period.[65]

Some *soli* dealt with the difficulties experienced by members who were ill. On December 7, 1619, the superior general wrote to Brother Giovanni Battista Picciolo at Imola in the Venetian province about how sorry he was to hear of the latter's illness. His advice is standard: take comfort in the knowledge that it is possible to serve the Lord also while unwell, and to obey the provincial's directives in all things. Many of the letters contain a mix of spiritual direction, offering comfort in disappointment or misfortune, and (in some cases) firm endorsement of the provincials' decisions, against which the authors of the *soli* appealed. It is remarkable how far along the hierarchy the superior general's replies traveled. These were not just letters reserved for the leaders of the Society, but for all of its members. For example, Superior General Vitelleschi replied to Brother Marco Benavere at Parma only ten days after having received his letter, in February 1620, about the latter's request to move from his current location, although it is not clear why: "I greatly desire your consolation, [but] the true path to securing it is not to change location, but to place everything once and for all in the hands of Holy God. . . . Therefore, my brother, let yourself rejoice in being governed by the Father Provincial."[66] A month later, Vitelleschi wrote again, this time persuaded to take action: "I received your fourth letter and in reply I say . . . it is necessary first of all, to act so that our hearts are quiet inside of us, that no matter where we are exteriorly, we will find that tranquility that can be obtained in this exile [that is, during our lifetimes], where there will always be opportunities to suffer." He added, however, that he had written to the father provincial to ask "if he might be able to find some place for you in the Province of Milan: and I am certain that he will not fail to console you as much as he can." He concluded his letter by asking Brother Benavere "to pray for me."[67]

Several *soli* were sent to provincials on matters of governance. In one case, a confidential letter was sent to the provincial of Parma in 1620 concerning an internal disagreement, for which Vitelleschi held the provincial partly responsible. "Nothing has been done about it," he wrote curtly. He added that he was not writing his current letter out of doubt regarding his correspondent's prudence, "but to remind you that the more *soave* [kindly] solution that you can find, the better it will be."[68]

One of the *soli* from 1557 explains to the rector of the college at Loreto that a certain "Paolo originally was called Urbano, and due to the fact that people from his city were annoying him, he is being sent away from Rome, and his name has been changed." In the next letter, the superior general addresses another delicate topic: a Jesuit reported to have been speaking about the devil late at night. Three years later, in 1560, the general wrote about another member, Baldassar Melo, who "needs to be kept down on account of his nature: he would be capable of many things, but for now it is not appropriate to entrust anybody to his care or guidance. Instead, he should take care of himself."[69]

Several *soli* were exchanged with Jesuits serving in Asia. These letters carried a greater potency than those from closer to home for the distance they traveled and the emotions they likely evoked in the superior general in dealing with his confreres so far away. In these letters, the scope, seriousness, and risks involved in the task that faced the missionaries, and the Society that supported them, are evident. The spiritual dimension of the *soli*—to provide fraternal support, fatherly guidance, consolation, and reinforcement of the Society's mission are reflected in the repeated phrases that appear in them. In January 1595, Superior General Acquaviva wrote to the future provincial of Malabar, Alberto Laerzio, at that time based in Goa: "It is clear to see the holy zeal that Our Lord gives you for His holy service, and the good of the Society." He wrote similar words of encouragement a few days later in his letter to Organtino Gnecchi-Soldo, one of the Jesuit leaders in Japan. These letters clearly were not taken lightly and even in repetition were not merely formulaic; they must have been akin to precious objects, like the relics that circulated throughout the worldwide Society, since many took several years to arrive. The precariousness of the overseas mission and the circumstances of the men working there were amply acknowledged in the superior general's correspondence. Acquaviva wrote to Gnecchi-Soldo in Japan in 1595 how "I received [your letter] of 4 October of '92 [three years before], and in it I saw to my consolation the holy zeal with which you uphold your divine service and the good of the Society also shown by the news you give me related to Father Alessandro [Valignano]."[70] These late-arriving letters may not have helped the Society to run smoothly, but their rarity gave them another kind of valuable currency; this was not lost on the correspondents, no matter how frustrating for the administrative needs of the Society these delays must have been.

Of course, the secret nature of these *soli* also meant that they contained serious and confidential material specific to the individual correspondent. For example, Acquaviva commented on Laerzio's lament concerning "the little attention that is paid to the conversion of the Gentiles," which news, wrote the superior general, "gave me great pain, since it is something so important, and especially to our own Institute, and vocation." He outlined the steps that he was taking from Rome: "I want to hope that with the directives that we are sending about it to the Father Provincial an effective solution will be put in place." To Gnecchi-Soldo, instead, Acquaviva confirmed that "we do not fail to advise him about what is suitable" from Japan, adding wryly, "especially about matters concerning expenses and loans." He went on to advise moderation in these areas, a theme that he addressed in more detail in one of his *soli* addressed directly to Visitor Valignano, written two days later.[71] In his letter to Laerzio, further, Acquaviva seemed to play the role of mediator and advocate from one group of missionaries in India to another, using his privileged position as superior but also as the sole recipient of these secret letters, to explain the reasons for the failed mission to Mughal lands in north India, addressed to his confrere in the expanding Malabar mission of the south. His own nephew, Rodolfo Acquaviva (1550–1583), had been martyred after his return from the Mughal court, along with four other Jesuits, in Cuncolim near Goa in 1583. Superior General Acquaviva lamented to Laerzio the return of the Jesuit fathers from north India in defeat; he worried that "many souls [in the Mughal territories] now are entombed in the darkness of faithlessness, even if, according to what they write to me, those fathers indicated that the reason for their return was the little hope that they had of being able to produce that fruit that was expected."[72]

This chapter has explored the distinctive nature of Jesuit documentary production and the wealth of extant material that contains individual and personal perspectives on the self and on fellow Jesuits from the first century of the Society's operations. The individuality of these Jesuits can be recovered at least partially, as well as their institutional setting ("how things worked"), constituting a remarkable textual record of early modern attitudes, mentalities, and opinions, as well as the inner workings of the Society. These were not just administrative documents but were also textual evidence of the tenets of the *Constitutions* and *Spiritual Exercises* applied in practice and functioning as their heirs. Like their illustrious predecessors, these documents drew together the spiritual underpinnings for a vocation and life in the Society, to facilitate the workings of a mobile entity, at whose center was each individual, itinerant and apostolic, and whose records were meticulously and intentionally preserved: the *Spiritual Exercises,* one might say, in practice and embodied.

5

Deaths and Departures

*E*very Jesuit who entered the Society also left it. The majority departed on their death, but a sizable minority left voluntarily or were dismissed. Like all periods in a Jesuit life, this one was well documented, from accounts of early departures and dismissals, to memoirs written by members at the end of their lives, to the many records about Jesuits who died within the Society and those who died outside it after having abandoned it. These texts brought a Jesuit life full circle, and, like all of the biographical texts, from entry onward, carried in them the Society's genetic traits, each one encoded with elements of its foundational documents.

Most managed to remain and die within the community of Jesuits; according to the spiritual understanding of the Society, they never really left. The textual accounts that provide access to the wide variety of circumstances, including the chaos that regularly marked both departures from the Society and the end of human life within it, raise questions about the Society itself. How did it manage this phase in a Jesuit life? How did individuals fare, and what was the institutional framework for dealing with departures and deaths? What can the texts tell us about both of these things?

The Society's biographical texts permit an exploration of how their authors carefully excluded some members from the body of the Society and allowed others to remain in it through spiritual communion. Like the many figurative depictions of both living and dead Jesuits presented together within the same painting or engraving, dedicated texts sought to bridge these dimensions and view them as part of a seamless whole. They functioned like the familiar image of the "Ignatian tree"—with its roots and branches reflecting the worldwide Society in all of its members, past, present, and future (see Figure 1). Yet unlike the idealized version in visual representations, the tree of the Society recorded in the biographical documents contained evidence of disease, decay, and death, as well as growth, health, and life.

Leaving the Society

The *Constitutions* dealt with the question of what to do when those who had entered the Society were deemed not suitable to remain in it. Part 2 contains a chapter entitled "The dismissal of those who were admitted but did not prove themselves fit." It opens with the following words:

> Just as it is proper, for the sake of the end sought in this Society, the service of God our Lord by helping souls who are His, to preserve and multiply the workers who are found fit and useful for carrying this work forward, so is it also expedient to dismiss those who are found unsuitable, and who as time passes make it evident that this is not their vocation or that their remaining in the Society does not advance the common good.

While the *Constitutions* stated that if the reason was serious enough to warrant it, "no matter how advanced the incorporation may be, in some cases, anyone can and should be separated from the Society." However, "The more fully one has been incorporated into the Society, the more serious ought the reasons to be." Each case of possible dismissal was to "proceed with much consideration and weighing in our Lord."[1]

The grades of reasons for being dismissed were identified to be offense to God (occult); disruption to the Society; and bodily or spiritual weakness, such that "he could not carry on the labor which is required in our manner of proceeding in order to serve God our Lord by that way." In the case of this third reason for dismissal after conditional entry, despite a known illness, "when he is seen not to improve and it seems he will not be able to carry forward the labors of the Society in the future, it will be possible to dismiss him, while giving him aid after he has left the house, as true charity requires."[2] A fourth cause for dismissing a Jesuit was "if his remaining is seen to be contrary to the good of others outside the Society." The following directive was given about how to dismiss members: the Jesuit should be sent away with kindness—"with as much love and charity as possible," and to "try to give him direction whereby he may find another good means to serve God in religious life or outside it."[3] There is a great deal of documentary evidence, some of it discussed here, that shows that departures did not always conclude well, were often litigious, and caused much bitterness on both sides, providing concrete examples of the letter of the *Constitutions* not always being followed.

In terms of individual members' observance of the *Constitutions*, their prescriptions were not enforced under pain of sin; this was in line with Thomas Aquinas's teachings and with the rules of other religious orders, with the aim of avoiding placing unreasonable expectations on members. However, unlike the Dominicans and the Benedictines, which had penal codes (and physical spaces for enforcing them), the Society had none. As Antonio M. de Aldama notes, the term "punishment" did not occur in the founding documents concerning correction from error. Ignatius instead drew on scriptural notions concerning the charity of the Holy Spirit as a guide to correcting behavior: "In place of the fear of giving offense [or of the penalty] there should arise a love and desire of all perfection." Penances of course could be imposed; troublesome members could be moved to another location, and those deemed unfit were to be dismissed.[4]

The *Constitutions* paid less attention to those who left of their own accord than it did to dismissals: "In the case of those who leave without permission, if they were previously regarded as little suited to the Society, there will be no need to take measures to bring them back to it." However, "If these subjects are such that it seems a service to God our Lord not to let them go in this way, especially if it is clear that they left through some strong temptation or when misled by others, diligent measures can be taken to bring them back." Among the reasons for departures in the *Constitutions*, there was no room given to a middle ground, such as incompatibility—simply not being a good "fit" for the Society; either members were considered to hold no particular value to the aims of the Society (unfit) or, if deemed suitable, they should be encouraged to come back. The *Constitutions* did acknowledge, however, that in the case of good men who left for other orders, no litigation should be entered into to win them back.[5]

The balance of the *Constitutions* weighed in favor of viewing those who left the Society as dismissals, and that was how they were classified in the records about such Jesuits, regardless of the reason—as *dimissi*. For example, taking as a sample all Jesuits in Rome whose names started with the letter "A," drawn from an ambitious alphabetical list of all Jesuits in Italy between 1619 and 1628, the following configurations emerge: of forty-three coadjutors, six had died, one had been dismissed (the reason was not given), and one had been sent to Veneto. Of the sixty-eight other Jesuits listed (professed priests of three and four vows, including spiritual coadjutors), nine were deceased, two had been dismissed, eleven had been sent to other parts of Italy and Europe, and five were sent overseas (one to Mexico, and the rest to the Portuguese Indies). Just over 2 percent of this sample was among the *dimissi*; the majority of departures were accounted for by missions to other provinces and through death.[6]

Who, then, were these *dimissi*? And what kinds of Jesuits left the Society? There is one particularly rich source of information from the Italian provinces, which lists all of those who were dismissed between 1573 and 1640, around 700 all together in this almost-seventy-year span—so an average of just over ten dismissals per year.[7] Salvatore Castelano was let go for being too ill for the demands of the Society, and Giovanni Pietro Massario was sent away because of extreme family hardship. In the year 1575, Enea Ferrarese had been in the Society for only two and a half months when he was dismissed, despite his virtue: "Nonetheless, in the name of charity, on the advice of doctors, we dismissed him for having the beginning of a dangerous physical infirmity, hoping in this way that he can better recover his health or else live a longer life [than if he were to live as a member of the Society]." The next year, 1576, Luca Micalopoli from Messina was sent away "for not having sufficient physical strength for the labors that being with this Institute entails, and for the quality of the [spiritual] exercises with which it would have been appropriate to engage, we have judged that he will be able to serve God better outside our Society." In the same year, a *dimissoria* was granted "to Giovanni Giorgio Scalpiccia, to enter the religion of St. Francis [the Franciscan Order]." In 1581 the following was recorded about Giovanni Andrea Monfellino: "[He] had lived for some years in our Society, nevertheless ... he had not made any profession [of vows] within it, and in right respect towards the faculties conceded to us by the Holy Apostolic See, we have let him go from our Society, free of every obligation, and in faith."[8]

We know that many who entered the Society did not remain. Over 50 percent of novices entered as former students in Jesuit colleges; many college students sought entry but were refused; in some areas there was not enough money to support them, and dowries were not accepted. First companion Alfonso Salmerón (1515–1585) accepted two men at Belluno in 1549 but told others they would have to wait until they could be supported financially. At the same time, there was more demand for Jesuit works than there were members: large colleges struggled to find finances and manpower to keep them running. In 1565 there were 3,500 Jesuits worldwide and 130 educational institutions; in 1575 there were 3,905 members and 210 colleges.[9] Many departed. In the case of Italy, these have been calculated between 1540 and 1565 (the records list all departures as dismissals, but unfortunately do not specify whether these persons were expelled or left voluntarily): 366, or just under 35 percent, departed (calculated out of 1,053 members). This can be further broken down: roughly 22 percent had been in the Society for under two years as novices; 46 percent left over the next seven years (after the novitiate but before full integration into the Society); finally, approximately 29 percent left after ten years or more. In terms of grade, 60 percent were scholastics (still in formation and not yet ordained); of the 832 ordained members, 17 percent left.[10] This compares with the Province of Goa (1588–1594), where twenty-six, or roughly 14 percent, of its members were dismissed (about three or four per year). For Japan between 1554 and c. 1595, while precise numbers remain uncertain, roughly twenty-five departed or were dismissed from the Society prior to the large-scale persecutions that began at the end of that century. The Province of Brazil (1556–1675) recorded one-quarter to one-third departures with respect to the number of admissions (most were in formation or brothers; less than 20 percent were priests, and none had taken the fourth vow). These figures compare to departures from a later period (1712–1761) for the Province of France (31 percent).[11]

Where did these men go? In his study of the French Jesuits, A. Lynn Martin found that many considered leaving to become Carthusian monks to escape "the burden of the Society"—its active life—although none did in the end: they remained or left religious life altogether. (Ignatius had stipulated that if they wanted to go to another order, it should be to the Carthusians, who were admired by Ignatius for their strict religious lifestyle.) That the Carthusians were an appealing option for Jesuits considering leaving the Society chimes with Thomas V. Cohen's finding that in the early questionnaires about the reasons for joining, discussed in Chapter 1, a very large number of respondents indicated separation and safety from the outside world; the Society, for some, evidently did not provide enough distance from the world. Yet Miriam Turrini sees a possible contradiction between Cohen's findings about Jesuits in the Nadal surveys of the mid-sixteenth century seeking to leave the world, and many members' stated desire a century later, in the questionnaires from 1640s, to go to the "Indies" and die a martyr. In the early years, the active apostolates of the Society possibly had not been fully apprehended by those seeking entry; hence their disappointment and desire to leave or transfer to a different religious order. (This is borne out in the case studies analyzed by Martin.) In the later years, the distinct Jesuit active style was more fully understood. Turrini posits that this contradiction can be explained by the time that had elapsed between these records and the changes in the Society, including its missionary and martyrological identity. This important theme of change over time relating to Jesuit vocations and other records about the different phases of life in the Society should be kept in mind as we proceed with our analysis here.[12]

There were many reasons why some abandoned their life in the Society of Jesus. One set of records titled "Departures from the Society, 1588" lists a variety of motivations for departure—some dismissed, others not—recorded in Rome about subjects from all over Italy, around thirty in all. The Sicilian Giovanni d'Ama left "because of the poverty of his [relatives]." Several simply were voluntary, without providing the reason: Alessandro Fioravanti was given license to leave—that is, "*licentiato* at the beginning of April before Easter, having asked to depart from the Society." Some left without giving notice: the German coadjutor, Giovanni Dolf, is recorded as having "left without license." Some entries note that a letter of resignation—*dimissione*—had been sent to the provincial; these letters provided the basis for processing licenses for voluntary departures. Of the roughly thirty Jesuits listed in this source, most have an accompanying note that a license—*patente*—had been granted (sent to the provincial or rector, depending on the person in question). One entry mentions that permission was not granted to a Jesuit from Naples who wished to be released to help his relatives, but that if permission subsequently were to be granted, Father Provincial Fabio de Fabii could provide it. The Sicilian Leonardo Catania, on the other hand, "was *licentiato* in Bivona, in Sicily, on 12 May 1588, having fallen into temptation ... having spoken badly and created confusion."[13]

Family need was an extremely common reason for departure: the superior general's correspondence in April 1601 records how the general had informed the provincial of Sicily, in Palermo, that he had written to the Messina College rector, Father Cesare Corto, about a Father Salvarezza, who had found himself obliged to take care of his orphaned nieces, "which, while it is a pious work, it is not however something that is permissible for one who is in the Society."[14] Among the general's *soli* concerning the province of Sicily is one letter from 1604 addressed to Provincial Giacomo Domenichi (1558–1626). Claudio Acquaviva wrote the following directive about an unnamed person and a transgression of unclear nature:

> It seems necessary that Your Reverence make some kind of demonstration about it, if it is public as an example for others, and for the edification of those who know about it, and also as a correction for that Father, for whom—even though he would well deserve to be expelled from the Society for the gravity of his guilt, which shall be conveyed to him—nevertheless, this time, the punishment for correction that Your Reverence considers fitting to the circumstances will be sufficient.

Superior General Acquaviva referred in the same letter to a second case relating to another unnamed Jesuit:

> [It] is more unpleasant and it is difficult to apply a remedy. I say that, this being a case for the Inquisition, I doubt neither Your Reverence nor I can deal with it, and removing him from Sicily or dismissing him [from the Society], besides the fact that we cannot do so because this Inquisition is subject to that of Spain, would expose him to danger.

Acquaviva therefore advised that, consulting with a local inquisitor "*nostro amico*" could help them decide the next step. Based on the advice they received, he reasoned, they could then deliberate on where it might be possible to send him, either to punish him or to leave him to face judgment that would be handed down *in Dominio*, "because a better way for now does not occur to me. In the meantime, I praise Your Reverence for what you have done to remove him from that place and circumstances, and do not fail to keep an eye on things."[15]

Two years later, in 1606, Acquaviva wrote to the provincial of Sicily about another difficult case concerning Father Paolo Giuliani: "As already written, we shall await the truth of the matters imputed to him, on the basis of which we will deliberate about him; clearly he is not for us and if he says that he wishes to come to Rome, do not let him do so under any circumstances."[16]

The above letters of 1604 and 1606 were reserved for the eyes of the superior general and his correspondent, the Sicilian provincial; they belonged to the category of letters already discussed, called *soli*, of which both those received by and sent from the general survive in the Roman Jesuit archive. They included deliberations about problem situations and who should be let go or retained. In one such letter, with an illegible year (at the beginning of the seventeenth century), the superior general wrote about a Jesuit who was to be dismissed from the Society, advising tautly

> that if he wants to know the reason for his dismissal, he should read the *Constitutions*, where he will find that it is not good—neither for him nor for the Society—for him to stay in this religion [that is, to remain a Jesuit]; and that if the Father

himself knows the reasons, apart from his indispositions of melancholy and heart problems, for the Society, we know them [the reasons] and that he should recall his vows, with which he was duty-bound to the Society.[17]

The *soli* also contain evidence of many Jesuits leaving without notice. The vicar general governing the Society in 1565—Superior General Laìnez had died in January, and Francis Borgia was elected in July of that year—wrote to the rector of Forlì about one Jesuit who had left the Society without permission and had returned to his home. He advised that the Jesuit in question should be sent to Rome, where he could be interviewed properly about the situation, presumably either to reenter or to be given a license to leave.[18]

The *soli* include an extraordinary case of a college student who had been expecting to enter the Society, only to have his hopes almost dashed through a misdemeanor, followed by the possibility of a second chance. The case, reported through the *soli* by the rector of the Jesuit college at Loreto, involved a possible homosexual act or some other forbidden activity by means of a "seduction." A certain Andrea appears in the 1560 *soli* as a shoemaker, who, having been judged as "modest and virtuous and also intelligent," had been given the opportunity to study at the Jesuit college. However, he had "caused certain disorder as the result of a seduction on the part of another (who was sent away)." Andrea was also dismissed (*licentiato*) as a result. However, Andrea's many "tears" and the rector's own "compassion" were such that it was decided that the "hope" of entering the Society should not be denied him. He was sent to Venice, where he was assigned to work his trade outside the Society but under the watchful eye of the Jesuit provincial of Lombardy, Father Benedetto Palmio. The purpose of the superior general's letter on the matter was his determination that if his virtue were to warrant it, "in time it will be possible to admit him and to give him another name."[19]

This Society of Jesus, with its living members (and in the case of Andrea, would-be members) intended as a single body, could not always stay whole without removing some from it. The documentary evidence that made up the Society's edifice permitted its authors to enact this process, carefully excluding some Jesuits from its membership—but not cancelling them from the record. In many cases, they remained visible.

For the leadership, however, separation was a necessary price to pay in its efforts toward keeping the health of the whole, even if the textual traces of this exclusion remained, providing evidence, too, of second chances for some.

Giovanni Battista Eliano and Jesuit Life Writings

Most men who joined the Society remained in it until their death. Several of these marked their final years with a further self-narrative text: autobiographical accounts about the circumstances, nature, and main events of their vocation and lives as Jesuits. These memoirs were made at the request of superiors, who themselves were enjoined to identify and procure remarkable life stories in their provinces for posterity and as part of the history-writing projects to which the whole Society was expected to contribute. The first such account, or *Acta*—known as the *Autobiography*—was dictated to a confrere by Ignatius at the request of his companions just before his death, focusing above all on his conversion and decision to start a new "Society" dedicated to the "help of souls."[20]

These writings spring from the discernment process described and practiced in the *Spiritual Exercises*, pointing to the objective of each Jesuit both to develop along his own individual path (these men were described in the Rules for the Discernment of the Spirits in the *Spiritual Exercises* as those "who are progressing from good to better in the service of God our Lord") and to become part of the collective narrative about what it meant to be a Jesuit. At the same time, the writings served the purpose of providing examples for emulation by younger and future Jesuits. They have been the focus of a number of recent studies, and they have provided important biographical information about individual Jesuits, such as that about Giovanni Battista Eliano (1530–1589), to whose story we turn now.[21]

This Jesuit's life story was considered sufficiently remarkable and worthy to warrant an autobiographical account. Eliano is a distinctive figure for a number of reasons: he is known as the only Jesuit in the early modern period to have been born a Jew, with the name Elia; he was also very widely traveled. A native Roman, before his conversion as a young man he lived in Venice under the guidance of his grandfather, the celebrated Hebrew grammarian and lexicographer Elia Levita (1472–1549), with whom he traveled to Germany. Aside from his studies and journeys with his grandfather, he also traveled with his parents on business to Constantinople, Egypt, and Palestine. After arriving in Venice to try to convince his elder brother on behalf of his family to reconvert to Judaism from Catholicism, Eliano himself underwent an intense conversion in 1551 at the age of twenty-one and entered the Society. He made several missions for the Society back to Egypt (to the Coptic Church), then to Lebanon (among the Maronites), and spent time on Cyprus after a shipwreck. He was multilingual too: he taught Hebrew and Arabic at the Collegio Romano. His main extant writings are in Latin, Italian, and Arabic, although he was proficient in several more languages.

Unsurprisingly, Eliano is familiar to scholars. The writings with which Eliano was associated are noteworthy. One of the most important is what is considered the first illustrated catechism for illiterates, published with brief captions in Italian in 1587 but translated into many languages subsequently with widespread success. There is also a text of Christian doctrine, in Arabic, probably produced in collaboration. Most of his work was in the translation of texts, especially church documents mainly into Arabic. One hundred of his letters are also extant from the missions he was involved in, written in several languages; much of this correspondence has been published along with other documents concerning the missions themselves, in *Monumenta Missionum Societatis Iesu*.[22]

The most relevant of his writings for our purposes is Eliano's self-narrative text, or conversion narrative. Eliano's account is preserved among the Society's "Vocationes Illustres," a variant of the life writings (*Vitae*) that were common in the Society of Jesus, usually circulated in manuscript. There are two manuscript versions (at ARSI: *Hist. Soc.* 176, fols. 119–145 and 146–160). The first is the most complete; the second is less legible and constitutes a segment of the first (from partway down fol. 128 to fol. 160, about the mission to Cairo and the patriarch of Alexandria). While both manuscripts conclude with the date—January 24, 1588, the Feast of the Conversion of St. Paul—and the name of the author, only the first version has an autograph signature, "Giovanni Battista Romano." In the analysis that follows, the title "Vocatione" has been given to this unnamed text, on the basis of the first line, which states, "The desire, which Your Reverence has always shown in wishing that

I write my *vocation* to the Faith, and to the holy Religion" (emphasis added).[23]

Part of the conversion genre of the Reformation and post-Reformation era, Eliano's belonged within its subgenre: the Ignatian one.[24] The work was destined not to be published until the modern era. In this, it resembles somewhat the *Autobiography* of Ignatius (his last work, recounted between 1553 and 1555), which was not published until 1731 (and only then, in Latin translation): it included difficult topics for the Society, such as Ignatius's investigations by the Inquisition and his youthful "vanities." In a similar vein, Eliano's Jewish identity was a sensitive subject, and by the time he came to write his "Vocatione," the Society was only a few years away from its 1593 decree banning all candidates of Jewish origin from entering.

Whatever the reason for its remaining in manuscript, the well-prepared and presented format of Eliano's work point to its possible composition as a manuscript work from the outset, intended for internal circulation among his fellow Jesuits and for the Society's posterity (and not for publication), as was the case for many Jesuit writings. Works did not have to be published to have been utilized extensively and known well by the Jesuits, although its level of circulation in this way is unknown. More generally, Eliano's account belongs to those texts intended for spiritual edification and emulation by fellow Jesuits, and for assistance in the process of institutional history making, the importance of which this still-young Society was keenly conscious.

The autobiographical narrative runs for twenty-six pages; it was written in 1588, only one year before Eliano's death at fifty-nine years of age. It was addressed to Claudio Acquaviva and produced on the superior general's request. Eliano introduced his text with the conventional modesty, claiming to be writing his story *malvolontieri* (reluctantly) and out of obedience to Acquaviva—"in this I will obey you."[25] The action revolves around Eliano's conversion and its immediate effects, so the text should be read as a conversion narrative rather than as an autobiography in the sense in which we understand that genre. For example, the period covering his childhood, conversion, and joining the Jesuits takes up almost half the work—close to five folios. The rest of the account is concerned with his first mission to the Coptic Church in Cairo, which was abortive and ended in an almost fatal shipwreck. Like Ignatius's so-called *Autobiography*, Eliano's account ceases abruptly, with his return to Italy in the year 1563. The remaining twenty-five years of his life up to the time of writing (including subsequent missions to the Eastern Christian Churches) are passed over in a few short paragraphs.

One of the most striking aspects of Eliano's text is that it is gripping; it is also personal, even intimate, especially the long section dealing with the period before and including his conversion. His narrative style contrasts markedly, for example, with that of Antonio Possevino's autobiography (1604), a near neighbor in the Roman Jesuit archive's collection of "Vocationes Illustres." The life of this remarkable Jesuit propagandist, who set alight the courts of most of Europe with his pro-Catholic polemics, is recounted by Possevino himself almost entirely in terms of the dry aspects of the politics with which he was so engaged.[26] That is not so with Eliano, who writes with an elegant prose style and a strong narrative ability.

The story of conversion that Eliano recounts brings to the surface three prominent themes: the first is divided loyalties and youthful rebellion; the second is the appeal of belonging to a (Christian) elite and leaving behind a minority (Jewish) status; and the third is doubt, desolation, and the guilt and risk associated with renouncing one's origins. All converge on the question of identity, providing a window also more broadly onto how identity in this period might be negotiated and indeed negated and with what consequences, both individual and collective. Clearly the account fits a Jesuit conversion pattern, so it also reveals how individual identity *should* unfold according to the norms and expectations of the Society. It is this intersection between the institutional framework in which the text was generated and the individual elements within it that are of interest here.

Following the chronology set out in the account, the first theme is concerned with divided loyalties and the youthful rebellion that marked Eliano's experience of conversion, first as a scandalized observer (when his brother left Judaism for Christianity) and then as a neophyte himself. Eliano's elder brother Yosef was the first in the family to convert to Christianity, after which he took the name Vittorio. Soon after his conversion, and on the death of their famous grandfather (who had disowned him), Vittorio's loyalties were so divided that he nearly put an end to his rebellion and had decided to return to Cairo with his family (where they had been based for their business interests). Instead, Eliano wrote, "As we were departing, my brother could not be found." This kind of obstinate disobedience was very difficult for a family to recover from; as Eliano observed, "Amongst the Jews, the household that has a Christian family member is infamous; for this reason we all decided not to manifest our infamy to the Jews of Cairo." Even after Eliano returned to Venice subsequently, in 1551, with the express aim of reconverting his brother to Judaism, the dishonor that this contact would bring him among his fellow Jews made him shirk the task: "Fearing for my reputation among the Jews, I sought to avoid attending to the business with my brother."[27] Honor and reputation were at stake at every turn.

The rabbi in Venice, Achiba, is presented in Eliano's account as having defined and witnessed the youth's path to desertion of his religion by birth. The twenty-one-year-old Eliano visited the rabbi during his own period of doubt to discuss those passages in the Jewish Scriptures that predicted the coming of the Messiah (especially the book of Daniel, chapter 9). When Eliano questioned him about them, the rabbi became furious. He underlined especially the danger of youthful curiosity; as Eliano recounts, "He reprimanded me strongly, that someone as young as me would look for such things, adding: perhaps you would like to go and fall, and ruin yourself, just as your brother has done?"[28] In order to take his step, Eliano had to turn his back on such figures of authority and their readings of the sacred texts, bringing shame on his family and his community in doing so.

The second pertinent theme of the conversion narrative under discussion here is the appeal of belonging to the (Christian) elite and of leaving behind a (Jewish) minority status, and the rewards that would come with becoming a member of the dominant group. Eliano clearly was enthralled by his brother's Christian circle, made up of "other gentlemen" and "other learned men," including the Venetian nobleman Giovanni Battista Contarini, whose confessor was the Jesuit André des Freux (c. 1515–1556). Eliano recorded their discourses on the Christian faith as having "entered into my heart." In addition to the company and conversation of these learned elite Christian gentlemen, the Jesuits in Venice also played a decisive part in Eliano's conversion; he was particularly impressed "seeing them all so modest, and devout, and reverent, which I had never seen before, neither among the Jews, nor among the Christians."[29]

In addition to the apparent thrill of being courted by Venice's Christian elite, what Eliano seems to be recalling here is a meeting of youth with youth: at the time of Eliano's conversion—1551—the Jesuits had been in Venice only a few years; the Society itself was little more than a decade old, drawing Eliano and many other young men to it as a new, dynamic, and attractive presence in the city. As we have seen elsewhere, this was a common feeling among Jesuits describing why they joined the Society. But for Eliano, there was the added attraction that the Society was a conduit to an elevated Christian cultural and intellectual world offering a wide horizon that was different from that of the Jewish minority elite to which he belonged. That it was not just the Jesuits but also Venice's own secular elites who were working to try to bring Eliano into their fold (by way of Contarini and his friends) must have been quite irresistible to a young man whose zeal, as well as possibly ambition and style, aligned so much with that of the still-emerging Society of Jesus.

The third theme with which Eliano's narrative deals at some length is doubt: the desolation, guilt, and risk associated with leaving one's original faith community to join another. As he moved closer to conversion, Eliano entered a spiritual and ritual vacuum. He wrote, "Being thus suspended, I already was not practicing often in the synagogue of the Jews." Eliano responded to this tension by considering returning to his people:

> Since in September there were many Jewish festivals, there were times when I was tempted to leave and go to the synagogue, and throw myself at the feet of all the Jews to ask their pardon for the scandal that I had caused them in not having come to the synagogue during those holy days and how I had been too curious in seeking the things of a different law from the one into which I was born and raised.[30]

He continued: "At the time I found myself in great confusion, seeing that I was in a state of being neither Jewish nor Christian." This suspension between two worlds must have been terrifying for someone of his time.

Des Freux, who was in Venice to help with the founding of the college there, reported on the conversion of Eliano in a letter to Ignatius in 1551:

> That Jew... a youth of twenty years, of very good intelligence and judgment, and very well versed in the Hebrew Scriptures, having been with us, as one of our brothers for more than a month, finally by the grace of God, through orations, study, debates and good discussion, understood truth and received Holy Baptism with great solemnity; and now that it has been proposed to him to choose some occupation for his maintenance and living arrangements, he says that he would feel lost in leaving the house, and he begs that we keep him here to live in obedience to the Society.[31]

Clearly, the impact could be truly devastating for the family of a convert. Eliano wrote about his return to Cairo with the Jesuit mission to the Coptic Church, which included a meeting with his mother: "Since my mother had received the news while she was still alive—not having seen me, nor had any news of me for thirteen years—she begged to speak to me, hoping that, on my seeing her and hearing her voice, she would have convinced me to stay in Cairo, to return to my vomit" (thus employing a common scriptural phrase, from Proverbs and 2 Peter, usually reserved for apostates). With these words, quoting Scripture—both from the Jewish and Christian traditions, in reference to people who return to old errors—and at this point in his story, Elia the Jew becomes Eliano the Christian, ready to take his rebellion to a permanent state by renouncing the faith of his birth as well as his mother through whom he inherited that religion.

The Jewish community in Cairo nearly succeeded in having Eliano killed in the same episode, but it is this repudiation of his mother's entreaties that more decisively marks his transition from one world into another. From a human point of view, this section of his account is tragic; from the religious standpoint from which Eliano was writing, it marked a new life, a kind of rebirth. It is interesting to notice that at a later stage in Eliano's life, the severity of these divisions had softened somewhat through familial reconciliation.[32] During his second mission to Cairo in the 1580s, Eliano wrote to Superior General Claudio Acquaviva on

March 18, 1583 (five years before he wrote his "Vocatione"), about how he had been in hiding to avoid being recognized by the Jews, whereas he was reassured by his sister, who contacted him after more than thirty years and in a touching meeting told him that he was now respected by the community: "I went to visit her; and she ... remained for a while without being able to speak, and crying.... She told me not to be afraid of the Jews who all know about me, for they have no intention of harming me.... And so in fact I have seen that they are very respectful towards me."[33]

This familial reconciliation and the regaining of respect on the part of the original community provided for Eliano the means to show that, despite the convulsions of his life brought on by his conversion, family and social order were restored somewhat—values by which the Society for whom he was writing set great store. In this account (whether it was the case or not), even the Jews respected this convert's choice to leave their shared religion and embrace Christianity. In providing this frame, apart from its clear religious intent, Eliano's account reflects that this was not a revolutionary institute seeking to overturn the established order of things. Eliano and his fellow Jesuits were obliged to follow the rule set by Ignatius himself, to "think with the Church" and to obey the rules already in place. These implied the cornerstones of early modern society as well, including where possible familial and social norms in addition to ecclesial ones.

While this conversion text, which was also as a vocation narrative, barely touches on Eliano's missionary work as a Jesuit, we can see its roots and his subsequent formation and personal trajectory as the natural outcomes of his process of conversion and vocation—through these, Eliano came to construct a new self, an identity forged in a new mold. Of course, Eliano presents an idealized self and uses tropes common to conversion narratives, leaving out many of the unsavory aspects and consequences of his religious choice. What he clearly underlines is that this is a story about the negation of the self as much as it is about the construction of the self; one had to be destroyed—at least partially—in order for the other to be brought into existence. This is a point about which Eliano appears to be profoundly aware. Clearly, he wished his account to be instructive for the religious life of a Christian; the result is that it also tells the modern observer something about the process by which some individuals in the early modern period negotiated the complex, often divided worlds that they traversed physically, linguistically, culturally, and theologically, and the painful price that was paid by some to cross boundaries and live between discordant worlds. Such a message was a model to others who may have experienced similar ruptures, if less dramatic ones than Eliano's. In his case, the dissonance that can be observed outwardly started inwardly with the self: it is here, in the recorded interior life of figures like Eliano, that investigations into the period's cosmopolitan features may profit from deeper research.[34]

Deaths and Legacies

Like other phases of life in the Society, the final one, death, was scrupulously recorded. Little wonder, for two obvious reasons: First, it was a constant feature of premodern life for all age groups, with low life expectancy being the norm (especially for women)—meaning that, also for the Society, death had to be planned for from the outset. Second, consistent record-keeping was not yet a feature of premodern states, so a religious institute's role in generating such records was expected, and indeed upheld in the case of the Society, with respect to producing and conserving records about the deaths of its members.[35]

In terms of death rates according to grade, region, and age, some data is available, although these have not yet been calculated for Italy. According to Dauril Alden, the average age at death for Jesuits in China up to 1640 hovered between fifty-five and sixty-three; for Japan (counting parts of Southeast Asia), the average age at death for Jesuits was abysmally low, between thirty-three and forty-three (although before the Japan persecutions it was fifty-seven). Alden's data is patchier for Jesuits in other parts of the Portugal assistancy (including in Portugal itself), where the average age at death appears to be similar or slightly higher than that for China.[36]

All of the Society's foundational documents deal with the subject of death at length. The first document (in chronological terms)—the *Spiritual Exercises*—sets out the Christian distinction between two deaths, the death of the body and the death of the soul. The first is to be welcomed if the soul is in communion with God, and the second—that is, a soul in a state of sin and destined to be shut out from God for eternity—is to be avoided at all costs. According to this view, the centerpoint for dealing with the two types of death, of course, is Christ. His physical death and resurrection saved humans from their destiny of spiritual death through sin—that is, he "passed from eternal life to death here in time, and to die in this way for my sins." Thoughts of "pain, sorrow, and tears for our sins" provided the conditions for ridding oneself of the obstacles to the right path indicated in the *Exercises:* "seeking and finding God's will in the ordering of our life for the salvation of our soul." This way of thinking creates a paradox that helps to set the subject of death in context, not just in terms of the Christian tradition to which this worldview belongs but also for the Jesuit documents under analysis here. It is encapsulated in this meditation from the second week of the *Exercises:* When the "service of God our Lord and the salvation of my soul" are in harmony, "I do not desire or feel myself strongly attached to . . . a long life rather than a short one."[37]

Ignatius's correspondence bears this attitude out. He wrote many letters of consolation to friends and family regarding the extremely common occurrence of death among acquaintances of all ages. Several of these letters were addressed to women; the earliest extant letter by Ignatius, to Inés Pascual, written in Barcelona and dated December 6, 1524, dealt with the death of his friend's female companion, among other misfortunes (which Ignatius assumed included "the enemy of human nature [the devil] and his incessant temptations"). Ignatius wrote empathetically that "I can well imagine . . . you are feeling overwhelmed." He advised Pascual that this feeling should not end there—"For the love of God our Lord try to keep going forward"—but with resolution, which was to be found by "placing the Lord's praise ahead of everything else."[38] In 1539, Ignatius wrote to his sister-in-law, Magdalena de Loyola y Aaroz, on the death of her husband, the brother of Ignatius, Martín García: "Upon hearing" the news, "I immediately did the best thing I could do for any person: I said Mass for his soul. . . . We should not weep while he rejoices. . . . Instead we should look to ourselves—for we will come to the same point as he—and live in such a way during this life that we may live forever in the other." To Teresa Rejadell, on the loss of her friend, Sister Luisa, in 1543, Ignatius wrote that "God's will has been fulfilled in withdrawing from the present trials of this life your sister (and our own in our Lord)," adding, "If I were to go on at length with words of consolation I would feel I was insulting you, since I am sure that you conform yourself as you ought to the perfect and everlasting providence which solely looks to our greater glory."[39]

These letters help us to understand Ignatius's—and more broadly Christian—thought in that specific time and place. While his fellow Jesuits naturally were not privy to these letters that Ignatius sent, they could trace the same views into their own primary guide for their life and spirituality, the Ignatian *Spiritual Exercises*. They also had ready access to that other guide for their lives as Jesuits, the *Constitutions*. This text deals with the death of its members in a number of ways. The main section on the subject is in part 6—"The personal life of those already admitted or incorporated into the Society"—at chapter 4, with the title, "The help given to the dying members and the suffrages after death." It states: "At the time of his death, each member ought to strive earnestly that through him God our Lord may be glorified and served and his fellowmen may be edified." The community of Jesuits was expected to be involved in the death of one of its members: "Besides others who may enter to see the sick man die . . . some ought to be especially assigned to keep him company." The physical and mental difficulties as well as the spiritual risks of dying were addressed: "Sickness is often such that it greatly impairs the use of the mental faculties; and through the vehement attacks of the devil . . . the passing away itself is such that the sick man needs help from fraternal charity." Only trusted members should be present in the event of "delirium," when "there is neither blame nor merit for what they say." After a Jesuit's death, a Mass is to be said for his soul, continuing "this subsequently, according to the judgment of the superior."[40]

In terms of record keeping, the *Constitutions* advise that the catalogues must provide information that includes deceased members. Each college and house was to send to the provincial on a regular basis "a brief list in duplicate of all who are in that house, and of those who are now missing because of death or some other cause," who in turn should "send to the general the copies of the lists from each house and college."[41]

These lists are in abundance; some were compiled as discrete records with information solely about the deceased. (Many of these are now preserved in ARSI at *Hist. Soc.* "Defuncti," or, for the Italian sources,

"Defunti"). One striking feature of the records about Jesuit deaths is the youth of many listed. In 1568 the following simple entry was recorded about the death of one of the Society's most famous saints, as well as one of the youngest: "On 15 August was commended the soul of brother Stanislaus Kostka, Polish, deceased at S. Andrea in Rome on the said day of '68." He was only eighteen, and his death took place less than one year after his entry to Rome, in October 1567.[42]

Other deceased Jesuits named in documents pertaining to their entry to the Society were analyzed in Chapter 2. Pietro della Torre had arrived at the novitiate on September 6, 1556. His entry record stated this:

> He came to the house on 6 September 1556; he was examined to be indifferent, having none of those impediments proposed in the *examen*, he showed himself to be ready for everything that was proposed to him. He brought with him a biretta, a velvet padded tabard . . . a pair of hose in the style of a soldier, four shirts, a travelling hat . . . ; he brought with him, further, a sword, a pair of gentleman's boots with spurs.

Less than one year later, he was listed among those who had died in the Roman Province ("nel Collegio [Romano]") on August 15, 1557.[43]

The *Constitutions* stipulated that in some cases on a Jesuit's death, "a notice should be sent to the other places of the Society which the Superior thinks proper," so that prayers might be offered and "charity may be shown in our Lord toward the departed no less than toward the living." ARSI holds records of exactly such practices, where directives for intercessory prayers were given. Some prescribed prayers were for figures mentioned already a number of times in this book, such as for Benedetto Palmio in 1598: "on 25 November, all of the Provinces of Italy were ordered to have every priest say three masses and every brother three rosaries for the soul of Padre Benedetto Palmio [name underlined], deceased in Ferrara on [November] 14, having been Assistant for Italy, and also the Provinces outside of Italy were ordered to have every priest say one mass and every brother one rosary."[44]

The collective identity that we have observed among members thus extended to those who were deceased; this ongoing institutional unity was manifested not just in masses for individual deceased members but for entire groups as well. Once again, the Society's documents were the midwife for delivering the care of these deceased members into the hands of the living ones. The first folio of *Hist. Soc.* 43 opens with a manicule (see Figure 3 in the Introduction to this book), with the index finger partly transformed into a quill pen, as if to illustrate the inseparability of the Jesuit with his written record—about himself and his fellow members of this Society. The manicule points to a serious subject: prayers for the dead. In particular, those Jesuits who had died in Scotland and Ireland that year were to receive prayers for their souls in the Province of Rome. The 1629 entry states: "23 March Our Paternity ordered for 'ours' in Scotland, who are deceased in that mission, that in this Province of Rome two masses must be said by the priests for every deceased: and two rosaries, by every brother and three by those in the Professed House, as for members of this House and Province. And two masses, and two rosaries for those who die in Ireland.[45]

The city of Rome held a particular significance for the saying of prayers and masses for departed members, special intentions, and even for entire cities. Jesuit sites in the city were the location for these Roman devotions. For example, the records for 1599 included the following entry: "On 4 February, it was ordered for our places [that is, Jesuit communities] in Rome that the city of Lisbon now oppressed by the Plague be recommended in masses and prayers to Our Lord God." The long lists of requests for prayers in these records—for persecuted lands, for protectors and benefactors, kings, queens, popes, entire nations, and single Jesuits imprisoned by the "heretics"—with the Jesuit sites of Rome at the frontline as locations for the prayers—are a fascinating mixture of current affairs, commentary on their significance for the Society, and a window onto the community of Jesuits in Renaissance Italy and beyond, living and dead.[46]

As Ignatius knew only too well, however, not all deaths were good deaths, as we see from his *Spiritual Exercises* and even the *Constitutions*. A special place in the documentation of the Society was reserved for the bad deaths of those who abandoned the Society. Stories of the unfortunate ends of Jesuit "deserters" recur in numerous places in the Roman Jesuit archive. They are a remarkable example of the use of such documents to "edify" the Society's members, in this case, by warning them of the many dangers of abandoning their vocation. In one of these *faldoni* (which includes an aptly named set of records, the "Tristes Annuae"), a sheaf of documents carries the title "Infelices exitus desertorum Societatis Iesu etc. ss. XVI–XVII." The first of these warns against the temptation of not believing such tales. It tells of a young Jesuit who left the Society and scorned his *confratelli,* who say about the "'other Jesuits who have left . . . that whoever leaves the Society comes to a bad end. I have ended up really well.'" The account continues: "In that same year, the revolution took place in Naples." During the upheavals and violence, that former Jesuit's head was found on a rock.[47]

Ignatio Vergilio was a former Jesuit who had been a coadjutor but was dismissed in 1616:

> He turned up in Loreto where, either there or possibly elsewhere, he took a wife, [and where] he was practicing his trade as Barber [and other activities]. . . . He became reduced to such extreme misery that to survive, being deprived of any other substance, he was making bread with ash of vine scraps and, in eating it, his body bloated to such a point that it burst and he died. His exit from the Society was in 1616 at the college of Montepulciano.[48]

A similar collection of texts is located at *Vitae 5* in ARSI and called "Examples of those who, having left the Society, came to a bad end, or greatly regretted it." One Jesuit left to become a brother of S. Agostino; he moved to Sicily, where he was killed by thieves and "having been buried badly, his body was devoured by dogs." Another, Giovanni Cola Rossi, had been in the Society nine years, and was a priest, when he asked to leave. A few months later—perhaps in exasperation, or "others say in madness," he threw himself from a *loggia* "four floors high, down into the piazza that in Naples they call fish rock [after a fountain built there in 1578]," where he died immediately; the writer adds, perhaps for authenticity, "about which Father Luca Spinelli wrote from Naples." Yet another story from 1596 tells of a Jesuit who had finished his studies but was not promoted to the priesthood like his companions. His superiors tried to guide him and correct him, but he left the Society and complained widely to his friends about his treatment; he ended up in prison, where he later died.[49]

Yet another source on the subject, at ARSI, *Vitae* 129—called "Outcomes of some departures from the Society"—is a manuscript whose physical appearance and presentation suggest that it was intended for circulation and possibly publication. A subtitle further explains the subject: "Woeful outcomes of some who either left the Society, or, called by God to the Society, did not enter, or else they caused those who were called not to enter or to depart from it. Part I."[50] The text states that, in setting out the accounts, it draws on multiple authors, authorities, and sources, such as first companion Pedro de Ribadeneira (1526–1611), distinguished fellow Jesuits (Loreto college rector Oliviero Manareo [1560–1605] and German superior Lorenz Keppler [1605–1688]), *Istorie della Compagnia,* published *Lettere Annue,* and letters written to the superior general.[51] The first two accounts pertain to Jesuits in Spain and France. A third account, set at the dawn of the Society, in 1541, tells of "a certain Giacomo born in Rome." He is identified as one of the first to go and set up the Jesuit college in Coimbra; then, returning to Rome, he wanted "to change to another more sour religion [that is, a more austere religious order than the Jesuits], where he could give himself over to the idleness of contemplation." That was how the demon tricked him, the author explains, adding that he was originally from a poor family, perhaps helping to explain the temptations that came next. He left the Jesuits and, while waiting with the intention to join another order, he entered the service of a gentleman, where he got to wear white silk stockings, which he showed off to Ribadeneira when he ran into him. A few days later, "the hand of God" visited him with a severe fever, and he languished "in the hospital of St. John Lateran," where he died.[52]

Another story tells how one Jesuit loved his mother too much and left the Society on account of it. He later died prematurely. Another Jesuit left to get married; as soon as he did so, he got sick and died.[53] One account even tells of a case of atheism in 1659, which is the last date recorded for this collection of texts:

> Brother Cristiano Sassone, after leaving the Society, apostatized from the faith, believing in nothing, nor even that there was providence, or that the soul was immortal, nor in baptism, nor the other sacraments. And he came to such blindness that he denied even God being in the world, and he became entirely Atheist. He wrote against the whole Christian Religion. For this, he came to be hated by all; even the heretics expelled him from their gatherings, despite treating him well at the beginning.

The account stated that he readily spoke against the pope and the Catholic Church. However, as a result of his many misfortunes, "he returned to his vomit and was burned."[54]

Of course, reality included more variety than the authors of these accounts would have liked. A. Lynn Martin found that some former Jesuits established good opportunities for themselves. The explanation he gave for this is that "the Society's training gave men the means to gain their livelihood elsewhere," including three paths that he identified in his case studies from sixteenth-century France: "teaching, entering the court of high-ranked religious prelates or secular princes; obtaining ecclesiastical office."[55] The fact that those who chose to leave were not permitted, in the documents at least, to come to a good end is a graphic reminder of the limits to individual agency as a Jesuit; beyond some limits, that individual, together with his free choice, was cut off. The very name given to the documents about separation from the Society testifies to the fact that there was no such thing as voluntary departure, only *dimissi*. The result produced blurred lines in these texts between edifying stories and factual events.

For those who stayed, a "good death" within the Society might well be recorded for posterity. Some reports were for internal circulation, such as that of the death of Paolo Battista da Camerino, who traveled east with Xavier in 1541 but who stayed behind in Mozambique (at the governor's request) and arrived later in India, where he became hospital director and Xavier's deputy in Goa, superior of the Jesuits there during Xavier's absences, and finally his successor as mission superior. He shared this role with Antonio Gomez, whom Xavier later dismissed for his tough anti-Indian stance. He was mentioned in a letter to Ignatius, sent from Quilón in 1551 by fellow Italian Niccolò Lancillotto, superior for South India (Fishery Coast, Travancore, São Tomé): "Of M. Paulo, whom we have as superior here, it is not possible to say how much he travails in the service of God, spending all day and a large part of the night, constantly over many years until the present day: his constancy amazes. He is a man of few words and many works."[56] Just under a decade later, Paolo di Battista's death in early 1560 was recalled by Luís Fróis in his letter from Goa to the Jesuits of Portugal dated December 1, 1560: "Our Lord took from us for himself our good, old, and blessed Father *Miser* Paolo, after a lengthy illness, during which everyone was edified with the perfume of his virtue and religious patience. His passing took place with as much peace and serenity as the interior peace that he himself had with God in his soul."[57]

As Ignatius predicted, however, the actual experience of illness and death did not always fit within ideal portraits of patient suffering. Niccolò Lancillotto, who wrote the glowing report about Paolo di Battista (and whom he predeceased by two years), himself suffered from severe pulmonary disease in India from 1546, and he wrote of it in his letters back to Rome. The Fishery Coast superior, Lancillotto wrote to the Society's (and Ignatius's) secretary, Juan Alfonso de Polanco:

> I am so weak that the body cannot do what the spirit desires. But a vein has split in my chest, which means I often lose a large amount of blood. I can neither study, nor teach, nor even assume the tasks that my role requires. It seems that I have been born only to be a burden to others.[58]

Lancillotto mentioned his illness again in a letter written the year before his death, in 1556, this time to Ignatius, his own spiritual "father," who had personally admitted him to the Society the year after its founding. The letter was written only six months before Ignatius's own death and would not have reached him in time: "I was seriously ill in Quilón and, because it seemed to me that I was close to death, I went to Goa.... I very much wanted to die among these Fathers and Brothers of the Society." His traveling companion, Jerónimo Fernandes, wrote about Lancillotto's painful journey back to Goa to prepare for death: "I left from Quilón with him—he was very sick—travelling by the river that flows to Cochin, in a canoe.... And how much he suffered in this journey, God our Father knows." Clearly struggling with feelings of hopelessness, Lancillotto wrote:

> Every year I die and I don't ever die. God be praised always. From when I find myself in this agony and travail, so many valorous, robust, and virtuous Jesuits have died who procured a great service to our Lord; and I, useless tree and without any fruit, continue to occupy the ground without profit in the vineyard of the Lord.[59]

He finally died on April 7, 1558—and it was reported as a "good death." Antonio da Costa wrote to the Portuguese Jesuits in Goa: "In the hour of his passing, he gave clear testimony that he was certainly a servant of

God during his life, because the same patience he had in life, with all of his labors and illness, was present in his last hour." This Jesuit, whose letters revealed a man on the edge of despair and in excruciating physical pain, was transformed in these accounts into a saintly one, with the dramatic and harsh Indian environment as backdrop bringing his merits into relief even further.[60] Lancillotto kept his place among the branches, fruits, and leaves of the large tree that was the Society and whose roots lay with his own spiritual father, Ignatius, as well as with his teacher's most important written work, the *Spiritual Exercises*.

This example concludes the book's aim to follow the full arc of a Jesuit life, from entry to death. The final documents, about desertions and departures—a kind of death—and physical death, both those that were good and those that were bad, reveal that every Jesuit was considered to be ever-present to each other—living, dead, near, far, single, or grouped together. The bad had to be cut away from the living "tree" of the Society; they became illegitimate but, crucially, in many cases their record survived. For those Jesuits who remained, the Society was like a family. In this sense, the Ignatian tree represented the Society as both a spiritual and a genealogical family tree. Like many families with access to the literature and traditions of Renaissance culture, members of the Society recorded their works, thoughts, spiritual insights, experiences, longings, failures, travels, and stories—from entry to end of life—carefully preserving their accounts for the generations of Jesuits who would come after them.

Afterword

Writing Jesuit Lives

*T*his book has enlisted a combination of self-narrative texts and administrative documents about individual members—collectively called biographical documents—to reconstruct Jesuit life in Italy in the first century after the founding of the Society of Jesus. Some of these Jesuits also traveled widely. The contours have been drawn not through the life of a single person or from an institutional standpoint, but from the perspectives of the individual Jesuits themselves as they were recorded in these texts. In so doing, the book has aimed to open a window onto Jesuit experience and the collective framework within which it was manifested. It has sought thereby to provide an intersecting point from which to observe Jesuits and their Society and, more broadly, the relationship between individual and communal lives in the early global age.

The analysis presented in this book has shown that a number of factors gave rise to a highly specific and intensive use of written records in Jesuit practice. These included the particular charism, or defining feature, of the Society of Jesus, which envisaged an active (often itinerant) mission "to help souls" that was free from the rules and regimen typical of other orders; its far-flung organization and at the same time centralized and hierarchical structure; its method for individuals to discern their specific path through the Ignatian *Spiritual Exercises*, continued in Jesuit life through the regular examination of conscience, and written and spoken accompaniment by others through those practices; and, finally, its comparative lack of history in the vast constellation of Catholic Christendom. All of these factors contributed to the creation, to use Brian Stock's classic formulation, of a "textual community," with a distinct genetic code traced to its foundational documents—especially the *Exercises* and the *Constitutions*—and branching out like a tree, by way of its "roots" and "leaves," and in innumerable forms and applications, of which this book has attempted to provide a sense.

To this end, the book has aimed to present a portrait on two levels: of the early Society of Jesus through its members and through their writings, and, as a consequence, of the archive that has furnished the tools for this study: the Archivum Romanum Societatis Iesu (ARSI). Within the limits of the book's scope it has drawn together a selection of documents that pertain to individual Jesuits preserved at ARSI, whether in their own words or in those of others, to retrace Jesuit lives from entry to departure and to connect them to the specific objectives for which they were produced and preserved.

The texts analyzed in this book functioned in three main ways: they provided in paper form the "monastic walls" that the Jesuits lacked; they laid the material and textual foundations in the construction of a historical memory and spiritual community; and they facilitated the organization of the Society, which was hierarchical, to be sure, but also interactive, consultative, and—what has been termed in this study—"dialogic." With this term, the book has attempted to outline the mechanisms of an exchange, on paper, between unequal parties—according to the principal of obedience that underpinned the Society's operations—as well as that of individual discernment enjoined on every member of the Society through prayer, meditation, and accompaniment. The interactive dynamic that these documents are expression of had the aim of aligning each member's individual strengths and inclinations with the objectives of the Society, which identified Jesuits both collectively and singly as working in the world for the greater glory of God.

The system was highly practical, but it was also ambitious. What this study has shown is that the documents served the Society's aim to draw out individuals' highest potential for a common purpose: Through a process of dialogic exchange that the documents facilitated, the Society represented a life choice that many apparently found attractive, given the thousands of men who flocked to make it. A large number of these, as laymen, could have expected to play leading roles as household heads and members of elite dynasties, with wide responsibilities and a great deal of influence. They preferred to become Jesuits instead, where, quite possibly, they saw even greater opportunities—for the Society and its aims, and for themselves and their well-being, which in this period meant their souls, and their hopes for their salvation and that of those to whom they ministered, near or far. Because the Jesuits' mission was to be in the world, this was where they lived out their vocation and pursued their objectives.

This religious institute of clerics regular was founded by a nobleman who had been wounded in battle and had undergone a dramatic conversion that prompted him, together with his elite companions, to wish to travel as profoundly as possible—as much into the spiritual realm as into the physical one and wherever there was a need. It was a new Society for its time, with a specific worldview. Within a clear hierarchical structure, its organization also assumed a great deal of individual agency, and, as was perhaps quite natural to their worldview, the founders developed mechanisms for the practice of that agency for each one of its members. Apparently young men, elites and not, understood something of this feature of the Society and were drawn to join it.

What of the members who chose to enter this Society rather than remain men of the world? A central aim of this book has been, not just to explore "how things worked"—with what foundations, what means, to what end, and with what impact—but also to bring individual Jesuits and their written perspectives into view. The result of this exploration has revealed as much variety as is imaginable. Some were illiterate, others arrived with a horse, some with nothing, and others with a fur-lined coat; many came from over the Alps to escape religious conflict; others came from closer to home with the wish to leave familiar surroundings and relatives and go to the "Indies." Still others were drawn to join by the example of Jesuits whom they had met or who had taught them. Many left before their full incorporation; most stayed.

Until the papal suppression of the Society, the process of joining, working, and dying in the Society was handed down from one generation to the next. The fact that the Ignatian tree was gradually cut during the eighteenth century and abruptly severed by a papal bull between 1773 and 1814 is not the subject of this book. Yet it is interesting that from our contemporary standpoint, and despite that dramatic hiatus, the presence of a Jesuit pope, Francis, on the world stage today is a reminder that he and his fellow members of the Society of Jesus continue to recognize Ignatius and themselves as roots and branches of the same tree that was planted in 1540 and whose first century has been the subject of this book. The Jesuit genetic code traced in these pages, through the transient lives of individual members, is visible and preserved in their texts. In writing their letters, petitions, and reports, the Jesuits seemed to have understood something of this and about their place as single parts in a larger whole to which they bound their lives: the Society of Jesus. In the words of an otherwise unknown Jesuit—but for his documentary testimony that was left and preserved—being a Jesuit in Renaissance Italy and the early global age offered a compass in "this Life" that "I see . . . is fleeting like the Wind."[1]

NOTES

ACKNOWLEDGMENTS

INDEX

NOTES

INTRODUCTION

1. Rome, Archivum Romanum Societatis Iesu (hereafter ARSI), *Rom.* 171 ("Vocationi"), fol. 70r; ARSI, *Rom.* 173 ("Ingressus Novitior. 1631-1675"), fols. 34v-35r (December 1637): "un capello, un mantello di saetta di Milano ... un paio di calzoni ... 6 camiscie ... doi pare di scarpe ... un fucile." Giovanni Raffaele de Ferraris signed his consent to the accuracy of this list with his own hand; ARSI, *Fondo Gesuitico* (hereafter *F.G.*) 742 ("Indipetae"), fol. 36r (petition of Giovanni de Ferraris, April 30, 1639): "demeriti ... la povertà di spirito, l'età e debboli forze"; ARSI, *Rom.* 57 ("Romana Catal. Triennal. 1636-1639"), fol. 213r (*secundus catalogus,* 1639); ARSI, *Hist. Soc.* 47, fol. 38r (record of death on April 2, 1642). All translations are my own unless otherwise indicated. Note that for transcriptions from archival documents, scribal abbreviations have been silently expanded (for example, V. P. has been transcribed as Vostra Paternità; common abbreviations used within the Society also have been expanded, such as Comp.a, transcribed as Compagnia, and P.le, rendered as Provinciale). Some original punctuation marks and accents have been modernized or removed to assist legibility; in general, well-known names have been given in their most familiar English form. Otherwise, original spellings of words and names that may deviate from their native or modern forms have been given as they appear in the documents.

2. For ARSI, see Edmond Lamalle, "L'Archivio Generale della Compagnia di Gesù," *Archiva Ecclesiae* 24-25, no. 1 (1981-1982): 89-120; Flavio Rurale, "... lo sguardo o la mano del generale: Problemi e prospettive di ricerca nell'Archivum Romanum Societatis Iesu," in *Gli archivi per la storia de gli ordini religiosi: Fonti e problemi (secoli xvi-xix),* ed. Massimo Carlo Giannini and Matteo Sanfilippo (Viterbo: Edizioni Sette Città, 2007), 93-110; Robert Danieluk, "Archivum Romanum Societatis Iesu: Un luogo privilegiato per lo studio dell'attività evangelizzatrice dei gesuiti," *Archiva Ecclesiae* 53-55 (2010-2012): 221-254. Ignatius of Loyola has been studied extensively. A recent biographical history is Enrique García Hernán, *Ignacio de Loyola* (Tres Cantos, Madrid: Taurus, 2013). Known collectively as the first companions—nine of whom formed a group in Paris under the leadership of Ignatius during their studies there, and where their first

steps to forming a religious institute were taken in the 1530s—they are: Francis Xavier, Diego Laínez, Pierre Favre, Alfonso Salmerón, Simão Rodrigues, Nicolás Bobadilla, Claude Jay, Paschase Broët, and Jean Codure. Two key figures who did not join the first companions in Paris but who were leading protagonists in the Society's early history, and collaborators with Ignatius, were Juan Alfonso de Polanco and Jerónimo Nadal. In general, biographical information and accompanying bibliography for the very well-known Jesuits in this study are not provided. For the less well-known Jesuits, I have attempted to signal readily accessible biographical data, such as when they appear in the *Dizionario biografico degli italiani*, available at https://www.treccani.it/biografico (hereafter *DBI*, followed by the relevant volume number and author), and the *Diccionario histórico de la Compañía de Jesús*, ed. Charles E. O'Neill and Joaquín Maria Dominguez, 4 vols. (Rome and Madrid: Institutum Historicum Societatis Iesu [hereafter IHSI] / Universidad Pontificia Comillas, 2001) (hereafter *DHCJ*, followed by the relevant volume number, page number, and author). For bibliographical resources relating to many of the Jesuits and themes mentioned in this study (but which are not specified), see Carlos Sommervogel et al., *Bibliothèque de la Compagnie de Jésus*, 12 vols. (Bruxelles-Paris: Picard, 1890–1932); László Polgár, *Bibliographie sur l'histoire de la Compagnie de Jésus (1901–1980)* (Rome: IHSI, 1981-1990); "The Bibliography on the History of the Society of Jesus," published annually in the journal *Archivum Historicum Societatis Iesu* [hereafter *AHSI*]; The Jesuit Online Bibliography, https://jesuitonlinebibliography.bc.edu.

3. Ulrike Strasser, *Missionary Men in the Early Modern World: German Jesuits and Pacific Journeys* (Amsterdam: University of Amsterdam Press, 2020), 53–54, discusses (and provides an example of) the genealogical tree in Jesuit iconography, including its classical and other predecessors in religious orders. In the Jesuit context, Strasser highlights the tree's patrilineal representations (with Ignatius as progenitor), as well as its geographical ones (depicting the expansion of the Society). A very similar image to the one chosen for this book, and from the same work by Kircher, is discussed in detail in Steven J. Harris, "Mapping Jesuit Science: The Role of Travel in the Geography of Knowledge," in *The Jesuits: Cultures, Sciences, and the Arts, 1540–1773*, ed. J. W. O'Malley, Gauvin Alexander Bailey, Steven J. Harris, and T. Frank Kennedy, 2 vols. (Toronto: University of Toronto Press, 1999, 2006), 1:219. Harris recalls the origins of genealogies from the Old Testament, sometimes represented in arboreal form. The most representative artefact marking the Society's celebration of its first century is the 1540 *Imago primi saeculi*, a large, lavishly illustrated folio volume of emblem art produced by the Flanders-Belgium Province, republished in a modern edition: John W. O'Malley, ed., *Art, Controversy, and the Jesuits: The Imago primi saeculi (1640)* (Philadelphia: Saint Joseph's University Press, 2015). For the suppression and restoration of the Society of Jesus, see Pierre-Antoine

Fabre, Patrick Goujon, and Martín María Morales, eds., *La Compagnie de Jésus des Anciens Régimes au monde contemporain (XVIIIe–XXe siècles)* (Rome: École Française de Rome and IHSI, 2020).

4. Monograph studies include A. Lynn Martin, *The Jesuit Mind: The Mentality of an Elite in Early Modern France* (Ithaca, NY: Cornell University Press, 1988); Jennifer Selwyn, *A Paradise Inhabited by Devils: The Jesuits' Civilizing Mission in Early Modern Naples* (Rome and Aldershot, UK: Ashgate/IHSI, 2004). The title, if not the contents, of the book by Jean Lacouture, *Jesuits: A Multibiography,* trans. Jeremy Leggatt (Washington, DC: Counterpoint, 1995; orig. pub. 2 vols. in French, 1991-1993), identifies—in a broad treatment for general readership—the promising features of collective biography for Jesuit history.

5. Examples of Jesuit biographies and institutional histories appear throughout this study; the classic overview of prosopographical history is Lawrence Stone, "Prosopography," *Daedalus* 100, no. 1 (1971): 46–79.

6. In the modern period, the *Constitutions* were edited and published in *Monumenta Ignatiana: Sancti Ignatii de Loyola Constitutiones Societatis Jesu . . .* , 3 vols. (Rome: IHSI, 1934–1938). Hereafter, quotations using the standard citation format—*Const.*, followed by the relevant paragraph in square brackets—are from the modern English edition, *The Constitutions of the Society of Jesus: Translated, with an Introduction and a Commentary,* ed. and trans. George E. Ganss (St. Louis: Institute of Jesuit Sources, 1970), [668].

7. For entrants in Rome: ARSI, *Rom.* 170, 171a, 172, 173 ("Ingressus Novitiorum"), discussed more fully in Chapter 1 of this study; for Italy: Mario Scaduto, *Catalogo dei Gesuiti d'Italia 1540–1565* (Rome: IHSI, 1968); for worldwide members: Dauril Alden, *The Making of an Enterprise: The Society of Jesus in Portugal, Its Empire and Beyond, 1540–1750* (Stanford, CA: Stanford University Press, 1996), 17. For the Society's governance and the normative texts that underpinned it, see Markus Friedrich, "Jesuit Organization and Legislation: Development and Implementation of a Normative Framework," in *The Oxford Handbook of the Jesuits,* ed. Ines G. Županov (New York: Oxford University Press, 2019), 23–43. For an overview of the relevant scholarship on Jesuits in Italy, see Kathleen Comerford, "The Historiography of Jesuits in the Italian Peninsula and Islands before the Suppression," in Jesuit Historiography Online, http://dx.doi.org/10.1163/2468-7723_jho_COM_192580.

8. Flavio Rurale, "Un'identità forte? A proposito di tre studi recenti sulla Compagnia di Gesù," in *Anatomia di un corpo religioso: L'identità dei gesuiti in età moderna; Annali di storia dell'esegesi* 19, no. 2, ed. Franco Motta (2002): 359. In the just-cited volume, the evocative image of the letters and papers in the Society of Jesus standing in place of chapter meetings and monastic edifices is a recurring theme in several essays: Motta, *Anatomia di un corpo religioso.*

9. The modern edition of the *Spiritual Exercises* is in *Monumenta Ignatiana: Exercitia spiritualia S. Ignatii de Loyola et eorum directoria,* ed. J. Calveras and C. de

Dalmases, rev. ed., Monumenta Historica Societatis Iesu (hereafter MHSI) 100 (Rome: IHSI, 1969), 1:140–417 (hereafter identified as *Sp. Ex.*, using standard identifying paragraphs in square brackets). English quotations in this study are from *Ignatius of Loyola, The Spiritual Exercises and Selected Works*, ed. George E. Ganss (New York: Paulist Press, 1991), 113–214; the relevant quotation is at [231].

10. *Const.*: "Aids toward the union of hearts" is the title of chapter 1, in part 8, from where the quotes are drawn: [655–676]. Marc Fumaroli helpfully characterized the early Society as being animated by both centripetal and centrifugal forces: "Renaissance Rhetoric: The Jesuit Case," in O'Malley et al., *The Jesuits*, 1:90–106. This dynamic is reflected in its documentary production. The term used here, "dialogic," was enlisted by Carlo Ginzburg to describe recorded interactions that, despite the often unequal power dynamic between authors and their subjects, can provide useful means for understanding both—precisely because the more powerful group sought to not just govern but also understand its subjects. This was the case for the Society's leadership that produced and solicited records about and by individual Jesuits to understand them better. These dialogic features of historical records provide rich material for historians: Carlo Ginzburg, "The Historian as Anthropologist," in his *Clues, Myths, and the Historical Method*, trans. John and Anne C. Tedeschi (Baltimore: Johns Hopkins University Press, 1989), 156–164.

11. *Const.* [655]; *Sp. Ex.* [231].

12. John W. O'Malley, *The First Jesuits* (Cambridge, MA: Harvard University Press, 1993), 2–3, 9.

13. The 1573 text of the *Formula scribendi* is in *Monumenta Missionum Societatis Iesu;* [vol. 21,] *Missiones Orientales: Documenta Indica*, [vol. 9,] *1573–1575*, ed. Josef Wicki, MHSI 94 (Rome: IHSI, 1966), 717–722 (hereafter, abbreviated titles of works in this series are cited as *Documenta Indica*). The early versions of writing guides are discussed in Mario Scaduto, *Storia della Compagnia di Gesù in Italia* [in 5 vols.]: *L'Epoca di Giacomo Lainez, 1556–1565:* [vol. 3,] *Il governo* (Rome: La civiltà cattolica, 1964), 217–226. A valuable overview of Jesuit letters, and the various iterations of the *Formula scribendi*, including an updated bibliography, are in Paul Nelles, "Jesuit Letters," in Županov, *The Oxford Handbook of the Jesuits*, 44–70 (49 and notes).

14. Juan Alfonso de Polanco, "Istruzioni del 1547": "20 considerazioni spirituali, per promuovere e mantenere la pratica regolare della scrittura epistolare indirizzata al Padre Generale"; "la prima ragione [per l'accuratezza nella scrittura] è l'unità della Compagnia, la quale per vocazione è dispersa in varie parti, ed assai più che qualsiasi altro [ordine] necessita di comunicazione per tenerla insieme come una, e ciò è attraverso continue lettere," quoted in Italian translation in, Scaduto, *Storia della Compagnia di Gesù in Italia*, 3:220.

15. Wiktor Gramatowski, "Jesuit Glossary: Guide to Understanding the Documents, English Version," trans. Camilla Russell (orig. in Italian, 1992) (ARSI, 2014), 5, http://www.sjweb.info/arsi/documents/glossary.pdf.
16. On these questions, see J. Michelle Molina, *To Overcome Oneself: The Jesuit Ethic and Spirit of Global Expansion, 1520–1767* (Berkeley: University of California Press, 2013), 6. Molina's own work fruitfully places Spain and New Spain within a single frame for analysis. Others have studied certain Jesuit missionary endeavors under the same analytical umbrella and collapsed the vast geographical distances between areas where there was a coherent missionary style developed in very different locations. See Ana Carolina Hosne's study of the mutual influence between Jesuits in South America and China, *The Jesuit Missions to China and Peru, 1570–1610: Expectations and Appraisals of Expansionism* (London: Routledge, 2013); see also Takao Abé's analysis of the Jesuits between New France and Japan, *The Jesuit Mission to New France: A New Interpretation in the Light of the Earlier Jesuit Experience in Japan* (Leiden: Brill, 2011). The connectivity between regions, and the influence of the wider world on European Catholicism, extends beyond Jesuit studies, on which see Simon Ditchfield, "The 'Making' of Roman Catholicism as a 'World Religion,'" in *Multiple Modernities? Confessional Cultures and the Many Legacies of the Reformation Age,* ed. Jan Stievermann and Randall Zachmann (Tübingen: Mohr Siebeck, 2018), 189–203.
17. Two case studies where these sources are very effectively used to trace individual Jesuit lives from beginning to end (Francesco Guerrieri and Niccolò Orlandini) are Mark A. Lewis's study of the Jesuits and the humanistic tradition, "The Jesuit Institutionalization of the *Studia Humanitatis:* Two Jesuit Humanists at Naples," in *The Renaissance in the Streets, Schools, and Studies: Essays in Honour of Paul F. Grendler,* ed. Konrad Eisenbechler and Nicholas Terpstra (Toronto: Centre for Reformation and Renaissance Studies, 2008), 87–100; and Selwyn, *A Paradise Inhabited by Devils.*
18. Paul Grendler's many studies are the most important sources for the early history of Jesuit education. Except for a case study in Chapter 5 (which illustrates the Jesuit autobiography as an end-of-life example of the documents analyzed here), the book is not concerned with the Jesuit first-person memoir, or autobiography. A useful overview of this genre, and a valuable chronological list of the most significant early examples of it in the Society, is in Lorenzo M. Gilardi, "Autobiografie di Gesuiti in Italia (1540–1640) Storia e interpretazione," *AHSI* 64, no. 127 (1995): 3–38. Gilardi argues that Jesuit autobiographical documents reveal "a new space of interiority" because of their interest in the "perception of various spiritual movements, recognised by an interior sensitivity that is matured and evolves through the different events of history ('un nuovo spazio di interiorità';

'[la] percezione dei vari movimenti spirituali, riconosciuti da una sensibilità interiore che è maturata ed evoluta attraverso le diverse vicende della storia (p. 8).'" At pp. 34–35, Gilardi ties the Jesuit autobiographical narrative genre to the practices associated with the Jesuit mental prayer method, in contrast to the use of the divine office by other institutes. My study identifies that added to the documents' expressions of interiority was an interactive dynamic between their author and the ever-present addressee.

19. In the English-reading world of Jesuit historical research, the Jesuit John W. O'Malley opened the path to postconfessional and non-Jesuit interest in the Society's history through his many single-author publications and through his influential coedited two-volume work, *The Jesuits*. Subsequently, Robert Maryks has been a driving force in harnessing the dynamism in Jesuit historical research, especially as editor of a number of recent publication initiatives with Brill (and with the Institute for Advanced Jesuit Studies at Boston College until 2018). These include the *Journal of Jesuit Studies* (established in 2014), the book series Jesuit Studies (from 2013), and Jesuit Historiography Online, which provides access to themed appraisals of the latest scholarship and new directions in the field (https://referenceworks.brillonline.com/browse/jesuit-historiography-online).

20. A useful genealogy of apologetic Jesuit writings is provided by John O'Malley, "The Historiography of the Society of Jesus: Where Does It Stand Today?," in O'Malley et al., *The Jesuits*, 1:3–37. For the anti-Jesuit traditions, see Thomas Worcester, "Anti-Jesuit Polemic," in *The Cambridge Encyclopedia of the Jesuits*, ed. Thomas Worcester (New York: Cambridge University Press, 2017), 30–35; Sabina Pavone, "Anti-Jesuitism in a Global Perspective," in Županov, *The Oxford Handbook of the Jesuits*, 833–853. The initial signs of a "Jesuit turn" in early modern historical studies were identified in the review essay by Simon Ditchfield, "Of Missions and Models: The Jesuit Enterprise (1540–1773) Reassessed in Recent Literature (Review)," *The Catholic Historical Review* 93, no. 2 (2007): 325–343. The attraction to Jesuit topics in historical research was very well captured by Emanuele Colombo in "Gesuitomania: Studi recenti sulle missioni gesuitiche (1540–1773)," in *Evangelizzazione e Globalizzazione: Le missioni gesuitiche nell'età moderna tra storia e storiografia*, ed. Michela Catto, Guido Mongini, and Silvia Mostaccio, special issue, *Biblioteca della Nuova Rivista Storica* 42 (2010): 31–59. For an updated treatment of Jesuit scholarship, see Paul Shore, "The Historiography of the Society of Jesus," in Županov, *The Oxford Handbook of the Jesuits*, 759–782.

21. *Const.* [547]: "as if he were a lifeless body." Luce Giard, ed., *Les jésuites à la Renaissance: Système éducatif et production du savoir* (Paris: Presses universitaires de France, 1995); Pierre-Antoine Fabre and Antonella Romano, *Les Jésuites dans le monde moderne: Nouvelles approches* (Paris: Albin Michel, 1999), 253.

22. Ditchfield, "Of Missions and Models," 325–343. On this subject see also Silvia Mostaccio, "A Conscious Ambiguity: The Jesuits Viewed in Comparative Perspective in the Light of Some Recent Italian Literature," *Journal of Early Modern History* 12, no. 5 (2008): 409–441.
23. These questions underpin much of the analysis of several leading scholars in the field, such as monograph studies: Silvia Mostaccio, *Early Modern Jesuits between Obedience and Conscience during the Generalate of Claudio Acquaviva (1581–1615)* (Aldershot, UK: Ashgate, 2014); Prosperi, *La Vocazione;* and (in part) Guido Mongini, *Maschere dell'identità: Alle origini della Compagnia di Gesù* (Rome: Edizioni di storia e letteratura, 2018). For an important essay collection on the theme see Fernanda Alfieri and Claudio Ferlan, eds., *Avventure dell'obbedienza nella Compagnia di Gesù: Teorie e prassi tra XVI e XIX secolo* (Bologna: Il Mulino, 2012).
24. *Sp. Ex.* [230], [252], [177], and [231].
25. The magisterial treatment of this subject is Joseph de Guibert, *La spiritualité de la Compagnie de Jésus: Esquisse historique* (Rome: IHSI, 1953). Themed treatments of the centrality of spirituality in Jesuit history include John O'Malley, "Early Jesuit Spirituality: Italy and Spain," in O'Malley, *Saints or Devils Incarnate? Studies in Jesuit History* (Leiden: Brill, 2013), 121–145; Patrick Goujon, "Elites and the Constitution of Jesuit Identity," in Županov, *The Oxford Handbook of the Jesuits,* 176–192; Nicolás R. Verástegui, "The Importance of Archives in the History and Spirituality of the Society of Jesus according to Its 'Way of Proceeding,'" in *"Scriptis tradere et fideliter conservare": Archives as "Places of Memory" within the Society of Jesus* (Rome: General Curia, 2003), 25–47. For its history and historiography, see John W. O'Malley and Timothy O'Brien, "The Twentieth-Century Construction of Ignatian Spirituality: A Sketch," *Studies in the Spirituality of Jesuits* 52, no. 3 (2020): 2–40.
26. On this theme, with particular relevance to this study's documentary focus, see Gabriella Zarri, "Gender and Religious Autobiography between the Reformation and Counter-Reformation: Typologies and Examples," in *Saints, Scholars, and Politicians: Gender as a Tool in Medieval Studies; Festschrift in Honour of Anneke Mulder-Bakker,* ed. Mathilde van Dijk and Renée Nip (Turnhout: Brepols, 2005). For useful frameworks for viewing early modern masculinity, see Alexandra Shepard, *The Meanings of Manhood in Early Modern England, 1560–1640* (Oxford: Oxford University Press, 2003).
27. For an overview of the subject, see Mary Laven, ed., *The Jesuits and Gender: Body, Sexuality, and Emotions,* special issue, *Journal of Jesuit Studies* 2, no. 4 (2015). The first monograph-length study dedicated to Jesuit history with respect to gender and the history of masculinity—together with global/world history—is Strasser, *Missionary Men:* the chosen lens for exploring "the importance of the larger world to the making of early modern European manhood" (28) are "emotions, religious media, and male

mimesis" (19). Despite the different interpretive frame, questions, and sources presented in the study that follows, it is interesting to note a similar set of findings in terms of the connectedness of members that was not always tied to a specific place but instead could be established between Jesuits wherever they were, touching on a defining characteristic of the Society.

28. While most religious orders created female branches, the Jesuits distinguished themselves by deciding not to do so, after some early initiatives in that direction. The reason given for their final decision was that women were not suited to the active "apostolates" (or spheres of activity) envisioned for members of the Society. It should be borne in mind that this decision was not necessarily radical. At the time of Ignatius, the exclusion of women did not have to be justified; it was assumed, and therefore a nonissue. See this point, about female exclusion in the medieval context, in Ruth Mazo Karras, *From Boys to Men: Formations of Masculinity in Late Medieval Europe* (Philadelphia: University of Pennsylvania Press, 2003), 154.

29. See Silvia Mostaccio, "A Gendered Obedience: The Spiritual Exercises by Jesuits and by Women; Two Case Studies and Their Context," in Mostaccio, *Early Modern Jesuits,* 105–154. For the Jesuits and women in religious life, see the discussion of perhaps the most unusual case (and ecclesiastical silencing) of Mary Ward and her followers in the seventeenth century in Laurence Lux-Sterrit, "Mary Ward et sa Compagnie de Jésus au Féminin dans L'Angleterre de la Contre-Réforme," *Revue de l'histoire des religions* 225, no. 3 (2008): 393–414.

30. See Olwen Hufton, "Altruism and Reciprocity: The Early Jesuits and Their Female Patrons," *Renaissance Studies* 15, no. 3 (2001): 328–53; Elizabeth Rhodes, "Join the Jesuits, See the World: Early Modern Women in Spain and the Society of Jesus," in O'Malley et al., *The Jesuits,* 2:33–49; Carolyn Valone, "Women on the Quirinal Hill: Patronage in Rome, 1560–1630," *The Art Bulletin* 76, no. 1 (1994): 129–146.

31. Classic leading studies include, for example, Paolo Prodi, *Disciplina dell'anima, disciplina del corpo e disciplina della società tra madioevo ed età moderna* (Bologna: Societa editrice il Mulino, 1994); Paolo Prodi and Wolfgang Reinhard, eds., *Il concilio di Trento e il moderno* (Bologna: Societa editrice il Mulino, 1996); Wietse de Boer, *The Conquest of the Soul: Confession, Discipline, and Public Order in Counter-Reformation Milan* (Leiden: Brill, 2001).

32. There is a great deal of stimulating work on the complex questions of the relationship between Jesuit notions of the self and the history of interiority, subjectivity, and modernity: see especially Michelle Molina, "Technologies of the Self: The Letters of Eighteenth-Century Mexican Jesuit Spiritual Daughters," *History of Religions,* 47, no. 4 (2008): 282–303; Michelle Molina, *To Overcome Oneself: The Jesuit Ethic and Spirit of Global Expansion, 1520–1767* (California: University of California Press, 2013); Moshe Sluhovsky, "St. Ignatius Loyola's *Spiritual Exercises* and Their Contribution to Modern Introspective Subjectivity," *Catholic Historical Review* 99, no. 4 (2013): 649–674;

Moshe Sluhovsky, *Believe Not Every Spirit: Possessions, Mysticism, and Discernment in Early Modern Catholicism* (Chicago: University of Chicago Press, 2007). A key and somewhat related line of research is the history of emotions, brought to bear on Jesuit history, for example, in Yasmin Haskell and Raphaële Garrod, eds., *Changing Hearts: Performing Jesuit Emotions between Europe, Asia, and the Americas* (Leiden: Brill, 2018).

33. The *Spiritual Diary* was published under the heading "Ephemeris S.P.N. Ignatii" in *Monumenta Ignatiana, ex autographis vel ex antiquioribus exemplis collecta: Series tertia; Sancti Ignatii de Loyola Constitutiones Societatis Jesu...*, ed. Arturo Codina, MHSI 63 (Rome: IHSI, 1934), 1 [of 4]: 86–158, partly reproduced in English translation in Ganss, *Ignatius of Loyola*, 229–270. The standard modern edition of the so-called Ignatian *Autobiography* is in *Fontes narrativi de S. Ignatio de Loyola et de Societatis Jesu initiis,* vol. 1, *Narrationes scriptae ante annum 1557,* ed. Candido de Dalmases and Dionisio Fernandez Zapico, MHSI 66 (Rome: IHSI, 1943), 354–507. The English translation used here (by Parmananda R. Divarkar) is in Ganss, *Ignatius of Loyola*, 65–111.

34. Mongini, *Maschere dell'identità,* explains the relationship between the Society's founding companions (especially through Ignatian thought) and heterodox religious currents in the sixteenth century, with its various consequences. For the many convergences in religious thought and associations centered on "the Christian life" in the sixteenth century (including among those viewed as theologically transgressive), see Querciolo Mazzonis, *Riforme di vita cristiana nel Cinquecento italiano* (Rubbettino: Soveria Mannelli, 2020), with a discussion in chapter 4 of, among others, Ignatius and the early Jesuits.

35. Analysis of the genre, both in terms of historiographical origins and application to the premodern period, are traced in Rudolf Dekker, ed., *Egodocuments and History: Autobiographical Writing in Its Social Context since the Middle Ages* (Hilversum: Verloren, 2002); see also Mary Fulbrook and Ulinka Rublack, "In Relation: The 'Social Self' and Ego-Documents," *German History* 28, no. 3 (2010): 263–272. For early modern usages, see Geoff Mortimer, *Eyewitness Accounts of the Thirty Years War, 1618–48* (Basingstoke, UK: Palgrave Macmillan, 2002). For an analysis of this document type in the Tridentine context, see Adelisa Malena, "Ego-Documents or 'Plural Compositions'? Reflections on Women's Obedient Scriptures in the Early Modern Catholic World," *Journal of Early Modern Studies* 1, no. 1 (2012): 97–113. See also Miriam Turrini, "La vocazione esaminata: Narrazioni autobiografiche di novizi gesuiti a metà Seicento," *Archivio italiano per la storia della pietà* 28 (2015): 311–388 ("la questione di un io che nell'età moderna si definisce in perenne rapporto con un'alterità, con reti e con modelli di compimento del sé ricevuti"), quotation at p. 367.

36. Brian Stock, *The Implications of Literacy: Written Language and Models of Interpretation in the Eleventh and Twelfth Centuries* (Princeton, NJ: Princeton University Press, 1983); Benedict Anderson, *Imagined Communities: Reflections*

on the Origin and Spread of Nationalism (London: Verso, 1983), which is methodologically relevant, although applied by Anderson to a later period.

37. Juan Alfonso de Polanco, "Chronicon Societatis Iesu," in *Vita Ignatii Loiolae et rerum Societatis Jesu historia*, vols. 2-6 (Madrid: A. Avrial, 1894-1898), partially available in English in *Year by Year with the Early Jesuits (1537–1556): Selections from the "Chronicon" of Juan de Polanco, S.J.*, trans. and ed. John Patrick Donnelly, SJ (St. Louis: The Institute of Jesuit Sources, 2004).

1. VOCATION AND ENTRY

1. The archival sources that underpin the analysis are: entrance records, located at ARSI, *Rom*. 170, 171a, 172, 173 ("Ingressus Novitiorum"; each of the four folders has a slight title variation on the most representative used here and ascribed to *Rom*. 171a); and vocation questionnaires at ARSI, *Rom*. 171 ("Vocationi").

2. Mario Scaduto, *Catalogo dei Gesuiti d'Italia 1540–1565* (Rome: IHSI, 1968), with, at p. x, a descriptive overview of the individual information provided throughout the book about single Jesuits. For further analysis of this data in terms of different grades and other measurable characteristics about these Jesuits, see Ladislaus Lukás, "De graduum diversitate inter sacerdotes in Societate Iesu," *AHSI* 37, no. 74 (1968): 239-312 (for foreign and Italian member numbers, pp. 311-312).

3. Miriam Turrini, "Poco oltre la soglia: racconti autobiografici di aspiranti gesuiti a metà Seicento," *Studi storici* 55, no. 3 (2014): 585-614; Miriam Turrini, "La vocazione esaminata: Narrazioni autobiografiche di novizi gesuiti a metà Seicento," *Archivio italiano per la storia della pietà* 28 (2015): 311-388.

4. Miriam Turrini, "La vita scelta? Appunti per una storia della vocazione in età moderna," in *Dai cantieri della storia: Liber amicorum per Paolo Prodi*, ed. Gian Paolo Brizzi and Giuseppe Olmi (Bologna: CLUEB, 2007), 145-159; Adriano Prosperi, *La vocazione: Storie di gesuiti tra Cinquecento e Seicento* (Turin: Einaudi, 2016); Thomas V. Cohen, "Why the Jesuits Joined, 1540-1600," *Historical Papers/Communications Historioques* 9, no. 1 (1974): 237-258. For vocations in the French context, see A. Lynn Martin, *The Jesuit Mind: The Mentality of an Elite in Early Modern France* (Ithaca, NY: Cornell University Press, 1988); for vocations to the Society generally, see John W. O'Malley, *The First Jesuits* (Cambridge, MA: Harvard University Press, 1993), 44-45, 65-68, 157-159. Relating to the missions in non-European lands, see Aliocha Maldavsky, *Vocaciones inciertas: Misión y misioneros en la provincia jesuita del Perú en los siglos XVI y XVII* (Madrid: CSIC, 2012); and within the missionary context of Europe, see Lucy Underwood,

"Youth, Religious Identity, and Autobiography at the English Colleges in Rome and Valladolid, 1592-1685," *Historical Journal* 55, no. 2 (2012): 349-374.

5. For the history of the novitiate in the Society, see Manuel Ruíz Joardo, *Orígens del noviciado de la Compañía de Jesús* (Rome: IHSI, 1980), and for Rome specifically, see p. 88. See also O'Malley, *The First Jesuits*, 356, 360-361. For the origins of separate quarters for novices, and for the nature of life there, see Peter J. Togni, "Novices in the Early Society of Jesus: Antonio Valentino, S.J., and the Novitiate at Novellara, Italy," in *Spirit, Style, Story: Essays Honoring John W. Padburg, S.J.*, ed. Thomas M. Lucas (Chicago: Loyola Press, 2002), 227-267. There is an evocative and chronologically useful note in ARSI, *Rom.* 173, fol. 17v: "Note that the house of profession at S. Andrea on Monte Cavallo began on 20 September 1565 (Nota che la casa di professione in S. Andrea a Monte Cavallo cominciò alli 20 di settembre 1565)."

6. For the connection between Jesuit schools and vocations to the Society, see O'Malley, *The First Jesuits*, 54, and on the apostolate more broadly, see Paul F. Grendler's many studies on the early history of Jesuit education. A very useful analysis of the interior (spiritual) and exterior (practical) dynamics that informed Jesuit vocation, admission, and identity, with the *Spiritual Exercises* touching on all of these spheres, is Patrick Goujon, "Elites and the Constitution of Jesuit Identity," in *The Oxford Handbook of the Jesuits*, ed. Ines G. Županov (New York: Oxford University Press, 2019), 176-192. For the problems associated with determining the grades of membership, and the inevitable hierarchical meanings attributed to these grades in their application as a largely unintended consequence of Ignatius's formulation, see O'Malley, *The First Jesuits*, 345-348, and Mark A. Lewis, "The Jesuit Institutionalization of the *Studia Humanitatis*: Two Jesuit Humanists at Naples," in *The Renaissance in the Streets, Schools, and Studies: Essays in Honour of Paul F. Grendler*, ed. Konrad Eisenbechler and Nicholas Terpstra (Toronto: Centre for Reformation and Renaissance Studies, 2008), 87-100 (esp. 96-97). For the quoted figures, see Lukás, "De granduum diversitate," 311-312.

7. For a useful overview of the path to full incorporation into the Society (allowing for some regional and chronological variation), see D. Gillian Thompson, "The Jesuit Province of France on the Eve of Its Destruction in 1762," *AHSI* 87, no. 143 (2018): 3-60 (see pp. 14-15).

8. Aside from the Ganss edition and translation of the *Constitutions*, enlisted for quotations of the document throughout this study, another valuable work on the text is Antonio M. de Aldama, *The Constitutions of the Society of Jesus: An Introductory Commentary on the Constitutions*; trans. Aloysius J. Owen (1979; repr., Rome and St. Louis: Centrum Ignatianum Spiritualitatis/Institute of Jesuit Sources, 1989). For the core characteristics of the

Constitutions and how they related to Jesuit formation and development in the Society, see O'Malley, *The First Jesuits,* 337.
9. *Const.* [147–148], [151–152]. The Gospel story about Martha is at Luke 10:38–42.
10. *Const.* [153], [157–160]. Numerical data is from Lukás, "De granduum diversitate," 311–312. For studies of the Jesuit mind and body, see especially the work of Fernanda Alfieri, for example (in English), "Tracking Jesuit Psychologies: From Ubiquitous Discourse on the Soul to Institutionalized Discipline (16th–20th Centuries)," in Županov, *The Oxford Handbook of the Jesuits,* 783–810.
11. Lukás, "De granduum diversitate," 311–312.
12. *Const.* [161].
13. Goujon, "Elites and the Constitution," 176–192.
14. Shelly MacLaren, "Shaping the Self in the Image of Virtue: Francesco da Barberino's 'I Documenti d'Amore,'" in *Image and Imagination in the Religious Self in Late Medieval and Early Modern Europe,* ed. Reindert L. Falkenburg, Walter S. Melion, and Todd M. Richardson (Turnhout, Belgium: Brepols, 2007), 71–95 (p. 89).
15. Dilwyn Knox, "*Disciplina:* The Monastic and Clerical Origins of Civility," in *Renaissance Culture and Society: Essays in Honor of Eugene F. Rice Jr.,* ed. John Monfasani and Ronald G. Musto (New York: Italica Press, 1991), 107–135 (p. 109).
16. *Const.* [177–189]. For further discussion of what were considered negative attributes of candidates, see Cohen, "Why the Jesuits Joined," 245–246, and for analysis with colorful examples, see Mario Scaduto, *Storia della Compagnia di Gesù in Italia* [in 5 vols.]: *L'Epoca di Giacomo Lainez:* [vol. 3,] *Il governo, 1556–1565* (Rome: La civiltà cattolica, 1964), 385–386.
17. *Const.* [163–189].
18. Togni, "Novices in the Early Society," 229–241 (p. 232). Jesuit visitors were appointed by the superior general to conduct ad hoc visitations—that is, assessments, meetings with members, and inspections—of provinces and their various works.
19. The original text is in ARSI, *Inst.* 111a, and reproduced, with an introduction, in Mario Scaduto, "Il 'Libretto consolatorio' di Bobadilla a Domènech sulle vocazioni mancate (1570)," *AHSI* 43, no. 85 (1974): 85–102; it is also discussed and quoted in English translation in Togni, "Novices in the Early Society," 231. One of the first Jesuits who was not among the original companions, the Spaniard Juan Jerónimo Doménech held key roles in the new Society, including provincial of Sicily three times: 1553–1561, 1562–1568, and 1570–1576: *DIICJ* 2:1135–1136 (F. B. Medina).
20. O'Malley, *The First Jesuits,* 56; A. Lynn Martin, "Vocational Crises and the Crisis in Vocations among Jesuits in France during the Sixteenth Century,"

The Catholic Historical Review 72, no. 2 (1986): 201–221 (pp. 205–206). According to Mario Scaduto's research, the main reasons for not allowing candidates to enter at all were being too young and too uneducated; family consent was preferable but not necessary: *Storia della Compagnia*, 3:387.

21. Togni, "Novices in the Early Society," 243.
22. De Aldama, *The Constitutions of the Society*, 21–22, 58. The importance of the *General Examen* for the early Society, and in its transition to an established religious institute, is reflected in the fact that the publication of the *Constitutions of the Society* in 1558 was to begin in the first instance with that of the *Examen*: Scaduto, *Storia della Compagnia*, 3:190–191.
23. For Nadal's additional instructions, see Jerónimo Nadal, "De Admittendis ad Societatum," in "Instructiones (1562)," reproduced in *Epistolae mixtae ex variis Europae ab anno 1537 a.d. 1556 scriptae...*, 5 vols. (Madrid: A. Avraial, R. Fortanet, 1898–1901), 4:547–552 (doc. 61). Concerning apparel on entry, see the *General Examen, Const.* [19]. See also *Const.* [190–203]. On admission to probation, see commentary by Ganss in his introduction, *Const.*, 36–37.
24. *Const.* [200].
25. The four folders are: (1) ARSI, *Rom.* 170 ("Novitii in Dom. Prof. admissi 1556–1569"), 107 folios concerning over 600 entrants; (2) ARSI, *Rom.* 171a ("Ingressus Novitiorum 1569–1594"), 172 folios concerning about 1,140 entrants; (3) ARSI, *Rom.* 172 ("Ingressus Novitiorum ab anno 1594 usque ad 1630"), 270 folios, 1,520 entrants; (4) ARSI, *Rom.* 173 ("Ingressus Novitiorum 1631–1675"), 184 folios in total, with 80 entering before 1640. They are presented here for the first time as the subject of a focused analysis. For comparison, see similar entrance records for Naples: ARSI, *Neap.* 178 ("Ingressus Novitiorum, 1587–1678").
26. *General Examen, Const.* [2], and commentary on pp. 76–77n9.
27. ARSI, *Rom.* 170, fol. 2r: "Venne in casa alli 8 di Giugno 1556, fu essaminato per coadiutore temporale, et non havendo alcuno dell'impedimenti, se mostrò pronto a tutto quello che'gli fu esposto nell'essamine."
28. ARSI, *Rom.* 173, fol. 76: "Francesco Lana Bresciano venne a S. Andrea a dì diece di novembre 1647 portò un Cappello, una zimarra di panno nero, un par di calzoni Giubbone e Mantella di Panno di Spagna, due pari di Calzette di seta uno leonato, e l'altro nero, Camiscie cinque sottocalzetti pari 4, scarpini pari 4, fazzoletti diece lenzoli par uno sciugatore uno, Collari cinque manichetti pari cinque pianelle par uno, scarpe par uno, scopetta da testa una, Pettine uno, Un berettino di raso nero un baullo. Io Francesco Lana affermo quanto sopra." See *DBI* 63 (C. Preti).
29. ARSI, *Rom.* 173, fols. 32r, 40r, 88r. For Nicolò Mascardi (1624–1674), see *DHCJ* 3:2552–2553 (J. Baptista, C. J. McNaspy); Francesco Maria Gonzaga was a member of the Castiglione cadet branch of the Gonzaga of Mantua.

30. ARSI, *Rom.* 172.
31. ARSI, *Rom.* 170, fol. 85r (July 2, 1566): "Non saper scrivere." For the role of coadjutor in the Society, see O'Malley, *The First Jesuits*, 60.
32. *Const.* [201], and accompanying commentary by Ganss, 138n.
33. ARSI, *Rom.* 170, fol. 36r: "Venni in casa alli 6 di gennaro 1560 fui esamminato per coadiutor temporale... portai meco un tabarro negro." For Giovanni Francesco Stefanoni (c. 1541-1612), see Maria Iris Gramazio, "Gesuiti italiani missionari in Oriente nel XVI secolo," *AHSI* 66, no. 132 (1997): 275-300 (294). Despite this difficult start in terms of his writing ability, one of his letters was published in a 1582 collection from Japan: Luís Fróis et al., *Breuis Iapaniae insulae descriptio*... (Cologne: In Officina Birckmannica, 1582).
34. ARSI, *Rom.* 170, fol. 41v: "Io Roberto venni in casa alli 20 di settembre 1560 fui esaminato per indifferente, et non trovandosi impedimento alcuno mi offersi pronto a fare ogni cosa, che da superiori mi sarà comandato. Portai meco un tabarro negro, 4 camicie, fazzoletti 10 sciugatori 3, pedali 3 para, scuffie 3." For Bellarmine, see Franco Motta, *Bellarmino: Una teologia politica della Controriforma* (Brescia: Morcelliana, 2005); Stefania Tutino, *Empire of Souls: Robert Bellarmine and the Christian Commonwealth* (New York: Oxford University Press, 2010).
35. O'Malley, *The First Jesuits*, 60. For the concept of "indifference" in these vocation statements and Ignatian thought, see, for example, Thomas V. Cohen, "Molteplicità dell'esperienza religiosa tra i primi 1259 gesuiti, 1540-1560," *Annali Accademici canadesi* 1 (1985): 7-25 (16n).
36. ARSI, *Rom.* 171a, fol. 62r: "Quest'inventario del 4 giugno 1579 è l'ultimo nel quale ricorre la formula 'fu esaminato per coadiutore = ovvero l'altra = fu esaminato = per indifferente.'"
37. For example, one entrant's record mentions a sword and another a firearm (ARSI, *Rom.* 173, fols. 53r, 35r). Francesco Gomez (Francisco Gómez) arrived with his horse on February 19, 1558 (ARSI, *Rom.* 170, fol. 17r). In imitation of the poor, who traveled on foot by necessity, and in view of the association of horses with wealth above the station of poverty, *Const.* dealt with the subject [575-576]: "Ordinarily no mount will be kept for any member of the Society itself, either superior or subject unless it should be because of constant infirmities or of urgent necessities in regard to public business." *Const.* [576]. See also De Aldama, *The Constitutions of the Society*, 233.
38. For the requirement of producing lists of possessions on entry, see *Const. General Examen*, [57]; ARSI, *Rom.* 172, 0v: "In questo stesso libro è bene lassarci margine per scriverci le sudette robbe quando partendo alcuno se le restituiscono, overo quando nel termine de doi anni o doppo fatti li voti con voluntà dei proprii padroni si distribuissero fuori." For the require-

ment of poverty and the renunciation of goods and property, see *Const.* [533–534], [570–572], [574–581]. See also O'Malley, *The First Jesuits,* 350, and De Aldama, *The Constitutions of the Society,* 233, with a useful discussion of *Const.* [570].
39. ARSI, *Rom.* 171a, fol. 88v: "a Valentino fu data licenza et hebbe tutte le sue robbe et denari." ARSI, *Rom.* 171a, fol. 97r: "fu mandato in casa sua Domenico et hebbe tutte le sue cose." ARSI, *Rom.* 171a, fol. 97r: "hebbe le sue robbe et fu licenziato." These entries were crossed out, with a line running diagonally through them.
40. *General Examen, Const.* [53]. Chapter 4 of the *General Examen* is at *Const.* [53–62].
41. See De Aldama, *The Constitutions of the Society,* 42.
42. *Const.* [565], [570], and [572] stipulated that no property was to be owned by an individual nor any payments or financial benefits be accorded any individual. See O'Malley, *The First Jesuits,* 349.
43. For the many circumstances and causes of family disapproval surrounding sons' vocations to the Society, see Adriano Prosperi, "Il figlio, il padre, il gesuita: Un testo di Antonio Possevino," *Rinascimento* 53 (2013): 111–155; Prosperi, *La vocazione,* especially parts 2 and 3; and Martin, *The Jesuit Mind,* chapter 11.
44. For forced entry into religious life in the period, see Anne Jacobson Schutte, *By Force and Fear: Taking and Breaking Monastic Vows in Early Modern Europe* (Ithaca, NY: Cornell University Press, 2011).
45. ARSI, *Rom.* 170, fol. 4v (Antonio Poretta): "una casacca di panno grosso nero siciliano vecchia senza maniche . . . due gioponi bianchi con le sue maniche vecchi, rotti nelle maniche . . . due camise vecchie rotte: un officiolo della Madonna vecchio, l'imagine di Santo Iacopo, un capello di feltro molto vecchio"; "fu accettato per cuoco perpetuo." Poretta signed his name and brief statement of assent in a barely legible scrawl.
46. "Una corona d'oro"; "quattro casse di robbe." ARSI, *Rom.* 170, fol. 84v. For brief biographical overviews of Alessandro Valignano, see *DBI* 98 (Giovanni Pizzorusso); *DHCJ* 4:3877–3879 (H. Cieslik, J. Wicki).
47. ARSI, *Rom.* 170, fol. 92v.
48. The full transcription is: "Venne in casa a 17 di Febraio 1567 et fu essaminato per indifferente: et non havendo impedimento alcuno si mostrò pronto a fare quanto nell'essame gli fu proposto. Portò seco una cappa nera buona, un par di guanti, un par di scarpi." ARSI, *Rom.* 170, fol. 89r.
49. The importance of long-standing connections (indeed, almost certainly friendships) such as those between Acquaviva, Valignano, and de Fabii in terms of the governance and overall culture and policies of the Society is analyzed in more detail in, Camilla Russell, "Japan, India, or China? The Uncertain Steps of Sabatino de Ursis's Mission to Asia," in *La via dei libri:*

Sabatino de Ursis [熊 三 拔] *e le contaminazioni culturali tra Salento e Cina nei secc. XVI–XVII,* ed. Paolo Vincenti (Lecce: L'Idomeneo-Università del Salento, 2020), 41–58.

50. "Ogni cosa usata." ARSI, *Rom.* 171a, fol. 89v. To date, scant research has focused on the sixth superior general, Muzio Vitelleschi. For biographical overviews, see *DBI* 99 (Simona Negruzzo); *DHCJ* 4:1621–1627 (M. Fois); for his writings, see Carlos Sommervogel et al., *Bibliothèque de la Compagnie de Jésus,* vol. 8 (Bruxelles-Paris: Picard, 1898), 848–852.

51. The listing of books gradually diminishes partway through ARSI, *Rom.* 172 (1594–1630); there are no books mentioned in ARSI, *Rom.* 173 (1631–1675). Giovan di Moraga [Malaga] is the first entrant recorded in these documents at ARSI, *Rom.* 170, fol. 2r, with a long list of books: "Libri, un libro di Architettura...un offitio della Madonna...in lingua spagnuola...un altro officio piccolino pur della Madonna in lingua italiana, una bibbia in lingua italiana insieme col testamento..." For Giovanni di Polo da Villa, see ARSI, *Rom.* 170, fol. 3r: "un officiolo, et un Rosario della Madonna." For Camillo Vannuzo, see ARSI, *Rom.* 170, fol. 11r–v.

52. ARSI, *Rom.* 170, fol. 14r (name illeg.); ARSI, *Rom.* 170, fol. 20v (Gioan Maria Gratiani) [the whole transcription is]: "doi camiscie nove 3 fazzoletti, un gippon de tela foderato, novo, un par de calze vecchie, un par de scarpe usate, un saio et una cappa nera nova, una barretta usata nera. L'Epistole di Platone Greche. Clenardo greco. Il primo libro de l'Iliade de Homero Greco. Dyonisio Carthusiano de 4 novissimis Latino. Gioan Gerson Latino con Innocentio papa insieme ligato, Don Jeronymo sirino de la divina gratia volgare. Uno officiolo della Madonna. Uno calamaro. L'Odyessea d'Homero intiera greco."

53. ARSI, *Rom.* 170, fol. 46r (Joseph de Mazancourt).

54. ARSI, *Rom.* 171a, fol. 96r (Francesco Sulyok, entrant number 778, in the year 1584); ARSI, *Rom.* 170, fol. 59r (Giovanni Bruneo de Senas): "Venne di Loreto...dove fu mandato da Napoli in peregrinatione, et non portò seco niente"; ARSI, *Rom.* 173, fol. 34v (Guglielmo Scharp); ARSI, *Rom.* 173, fol. 53v (Francesco Wisenbach); ARSI *Rom.* 171 fol. 231r: "asai richi"; ARSI, *Rom.* 173, fol. 88r (Francesco Maria Gonzaga): "un cappello, un mantello di panno di Spagna, una veste di saietta di milano, una cinta di seta...e calzoni di saia inglese leonato oscuro."

55. Recent decades of scholarship on the subject of clothing have provided insight into its role in signifying many elements in a person's social position, age, professional status, and provenance. Ludovica Sebregondi, "Clothes and Teenagers: What Young Men Wore in Fifteenth-Century Florence," trans. Konrad Eisenbichler, in Eisenbichler, ed., *The Premodern Teenager: Youth in Society, 1150–1650* (Toronto: Centre for Reformation and Renaissance Studies, 2002), 25–50 (27–28); Timothy McCall, "Brilliant

Bodies: Material Culture and the Adornment of Men in North Italy's Quattrocento Courts," *I Tatti Studies in the Italian Renaissance* 16, no. 1/2 (2013): 445–490; Ulinka Rublack, *Dressing Up: Cultural Identity in Renaissance Europe* (Oxford: Oxford University Press, 2010).

56. *General Examen, Const.* [19], with Ganss commentary at pp. 84–85; see also *Const.* [190–203], with Ganss commentary at pp. 135–139.

57. ARSI, *Rom.* 172, fol. 37v (Mario Squadrini); ARSI, *Rom.*, 171a, fol. 45v. In the case of Squadrini, he appears in the documents again as an applicant for the missions; several catalogue entries detail his progress in the Society and there is a report about his suitability for the missions. He left for Goa in 1603, only three years after his first appearance in the entrance records as a new novice.

58. Elisabeth Salter, "Reworked Material: Discourses of Clothing Culture in Early Sixteenth-Century Greenwich," in *Clothing Culture, 1350–1650: The History of Retailing and Consumption,* ed. Catherine Richardson (Aldershot, UK: Ashgate, 2004), 182–183.

59. Catherine Richardson, "'Havying nothing upon hym saving onely his sherte': Event, Narrative, and Material Culture in Early Modern England," in Richardson, *Clothing Culture,* 209–221 (p. 214).

60. *Const.* [190].

61. *General Examen, Const.* [18]: This requirement to study and meditate on the *Constitutions* corresponded with the admission practice set out in the Benedictine Rule. See De Aldama, *The Constitutions of the Society,* 91.

62. *Const.* [198], [200].

63. The 1638 questionnaire for the twenty-two-year-old Fleming listed as "Antonio della Ferra" stated, "Interrogatorio da proporci a Novitii finita la prima probatione" (Questionnaire to be proposed to the novices upon completion of the first probation): ARSI, *Rom.* 171, fol. 84r; a similar annotation is at ARSI, *Rom.* 171, fol. 45r, for the 1637 questionnaire of Tommaso Rustici.

64. *General Examen, Const.* [34–51]. At [37], the text states, "If the parents are in present and extreme need of the candidate's aid, it is evident that such a one should not be admitted." "Parents" included close relatives, as borne out in the documentation under consideration here.

65. *General Examen, Const.* [38].

66. *General Examen, Const.* [51], and discussed in De Aldama, *The Constitutions of the Society,* 29–32.

67. See, for example, Underwood, "Youth, Religious Identity, and Autobiography," who found variations according to the subjects' religion of origin (parents and family) and their age, as well as important conclusions from these sources concerning the appeal of the Society for its perceived distinctiveness as a religious institute. See also O'Malley, *The First Jesuits,* 338–340, 362. For extant texts of the *General Examen* for the novitiate in the Polish

context during the same period, see Justyna Łukaszewska-Haberkowa, ed., *Examina novitiorum (Egzaminy nowicjuszów) jezuitów z Braniewa z lat 1569–1574* [*Examina novitiorum* (Exams of novices) of the Jesuits from Braniewo from 1569–1574) (Krakow: Akademia Ignatianum Wydawnictwo, 2012). My thanks to Miriam Turrini for this last reference.

68. Cohen, "Molteplicità dell'esperienza," 8. See also Cohen, "Why the Jesuits Joined."

69. Cohen, "Why the Jesuits Joined," 240. Surprisingly, Cohen found that candidates mentioned in large numbers the need for safety from the world and the desire to join the Jesuits to save their souls, rather than the more predictable evidence of the desire for an active apostolate and to save souls, terms in which the Society preferred to present itself.

70. *General Examen, Const.* [34]. The questions are at [34–52]. For the place of conscience and confessor in the entry process, see *General Examen, Const.* [23], discussed in Turrini, "La vocazione esaminata," 315–317.

71. ARSI, *Rom.* 171 ("Vocationi"). Turrini, "La vocazione esaminata," 318–319, conjectures that they were an experiment that was discontinued, probably introduced by the rector of the time, Giovanni Paolo Oliva (1600–1681, later superior general of the Society, 1664–1681). For biographical overviews, see *DBI* 79 (Flavio Rurale); *DHCJ* 2:1633–1642 (M. Fois). It certainly was common that some documentary production started and then stopped in the Society's administration and was tied to the initiatives of individual superiors. For example, see Chapter 2 about the short-lived dedicated assessments of Italian candidates for the "Indies."

72. For this connection between the *General Examen* and the vocation surveys, see Turrini, "Poco oltre la soglia," 591–592; and Turrini, "La vocazione esaminata," 315, 315n15.

73. ARSI, *Rom.* 171, fol. 68v: "A che si sente più inclinato, supposto l'indifferenza, Al Indie, o in Almagna, o in altra qual si voglia missione, o ministerio difficile di maggiore servitio, di Dio, aiuto suo, e de prossimi."

74. See the example of Nicola Consalvio [Consalvi] from May 8, 1641, ARSI, *Rom.* 171, fol. 222v: "Mi sono sentito sempre anco da piccolo inclinato . . . di andare all'India."

75. ARSI, *Rom.* 171, fol. 84v: "Ho inclinatione di andare in Engelterra ho in Hollande per respecto de la lingua et per essere pratico del modo di vivere loro."

76. ARSI *Rom.* 171, fol. 81r (Domenico Weibel): "zelo a aiutar l'anime, massime a instruir la giovventù e i semplici."

77. ARSI, *Rom.* 171, fol. 1r (Pietro Conti): "Ho sempre studiato."

78. Cohen, "Molteplicità dell'esperienza," 9. For the question of age among entrants, see O'Malley, *The First Jesuits*, 56; for life experience on entry see Scaduto, *Storia della Compagnia*, 3:259.

79. ARSI, *Rom.* 171, fol. 51r (Giovanni Luigi Saluzzo): "Ho due Fratelli et un Sorella che sono ancora Figli di Famiglia"; ARSI, *Rom.* 171, fol. 160r (Giovanni Battista Cattani): "fratelli giovani tutti mediocremente facoltosi"; ARSI, *Rom.* 171, fol. 162r (Uberto Spinola): "piu tosto poveri"; "Ho quattro fratelli religiosi et un secolare amogliato, Ho tre sorelle monache et una maritata sono mediocri ma piu tosto poveri"; ARSI, *Rom.* 171, fol. 133r (Paolo Ottolini): "al secolo"; "una buona heredità"; "passerà nel mio fratello Lelio."
80. ARSI, *Rom.* 171, fol. 207r (Costanzo Gubernali): "sono di facoltà mediocre anziché poveri"; ARSI, *Rom.* 171, fol. 51r (Giovanni Luigi Saluzzo): "veramente non lo so"; Saluzzo's longer vocation statement is at fol. 53r.
81. ARSI, *Rom.* 171, fol. 62r (Ludovico Lazarini): "Non ho facoltà nessuna per essere figlio di famiglia, et nato ultimo fra tutti li miei fratelli."
82. ARSI, *Rom.* 171, fol. 38r (Guglielmo Euskirchen): "Ho havuto diverse tentationi, come di poter fare magior frutto nel secolo, di non poter adiutare li parenti." For family expectations and disappointments concerning Jesuit vocations, see Prosperi, *La vocazione,* parts 2 and 3. For this theme, focusing on vocations to religious life in France, see also Barbara B. Diefendorf, "Give Us Back Our Children: Patriarchal Authority and Parental Consent to Religious Vocations in Early Counter-Reformation France," *Journal of Modern History* 68, no. 2 (1996): 265–307.
83. ARSI, *Rom.* 171, fol. 164v (Uberto Spinola): "con buona licenza de parenti che poca difficoltà mi fecero venni qui"; ARSI, *Rom.* 171, fol. 102r (Giacomo Antonio Scaravellini): "Dovevo dar la dote alli cognati, già ce l'ho data intieramente del mio guadagno"; "Ho tenuto scuola di gramatica et di musica, e di cimbalo molti anni, non ho studiato altro, che le somme de Canonisti"; "Ho il voto di castità per esser Sacerdote." Scaravellini's longer vocation statement is at ARSI, *Rom.* 171, fol. 103r-v: "per il peso delle sorelle"; "già che quella de Cappuccini non era più per me, come nella gioventù havevo desiderato, e procurato"; "senza più far caso di tante opinioni."
84. Turrini, "La vocazione esaminata," 321–322; Turrini, "Poco oltre la soglia," 601–606.
85. ARSI, *Rom.* 171, fols. 45r–46r (Tommaso Rustici): "di fuggire l'occasioni di peccare"; "se ha haute tentationi, o impedimenti, o allongamenti, da parenti dalli amici, dal mondo, o dal Demonio"; "Pocho allongamento per causa de miei ho havuto, qualche dilatione seguita e nata dalla mia pigritia."
86. ARSI, *Rom.* 171, fol. 145r: "Leggevo spesso la vita del nostro Padre S. Ignatio, e di S. Francesco Xaverio, e del B. Stanislao [Kostka], quando al mio Paese [Subiaco] vedevo un Gesuita mi pareva sempre vedere un Angelo."
87. ARSI, *Rom.* 171, fol. 191v: "fin'ché haverò fiato, sarò obedientissimo perché questa Vita vedo che se ne fugge come Vento."

88. ARSI, *Rom.* 171, fols. 62r–63r (Ludovico Lazarini): "Ho inclinatione a volere imitare S. F. Xaverio"; "A questo effetto particolarmente sono entrato nella Compagnia perché sono spesso ingiurati et calumniati"; "tentationi del Demonio in gran numero"; "sono andato per 3 anni ogni sera alla congregatione del Padre Petro Garavita." See a biographical overview of the founder of the Caravita Oratory in Rome (1587–1668), at *DHCJ* 2:1808 (D. Chianella).
89. ARSI, *Rom.* 171, fol. 74r (Giovanni Battista De Schuldthaus): "mi ellessi la Compagnia di Giesù non dubitando punto ch'essa sarebbe per me più sicura barcha per arrivar al porto della perfettione"; ARSI, *Rom.* 171, fols. 37r–38v (questionnaire and vocation statement, Guglielmo Euskirchen): "sono sacerdote"; "considerando li pericoli et molte occasioni di peccare, che soprastanno a gli Ecclesiastici secolari nella funtione delli loro offitii, e li pochi aiuti ch'hanno per risistere alle continue tentationi"; ARSI, *Rom.* 171, fol. 56r (Francesco Eschinardi): "havendo io sempre desiderato una vita regolata, et dove non si abada a rispetti humani."
90. Turrini, "La vocazione esaminata," 318–319. The article presents a detailed analysis of the vocation statements.
91. ARSI, *Rom.* 171, fols. 45v–46r: "A queste dimande risponda ciascheduno di suo pugno"; "Nome, Cognome, età et patria propria... Le horigini e motivi della vocatione alla Religione in commune, et alla Compagnia in particolare." These notes were provided in relation to the vocation of Tommaso Rustici, twenty years old, from Lucca.
92. See, for example, ARSI, *Rom.* 171, fol. 50r (notes for the vocation statement of nineteen-year-old Carlo Pessallo, July 1637): "Punti per scrivere la Vocatione." These notes for candidates' responses resemble the spiritual autobiographies produced in Poland (1574–1580) and studied by Joseph Warszawski, discussed in Cohen, "Why the Jesuits Joined," 242–247.
93. Turrini, "La vocazione esaminata," 323.
94. "Dalla lettione di certe vocationi scritte a mano di alcuni padri della Compagnia, essendo egli all'ora in età di 14 anni in circa." Girolamo Pichi, quoted in Turrini, "La vocazione esaminata," 327. Exemplars were circulating from the 1570s (327n68).
95. ARSI, *Rom.* 171, fol. 135r (Antonio Maria Galletti): "essendo stato per un pezzo in Roma impedito e minacciato con lettere dai miei e trattenuto dall'amici qui in persona, venendo anco mio zio qua per impedirmi, non potendo niuno impugnare alla gratia che Dio mi voleva fare, fui ricevuto dalla Consulta del P. Piccolomini Provinciale... Adesso sto contentissimo nella Compagnia." For Piccolomini, see *DBI* 83 (Sabina Pavone) and *DHCJ* 2:1629–1630 (M. Colpo). *Consultores* were appointed to assist Jesuit superiors, on which see Wiktor Gramatowski, "Jesuit Glossary: Guide to Understanding the Documents, English Version," trans. Camilla

Russell (orig. in Italian, 1992) (ARSI, 2014), 10, http://www.sjweb.info/arsi/documents/glossary.pdf.

96. ARSI, *Rom.* 171, fols. 131r-132r (Paolo Ottolini, with the whole relevant section quoted here): "atteso a negotii di mercante in Lucca, seguitando sempre qualche cosa delli medesimi studii [humanities] ... dalli 24 sinqui ho atteso all'amministrazione di un negotio in Messina"; "Mentre ero in Lucca l'anno 1631 et vissi la peste, in quelle miserie venni in qualche consideratione di lassare il mondo."

97. ARSI, *Rom.* 173 fol. 40r (Niccolò Mascardi); ARSI, *Rom.* 171, fol. 119r: "i talenti che Iddio mi havea dati"; Giuseppe Rosso, "Niccolò Mascardi missionario gesuita esploratore del Cile e della Patagonia (1624-1674)," *AHSI* 19 (1950), 3-74; *DBI* 71 (Paolo Broggio, who described him as "modello del missionario-esploratore-scienziato"); *DHCJ* 3:2552-2553 (J. Baptista, C. J. McNaspy).

98. ARSI *Rom.* 171, fol. 81r (Domenico Weibel): "certe vanità del mondo ... la guerra e perturbatione nella Germania ... s'accompagnorono finalmente le tentationi stando molto inchinato e dubbioso a entrar l'una altra Relligione ... i pericoli non solamente di perder la Vocatione ma anco la vita"; ARSI, *Rom.* 171, fol. 85r (Antonio della Ferra): "avendo girato la maggiore parte de l'Europe per tre quatre anni, et molti volti in periculo non solo del corpo ma ancora del anima ... di conoscere quello periculo così grandi et fue dui ho tre giorno senza potere mangiare con quelli pensieri." For the violent realities of youth culture in the early modern period, see Ottavia Niccoli's case studies from the criminal court proceedings preserved in Bologna (1590-1630), "Rituals of Youth: Love, Play, and Violence in Tridentine Bologna," in Eisenbichler, *The Premodern Teenager,* 75-94. As Niccoli observes, the difficult economic circumstances of the period meant that theft was a problem: "It was not theft, however, but violence that characterizes the behaviour of the young ... that at this time was endemic in the cities as well as in the countryside ... [and was] tied to their work ... or to frequent play altercations" (78). Educational institutions for boys also were a potential source of disruption and lack of discipline, which possibly also explains the appeal of Jesuit schools, which managed to forge identities of order and quality training. See Christopher Carlsmith, "Troublesome Teens: Approaches to Educating and Disciplining Youth in Early Modern Italy," in Eisenbichler, *The Premodern Teenager,* 151-171. For a comparative comment on the Jesuits, see p. 164, and for a fuller treatment of the Jesuit role in the educational culture of the early modern period see Christopher Carlsmith, "Struggling toward Success: Jesuit Education in Italy, 1540-1600," *History of Education Quarterly* 42, no. 2 (2002): 215-246.

99. Turrini, "La vocazione esaminata," 321: "I racconti ... potrebbero dunque porsi alla confluenza di due differenti punti di vista: da un lato il percorso

del candidato che cerca nella propria storia un filo rosso dall'altro l'esame della Compagnia che scruta la solidità di una scelta nella ricostruzione dell'itinerario soggettivo.... Un gioco delle parti, dunque."

100. The work of Michel de Certeau and, more recently, Silvia Mostaccio is helpful in plotting a middle path of interpretation concerning this dynamic: Michel de Certeau, *The Mystic Fable,* vol. 1, *The Sixteenth and Seventeenth Centuries,* trans. Michael B. Smith (Chicago: University of Chicago Press, 1992); Silvia Mostaccio, *Early Modern Jesuits between Obedience and Conscience during the Generalate of Claudio Acquaviva (1581–1615)* (Aldershot, UK: Ashgate, 2014).

101. ARSI, *Rom.* 171, fol. 2r (Pietro Conti): "per gratia particolare di Dio."

102. ARSI, *F.G.* 741 ("Indipetae"), fol. 116r (Pietro Conti): "spargere anco il sangue, se sarà di bisogno, per amore di Dio."

2. CANDIDATES FOR OVERSEAS MISSIONS

1. ARSI, *Rom.* 171 ("Vocationi"), fol. 68v: "Al Indie, o in Almagna, o in altra qual si voglia missione." I introduced the term "indiani" in an article about the Jesuit vocation and selection process for the overseas missions; some material and analysis from the article also appears in this chapter: Camilla Russell, "Becoming 'Indians': The Jesuit Missionary Path from Italy to Asia," *Renaissance and Reformation / Renaissance et Réforme* 43, no. 1 (2020): 9–50.

2. See the commentary in Antonio M. de Aldama, *The Constitutions of the Society of Jesus: An Introductory Commentary on the Constitutions,* trans. Aloysius J. Owen (1979; repr., Rome and St. Louis: Centrum Ignatianum Spiritualitatis/Institute of Jesuit Sources, 1989), chapter 2. For the central place of the overseas missionary apostolate in Jesuit self-understanding (and traceable in the *Spiritual Exercises*), see Charlotte de Castelnau L'Estoile, "Jesuit Anthropology: Studying 'Living Books,'" in *The Oxford Handbook of the Jesuits,* ed. Ines G. Županov (New York: Oxford University Press, 2019), 811–830 (esp. 811–813).

3. See Ronnie Po-Chia Hsia, ed., *A Companion to the Early Modern Catholic Global Missions* (Leiden: Brill, 2018), which includes a strong emphasis on the Jesuit enterprise. A key work that placed the Jesuits center stage in historical studies' "global turn" is Luke Clossey, *Salvation and Globalisation in the Early Jesuit Missions* (New York: Cambridge University Press, 2008). Notable surveys that have signposted developments in this field's vast historiography are Simon Ditchfield, "Of Missions and Models: The Jesuit Enterprise (1540–1773) Reassessed in Recent Literature (Review)," *The Catholic Historical Review* 93, no. 2 (2007): 325–343; Emanuele Colombo, "Gesuitomania: Studi recenti sulle missioni gesuitiche (1540–1773)," in *Evangelizzazione e Globalizzazione: Le missioni gesuitiche nell'età moderna tra*

storia e storiografia, ed. Michela Catto, Guido Mongini, Silvia Mostaccio, special issue, *Biblioteca della Nuova Rivista Storica* 42 (2010): 31-59; numerous entries in *Jesuit Historiography Online,* https://referenceworks .brillonline.com/browse/jesuit-historiography-online; and similarly in Županov, *The Oxford Handbook of the Jesuits.*

4. For the Jesuit missions in the Portuguese "Indies," see Dauril Alden, *The Making of an Enterprise: The Society of Jesus in Portugal, Its Empire and Beyond, 1540–1750* (Stanford, CA: Stanford University Press, 1996). Important region-specific studies of the Jesuits in Asia and the Pacific include Liam Matthew Brockey, *Journey to the East: The Jesuit Mission to China, 1579–1724* (Cambridge, MA: Harvard University Press, 2007); Ângela Barreto Xavier and Ines G. Županov, *Catholic Orientalism: Portuguese Empire, Indian Knowledge (16th–18th Centuries)* (Oxford: Oxford University Press, 2015); Ulrike Strasser, *Missionary Men in the Early Modern World: German Jesuits and Pacific Journeys* (Amsterdam: Amsterdam University Press, 2020).

5. For Jesuits sent to the East Indies, see Josef Wicki, "Liste der Jesuiten-Indienfahrer 1541-1758," *Aufsätze zur Portugiesischen Kulturgeschichte* 7 (1967): 269-297. For the Portuguese *Estado da Índia* and the *Padroado,* see Alden, *The Making of an Enterprise,* 25-27. For the various sources of financing for the Jesuit missions in Asia and America, see Hélène Vu Thanh, "The Jesuits in Asia under the Portuguese *Padroado:* India, China, and Japan (Sixteenth to Seventeenth Centuries)," and Frederik Vermote, "Financing Jesuit Missions," in Županov, *The Oxford Handbook of the Jesuits,* 400–426 and 128–150, respectively. Jesuits first arrived in Portuguese Brazil in 1549. In the Spanish sphere, they were established in Florida in 1566 (but had already left by 1572), Lima and Peru in 1568, Mexico in 1572, the Philippines in 1581, and Canada in 1611.

6. Francis Xavier to Simão Rodrigues in Portugal from Cochin, India, January 20, 1548 (quoted in English translation), in *Jesuit Writings from the Early Modern Period, 1540–1640,* ed. and trans. John Patrick Donnelly (Indianapolis: Hackett, 2006), 74. Xavier's boat *Santiago* carried two Portuguese and one Italian, the future mission superior in Goa and Xavier's successor in that role, Paolo Battista (or Paulo di Baptista) da Camerino; he was professed in 1548 in Goa, where he died in 1560. Mario Scaduto, *Catalogo dei Gesuiti d'Italia 1540–1565* (Rome: IHSI, 1968), 47; Maria Iris Gramazio, "Gesuiti italiani missionari in Oriente nel XVI secolo," *AHSI* 66, no. 132 (1997): 275–300 (276).

7. Flavio Rurale, "Un'identità forte? A proposito di tre studi recenti sulla Compagnia di Gesù," in *Anatomia di un corpo religioso: L'identità dei gesuiti in età moderna. Annali di storia dell'esegesi* 19, no. 2, ed. Franco Motta (2002): 357–367 (359).

8. For early plans to phase out European missionaries from the overseas missions, and subsequent Jesuit resistance to non-European membership,

see Alden, *The Making of an Enterprise*, 258-267. In the case of the Portuguese Assistancy, the need for recruits from Europe was greater for Asia than for Brazil, where local entry into religious life was more common and where missionary numbers were lower (in 1601, there were 276 Jesuits in Asia; in Brazil, there were 169 members in 1600). Fewer Italians were sent there too: in the period prior to 1615, a total of 143 Italians went to Asia, while only eight went to the Portuguese Americas (p. 203). The precise number of Italian missionaries in the Spanish Americas has not yet been calculated.

9. The address line of the letter sent by missionary to China, Sabatino de Ursis, to Portugal Assistant João Álvares illustrates this arrangement: "Assistente di Portogallo e delle Indie Orientali." ARSI, *Jap. Sin.* 14 II ("Iapon. Epist. 1600-1610"), fol. 317v (August 23, 1608). The presence of Italians such as de Ursis in China reflect the cosmopolitan makeup of the missionaries in Asia. For João Álvares, see *DHCJ* 1:89 (J. Vaz de Carvalho).

10. For Acquaviva, see Paolo Broggio, Francesca Cantù, Pierre-Antoine Fabre, and Antonella Romano, eds., *I gesuiti ai tempi di Claudio Acquaviva: Strategie politiche, religiose e culturali tra Cinque e Seicento* (Brescia: Morcelliana, 2007); Silvia Mostaccio, *Early Modern Jesuits between Obedience and Conscience during the Generalate of Claudio Acquaviva (1581-1615)* (Aldershot, UK: Ashgate, 2014); Pierre-Antoine Fabre and Flavio Rurale, eds., *The Acquaviva Project: Claudio Acquaviva's Generalate (1581-1615) and the Emergence of Modern Catholicism* (Boston: Institute of Jesuit Sources, Boston College, 2017). For Jesuit numbers in Asia, see Alden, *The Making of an Enterprise*, 46, 203-204.

11. See, for example, Francis Xavier from Goa to Ignatius of Loyola in Rome, April 9, 1552, in Donnelly, *Jesuit Writings*, 86. In Japan, the first three missionaries were Spaniards; the first Italians to arrive there were Giovanni Battista de Monte (1528-1587; arrived in 1563) and Alessandro Vallareggio (1529-1580; arrived in 1598). The first Jesuits to arrive on mainland China were Italians; this will be discussed in Chapter 3.

12. Alden, *The Making of an Enterprise*, 268.

13. For Valignano, see Josef Franz Schütte, *Valignano's Mission Principles for Japan*, vol. 1 in 2 parts, trans. John J. Coyne (St. Louis: Institute of Jesuit Sources, 1980); M. Antoni J. Üçerler, "Alessandro Valignano: Man, Missionary, Writer," *Renaissance Studies* 17, no. 3 (2003): 337-366; Adolfo Tamburello, M. Antoni J. Üçerler, and Marisa di Russo, eds., *Alessandro Valignano, S.I., Uomo del Rinascimento: Ponte tra Oriente e Occidente* (Rome: IHSI, 2008). For the office of visitor, see Alden, *The Making of an Enterprise*, 247-254; and for a discussion of the role, with a particular focus on Visitor André Palmeiro (1569-1635), appointed in 1617, see Liam Matthew Brockey, *The Visitor: André Palmeiro and the Jesuits in Asia* (Cambridge, MA: Harvard University Press, 2014). See also Thomas M. McCoog, ed., *With*

Eyes and Ears Open: The Role of Visitors in the Society of Jesus (Leiden: Brill, 2019).

14. For Jerónimo Nadal's attitudes, see Alden, *The Making of an Enterprise*, 267; for Xavier's attitudes, see, for example, Francis Xavier to Ignatius of Loyola, Cochin, January 27, 1545, quoted in English from M. Joseph Costelloe, ed., *The Letters and Instructions of Francis Xavier* (St. Louis, MO: Institute of Jesuit Sources, 1992), 114-115.

15. Alessandro Valignano to Everard Mercurian, Almeirim, January 7, 1574, in *Monumenta Missionum Societatis Iesu:* [vol. 21,] *Missiones Orientales: Documenta Indica,* [vol. 9,] *1573–1575,* ed. Josef Wicki, MHSI 94 (Rome: IHSI, 1966), 63: "poco zelo." Alessandro Valignano to Everard Mercurian, December 4, 1575, quoted in Gian Carlo Roscioni, *Il desiderio delle Indie: Storie, sogni e fughe di giovani gesuiti italiani* (Turin: Einaudi, 2001), 98: "in Europa si formano, per le lettere che da chi [da *qui:* dall'India] vanno, concetti molto differenti da quello che si ritrova, onde nasce che si raffreddano quando se veggono in queste parti."

16. Valignano's letters from the early period after his appointment as visitor are analyzed and quoted at length, in English, in Schütte, *Valignano's Mission Principles,* vol. 1, pt. 1. This research supports the argument by Jennifer Selwyn that, while mission was present from the beginning of the Society, it was in the later part of the sixteenth century that "an institutional missionary identity was forged" (Selwyn, *A Paradise Inhabited by Devils: The Jesuits' Civilizing Mission in Early Modern Naples* [Rome and Aldershot, UK: Ashgate/IHSI, 2004]), 136 and chapter 3 (for an elaboration of this argument). For the Society's fourth superior general, see Thomas M. McCoog, ed., *The Mercurian Project: Forming Jesuit Culture 1573–1580* (Rome and St. Louis: IHSI/Institute of Jesuit Sources, 2004). The Belgian, and first superior general not from Spain, was received into the Society by Ignatius; before his election to the generalate he was provincial of Flanders and then assistant to Germany. Overseeing a dramatic increase of the worldwide Society (from 3,000 to over 5,000 members in less than a decade) and bolstering the overseas missions were among the features of his tenure.

17. Valignano to Mercurian, Lisbon, February 8, 1574, in *Documenta Indica* 9:155-156: "se Vostra Paternità vuole davero essere signore della Compagnia nell'India, et che sia governata a suo modo, è necessario che vi sia commistione di nationi et non in picciol numero"; "Li nostri italiani sono pochi, ma sono buoni et io resto di loro molto consolato.... Questi sono fra tutti più accetti et, se Vostra Paternità desidera da dovero d'aiutar l'India, mandi alcuni buoni suggetti italiani, ma che sieno buoni et tali che sieno come pietre angulari tra queste due nationi."

18. Valignano to Mercurian, Lisbon, January 12, 1574, in *Documenta Indica* 9:84: "Regnat hic nonnisi 90 [spirito] di 94 [servitù] et di 227 [timore] et

li poveri 69 [Padri] et 71 [Fratelli] vengono a 306 [patire] quasi una misera b.o.d. [servitù]"; Valignano to Mercurian, 28/29 January 1574, in *Documenta Indica* 9:110, quoted also in Üçerler, "Alessandro Valignano," 342; "pensarono di cathechizar me et addoctrinarmi al lor modo acciò che governasse l'India con questo spirito che aqui tengono"; "il g.l.f. [governare] con f.g.g. [amore] è contro il b.m.o. [spirito] del P. Ignatio": this section from Valignano's letter of January 12 (partially quoted in English in my analysis) is in *Documenta Indica* 9:86.

19. Charles Burnett argues that Italian Renaissance humanism informed a Jesuit missionary style among members from Italy: "Humanism and the Jesuit Mission to China: The Case of Duarte de Sande (1547–1599)," *Euphrosyne: Revista de filologia Clássica* 24 (1996): 425–471; see also Antony Mecherry, *A Testing Ground for Jesuit Accommodation in Early Modern India: Francisco Ros SJ in Malabar (16th and 17th Centuries)* (Rome: IHSI, 2020), chapter 1. The outlines of this process, centered on what "the language arts inherited from Greece and Rome," are provided in Stuart M. McManus, "Jesuit Humanism and Indigenous-Language Philology," in Županov, *The Oxford Handbook of the Jesuits,* 737–758. The result, according to McManus, was a new "world philology," not universal (as its aims were) but nevertheless capable of interacting with "learned traditions from Asia, Africa, and the Americas" to produce hybrid, multidirectional knowledge systems, or what McManus calls "Indo-humanisms" (737–739). It provided the intellectual tools for the mission policy of accommodation.

20. For national configurations and numbers traveling east, see Wicki, "Liste der Jesuiten-Indienfahrer"; and Alden, *The Making of an Enterprise,* 267–277. Decree 130 of the first General Congregation records that "missions to the Indies are to be assisted," specifically that "the Portuguese fathers requested the assistance of the congregation. The response was that help would be supplied insofar as is possible": see *For Matters of Greater Moment: The First Thirty Jesuit General Congregations: A Brief History and a Translation of the Decrees,* ed. John W. Padberg, Martin D. O'Keefe, John L. McCarthy (St. Louis: Institute of Jesuit Sources, 1994), 100. The Portuguese Provincial Congregation Resolutions stated that Portugal would not send fully formed Jesuits or those demonstrating particular talents, who could perform greater service in Portugal than overseas. Acquaviva expressed his dismay, reminding his confreres of their well-known longstanding generosity in providing men of the highest ability from the assistancy (Brockey, *Journey to the East,* 231).

21. Gramazio, "Gesuiti italiani missionari," 275–276. For the fierce internal divisions in the Society at the time, see Michela Catto, *La Compagnia divisa: Il dissenso nell'ordine gesuitico tra '500 e '600* (Brescia: Morcelliana, 2009).

22. The main corpus of *Litterae indipetae* for the Old Society is located at ARSI, Fondo Gesuitico [hereafter F.G.] 732–759 ("Indipetae"). ARSI holds two indexes of the *Litterae indipetae,* one chronological (petitions from all prov-

inces) and one alphabetical according to author (Italian petitions only). Several thousand are located elsewhere in the archive, including many for the New Society (Pope Francis (1936–; r. 2013–), as the young Jesuit Jorge Mario Bergoglio, wrote an *indipeta* in the 1960s). The classic description of this source is Edmond Lamalle, "L'Archivio Generale della Compagnia di Gesù," *Archiva Ecclesiae* 24/25, no. 1 (1981–1982): 89–120 (104). The name given the petitions is a Latin contraction of "Petitions for the Indies." A selection of the following material and analysis appears in an earlier publication, "Imagining the 'Indies': Italian Jesuit Petitions for the Overseas Missions at the Turn of the Seventeenth Century," in *L'Europa divisa e i Nuovi Mondi: Per Adriano Prosperi,* ed. Massimo Donattini, Giuseppe Marcocci, Stefania Pastore, 3 vols. (Pisa: Edizioni della Normale, 2011), 2:179–189.

23. The number of petitions is unmatched by any other missionary order; for equivalent petitions in the Franciscan order, see Aliocha Maldavsky, "Administrer les vocations missionnaires: Les *Indipetae* et l'organisation des expéditions de missionnaires aux Indes Occidentales au début du XVIIe siècle," in *Missions Religieuses Modernes: Notre Lieu est le Monde,* ed. Pierre-Antoine Fabre and Bernard Vincent (Rome: École française de Rome, 2007), 45–70 (47–48). This is explained partly by the much more devolved and semi-autonomous appointment process among the mendicant orders. For Mexico, see Robert Ricard, *The Spiritual Conquest of Mexico: An Essay on the Apostolate and the Evangelizing Methods of the Mendicant Orders in New Spain, 1523–1572,* trans. Lesley Byrd Simpson (Berkeley: University of California Press; Cambridge: Cambridge University Press, 1966), esp. 61–82. For the non-Jesuit overseas enterprises more broadly, see Pedro Borges Morán, *El envío de misionaros a América durante la época espanol* (Salamanca: Universidad Pontificia, 1977); and Hsia, *A Companion to the Early Modern Catholic Global Missions,* 2018.

24. The Italian "Indipetae" are at ARSI, F.G. 752–751; Flanders-Belgium, F.G. 752–753; and Spain, 758–759. For applicants from Italy, see Alessandro Guerra, "Per un'archeologia della strategia missionaria dei Gesuiti: Le Indipetae e il sacrificio nella 'vigna del Signore,'" *Archivio italiano per la storia della pietà* 13 (2000): 109–192; for Naples, see Jennifer Selwyn, *A Paradise Inhabited by Devils: The Jesuits' Civilizing Mission in Early Modern Naples* (Rome and Aldershot, UK: Ashgate/IHSI, 2004); for applicants in the eighteenth century, see Capoccia, "Le destin des Indipetae au-delà." According to Lamalle, "L'Archivio Generale," 102, one of the reasons for the small number of *Indipetae* from France and Portugal was that the superior general's involvement was not required or expected for Jesuits who were sent to regions within their home assistancy. This could explain the relatively lower number of petitions from Spain, too, compared with Italy (most Spaniards, like Portuguese, traveled within their own assistancy). For possible reasons for the small number of Portuguese petitions, see

Charlotte Castelnau L'Estoile, "Élection et vocation: Le choix de la mission dans la province jésuite du Portugal à la fin du XVIe siècle," in Fabre and Vincent, *Missions Religieuses Modernes,* 21–43 (24): these simply may not have survived (some petitions are mentioned in the departure lists of Portuguese Jesuits, but they have not been located to date).

25. For an overview of the relevant scholarship, see Aliocha Maldavsky, "Pedir las Indias: Las cartas *indipetae* de los jesuitas europeos, siglos xvi–xviii, ensayo historiográfico," *Relaciones* 132 (2012): 147–181; Russell, "Becoming 'Indians,'" 19–22. Key studies according to core specified themes (in parentheses) are: (psycho-historical and among the first to tackle this source) Marina Massimi and André Barreto Prudente, *Um incendido desejo das índias* (São Paulo: Loyola, 2002); (geographically focused on Brazil, Peru, and the Philippines, and on candidates from Portugal, Spain, and Italy, in the last case, for the eighteenth century) several essays in Fabre and Vincent, *Missions Religieuses Modernes,* especially those by Capoccia, de Castelnau L'Estoile, Fabre, and Maldavsky; (on individual petitioners) Giovanni Pizzorusso, "Autobiografia e vocazione in una littera indipeta inedita del gesuita: Pierre-Joseph-Marie Chaumonot, missionario in Canada (1637)," in Donattini et al., *L'Europa divisa e i Nuovi Mondi,* 2:191–202; Claudio Ferlan, "Candidato alle Indie: Eusebio Francesco Chini e le 'litterae indipetae' nella Compagnia di Gesù," in *Eusebio Francesco Chini e il suo tempo: Una riflessione storica* (Trent: FBK Press, 2012), 31–58; Elisa Frei, "The Many Faces of Ignazio Maria Romeo, SJ (1676–1724?), Petitioner for the Indies: A Jesuit Seen through His *Litterae Indipetae* and the *Epistulae Generalium,*" *AHSI* 85, no. 169 (2016): 365–404; (for their administrative function) Colombo, "Gesuitomania"; (for their literary value and their themes of escape, martyrdom, and world evangelization) Roscioni, *Il desiderio delle Indie;* Adriano Prosperi, *Tribunali della coscienza: Inquisitori, confessori, missionari* (Turin: Einaudi, 1996), 586–599.

26. ARSI, *F.G.,* 733, fol. 68r (Francesco Corsi, Collegio Romano, February 2, 1590): "il Signore mi ha dato desiderio"; "chiamandomi egli interiormente"; "indifferente ad obedire a tutto quello che Vostra Paternità giudicherà esser maggior gloria sua." The 1599 Catalogue for Goa lists Francesco Corsi as a theology student: ARSI, *Goa.* 28 ("Elenchus missorum in Indiam Orient. 1541-1610"), fol. 13r.

27. ARSI, *F.G.* 734, fol. 14r (Donato Antonio Sementi, Naples, February 28, 1607): "guardando la moltitudine dell'Indie, che per mancamento di operarii sono, per dir così, quasi rubuttate dal Cielo nelle Tenebre dell'Inferno, non posso fare che grandemente non mi commova: per la qual cosa bisogna poi, che mi risolva tutto in lagrime, et sospiri."

28. ARSI, *F.G.* 733, fol. 301r, quoted in Roscioni, *Il desiderio delle Indie,* 77 (Giuseppe di Maio [no place], May 29, 1605): "un dì vedendo due ritratti, l'uno del Beato Nostro Padre Ignazio et l'altro del Beato Francesco Xaverio,

della qual vista mi penetrò dentro al cuore et mi accese un desiderio di patire e morire per Christo."

29. See also ARSI, *F.G.* 733, fol. 64r (Giacomo Antonio Colacino, Naples, September 5, 1597): "i gridi de i compagni che dimandano aiuto *in captura piscium,* intonano continuamente nelle mie orecchie"; ARSI, *F.G.* 733, fol. 46r (Francesco Buzomi (Buzome, Busomi), Naples, July 6, 1595): "sentii appresso tanta motione nel'udir l'ultime lettere del Giappone." Buzomi wrote again on May 20, 1603: ARSI, *F.G.* 733, fol. 256r, with the secretarial annotation on the address page "cavato (extracted)." While the impact of the letters from the overseas missions cannot be doubted, interestingly, the petitioners mention them rarely, preferring to ascribe their vocation to a spiritual calling and referring instead to the example of the early Christians and, at most, Xavier (but no other near-contemporary Jesuits) as their primary inspiration: Russell, "Imagining the 'Indies,'" 182-184. For Buzomi (1576-1639), see *DHCJ* 1:586 (J. Ruiz-de-Medina). He was one of the founding members of the Cochin-China mission. He is mentioned in a list of other short-listed candidates, dated a few days after his petition had been extracted and compiled on May 23 and 24, 1603, *F.G.* 733, fols. 259r-261v.

30. ARSI, *F.G.* 734, fol. 7r (Giovanni Rho, Como, January 10, 1607): "di andare all'Orientali, come Occidentali, come anche fra Turchi . . . però parmi d'esser ciamato particolarmente alla China, overo al Giappone." His younger brother was the China missionary Giacomo Rho (1592-1638). Giovanni was destined to remain in Italy as a prolific preacher, orator, and polemicist, as well as provincial of Rome and Naples: *DBI* 87 (Giovanni Pizzorusso). For Renaissance humanism, the mission policy of accommodation, and Italian Jesuits in the overseas missions, see Burnett, "Humanism and the Jesuit Mission." In a related vein, de Castelnau L'Estoile, "Jesuit Anthropology," 812, discusses how the education apostolate's "duty of intelligence" informed encounters with distant lands and their peoples. See also Colombo, "Gesuitomania," 41.

31. Edward W. Said, *Orientalism* (New York: Pantheon, 1978). An important framework for further developing the research potential of what I call "spiritual Orientalism" in the early modern world is Barreto Xavier and Županov, *Catholic Orientalism;* see also de Castelnau L'Estoile, "Jesuit Anthropology," 811-830, who outlines "the entanglement of scholarly and religious dimensions" that impelled Jesuits toward a unique brand of "missionary knowledge" (811).

32. For martyrdom in the early Society of Jesus, see, for example, Camilla Russell, "Early Modern Martyrdom and the Society of Jesus in the Sixteenth and Seventeenth Centuries," in *Narratives and Representations of Suffering, Failure, and Martyrdom: Early Modern Catholicism Confronting the Adversities of History,* ed. Leonardo Cohen (Lisbon: Centro de Estudos de História

Religiosa: Universidade Católica Portuguesa, 2020), 67-99; ARSI, F.G. 733, fol. 77v (Vespasiano Bonamici, S. Andrea, September 23, 1598), quoted in Russell, "Early Modern Martyrdom," 93: "Undeci anni sono stato nella compagnia, et sempre in aggi, mangiato bene, vestito bene, et commodo per tutti i luoghi, et finirò la vita mia in un letto; è possibile? Io finire la vita in un letto, et Christo in croce?" In his January 7 letter to Mercurian, quoted above, Valignano wrote of candidate Vincenzo Lenoci, "He does not want to go if not to Japan (non vuole andare se non al Giappone)," *Documenta Indica* 9:62.

33. ARSI, F.G. 734, fol. 98r (Angelo Rossi, February 29, 1608): "quelle povere animelle"; ARSI, F.G. 734, fol. 51r (Giulio Aleni, December 2, 1607): "quelle povere, et abbandonate genti dell'India."

34. ARSI, F.G. 733, fol. 12r (Francesco Pavone, Naples, June 24, 1590): "la mia età, che è di venti... havendo io in questa età tempo d'imparar la lingua, e dopo operar alcuna cosa in servitio di Dio"; ARSI, F.G. 733, fol. 11/1r (Nicolò Mastrilli, Naples, June 24, 1590): "sano"; "[di] saper la lingua spagnola"; the full phrase reads thus: "haver qualche abilità a qualche lingua straniera per haver appreso in breve tempo la spagnola senza molto aiuto né metodo." For Marcello Mastrilli, see *DBI* 72 (Paolo Broggio); *DHCJ* 3:2566-2567 (E. Fernández G., J Baptista).

35. ARSI, F.G. 733, fol. 11r (Alonso di Cordova, Naples, June 24, 1590): "la molta necessità che c'è nella China di pittori e intagliatori"; "per amor di Giesù Christo non se ne dimentichi [...e] disprezzi... questa mia domanda"; ARSI, F.G. 733, fol. 12r (Pavone): "in quanto a me mi conosco indegno di questa gratia."

36. ARSI, *Rom.* 172 ("Ingressus Novitiorum ab anno 1594 usq. ad 1630"), fol. 37v (Mario Squadrini's entry is dated in June 1600, one month after his arrival): "Portò seco una casacca et calzoni di saglia drappata di seta, capello di feltro: giuppone di cianbellotto bigio, calzette di lane bionde, un paro di calze lise, un fazzoletto, una camiscia, un paro di scarpini, un paro di scarpe. Io Mario Squadrini affermo come di sopra"; ARSI, F.G. 732, fol. 123r (Mario Squadrini, no place or date): "io esposi a Vostra Paternità come il Signore Dio per sua infinita misericordia (oltre all'havermi chiamato a questo Santo Instituto) si era degnato chiamarmi aservirlo nell'Indie... Ma per che Sua Paternità in me tiene il luogo di Giesù Christo nostro Signore a lei si aspetta di adempire tal vocatione."

37. For Pietro Lucari, see ARSI, *Neap.* 105 ("Neapol. Cat. Brev. Triennales, 1651-1662"), fol. 105v (notice of his death); ARSI, *Rom.* 173 ("Ingressus Novitior 1631-1675"), fol. 41v (February 2, 1639); ARSI, *Rom.* 171 ("Vocationi"), fol. 138r: "Ha governato la casa, e ha havuto cura dei negotii... et ha studiato la magior parte dai Padri della Compagnia"; (fol. 138r) "passati sei mesi di nuovo conobbe la volontà di Dio"; (fol. 138v) "Per adesso se Dio non vorrà altrimenti si sente inclinato supposta l'indifferenza alli Paesi del Turco,

particolarmente per haver la lingua con la quale potrebbe servir Idio et aiutar il prossimo in quei paesi"; (fol. 139r), regarding the shipwreck and his vocation to serve, although not specifically in the Indies.
38. ARSI F.G. 743, fol. 153r (Pietro Lucari, [no place or day] August 1641): "Tutte quelle parti dell'India ... per me sono più meritorie, che queste d'Europa"; ARSI F.G. 743, fol. 299r (Pietro Lucari, Collegio Romano, December 2, 1641) "occasione ... la quale rarissime volte si rappresenta, però prego ... che prima che parta il Procuratore mi ammetta nel numero degli altri missionari per la Cina." Procurators had many functions—chiefly, looking after the organizational work of the Society in their area, including the movement of personnel, goods, paperwork and correspondence, and financial management.
39. For Pietro Conti, see ARSI, *Rom.* 173, fol. 25r (S. Andrea entrance record); ARSI, *Rom.* 171, fol. 1r (vocation statement, February 23, 1636) and quoted in Russell, "Early Modern Martyrdom," 94: "alle Indie, et al Giappone, ma se di là c'è paese aprire la strada col mio sangue, dove mai né Padri, né Altri poterono penetrare"; ARSI, F.G. 741, fol. 116r (petition sent from Collegio Romano, May 25, 1638).
40. ARSI, F.G. 742, fol. 36r (Giovanni Raffaele de Ferraris, Collegio Romano, April 30, 1639): "gratia di seguir il figliuolo nelle Indie ... e darmi campo di sacrificar a Sua Divina Maestà questa misera vita e quei pochi giorni che mi restano ... l'ignoranza et inhabilità massime ad impresa così grande a lei troppo note." For his son, Giovanni Francesco de Ferraris (Ferrari), see *DBI* 46 (Giuliano Bertuccioli).
41. ARSI, F.G. 733, fol. 11/1r (Nicola Mastrilli, Naples, June 24, 1590): "de gli altri superiori sto suspetto perché come veggo e conosco mi amano di un certo amore che forse potrebbe ciò impedirmi."
42. Josef Wicki, "Liste der Jesuiten-Indienfahrer 1541-1758," *Aufsätze zur Portugiesischen Kulturgeschichte* 7 (1967): 252-450 (279-287); Capoccia, "Le destin des Indipetae," 89-110.
43. ARSI, F.G. 732, fol. 130r-v (Andrea Simi [no place or date]).
44. For this last point, see Maldavsky, "Administrer les vocations missionnaires," 70; de Castelnau L'Estoile, "Élection et vocation," 31.
45. ARSI, F.G. 734, fol. 14r (Donato Antonio Sementi, Naples, February 28, 1607): "o Padre mio questo è un negotio di grandissima importanza ... o Padre, Padre mio ... per i meriti del Nostro Santo et Benedetto Padre Ignatio che mi faccia quattro righe di lettera in risposta per mia consolatione"; (from the superior general's correspondence, about Benedetto Turri, April 1599) ARSI, *Neap.* 6 I ("Epist. Gener. 1599-1600"), fol. 44r: "Vostra Reverenza ... lo saluti et consoli."
46. Notes in the margins of the generals' copy letters on occasion indicate the subject (such as a petition to the Indies), which helps the researcher a little, as do some basic archival finding guides provided for some volumes of

these sources, which, however, tend to list names only. Cross-referencing between these names and similar alphabetical lists provided for the Italian petitioners for the 'Indies' also help identify relevant letters. See, for example, ARSI, F.G. 733, fol. 64r, which mentions that the superior general replied to the candidate; ARSI, FG, 733, fol. 145v (Giacomo Cardano, Milan, August 4, 1602) contains an administrative annotation on the address page, "Extracted; greeting sent" [from the superior general] ("cavato; fatto salutare"); see also ARSI, F.G. 733, fol. 11r (Alonso di Cordova, June 22, 1590), mentioning replies sent from the superior general.

47. The first publication on this source is Frei, "The Many Faces of Ignazio Maria Romeo." See also Russell, "Becoming 'Indians,'" 26–33. A study of Polish petitioners for the Indies includes a chapter about these replies; the Polish-language study has been reviewed in English: Robert Danieluk, "Review of Miazek-Męczyńska, *Indipetae Polonae, kołatanie do drzwi misji chińskie*" (Poznań: Wydawnictwo Naukowe Uniwersytetu im. Adam Mickiewicz University Press, 2015), *AHSI* 85, no. 170 (2016): 573–577.

48. General Acquaviva's reply to Giulio Orsino is dated August 2, 1603: ARSI, *Neap.* 7 ("Epist. Gen. 1602–1605"), fol. 173r: "[l']offerta che rinova con tanto affetto d'andar al Giapone"; "sì lungo viaggio."

49. Giulio Orsino's petitions are at ARSI, F.G. 733, fol. 93r (Collegio Romano, May 23, 1600): "d'andare tra gente infedeli et especialmente al Giappone, o vero alla China"; fols. 102r–103v (Collegio Romano, December 3, 1600): "come in Turchia molti per la fede di Christo patir solevano crudelissimi tormenti"; fol. 133r (Naples, November 27, 1602): "per conto del mio negotio dell'andare al Giappone." His requests for the Indies are analyzed in Roscioni, *Il desiderio delle Indie,* chapter 1.

50. General Acquaviva's replies to Orsino are at ARSI, *Neap.* 7, fol. 314v (October 9, 1604): "desiderii del divino servizio"; fol. 363v (February 19, 1605): "risposto altre volte"; "la sua poca sanità, e forze fanno la cosa un poco difficile." Orsino's name was included on a short list of candidates for the Indies (May 23, 1603, six months after his final petition), among the *Litterae indipetae* (ARSI, F.G. 733, fol. 259r); the author of the document mentions that the list had been compiled some time ago and that some of those mentioned on it "have already left" ("già sono andati").

51. Pietro Cornaro's petitions were sent from Parma: ARSI, F.G., 734, fol. 360r (March 31, 1611): "Io sono nato in Candia, se bene i miei parenti discendono da Venetia"; "mi ritrovo . . . di complessione molto robusto; d'anni 24, e studio physica. Di spirito e virtú però, che è quel che più importa, mi ritrovo molto povero, mi sento però havere un poco di desiderio d'acquistarne"; (June 24, 1611) fol. 368r: "Dubitando io, che non sia capitata alle mani della Paternità sua"; "sapendo che da lei dipende il tutto,

non ostante l'impedimento che vi è per l'Italiani"; "al quale si ricevano persone di grandissima virtù e dottrina."

52. ARSI, *Ven.* 6a ("Epist. Gener. 1607-1616"), fol. 211r (August 6, 1511); the relevant section of this letter is quoted here in full and in Russell, "Becoming 'Indians,'" 29–30: "tiene memoria di questa vostra offerta, quale per adesso non può haver luogo, essendosi come credo sappiate [crossed out "serrata la porta agl'italiani"] alcuni impedimenti communi per quelle parti, ma spero si aprirà... in breve et all'hora ci ricorderemo di voi. Intanto conservatevi nel vostro proposito et a perfettionarvi tuttavia più in ogni virtù."

53. General Acquaviva's two further letters to Pietro Cornaro are at ARSI, *Ven.* 6a, fol. 262r (December 15, 1612); and fol. 305r (March 22, 1614): "sento dispiacere, che li vostri parenti stiano in tanta necessità, che bisogni precisamente trasferirvi a consolarli."

54. ARSI, *F.G.* 733, fol. 46r (Francesco Buzomi, Naples, July 6, 1595); quoted in Russell, "Becoming 'Indians,'" 30-31: "essendo molto bisogno nella sua antiqua Chiesa"; "dalle lettere del Mogorr... l'ultime lettere del Giappone"; "conforme al consiglio de superiori facendo con orationi, digiuni, et altre mortificationi... et il P. Ricci prefetto di cose spirituali al quale haveo scoperti tutti i moti del animo, anco mi disse che la cosa era andata per buona strada."

55. ARSI, *Neap.* 6 I, fol. 62r (no day or month), quoted in Russell, "Becoming 'Indians,'" 30–31: "Indiani—saluti"; "Vostra Reverenza li saluti carissimamente... dicendoli come noi gli abbracciamo... et havremo a mente il loro desiderio che non manchino di pregare Iddio che ci inspiri."

56. The petitions, both from Naples, are at ARSI, *F.G.* 733, fol. 407r (August 4, 1606); *F.G.* 732, fol. 175r (no date): "il mio nome è Francesco Buzomi, e sono quello per chi il Procuratore dell' Indie ha con Vostra Paternità raggionato."

57. Allusions to Jesuit communities and individuals as families and as members of a family are scattered throughout the Society's reports, correspondence, and other records from the seventeenth century. For the German lands, see Frank Sobiech, *Jesuit Prison Ministry in the Witch Trials of the Holy Roman Empire: Friedrich Spee and His Cautio Criminalis (1631)* (Rome: IHSI, 2019). This is a promising theme for future research.

58. ARSI, *Neap.* 6 I, fol. 41v (April 3, 1599); quoted in Russell, "Becoming 'Indians,'" 31–32 (the full relevant section is quoted here): "Havevamo scritto a Vostra Reverenza che ci mandassi il P. Puerio quanto prima a Roma per le ["India" crossed out] Filippine;" "qualche difficoltà... poca sanità et qualche diminutione dello suo fervore... rimettendosi all'obedienza non si è partito... le dica che non si muova perché noi metteremo un altro in suo luogo non volendo mandare ad impresa sì grande

niuno che positivamente non vi senta affetto et desiderio." Girolamo Puerio's petition is at ARSI, F.G., 733, 42r (May 29, 1595).

59. ARSI, *Neap.* 6 I, fol. 43r (April 3, 1599); quoted in Russell, "Becoming 'Indians,'" 31–32: "conservi la vocatione dell'Indiani"; "ci dà ragguaglio di quei che hanno inspiratione d'andare all'Indie ci siamo consolati et Vostra Reverenza li conservi in questo buono spirito."

60. Some candidates' petitions for the Indies included brief notes on the address page, presumably made on arrival and after having been processed in Rome. These annotations began to disappear in the early seventeenth century, except for the occasional word, such as *cavato* ("extracted"), or *metterla al libro* ("to be put in the book [of the list of potential missionaries]"): see ARSI, F.G. 733, fol. 200v and fol. 202v, respectively. Such books with candidates' names appear to have been lost, except for a few extant lists discussed here—for example, ARSI, *Ital.* 173, fol. 2r–v: "Quelli che domandano l'Indie o altrove della Provincia Romana [1588-1594]."

61. ARSI, *Neap.* 6 I, 53v (April 30, 1599): "Circa il Padre Cicero già ho scritto al Padre Provinciale . . . che sia difficile contentare tutti."

62. ARSI, *Neap.* 6 I, 42r: "esortandolo a nutrir questo santo desiderio et accompagnarlo con le virtù a quello necessarie che noi l'havremo a mente."

63. Both of General Acquaviva's copy letters from 1599 are at ARSI, *Neap.* 6 I (fol. 66r): "Il desiderio di Vostra Reverenza, l'andar' all'Indie, ho caro che mel'habbiate proposto, io non mancherò di raccomandarlo al Superiore"; (fol. 68v) "Intanto il Padre Provinciale ha bisogno di voi in Provincia."

64. The reports are at ARSI, F.G. 732, 733; *Ital.* 173 ("Missiones et servitium . . ."). For similar reports produced in Portugal between 1592 and 1596, about candidates for the Brazil missions, see de Castelnau L'Estoile, "Élection et vocation," 26–28. The Italian reports are discussed briefly in Guerra, "Per un'archeologia," 161–163.

65. The Acquaviva copy letter of February 27, 1599 is at ARSI, *Neap.* 6 I, fol. 24v: "vorrei che facesse sopra ciò un poco di consideratione et ce ne proponesse parecchi di quelli che in questa santa inspiratione giudicherà più ferventi et più atti acciò bisognando chiamarne alcuni a questo effetto, possiamo farlo con più cognitione et sicurtà"; Giovanni Battista Carminata's 1600 report is at ARSI, F.G. 733, 105. (Folios 105–106 are numbered sequentially, without recto or verso.) (Sicily, October 15, 1600): "Conforme all'ordine, che mi diede Vostra Paternità per una sua li giorni a detro, mando l'informatione delli soggetti di questa provincia che l'hanno domandate l'Indie."

66. Very few later (and dispersed) reports are extant. See ARSI, F.G., 721, which contains one report dated from 1678 and another from the eighteenth century. In the first of the three folders (ARSI, F.G., 732) there are several reports, for the most part interspersed among Italian *Litterae indipetae;* the

folder contains mainly undated materials, which are chronologically traceable (and relevant to this study) by name, such as Alfonso Vagnone (1568–1640), who departed for China in 1603. There is also a small folder (ARSI, *Ital.* 173) with reports only (there are no petitions), about candidates from Rome, Veneto, and Milan. Archival notations date the contents from 1580; however, the earliest list of missionary candidates is dated 1588, and the earliest reports are from 1589. This analysis thus takes its starting point from the first reports of 1589. The reports in the third folder (*Ital.* 173) are the least detailed, although the names of several missionaries to Asia are included there.

67. Some reports are brief and on a single page; others are multipage documents about numerous candidates, such as the 1592 Neapolitan report on twenty-seven candidates: ARSI, F.G. 733, 27–37.
68. ARSI, F.G. 733, fol. 106v.
69. The 1591 report from Naples, written by the provincial, enlisted recommendations from the college rector: ARSI, F.G. 733, fol. 23r.
70. ARSI, *Ital.* 173, fol. 5v (reports about Giovanni Medaglia and Francesco Tezzoni, Milan, 1593/1594). For Bernardo Rossignoli, see Scaduto, *Catalogo,* 130; *DHCJ* 4:3417 (M. Ruiz Jurado). From a noble Piedmontese family, he entered the novitiate in Rome in 1563 against the wishes of his family; he was provincial of Milan (1592–1596; 1606–1611); Rome (1597–1600); and Venice (1601–1604).
71. See ARSI, *Rom.* 78b ("Cat. antiquiss. Ital. 1546–1577 [et varia usque ad 1600]"), fol. 106r: "Lista di quelli che potranno andare in Germania fatti dottori in Theologia" (c. 1569?); also, ARSI, *Rom.* 78b, 1565, fol. 124r, which contains a letter from the Loreto college listing "quei c'hanno la lingua francese." (The Jesuits entered France formally only in 1562; these documents may relate to the plan to send some members there.) For the vocation, recruitment, and selection process in the Society as a whole, see O'Malley, *The First Jesuits,* 51–90. For a case study and overview of the catalogues, discussed in Chapter 4 of this book, see A. Demoustier, "Les catalogues du personnel de la province de Lyon en 1587, 1606 et 1636," *AHSI* 42 and 43 (1973 and 1974); Paolo Broggio, *Evangelizzare il mondo: Le missioni della Compagnia di Gesù tra Europa e America (secoli XVI–XVII)* (Rome: Carocci Editore, 2004), 132n31. See also Wiktor Gramatowski, "Jesuit Glossary: Guide to Understanding the Documents, English Version," trans. Camilla Russell (orig. in Italian, 1992), Archivum Romanum Societatis Iesu (Rome, 2014), 6: http://www.sjweb.info/arsi/documents/glossary.pdf.
72. ARSI, F.G. 733, fol. 23r (report about Francesco Pavone, Naples, March 20, 1591): "sendo de primi della sua classe, et è specchio del Collegio di Napoli in ogni sorte di virtù."

73. See O'Malley, *The First Jesuits,* 60. According to Alden, *The Making of an Enterprise,* 504, temporal coadjutors were highly valued and sought after. This contrasts with Roscioni, *Il desiderio delle Indie,* 128, who cites the *Deliberationes* of 1575, recommending against sending coadjutors. On this question, see also Brockey, *Journey to the East,* 237.
74. The following reports are all located at ARSI, F.G. 733, fol. 25 / 1r (report about Barnaba d'Erma, Sicily, 1592): "ha poche lettere, come anco poco fervore; perciò non mi pare buono"; fol. 32 (no recto and verso) (Naples, April 1592): "non sa legere né scrivere . . . è di pochissimo ingegno." For Bartolomeo Ricci, see Hubert Jacobs, ed., *Documenta Malucensia II (1577–1606)* (Rome: IHSI, 1980) (MHSI, vol. 119; MMSI, vol. 39) 2:339n; in 1585, he was master of novices at Sant'Andrea and Sicily provincial between 1590 and 1594.
75. See a similar finding regarding Portuguese candidates for the Indies in de Castelnau L'Estoile, "Élection et vocation," 28.
76. Xavier to Rodrigues, January 20, 1548, quoted in English, in Donnelly, *Jesuit Writings,* 73–74.
77. ARSI, F.G. 733 (all following quotations are from this folder), fol. 33 (no recto and verso) (report about Lorenzo Stazzone, Naples, April 1592): "ha havuto dolor di petto, e sputato alle volte sangue"; fol. 25 / 1v (and fol. 4 [copy], Sicily, April 1592): "Il P. Benedetto Moleti seria stato buono perché tien zelo, gratia di predicare et trattare fruttuoso con i prossimi . . . ma come in gioventù hebbe il mal caduco, ancorchè poi sia stato bene, hora (com'ho detto altrove) se gli temono principii di paralisia" (directly after the report about Moleti is the glowing assessment of successful petitioner and missionary to China, Niccolò Longobardo, discussed in Chapter 3); fol. 23r (Francesco Pavone). ARSI, F.G. 733, "Ha patito qualche volta con poco di dolore di petto, ma non è stata cosa di momento." For Francesco Pavone, see *DBI* 81 (Sabina Pavone); *DHCJ* 3:3067 (A. Guidetti). A brief report about Nicola Mastrilli, including his slight health problems and many character and intellectual strengths, is on the *verso* of his letter, on the address page: fol. 11 / 1v (Nicola Mastrilli, Naples, June 24, 1590).
78. Quoted in O'Malley, *The First Jesuits,* 355, and Schütte, *Valignano's Mission Principles* 1:178–179, respectively.
79. ARSI, F.G. 733, fol. 17r (report about Pietro Martini, Jesuit College, Naples, January 1, 1591): "Non par tanto maturo per tal missione et mi pareria si provasse la sua riuscita per qualche altro tempo. Questo fratello sta nel novitiato né mai ha habitato in altro loco de nostri doppo l'entrata sua se forse non fusse per alcuni pochi giorni"; ARSI, F.G. 733, fol. 27 (no recto and verso) (report of Albertino di Catanzaro, Naples, 1592): "Ha talento in legere, et anco in predicare, et ha letto la dottrina Christiana in chiesa più d'un anno con molto frutto."

80. ARSI, F.G. 733, fol. 29 (no recto and verso) (report about Giovanni Palermo, Naples, 1592): "è mediocremente devoto, humile, e obediente, molto colerico, e presume di sé molto, e s'avanta, e dà poca edificatione, e sodisfattione"; ARSI, F.G. 733, fol. 25/1r (Sicily, 1592): "Il P. Antonio Cicala non ha sanità per tal viaggio, disaggi e fatighe; né meno ha stabilità d'animo per simil'impresa, però io non lo manderei." Antonio Cicala (1570–1629), became consultor with the Holy Office.
81. ARSI, F.G. 733, fol. 33 (no recto and verso) (report about Francesco Laccio of Monaciglione, Naples, April 1592): "di singolar devotione, et edificatione, et ha gran desiderio di patir per amor di Christo"; ARSI, F.G. 733, fol. 50r (report about Agostino Retava, Palermo, December 1592): "sa bene dell'arte sua di tagliare et dimostra principii de spirito et de maturità."
82. ARSI, F.G. 733, fol. 137r (report about Mario Squadrini, Rome, no date): "non contenta Sua Divina Maestà di averlo chiamato alla religione che anchora si è degnato chiamarlo alla maggior perfettione della salute dei prossimi: et havendo sopra ciò fatte molte orationi ... si sente finalmente con grandissimo affetto chiamato alla conversione degli infedeli."
83. For the importance of family networks in the vocation and appointment process for the overseas Jesuit missions, see Amélie Vantard, "Les vocations pour les missions *ad gentes* (France, 1650–1750)," PhD thesis, University of Maine, 2010, chapter 8. In her assessment of Portuguese candidates, de Castelnau L'Estoile similarly found that some candidates were turned back on account of family considerations, including applicants considered too wealthy or powerful, or those prevented from going on account of pressure from relatives ("Élection et vocation," 34–35). See also Frei, "The Many Faces of Ignazio Maria Romeo."
84. The reports are from ARSI, F.G. 733, fol. 27 (no recto and verso) (report about Stefano di Majo, Naples, 1592): "Non ha parenti poveri, tiene solo un fratello dottore, che non ha bisogno di lui"; fol. 28 (no recto and verso) (Albertino di Catanzaro): "Non ha parenti bisognosi"; fol. 19r (single report about Pietro Antonio del Guasto, Naples, March 15, 1591): "non par che habbi impedimento di parenti poveri; sì che ci pare atto per tal missione."
85. The long Neapolitan report of 1592 (ARSI, F.G. 733, fols. 27–37) contains a high number of coadjutors: ARSI, F.G. 733, fol. 32 (no recto and verso) (report about Giovanni Alfonso Sacco): "Ha madre e sorelle in qualche necessità, perché sebene prima li suoi stavano molto ricchi, hora sono cascati in povertà." These kinds of concerns likely informed the inclusion of a question about candidates' family circumstances in the interviews conducted on entry to the novitiate, on which, see, for example, ARSI, *Rom.* 171 ("Vocationi").

86. For an example of a successful family protest to keep a son home, see Frei, "The Many Faces of Ignazio Maria Romeo." For the stand-alone report about Pietro Antonio del Guasto, mentioned above, see ARSI, *F.G.*, 733, fol. 19r: "sì bene con incommodo di questa Provincia"; for that about Gasparo Taraninfa (Sicily, 1592), see fol. 25/1r: "È ben vero ch'habbiam pensato di proporlo per mastro de' novitii in Palermo."
87. *Sp. Ex.* [238].
88. The Milan report (compiled between 1593 and 1594) is at ARSI, *Ital.* 173, fols. 4r-7r (report about Giovanni Battista Laverna), 5r: "India o altra missione difficile." For Niccolò Levanto (c. 1564-1618), see Gramazio, "Gesuiti italiani missionari," 285-286: he arrived in Goa in 1594, was in Salsette and the Fishery Coast, and was rector of São Tomé, 1608-1609, and of Thane in 1616; he died in Malacca at the age of about fifty-five. For Carlo Spinola (1564/5-1622), see Gramazio, "Gesuiti italiani missionari," 293-294; *DBI* 93 (Daniele Frison); *DHCJ* 4:2623-2624 (R. Yuuki): First, he was sent to Brazil; he was captured in 1597 by English corsairs, along with fellow Jesuit Girolamo De Angelis. After some months in England, he was back in Lisbon in 1598 and the following year was in Goa. He entered Japan in 1602 and undertook many ministries there until he went into hiding at the outbreak of the 1614 definitive Christian proscription and expulsions. In 1618, he was arrested, imprisoned, and then martyred in 1623, during the so-called Great Martyrdom.
89. ARSI, *Gall.* 44 ("Epist. Secr. 1583-1602, Gall. Germ. Hisp. Lusit."), fol. 27r-v: "Desidero poi che Vostra Reverenza con ogni studio, e diligenza attenda a promovere ne' nostri fratelli lo spirito, poiché da quella educatione depende in gran parte il buon procedere de nostri nelli collegii, il che si bene è necessario in tutti i luoghi, particolarmente è in coteste parti dove havendo li nostri così alta impresa per le mani, com'è l'aiuto, e conversione di tante nationi hanno bisogno di spirito maggiore per poter poi trasfonderlo negl'altri." For Alberto Laerzio (1557-1630), see *DHCJ* 3:2257-2258 (J. Wicki); Gramazio, "Gesuiti italiani missionari," 285: Originally from Orte, near Rome, Laerzio entered the Society in 1576, left Lisbon, and arrived in Goa in 1579, where he was master of novices. He returned to Europe and worked as procurator in Rome until returning to India as vice provincial of Goa in 1602. Between 1605 and 1611 he was provincial of Malabar, and in 1620 he became visitor to China and Japan. He returned to Rome as procurator once more, and in 1624 he undertook a third voyage to India and then served again as provincial of Malabar in 1625-1629. He died in Cochin in 1630.
90. ARSI, *F.G.* 733, fol. 105 (no recto or verso) (Sicily, October 15, 1600): "non l'ho saputo, se non che l'ho fatto cavare dalle lettere che Vostra Paternità m'ha scritto in tempo del mio governo, quando a nome suo ho salutato o uno, o un altro fratello di questi che hanno tal desiderio, et sono li se-

guenti, comminciando dalli scolari"; "In tutti questi non trovo impedimento, perché mi pareno persone mature, et spirituali, et per quel che si ha visto, sono sani, et desiderosi di patire, solo rapresento a Vostra Paternità l'incomodo della provincia, perché tutti questi sono soggetti di poterla servire bene col tempo."

91. ARSI, F.G. 733, fol. 105 (no recto or verso) (report about Antonio Zumbo): "dopo finito, et difeso il corso di filosofia, ha fatto 4 anni di scola, et al presente studia il primo anno di Teologia."
92. See ARSI, F.G. 733, fol. 24/2 (fols. 24/1-2 are numbered sequentially, without recto or verso) (report about Alfonso Vagnone, Milan, 1592).
93. See the report about Vincente Galletti at ARSI, F.G. 733, fol. 106 (Sicily, October 15, 1600); for Benedetto Turri, see ARSI, F.G. 733, fol. 1r (Naples, 1589): "Benedetto Turri desidera andar all'Indie et di ciò ha scritto al Reverendissimo Padre Generale, et del medesmo ha parlato al Reverendissimo Padre Generale il P. Pietro Antonio Spinello nel mese di giugno dell'anno 1589. Questi ha ordinato il Nostro Padre che si scrivano nel libro di quelli che vogliono andare all'Indie." For Ottavio Lombardo (c. 1566–1627), see Gramazio, "Gesuiti italiani missionari," 286. He departed Lisbon in 1592 and served on the Fishery Coast in 1603, in Colombo in 1604, and in Cochin from 1605 to 1608. He died in Naples.
94. Brockey, *Journey to the East,* 55, 232; the case of Giulio Aleni is discussed in Chapter 3; for the report about Niccolò Levanto, see ARSI, *Ital.* 173, fol. 5v: "Partì finalmente ... col Padre Procuratore dell'Indie di Portugallo, Padre Francesco Monclaro."
95. ARSI, F.G. 733, fol. 27 (Stefano di Majo). The full transcription of this section of the report is: "È molto devoto, humile, e buon religioso, et ha desiderio di patire per amor di Christo. Ha molto zelo dell'anime, et inclinatione ad aiutar li prossimi, a confessare, far missioni, e la dottrina Christiana. Non ha parenti poveri, tiene solo un fratello dottore, che non ha bisogno di lui."
96. Numbers are based on the total Italians traveling east in the same years as those for whom a petition and/or a report survive. In the case of two missionaries, Mario Squadrini (who left for Goa in 1603 but did not proceed to China) and Alfonso Vagnone, both a report and a petition survive: twenty-three successful candidates have a documentary record about their vocation and selection process.

3. BEING A JESUIT IN THE "INDIES"

1. For the applied and mobile nature of a fixed Jesuit spirituality, see Rady Roldán-Figueroa, "The Mystical Theology of Luis de la Puente (1554–1624)," in *Brill's Companion to Jesuit Mystical Spirituality,* ed. Robert A. Maryks (Leiden: Brill, 2017), 54–81. For the meeting point between spirituality,

evangelization, and how they informed Jesuit proto-anthropology, see Charlotte de Castelnau L'Estoile, "Jesuit Anthropology: Studying 'Living Books,'" in *The Oxford Handbook of the Jesuits,* ed. Ines G. Županov (New York: Oxford University Press, 2019), 811–830, who observes how the Jesuits worked within a "strictly unitary religious framework, which boiled down to three propositions: creation is divine, there is only one human race, and all humans are called to become Christian" (811). This was the lens through which misson was understood, regardless of location. The Jesuit view of mission was distinctive: Pedro Lage Reis Correia, "Alessandro Valignano's Attitude towards Jesuit and Franciscan Concepts of Evangelization in Japan (1587-1597)," *Bulletin of Japanese/Portuguese Studies* 2 (2001): 79–108 (esp. 90-95), compares the Franciscan approach to its overseas enterprise with that of the Society. While of course there was a great deal of variation depending on the context and leadership on the ground, the Franciscans tended to maintain a messianic worldview aiming at purification from corruption, and a transcendent understanding of conversion. See also Stuart M. McManus, "Jesuit Humanism and Indigenous-Language Philology," in Županov, *The Oxford Handbook of the Jesuits,* 737-758. For the Jesuits, the project of salvation for oneself and others began in the physical world starting with helping wherever there was need. One of their fundamental tools in this aim was education, which, drawing on its Greco-Roman foundations transmitted through the Renaissance, consisted of a unitary cultural-linguistic system alongside the religious one that was applied wherever in the world the Jesuits went. The result was a discernibly Jesuit missionary culture.

2. Two region-specific examples of accessing non-Jesuit protagonists in the Society's China mission are Nicolas Standaert, *Chinese Voices in the Rites Controversy* (Rome: IHSI, 2012), and Nadine Amsler, *Jesuits and Matriarchs: Domestic Worship in Early Modern China* (Seattle: University of Washington Press, 2018).

3. The analysis in this section is based on, and further develops, the final part of my article, Camilla Russell, "Becoming 'Indians:' The Jesuit Missionary Path from Italy to Asia," *Renaissance and Reformation/Renaissance et Réforme* 43, no. 1 (2020): 9-50, and my earlier study focusing on successful petitioners for the China mission (with transcriptions of some documents quoted here): "Vocation to the East: Italian Candidates for the Jesuit China Mission at the Turn of the Seventeenth Century," in *Renaissance Studies in Honor of Joseph Connors,* ed. Machtelt Israëls and Louis Waldman, 2 vols. (Florence: Villa I Tatti, the Harvard University Center for Italian Renaissance Studies, 2013), 2:313–327. A useful study profiling Jesuit missionaries is Christoph Nebgen, "Missionaries: Who Were They?," in *A Companion to the Early Modern Catholic Global Missions,* ed. Ronnie Po-Chia Hsia (Leiden: Brill, 2018), 401–423 (including discussion of

the German petitions for the Spanish Indies in the seventeenth and eighteenth centuries, with reflections on the cultural stimuli for their production).

4. Among many studies of the early modern Jesuit China mission are Liam Matthew Brockey, *Journey to the East: The Jesuit Mission to China, 1579–1724* (Cambridge, MA: Harvard University Press, 2007); R. Po-Chia Hsia, *A Jesuit in the Forbidden City: Matteo Ricci, 1552–1610* (Oxford: Oxford University Press, 2010); R. Po-Chia Hsia, "Imperial China and the Christian Mission," in Hsia, *A Companion to the Early Modern Catholic Global Missions*, 344–364, dealing broadly with the Christian mission to China, with several relevant sections about the Jesuit presence there. Joseph Dehergne lists all Jesuit missionaries sent to China up to the nineteenth century, including their national provenance (relevant here are the Italians either side of the sixteenth and seventeenth centuries): *Répertoire des jésuites de Chine de 1552 à 1800* (Rome: IHSI, 1973), 399.

5. See ARSI, *F.G.* 732, 733, 734 ("Indipetae"), and *Ital.* 173 ("Missiones et servitium..."), where these successful candidates' names are listed and where their petitions and reports are dispersed.

6. Biographical notes are located in Dehergne, *Répertoire des jésuites,* 6–7 (Aleni), 153–154 (Longobardo), 238 (Sambiasi), 75 (de Ursis), 278 (Vagnone); see also (for Aleni, or Alenis) *DBI* 60 (Pietro Pirri) and *DHCJ* 1:72–73 (B. Luk); (for Longobardo) *DBI* 65 (Elisabetta Corsi) and *DHCJ* 3:2411 (J. Sebes); (for Sambiasi or Sambiase) *DBI* 90 (Elisabetta Corsi) and *DHCJ* 4:3481 (M. Zanfredini); (for de Ursis) *DBI* 39:498–500 (Giuliano Bertuccioli) and *DHCJ* 2:1063–1064 (D. Mungello); (for Vagnone or Vagnoni) *DBI* 97 (Elisabetta Corsi) and *DHCJ* 4:3867–3868 (J. W. Witek). Further name variations are Giulio Alenis and Sabatino de Orsi.

7. ARSI, *F.G.* 734, fol. 382/1r (Alfonso Vagnone, Milan, July 9, 1602; a copy of this petition in a later hand can be found at *F.G.* 733, fol. 143-1, 2, 3): "quelle povere anime de la China"; ARSI, *F.G.* 732, fol. 389r (report about Alfonso Vagnone, no date): The full section of the request reads, "Memoria al Reverendissimo Padre Visitatore per Alfonso Vagnone di raccomandare il suo desiderio d'andare all'Indie orientali a Nostro Padre, havendogliene già fatto fare due volte instanza."

8. ARSI, *F.G.* 733, fol. 249r (Giulio Aleni, Parma, May 16, 1603): "la vita istessa per aiuto di quelle povere anime"; ARSI, *F.G.* 734, fol. 259r (Francesco Sambiasi, Lisbon, February 27, 1609): "nelli maggiori travagli, et fatiche che per amor d'essa croce patirò"; ARSI, *F.G.* 733, fol. 249r (Giulio Aleni): "per aiuto di quelle povere anime... che sono in tante varie parti dell'India prive d'ogni aiuto spirituale."

9. ARSI, *F.G.* 734, fol. 382/1r (Alfonso Vagnone); ARSI, *F.G.* 734, fol. 259r (Francesco Sambiasi): "un povarello"; ARSI, *F.G.* 733, fol. 249r (Giulio

Aleni): "enormità de miei gravi peccati, vitii, et imperfettioni"; "quella gratia e talenti."

10. ARSI, F.G. 734, fol. 51v (Giulio Aleni, Collegio Romano, December 2, 1607): "Né deve dubitare della sanità, et forze, poiché per gratia del Signore mi son sempre sentito bene nella religione, e fuori, né ho hauto malatie, né indispositioni di momento"; ARSI, F.G. 734, fol. 383A (Alfonso Vagnone, Milan, August 20, 1602; a copy of this petition in a later hand can be found at ARSI, F.G. 733, fols. 147/1-2).

11. ARSI, F.G. 734, 142r (Francesco Sambiasi, Naples, June 6, 1608); ARSI, F.G. 734, fol. 109r (Francesco Sambiasi, Naples, March 20, 1608): "il mio Padre Rettore, et Dio"; ARSI, F.G. 734, fol. 109r; ARSI, F.G. 734, fol. 382/1r (Alfonso Vagnone); ARSI, F.G. 734, fol. 53r (Giulio Aleni, Collegio Romano, December 3, 1607): "mi ha promesso di arricordarsi di me a suo tempo; qual mi pare che sia hora." This petition was written on Francis Xavier's feast day, only the day after Aleni's earlier petition, cited above and dated December 2, 1607. For the Renaissance rhetoric of persuasion (which is enlisted in abundance in these letters), see Irene Fosi, "Rituali della parola: Supplicare, raccomandare e raccomandarsi a Roma nel seicento," in *Forme della comunicazione politica in Europa nei secoli XV–XVIII: Suppliche, gravamina, lettere,* ed. Cecilia Nubola and Andreas Würgler (Berlin and Bologna: Duncker & Humblot/Mulino, 2004), 329-349.

12. ARSI, F.G. 733, fol. 1, no recto or verso (report from the Sicily province about Niccolò Longobardo, September 1589): "virtuoso, zeloso et prudente"; fol. 25/1v (report by Bartolomeo Ricci, April 1592): "par bonissimo per la sanità, fervore et zelo. Questo è il primo anno di sua teologia con proposito che gli dovesse bastar il secondo."

13. For the 1588 nomination of Alfonso Vagnone for the missions, see ARSI, *Ital.* 173, fol. 4 (no recto or verso): Vagnone's name is mentioned in the Milan provincial list of mission candidates, dated between 1593 and 1594, at fols. 4, 5, 6. Three reports from the Milan province about Vagnone are at ARSI, F.G. 733, fol. 24/2 (no recto or verso) (March 30, 1592): "Alfonso Vagnone già philosopho di buon ingegno et giuditio, virtuoso et zelante dell'anime"; ARSI, F.G. 732, fol. 12v ([year only] 1594): "Alfonso Vagnone di buone forze se il catarro non lo fastidisse, assai spirituale"; ARSI, F.G. 732, fol. 389r (no date): "ha talento di conversare et aiutare i prossimi." This last report has no date; however, the age ascribed to Vagnone—twenty-nine—means that the report is from 1597.

14. ARSI, F.G. 733, fol. 25/1v (Longobardo): "Per esser nato nobile tien la madre, et una sorella per monacarse con molto poca sostanza. È vero che in casa sono due altri suoi fratelli, l'uno dei quali col suo valore mantiene tutti"; ARSI, F.G. 733, fol. 24/2 (Vagnone): "Ha madre e sorelle le quali se ben non stanno molto comode per disgratie occorse alla casa, tuttavia

fanno senza di lui et si può sperare che per l'avenire non havranno bisogno di lui."

15. ARSI, *F.G.* 733, fol. 116r (Salerno, January 28, 1601, report to unnamed recipient about Sabatino de Ursis, with postscript signed by Fabio de Fabii); "per amor de Dio, et della Madonna Santissima non manchi agiutarlo, et consolarlo in questo; poiché non può fare niente restando in questo modo, per il desiderio dell'andata"; "sperando grandemente essere agiutato da Vostra Reverenza in questo negotio; et ancora che lo voglia agiutare adesso con il Nostro Padre Generale accioché sia spedito con questi Procuratori di Goa, et de Giappone"; "[postscript:] assai mediocre"; "spirito et maturità"; "ha poca sanità." The two extant reports on Sabatino de Ursis are transcribed and analyzed in Camilla Russell, "Japan, India, or China? The Uncertain Steps of Sabatino de Ursis's Mission to Asia," in *La via dei libri: Sabatino de Ursis* [熊 三 拔] *e le contaminazioni culturali tra Salento e Cina nei secc. XVI–XVII*, ed. Paolo Vincenti (Lecce: L'Idomeneo-Università del Salento, 2020), 41–58. In this study, I conjecture that the main body of the January report may have been written by a Jesuit superior in Salerno, where de Ursis was based at the time, looking after a grammar school. For biographical references to Alberto Laerzio, see Chapter 2. For Francisco Vieira, see *DHCJ* 4: 3951–3952 (J. Ruiz-de-Medina). Procurators Laerzio and Vieira sailed with a large fleet of four ships: there were fifty-nine Jesuits, and a record number of thirty-one Italians (many destined for their missions of Malabar and Japan). Laerzio returned to work on the Malabar coast as provincial (1605–1611), whereupon he complained that less than a dozen of the Jesuits accompanying him, far fewer than he had expected, actually went with him to work at Cochin: Dauril Alden, *The Making of an Enterprise: The Society of Jesus in Portugal, Its Empire and Beyond, 1540–1750* (Stanford, CA: Stanford University Press, 1996), 236.

16. For Fabio de Fabii, see *DHCJ* 2:1367 (G. Mellinato). The entry of Sabatino de Ursis into the Society of Jesus, his vocation, selection, and networks relating to his mission to China, are the subject of the chapter by Davor Antonucci, "Prolegomeni alla biografia di Sabatino de Ursis," in Vincenti, *La via dei libri*, 12–40.

17. ARSI, *F.G.* 733, fol. 129r (report about Sabatino de Ursis, place and author not specified, May 17, 1601): "ricorda a Vostra Paternità che il suo desiderio fa sempre di andare nel Giappone." "Your Paternity" here refers to the Superior General, the only person in the Society to receive this title.

18. ARSI, *F.G.* 733, fol. 140/2 (no recto or verso) (report from Naples, naming, among others, Roberto de Nobili, 1601; signed by Provincial Fabio de Fabii). For de Nobili, see *DBI* 38 (Matteo Sanfilippo) and *DHCJ* 2:1059–1061 (S. Ponnad). A similar short-list report is at ARSI, *F.G.* 733, fols.

259r–261v (including Antonio Giannone, Francesco Eugenio, and Francesco Buzomo [or Buzomi, discussed in Chapter 2]). Not all of those short-listed were successful: Giulio Orsino (at fol. 259r), also discussed in the previous chapter, did not sail.

19. ARSI, *F.G.* 733, fol. 119r (noted on the petition of Giovanni Vincenzo Cafiero): "mostra spirito"; ARSI, *F.G.* 732, fol. 12v (report about Giulio Cesare Curione): "di buoni ingegno e spirito, et forze"; ARSI, *F.G.* 733, fol. 105r (report about Antonio Zumbo): "dopo finito, et difeso il corso di filosofia, ha fatto 4 anni di scola, et al presente studia il primo anno di teologia."

20. ARSI, *F.G.* 733, fol. 25 / 1v (copy) (report about "Geronimo" (Girolamo) De Angelis (where Longobardo is also named): "una sorella maritata et ricca"; "quest'anno ha incominciato la logica et ci riesce molto bene." For the extraordinary biographical details of Girolamo De Angelis (he went to Brazil in 1596 and was later captured by English corsairs; from England, he went to Lisbon in 1599, where he departed once more for the Indies, this time for Japan, where he arrived in 1602), see Maria Iris Gramazio, "Gesuiti italiani missionari in Oriente nel XVI secolo," *AHSI* 66, no. 132 (1997): 275–300 (281); *DBI* 33 (Giuliano Bertuccioli) and *DHCJ* 2:1050 (H. Cieslik).

21. Mario Squadrini's undated petition is at ARSI, *F.G.* 732, fol. 123r (the full transcription reads): "con tutto che me ne conoscessi, et conosca indegno ... desidero con tutto l'affetto del quore di conrispondere" (that is, he desires to rise to the challenge of his calling). Squadrini's undated report is at ARSI, *F.G.* 733, fol. 137r: "chiamato alla conversione degli infedeli."

22. ARSI, *F.G.* 734, fol. 259r (Sambiasi): "Rendo infinite grazie prima a Dio Nostro Signore ch'ha mosso Vostra Paternità a destinarme alla Cina, et poi a Lei ch'ha mandato in effetto questo divino volere."

23. See Liam Matthew Brockey, "Jesuit Missionaries on the Carreira da India in the Sixteenth and Seventeenth Centuries: A Selection of Contemporary Sources," *Itinerario* 31, no. 2 (2007): 111–132; Ulrike Strasser, "Braving the Waves with Francis Xavier: Fear and the Making of Jesuit Manhood," in Strasser, *Missionary Men in the Early Modern World: German Jesuits and Pacific Journeys* (Amsterdam: Amsterdam University Press, 2020), 79–111; the journey east as a rite of passage and the Xaverian model for overcoming the fears, privations, and dangers of the experience of sailing to the Indies are the focus of Strasser's analysis.

24. For Alessandro Valignano's entry record to the S. Andrea novitiate in Rome, see ARSI, *Rom.* 170 ("Novitii in Dom. Prof. admissi 1556–1569"), fol. 84v: "quattro casse di robbe ... una scatolina con una corona d'oro"; "pur d'oro, che pesarano oncie tre et una quarta."

25. Alessandro Valignano to Everard Mercurian, Almeirim, January 7, 1574 (about Francesco Vipera): "non si giudica atto per il bisognio della India," in *Monumenta Missionum Societatis Iesu:* [vol. 21,] *Missiones Orientales: Documenta Indica,* [vol. 9,] *1573–1575,* ed. Josef Wicki, MHSI 94 (Rome: IHSI, 1966), 61. The Roman Francesco Vipera (Bonato) (1542–1605) left for India with the same fleet as that of Valignano on March 21, 1574, and despite Valignano's strenuous espistolary protests. Their ships arrived in Goa in September 1574, but in November he had already departed again to return to Europe; he died in Rome. See Gramazio, "Gesuiti italiani missionari," 296, and much of the correspondence discussing his case, in *Documenta Indica* 9.

26. Alessandro Valignano to Everard Mercurian, Lisbon, January 24, 1574 (about Vincenzo Lenoci): "è stato sempre tenuto da tutti noi per molto pericoloso et travaglioso, se andava alla India, perchè tiene una qualità che, giunto in una città, la rivolta tutta sottosopra, non lascia cosa che vi sia per vedere, entra subito in diverse amicitie et visite di homini et di donne, abbraccia ogni sorte di negotio senza electione," in *Documenta Indica* 9:102. For Lenoci, see *DHCJ* 3:2332–2333 (F. Zubillaga/J. Sáez).

27. Alessandro Valignano to Everard Mercurian, Lisbon, January 24, 1574: "Bartolomeo Vallona è buona persona, sed non habet stabilitatem, et lasciamo, che giudichiamo tutti che non tiene quel che bisognia per l'Indie. Era venuto in tanto timore ... alla fine ... mi dicea che egli si era scordato in Roma di dire che solea patire grande malinconie et affanno di cuore et che, pensando di esser mandato al Giappone et in continue missioni, credeva di star sempre alegro; ma che hora, che gli era detto che si sarebbe stato nelli collegii, gli veniva grande malinconia; et mi disse tante altre fanciullarie, che erano da ridere.... Egli è buona persona, certo, ma non è per l'India," in *Documenta Indica* 9:105. For Bartolomeo Vallone, see Gramazio, "Gesuiti italiani missionari," 298.

28. Alessandro Valignano to Antonio Possevino, Mozambique, August 4, 1574: "Scrissi più volte a V.R. da Lisboa et hora gli scrivo più di dieci milia miglia lontano da quest'isola di Mozambiche, dove per la gratia di N.S. siamo arrivati alli 14 di Luglio 2 navi insieme con tanto prospero tempo et con tanta salute che non l'habbiamo più possuto desiderare" (*Documenta Indica* 9:375).

29. Francesco Palliola's letters are reprinted with an introduction in Pietro Manzi, "Carteggio familiare di P. Francesco Palliola, martire delle Filippine, 1640–1644," *AHSI* 33, no. 65 (1964): 44–89. The original letters are at Nola, Archivio della Famiglia Palliola, "Lettere del Padre Francesco Palliola." This analysis reproduces, with some variations, one section of my chapter, Camilla Russell, "Early Modern Martyrdom and the Society of Jesus in the Sixteenth and Seventeenth Centuries," in *Narratives and*

Representations of Suffering, Failure, and Martyrdom: Early Modern Catholicism Confronting the Adversities of History, ed. Leonardo Cohen (Lisbon: Centro de Estudos de História Religiosa, Universidade Católica Portuguesa, 2020), 67-99 (87-89). For hope in the afterlife, see Manzi, "Carteggio familiare di P. Francesco Palliola," 63: "con indulgenza nella morte"; "tutti li parenti in primo e secondo grado nostro." For Palliola, see, *DHCJ* 3:2959 (J. S. Arcilla).

30. Francesco Palliola to Father Matteo Maiorana, SJ, Seville, May 28, 1642: "il gloriosissimo S. Felice mi ha da far morir in altra maniera"; Francesco Palliola to Antonia Baiana, Cádiz, July 10, 1642: "Alcun[i gior]ni di viaggio sono stati pessimi per il caldo; il sangue... m'oscì dal naso"; "siamo in una nave 42 giesuiti; ad ognuno un poco d'acqua, che cosa è necessario. Iddio benedetto ci mantiene, che non moriamo... sinché piacerà a Sua Divina Maestà chiamarci, con quella morte che li piace, all'altra vita, a dove ci vidremo"; both letters are quoted in Manzi, "Carteggio familiare di P. Francesco Palliola," 77, 83.

31. Francesco Palliola to Antonia Baiana, "from Mindanao, in Iligan" (the Philippines), April 11, 1644: "un piccolo navicciuolo"; "se mosse tanta tempesta de mare che q[uasi] stavamo vicino per dare in terra... con grandissimo timor de altra gente inimica"; "Fu tanto el patir de un giorno particular por viagio de mar, que pansava morir del sangre del vomitar"; "Per fine sape V.S. quanto desidero che sia santa, tanto più quanto per inte[sa] che ha de pregar Dio per me, [c]ome farà, massime quando sto con jente infide[le], no perché temo de morir... che spero al Signor me farà questa gratia, che dii la vita per Sua Divina Maestà." In Manzi, "Carteggio familiare di P. Francesco Palliola," 85-86, 89.

32. Alessandro Valignano to Everard Mercurian, Goa, December 25, 1574: "Fu l'allegrezza di quelli che qui stavano et di quei che venivano tanta che non si può facilmente narrare," in *Documenta Indica* 9:480-533 (484).

33. Alessandro Valignano to Everard Mercurian, Goa, December 25, 1574: "venendo a tempo che stava la Compagnia nella India, per la morte di tanti et più principali, quasi distrutta, et per questo, tanto tra i nostri come fra fuoresteri, fu cognosciuta questa missione per una gratia et providenza di nostro Signor verso questa sua minima Compagnia molto amorosa et molto particolare," in *Documenta Indica* 9:480-533 (484).

34. *Const.* [655]; for the threefold features of the letters, see [655, 673] (dialogic), [673, 676] (factual), and [673, 675] (edifying).

35. Niccolò Longobardo to Claudio Acquaviva, Nanjing, May 14, 1613, ARSI, *Jap. Sin.* 15 II ("Iapon. Epist. 1611-1613"), fol. 270r: "che mi ordinò facesse il Padre Visitatore la mando adesso al nostro Padre Provinciale nel Giappone, conforme all'ordine dato nella *Formula Scribendi*."

36. Alessandro Valignano to Everard Mercurian, Mozambique, August 7, 1574: "et queste lettere saranno triplicate," in *Documenta Indica* 9:427.
37. Alfonso Vagnone to "P. Carlo Torniello, Italia, Milano, Dalla Cina," ARSI, F.G. 730 I ("Missiones Sinenses [1605-1699, Epistolae"]), letter 2 (unfoliated): "La lettera scrittami da Vostra Reverenza di Alessandria a 14 di novembre 1617 mi capitò alle mani questa [e]state di 1619"; Niccolò Longobardo to Claudio Acquaviva, Nanjing, May 14, 1613, ARSI, *Jap. Sin.* 15 II, fol. 269r: "per quel che tocca al governo di questa missione sinica;" "Come può occorrere che le lettere ch'ho scritto a Vostra Paternità negli ultimi tre anni, non gli siano capitate."
38. Matteo Ricci to Ludovico Maselli, Beijing, May 1605 (n.d.): "Non so far fine a questa lettera, ma già sta voltato il foglio e non vi è più luogo" (p. 380); Matteo Ricci to Claudio Acquaviva, Beijing, August 15, 1606: "orfani"; "dar conto a V.P. delle persone e negocii particolari"; "in lettera italiana, ricomanderò al p. Alfonso Vagnoni che lo facci lui, oltre il p. Nicolao Longobardi"; "sono tanti gli negocij di questa corte [Beijing] ... che sto continuamente affocato e non posso ritruovar tempo per scrivere," in *Matteo Ricci: Lettere (1580–1609),* ed. Francesco D'Arelli (Macerata: Quodlibet, 2001), 380, 423–424.
39. Matteo Ricci to Fabio de Fabii, Beijing, May 9, 1605: "Avrà V.R. udite le nove delle nostre cose per lettere di altri che stanno piú presso ai porti del mare, di dove partono le lettere per l'India e per Europa. ... A me povero, posto già vicino ai Tartari, assai lontano non solo dai nostri europei et indici amici, ma anco da compagni [anco] che stanno nella Cina, non mi resta che scrivere, se non volessi ripetere l'istesse cose un anno doppo l'esser là mandate da altri" (D'Arelli, *Matteo Ricci,* 381).
40. Matteo Ricci to Claudio Acquaviva, Beijing, August 15, 1606: "mi duolse non puoco restar questo tutto sopra le mie spalle, et avendo fatto instantia al p. visitatore specialmente per star così ligato, e non poter senza scrupoli governare la casa e le persone per lettere, senza poter vederli in presentia"; "Intorno alle persone di queste residentie, molte di loro né potei vedere di faccia a faccia" (the sense has been rendered that Ricci had limited contact with confreres in mainland China); "ha da tardare più un anno o doi se non fosse più" (D'Arelli, *Matteo Ricci,* 424, 426).
41. Matteo Ricci to Claudio Acquaviva, Beijing, August 15, 1606: (about Vagnone) "doi anni sono sta qua con molta diligentia, studiando lingua e lettere cinesi con assai frutto, et in tutto si è mostrato prudente e virtuoso con grande satisfatione del superiore della casa di Nanchino, dove stette"; (about Longobardo) "tre anni sono fece i voti di coadiutore per ordine del p. visitatore, ma sempre mi parse meritava egli assai più, e che deveria darseli la professione de' quattro voti ... quanto alle altre parti ci fa vergogna ad alcuni che qua stiamo con professione; e se non

fusse questa impresa in terre soggette a Portoghesi, dove mi pare non se deveriano fare facilmente superiori forastieri, parmi che nessuno sta in queste residentie, che meglio governasse questa impresa per il zelo e prudentia e humiltà che tiene" (D'Arelli, *Matteo Ricci*, 426). Matteo Ricci to Fabio de Fabii, Beijing, May 9, 1605: "p. Nicolò Longobardi, grande operario in queste parti, molto divoto di V.R. e copioso nello scrivere" (381).

42. Matteo Ricci to Claudio Acquaviva, Beijing, August 15, 1606: "E qui ho un altro compagno, Diego Pantoja, che doi anni sono mandò il p. visitatore fare la professione di quattro voti, che non ci ha data tanta edificatione... parmi sentirei vergogna esser questo professo, e, questi altri doi, coadiutori [that is, Longobardo and Vagnone]" (D'Arelli, *Matteo Ricci*, 427). For Diego Pantoja (1571–1618), see *DHCJ* 3:2966 (J. Sebes).

43. Matteo Ricci to Claudio Acquaviva, Beijing, August 15, 1606: "qua non habbiamo licentia per stampare, né da V.P. né dagli inquisitori della India.... Parmi che V.P. in questa terra deverebbe dar licentia al superiore della missione, libera per lasciar stampare i libri che i nostri facessero, dipoi di rivisti, e procurarci la licentia degli inquisitori della India, come tiene Giappone"; "I libri che qua facciamo non sono nove cose, ma tutto pigliamo di nostri libri quello che ci viene qui a proposito per la Cina e *solum interponimus iudicium in seligendo*" (D'Arelli, *Matteo Ricci*, 428, 429).

44. Matteo Ricci to Claudio Acquaviva, Beijing, August 15, 1606: "questi quattro o cinque libri miei"; "Delle cose de qua penso posso dire che già sta quasi secura la nostra stata nella Cina, non perché non vi fusse molto che aver paura con questa christianità, che già in quattro parti si va aumentando, cosa sì pericolosa in gente sospitiosa, ma, per quello che intendo della Cina, più sarebbe la loro paura bottarci fora della Cina, che il ritenerci dentro, parendogli che fora gli potessimo fare più male, sapendo tanto della Cina" (D'Arelli, *Matteo Ricci*, 428).

45. Matteo Ricci to Claudio Acquaviva, Beijing, August 15, 1606: "Una delle cose, con le quali più si assecura questa stata è con i libri che ho fatti; e così lo intendono i nostri, gli amici christiani e gentili; perché in essi veggono chiaramente che noi trattiamo di pace e virtude e obedientia ai principi, e non di guerra e ribellione"; "cosa molto particolare della Cina, tutte le sette farsi e dilatarsi più con libri che con sermoni, e gradi molto alti si danno per sole compositioni, senza parlar mezza parola" (D'Arelli, *Matteo Ricci*, 428, 429). At the end of his report (the letter is at pp. 423–429 of the modern Italian edition, quoted here), Ricci apologizes for having written such a long letter, for its genre, the *soli:* "I do not know if I was very long for *soli;* I ask Your Paternity to forgive me [Non so se fui molto lungo per *soli;* V.P. mi perdoni]" (429).

46. Matteo Ricci to Fabio de Fabii, Beijing, May 9, 1605: "Quest'anno posso dire che recevei due di V.R."; "che teneva quivi alcune cose che V.R. mi mandava... perché il corriere non poteva portare altro che lettere"; "E sappi che, non solo io, ma tutti i miei compagni, che solo di fama conoscono V.R., stanno molto edificati della sua carità; ché stando là in Europa sempre tanto occupata ne maggiori offitij della Compagnia, con tutto ciò si ricordi con tanto particulare affetto di un povero suo fratello, bottato qua nel fine del mondo fra infedeli; e ben intendo che le cause che ad altri sono di dimenticanza, come lo sono lo star lontano e fra sconosciuti, ai veri servi di Iddio sono di maggior e più efficace ricordanza. Con questi e simili agiuti viviamo qua contenti in sì tristi luoghi" (D'Arelli, *Matteo Ricci,* 381).
47. ARSI, *F.G.* 733, fol. 1 (no recto or verso): "virtuoso, zeloso et prudente." A longer study of Longobardo than the brief biographical entries mentioned above is Monica Juneja, Kim Siebenhüner, and Ronnie Po-chia Hsia, "Christian Conversion in Late Ming China: Niccolò Longobardo and Shandong," *Medieval History Journal* 12, no. 2 (2009): 275-301.
48. Niccolò Longobardo, "Copia d'una lettera del P. Nicolò Longobardi, scritta nel 1598, dalla Cina...," in *Copia d'una breve relatione della Christianità di Giappone...* (Venice, 1601), 39-72; "si può comparare con le più illustri, che si siano fatte fin'hora in queste parti dell'India, per le molte e molto rare qualità, che ha questa natione sopra tutti gli altri gentili" (40); "questo vastissimo regno della Cina" (39); "& è appunto come in Italia la lingua Romana corteggiana, che s'intende in tutti i regni d'Italia" (48); "Sono gli huomini molto industriosi e conseguentemente per lo più ricchi, e così anche il vivere a molto buon mercato" (49); "di me in particolare posso dire, che con quest'aria, studi, gente, e simili, sento tale convenienza e facilità, che mi pare d'essere in mezzo d'Italia" (39), and partly quoted in my essay, Camilla Russell, "Imagining the 'Indies': Italian Jesuit Petitions for the Overseas Missions at the Turn of the Seventeenth Century," in *L'Europa divisa e i Nuovi Mondi. Per Adriano Prosperi,* ed. Massimo Donattini, Giuseppe Marcocci, and Stefania Pastore, 3 vols. (Pisa: Edizioni della Normale, 2011), 2:179-189 (182).
49. Niccolò Longobardo to Claudio Acquaviva, Nanjing, May 14, 1613, ARSI, *Jap. Sin.* 15 II, fol. 269r: "poiché la mira principale e primaria l'havevamo posta nella conversione."
50. Longobardo to Acquaviva, May 14, 1613, ARSI, *Jap. Sin.* 15 II, fol. 269r-v: "nel mezzo della Christianità Europea"; "Sonno di bello ingegno e avvisati, prudenti e modesti, capaci e affettionati alle cose del spirito, tengono grande soggettione e rispetto verso i Padri, molto osservanti delle Regole, zelosi e applicati alla Conversione"; "fanno le sue processioni, frequentano le Prediche e sacramenti giusto come nel cuore di Portogallo."

51. Matteo Ricci provides an account of de Ursis, Valignano, and the China mission at the time in a letter to Claudio Acquaviva, Beijing, August 15, 1606: D'Arelli, *Matteo Ricci,* esp. 426–427.
52. Sabatino de Ursis to Portugal assistant João Álvares, Cambala [Beijing], August 23, 1608, ARSI, *Jap. Sin.* 14 II ("Iapon. Epist. 1600-1610") (the entire letter is at fols. 316r-v [with address on p. 317r-v]), fol. 316r: "sapendo quanto Vostra Reverenza desidera nove di queste parti... come infino adesso mi sono ritrovato (possiamo dire) di camino, non stando in loco determinato, non l'ho fatto, adesso... determinai scrivere queste due righe per dar la nova a Vostra Reverenza." The letter is discussed in Brockey, *Journey to the East,* 250.
53. ARSI, *Jap. Sin.* 14 II, fol. 316r (de Ursis to Álvares): "nel negociare l'entrare li Padri nella Cina, come nel pratticare coi Cinesi"; "il Padre Matteo Ricci, he già vecchio consumato già con tanti travagli, he grande il credito, e fama che tiene in tutto il Regno."
54. ARSI, *Jap. Sin.* 14 II, fol. 316r (de Ursis to Álvares): "questi tre... Padri studiano le lettere, e lingua Cinese con il Maestro Cinese già Christiano, che ogni giorno viene in nostra casa a leggere alli Padri, dalli quali si spera grande servitio di Nostro Signore essendo tutti di bonissima habilità."
55. ARSI, *Jap. Sin.* 14 II, fol. 316v (de Ursis to Álvares): "la Cina stava più piccola de qual che loro pensano, che gliè imaginare la Cina essere il mondo tutto"; "andassimo ambedue nel palazzo nel quale fummo ricevuti con molta cortesia, ci mostronno tutto il Palazzo, e altre cose, come Giardini, Case de Ucelli, Animali, lagune, e stagni pieni di pesci."
56. ARSI, *Jap. Sin.* 14 II, fol. 316v (de Ursis to Álvares): "Io in arrivando in questa casa incominciai a studiare la lingua e le lettere Cinesi con il Padre Matteo Ricci; la difficoltà delle lettere e lingua non è tanta quanto io imaginava; perché tutta la difficoltà consiste nella varietà della voce, essendo che con una sillaba v.g. Pa, chiamano più di ducento lettere tutte diverse, e che significano diverse cose... tutta la difficoltà consiste nel parlare... li nostri Padri imparano bene."
57. ARSI, *Jap. Sin.* 14 II, fol. 316v (de Ursis to Álvares). The full list of words and their explanations are as follows: "pā 鈀 carro de guerra (wagon of war); pà 把 pigliare (take); pá 霸 tiranno (tyrant); pā 捌 otto (eight); pâ 琶 viola (this the second character in pipa 琵琶, a classical Chinese instrument); pā 肥 ponte di legno (wooden bridge); pà 罷 sufficiente (sufficient) pá 怕 paura (fear); pă 汃 mormorio dell'acqua (a sound made by water)." My thanks to Daniel Canaris for his assistance with this part of the letter.
58. ARSI, *Jap. Sin.* 14 II, fol. 316v (de Ursis to Álvares): "l'istesso domando a Vostra Reverenza voglia fare con il Padre Fabio de Fabii, mio Maestro de Novitii, pregandolo mi voglia raccomandare al Signore, perché spero

che se per suo mezzo fui molte volte agiutato in Roma stando nel mezzo di tanti servi del Signore a S. Andrea; molto più sarò adesso, che la necessità, e il pericolo gliè maggiore; non scrivo adesso... con altra occasione lo farò."
59. Matteo Ricci to Ludovico Maselli, Beijing, May 1605 (n.d.): "molto tempo è che intendo quanto più agiuto ci dà christiani puochi e buoni che molti e imperfetti; e così li facciamo con molto essame e delecto [c]athechizandosi molto bene"; (the following sets out the full account of the convert's dream:) "Mi occorsero questi anni molte cose che scrivere di questi puochi christiani, ma non so se è bene scriver tanto che non paia volere ingrandire le nostre cose, se bene son certo che lo saprà per lettere di altri che penso le notò per scriverle. Uno fu che, non avendo mai udito parlare della Sma. Trinità che perché si facesse christiano, vide in sogno tre cappelle grandi di un tempio et in quella del mezzo una figura che gli dissero esser di Dio Padre; nell'altra un'altra figura, che gli dissero esser de Dio Figliuolo, nella terza non vide nessuna figura. Per tanto egli fece reverentia alle due prime, e quando si fece christiano riconobbe la dichiaratione del sogno" (D'Arelli, *Matteo Ricci*, 373, 375).
60. Matteo Ricci to Ludovico Maselli, Beijing, May 1605 (n.d.): "la Madonna con il Bambino nelle braccia, vestita di bianco" (D'Arelli, *Matteo Ricci*, 375). Dreams were a fundamental part of the evangelization and conversion process in China for a number of reasons connected to both sets of protagonists' European and Chinese cultures, on which see António Vitor Ribeiro, "Dreams, Visions and a Taoist-Christian 'Saint' in the Seventeenth-Century Jesuit Records of the China Mission," *AHSI* 88, no. 175 (2019): 103–133.
61. Matteo Ricci to Ludovico Maselli, Beijing, May 1605 (n.d.): "Questo Natale... in luogo della imagine del Salvatore... una imagine nova della Madonna di san Luca con il Bambino nelle braccia, pinto molto bene d'un giovane che sta in casa [G. Niva], che imparò in Giappone dal nostro p. Giovan Nicolò [Cola], e fu maraviglioso il contento che tutti hebbero con essa" (D'Arelli, *Matteo Ricci*, 373). For the artist Giovanni Cola (or Nicolao) (c. 1588–1626), who set up schools of art in Japan and was based mainly in Nagasaki and Arima before the definitive expulsion of all religious from Japan in 1614 (he died in Macao), see Gramazio, "Gesuiti italiani missionary," 280; *DHCJ* 1:838–839 (J. Ruiz-de-Medina).
62. Matteo Ricci to João Álvares, Beijing, May 12, 1605: "facciame V.R. carità di comunicare tutto questo con il p. Clavio, e dicali che già molti e molti Cinesi sanno il nome del p. Clavio" (D'Arelli, *Matteo Ricci*, 407). For Christopher Clavius (1537/1538–1612), the celebrated mathematician and astronomer, originally from Upper Franconia, who trained at Coimbra and taught at the Collegio Romano, see *DHCJ* 1:825 (F. A. Homann).

63. Filippo De Marini to Giovanni Luigi Confalonieri, in Tonkin (northern Vietnam, sent by the "seconda via [second way]"), no day or month (the year, 1654, is in a different hand, with notes about the contents, probably written after its arrival in Rome), ARSI, F.G. 721 II/IX ("Missione nel Tonchino"), fol. 78r: "chi non si parte già santo di Europa, s'inganna se crede, che arrivando qua, si farà qua santo"; fol. 78v: "Il nostro Christoforo Ferreira Provinciale che tanti anni fa posto al supplicio rinegò onde fu lasciato in sua libertà ha due anni che dicono sii morto Martire l'anno passato seppimo questa nuova, noi habbiamo fatto diligenza di saperla..." For biographical overviews of Giovanni Filippo De Marini, see *DBI* 38 (Giuliano Bertuccioli): De Marini was one of the few missionaries who returned to Europe (1661–1666), where he wrote the very successful volume on the region, *Delle missioni de' padri della Compagnia di Giesù nella provincia del Giappone, e particolarmente di quella di Tumkino: Libri cinque* (Rome, 1663). Many of his known difficulties in the region were at the hands of other missionaries, and one of his works was placed on the index of prohibited books. He was back in Macao in late 1666; in 1680, he was appointed visitor to Japan (that is, in its exiled state, based on Macao) and China. My thanks to Daniel Canaris for his advice about De Marini. For Cristóvão Ferreira, see Alden, *The Making of an Enterprise,* 136; *DHCJ* 2:1407–1408 (H. Cieslik).

64. Edward W. Said, *Orientalism* (New York: Pantheon, 1978).

65. Alfonso Vagnone to Carlo Torniello, Macao, March 25, 1619, ARSI, F.G. 730 I [unfoliated], letter 2: "contro la mia tenera cristianità"; "si viddero molti prodigi del cielo e della terra, e di tutti comparvero due comete grandi di straordinaria grandezza."

66. ARSI, F.G. 730 I [unfoliated], letter 2 (Vagnone to Torniello): "l'allegrezza che mi caggiona il sapere lo stato di quei miei carissimi Padri e fratelli, già che in questa vita non mi resta speranza di rivederli"; "mi sta stampato nella memoria... che di tutti tengo molto più che dei miei propri parenti"; (paraphrased in the text) "Padre Giacomo Filippo suo fratello... non ha mai trovato un'hora di ozio per scrivermi quattro parole. Vostra Reverenza glie lo dica, e faccia parte di questa mia"; "Quando si offrirà occasione comoda Vostra Reverenza mi mandi alcuni puochi christalli miniati di Milano, e li potrà inviare Vostra Reverenza al Padre Assistente di Portogallo in Roma, il quale ogni anno he solito mandarci tutto quello che vuole a Lisbona a tempo che partono le navi per l'India"; "E con questo finisco abbracciandolo col cuore finché ci rivediamo in Cielo."

67. Filippo De Marini to Giovanni Luigi Confalonieri, in Tonkin, n.d., ARSI, F.G. 721 II/IX, fol. 78v (quoting the full relevant section of the letter): "Non scrivo al Padre Giovanni Nicolò Marini mio fratello, supplico a Vostra Reverenza gli dii nuove mie; ho pure un altro fratello che entrò

nella Compagnia in Messina l'anno 1646 ... era fiacco non so se è vivo ... desidero che sappino nuove mie."
68. Alessandro Valignano to Antonio Possevino, Mozambique, August 4, 1574: "narra dell'India cose et verisimile et conforme a quel che gl'altri me dicono et senza monstrar passion," in *Documenta Indica* 9:376. For Ribera and Vallareggio, see more details in Chapter 4.
69. Donald F. Lach, *Asia in the Making of Europe*, 3 vols. (Chicago: Chicago University Press, 1965–1993), vol. 1, bk. 1, 261, 323–328, 430.
70. Luís Frois, *Relatione della gloriosa morte di XXVI. posti in croce per commandamento del Re di Giappone, alli 5 di Febraio 1597 ... Mandata dal P. Luigi Frois alli 15 Marzo al R. P. Claudio Acquaviva Generale ...* (Bologna, 1599), 7: "solamente scriverò quello che ho saputo da persone ... degne di fede, che à bocca, & per lettere ne hanno data certa, & distinta informatione di tutto quello, che qui dirò"; "gran consolatione, & edificatione, avvenuti in questa persecutione."

4. ON THE ITALIAN HOME FRONT

1. *Sp. Ex.* [135], [322].
2. Movement from Italy to other parts of Europe occasionally appears in the documents. See, for example, ARSI, *Rom.* 78b, fol. 106r: "List of those who could go to Germany, made doctors of Theology (Lista di quelli che potranno andare in Germania fatti dottori in Theologia [undated, 1560s])." In line with the book's aims, the analysis in this chapter focuses on the immediate and contemporary objectives of the documents' authors; with a few exceptions, it does not include such works as the summative and more literary *Relationi* and *Quadrimestri,* or the retrospectively written autobiographies and *Vitae.*
3. Edmond Lamalle, "L'Archivio di un grande Ordine religioso: L'Archivio Generale della Compagnia di Gesù," *Archiva Ecclesiae* 24/25, no. 1 (1981–1982): 89–120 (97). The wealth of archival documents for the first three decades is reflected in the published sources that are particularly plentiful for those decades, also because of the first years' obvious historical significance—for example, *Epistolae mixtae ex variis Europae locis ab anno 1537 a.d. 1556 scriptae ...*, 5 vols. (Madrid: A. Avraial, R. Fortanet, 1898–1901), and Mario Scaduto, *Storia della Compagnia di Gesù in Italia: L'Epoca di Giacomo Lainez, 1556–1565; Il governo* [vol. 3]; *L'azione* [vol. 4]; *L'opera di Francesco Borgia 1565–1572* [vol. 5] (Rome: La civiltà cattolica, 1964, 1974, 1992).
4. ARSI, *Ital.* 107–165 ("Epist. Italiae"), with an alphabetical index by author name at *Ital.* 165A. For a study of how the system worked, see Mario Scaduto, "La corrispondenza dei primi Gesuiti e le poste italiane," *AHSI* 19, nos. 37–38 (1950): 237–253; Paul Nelles, "Jesuit Letters," in *The Oxford Handbook of the Jesuits,* ed. Ines G. Županov (New York: Oxford University

Press, 2019), 44-72. The "Jesuit Glossary" provides the following entry: "Substitutus (Substit.): the secretary who provides the Society's assistants with summaries of the contents of correspondence sent to the superior general (except for those letters marked *soli*, destined for the general alone). Subsequently, it is this secretary's task to prepare a summary of the reply, which is written in the general's register of correspondence, in accordance with the period's official letter-writing practices. See *Inst. S.I.*, vol. 3, p. 718." Wiktor Gramatowski, "Jesuit Glossary: Guide to Understanding the Documents," trans. Camilla Russell (orig. in Italian, 1992), Archivum Romanum Societatis Iesu (2014), http://www.sjweb.info/arsi/documents/glossary.pdf.

5. Flavio Rurale, "Un'identità forte? A proposito di tre studi recenti sulla Compagnia di Gesù," in *Anatomia di un corpo religioso: L'identità dei gesuiti in età moderna; Annali di storia dell'esegesi* 19, no. 2, ed. Franco Motta (2002): 359. For the Society's "apostolic spirituality" and its historiography, see John W. O'Malley and Timothy O'Brien, "The Twentieth-Century Construction of Ignatian Spirituality: A Sketch," *Studies in the Spirituality of Jesuits* 52, no. 3 (2020): 2-40 (esp. 20).

6. *The Formula of the Institute, Const.* [3]. For the larger context of preaching, print culture, and other religious ministries in Tridentine Italy, see Emily Michelson, *The Pulpit and the Press in Reformation Italy* (Cambridge, MA: Harvard University Press, 2013); for Jesuits and other new religious orders, see 141-144; for mendicant and diocesan ministries in the generation after Trent, especially preaching, see 140-171. For Jesuit ministries, also known as apostolates, see John W. O'Malley, *The First Jesuits* (Cambridge, MA: Harvard University Press, 1993): much of the book is structured around the ministries. For a useful case study of one of these ministries, see Paul V. Murphy, "'Your Indies:' The Jesuit Mission at the *Santa Casa di Loreto* in the Sixteenth Century," in *The Renaissance in the Streets, Schools, and Studies: Essays in Honour of Paul F. Grendler*, ed. Konrad Eisenbichler and Nicholas Terpstra (Toronto: Centre for Reformation and Renaissance Studies, 2008), 210-227 (esp. 219-221). Murphy's discussion on the Jesuit presence at the Marian shrine of Loreto shows how the Jesuits' style of offering confession and penance with consolatory rather than disciplinary intent in the case of Loreto suited the many pilgrims who were seeking reconciliation with the Catholic Church, through absolution from "Protestant heresy" in the safety of the confessional, a privilege granted them by Julius III, who sent the Jesuits to Loreto in the first place. For a comprehensive study of this license to absolve heretics in confession rather than through diocesan tribunals or the Congregation of the Holy Office, see Jessica M. Dalton, *Between Popes, Inquisitors, and Princes: How the First Jesuits Negotiated Religious Crisis in Early Modern Italy*

(Leiden: Brill, 2020). Another central and understudied apostolate was prison ministry, on which see Frank Sobiech, *Jesuit Prison Ministry in the Witch Trials of the Holy Roman Empire: Friedrich Spee SJ and His Cautio Criminalis (1631)* (Rome: IHSI, 2019).

7. *Const.* parts 1–5 (steps to incorporation); *Const.* parts 6–10 (membership, apostolates, and governance). On becoming incorporated into the Society, members wrote a brief signed and dated statement that included promising obedience to God, the Virgin Mary, the (named) superior general, and the superiors of the Society, and stating the place where the vows were taken. The documentary records pertaining to members' final vows are valuable and help establish the timelines and grade levels of members. While this book has not included a detailed discussion of the rich records (nor indeed does there exist to date a dedicated analysis of them), they certainly warrant further attention. From the period covered by this book for the Italian Assistancy, see, for example, statements for the professed with three vows, at ARSI, *Ital.* 34, "Ass. Italiae professi 3 votorum 1582–1647."

8. As Lamalle, "L'Archivio di un grande Ordine religioso," 100, remarked, "St. Ignatius cared about this very much; or rather, he desired to see his catalogue updated every three months, to keep an eye on the mirror of available personnel (S. Ignazio ci teneva moltissimo; anzi desiderava veder il suo catalogo aggiornato ogni tre mesi, per conservare sott'occhio lo specchio del personale disponibile)"; for this directive, see *Const.* [676].

9. The introduction to this book discusses the mechanics of this dynamic as well as some historiographical features.

10. From the Jesuit perspective, see the relevant discussion in Antonio M. de Aldama, *The Constitutions of the Society of Jesus: An Introductory Commentary on the Constitutions,* trans. Aloysius J. Owen (1979; repr., Rome: Centrum Ignatianum Spiritualitatis; St. Louis: Institute of Jesuit Sources, 1989), 218–224, which also explores the famous Ignatian simile of obedience being like a lifeless body, "as though they would be a corpse (*perinde ac cadaver*)" [223]. For modern historical (and non-Jesuit) scholarly treatments, see the essays in Antonella Romano, ed., *Rome et la science moderne: Entre Renaissance et Lumières' études réunies par Antonella Romano* (Rome: École française de Rome, 2008), many of which present and illustrate the idea and practice of negotiated obedience in the religious, and especially Jesuit, sphere; Silvia Mostaccio, "'Perinde ac si cadaver essent': The Jesuits from a Comparative Perspective; The Tension between Obedience and *Prepresentar* in the Legal Documents of Religious Orders," in Mostaccio, *Early Modern Jesuits between Obedience and Conscience during the Generalate of Claudio Acquaviva (1581–1615)* (Aldershot, UK: Ashgate, 2014),

55-81; Markus Friedrich, "Ignatius's Governing and Administrating the Society of Jesus," in *A Companion to Ignatius of Loyola: Life, Writing, Spirituality, Influence,* ed. Robert A. Maryks (Leiden: Brill, 2014), 123-141 (133). My choice of term is discussed in the Introduction.
11. *Sp. Ex.* [351].
12. *Sp. Ex.* [351], [352], [365].
13. *Sp. Ex.* [370], [351], [353].
14. *General Examen, Const.* [116].
15. *General Examen, Const.* [131].
16. *Const.* [543], [627], discussed in de Aldama, *The Constitutions of the Society of Jesus,* 254-256. These reflections pertain to the book's historical focus on the Society's first century and do not extend to the many more themes, and extensive scholarship, concerning the foundational texts developed in other disciplines, such as theology and Ignatian spirituality.
17. Juan Huarte de San Juan's *Examen de ingenios para las ciencias* (1575), together with Gómez Pereira's *Antoniana Margarita* (1554) and Miguel Sabuco's *New Philosophy* (1587), were influential works of the Spanish Renaissance, including for the Society. My thanks to Dilwyn Knox for this research lead. See also Cristiano Casalini, "Discerning Skills: Psychological Insight at the Core of Jesuit Identity," in *Exploring Jesuit Distinctiveness: Interdisciplinary Perspectives on Ways of Proceeding within the Society of Jesus,* ed. Robert A. Maryks (Leiden: Brill, 2016), 189-211.
18. Juan Huarte de San Juan, *Examen de ingenios para las ciencias,* ed. Esteban Torre (Madrid: Editora Nacional, 1976), 61: "Y, porque no errase en elegir la que a su natural estaba mejor, había de haber diputados en la república, hombres de gran prudencia y saber, que en la tierna edad descubriesen a cada uno su ingenio, haciéndole estudiar por fuerza la ciencia que le convenía, y no dejarlo a su elección."
19. Cristiano Casalini, "Fertile Wit: The (Unwritten) Doctrines of Juan Huarte de San Juan and Chomsky's Intuition," *History of Education and Children's Literature* 7, no. 1 (2012): 575-587. Charles Keenan, "Possevino, Antonio," in *The Cambridge Encyclopedia of the Jesuits,* ed. Thomas Worcester (New York: Cambridge University Press, 2017), 634-635, provides a brief outline of Possevino's *Bibliotheca;* on Possevino and Zara, in relation to Huarte, see Cristiano Casalini, "Disputa sugli ingegni: L'educazione dell'individuo in Huarte, Possevino, Persio e altri," *Educazione: Giornale di pedagogia critica* 1, no. 1 (2012): 29-51.
20. See the Introduction to this book for the relevant historiography.
21. My thanks to Paul Begheyn, SJ, for his insights about the Society's likely appeal to the young men studied here for the prospect of working collectively on a shared enterprise that to their eyes would have carried noble and admirable objectives. Ulrike Strasser outlines the interlocking social,

cultural, and gender factors that intersected with the highly gendered European expansion beyond its borders and that, for the Jesuit part in this history, gave rise to a new and distinct "missionary masculinity" that impacted non-European and European cultures alike (Strasser, *Missionary Men in the Early Modern World: German Jesuits and Pacific Journeys* [Amsterdam: University of Amsterdam Press, 2020], 19).
22. *Sp. Ex.* [326], [327].
23. Anne J. Cruz, "Willing Desire: Luisa de Carvajal y Mendoza and Feminine Subjectivity," in *Power and Gender in Renaissance Spain: Eight Women of the Mendoza Family, 1450–1650,* ed. Helen Nader (Champaign-Urbana: University of Illinois Press, 2004), 177–193 (on desire and power, 178–180; on female resistance and negotiation in spheres ordinarily dominated by men, 178). After an abusive childhood recorded in her autobiography, and in return for her loyalty and support of the Society (she donated her large inheritance to the Society), Carvajal was permitted by the Jesuits to travel to England for the reconversion of Anglicans to Catholicism, only to die shortly after her imprisonment for her work (177–178). On martyrdom as a manifestation of agency, see 188.
24. These questions are discussed in Ruth Mazo Karras, *From Boys to Men: Formations of Masculinity in Late Medieval Europe* (Philadelphia: University of Pennsylvania Press, 2003), 160–162. Similarly, Emanuel Buttigieg, *Nobility, Faith, and Masculinity: The Hospitaller Knights of Malta, c. 1580–1700* (London: Continuum, 2011), 17, emphasizes that the celibate religious life was not incompatible with the masculine ideals of physical and military prowess. For the Jesuits specifically, see Ulrike Strasser, "Copies with Souls: The Late Seventeenth-Century Marianas Martyrs, Francis Xavier, and the Question of Clerical Reproduction," *Journal of Jesuit Studies* 2, no. 4 (2015): 558–585.
25. John Carmi Parsons found this in his study of instances of extraordinary and outlandish behavior among very young married noblewomen that was normalized on account of their married and high social status, so that their ages were subordinated to their married status; this status identified them as women, not the girls they in fact were. Apparently reliable categories—"chronological age, biological capacity, social status, [and] social behavior"—were observed to be fluid and contingent on how each characteristic interacted with the other in the life of an individual: John Carmi Parsons, "The Medieval Aristocratic Teenaged Female: Adolescent or Adult?," in *The Premodern Teenager: Youth in Society, 1150–1650,* ed. Konrad Eisenbichler (Toronto: Centre for Reformation and Renaissance Studies, 2002), 311–321 (see esp. 311–313, 315, 319). Carmi Parsons observes, "We might well ask whether women's ages were perhaps more likely to be reckoned relationally than chronologically" (315).

26. Francesco Palmio to Diego Laínez, Bologna, October 4, 1564, ARSI, *Ital.* 125 ("Epist. Italiae 1564–1565"), fol. 95r (about Giacomo Croce): "pareva impossibile che uno giovanotto come lui haverne potuto fare una oratione sì bella . . . ha monstrato che, se bene non ha barba in viso che non gli mancha nel cervello"; Benedetto Palmio to Diego Laínez, Forlì, August 22, 1561, ARSI, *Ital.* 118 ("Epist. Italiae 1561 II"), 210r: "nella bontà, et nella maturità dei costumi, so con queste conditioni se fussi barba sapia Vostra Reverenza che importarebbe assai"; "se, con queste condizioni, li fusse barba . . . importarebbe assai," both partially quoted in Scaduto, *Storia della Compagnia*, 4:459, who argues that the issue in these letters was the physical beard, not age. I argue that the youth of these Jesuits is what is meant here, transmitted visually through the lack of a beard. For medieval views on the various ages of males, mostly carried through to the early modern era, see Mazo Karras, *From Boys to Men*, 12–17. For Francesco Palmio, who was from a noble family and whose many and highly visible activities for the Society centered around Bologna, see *DHCJ* 3:2693. For his younger brother, Benedetto Palmio, see *DHCJ* 3:2692–2693 (M. Zanfredini): he entered the Society in 1546 and cofounded the first Jesuit college in Messina, and then in Padua. During his term as Lombardy provincial (1559–1565), he was invited to preach in Milan by Carlo Borromeo. Under Superiors General Laínez and Mercurian, he served as Italy assistant.
27. Peter J. Togni, "Novices in the Early Society of Jesus: Antonio Valentino, S.J., and the Novitiate at Novellara, Italy," in *Spirit, Style, Story: Essays Honoring John W. Padburg, S.J.*, ed. Thomas M. Lucas (Chicago: Loyola Press, 2002), 227–267 (231).
28. *Const.* [757] stipulates that provincials be appointed, as a guideline, for three years, so there was quite a regular turnover of personnel and the need for current information about them.
29. Chapter 1 introduces this genre of Jesuit writing as well as its historiography. See also Gramatowski, "Jesuit Glossary." For the "Informationes" about Jesuits in Venice, see ARSI, *Ven.* 36 ("Cat. Trien. 1573").
30. ARSI, *Ital.* 3 ("Ass. Italiae Gradus 1542–1582"). These had the purpose of identifying members according to their grade, evolving into separate records for each grade, for example, ARSI, *Ital.* 4 ("Ass. Italiae Profes. 4 Votor. 1581–1599").
31. ARSI, *Rom.* 78b ("Cat. antiquiss. Ital. 1546–1577 [et varia usque ad 1600]"), fol. 4r; see also ARSI, *Rom.* 78c ("Cat. Dom. Prof. Rom. 1549–1730").
32. ARSI, *Rom.* 78b, fols 7r–8v. Founded in 1551, the Collegio Romano had 112 members by 1555, from faculty to students: O'Malley, *The First Jesuits*, 54.
33. ARSI, *Rom.* 78c; ARSI, *Rom.* 78b, fols. 163r–164v: "Informatione de la qualità delli padri et fratelli di Loreto numero 42."
34. ARSI, *Rom.* 78c, fol. 20 (reproductions of original, with data only on recto); ARSI, *Rom.* 78c, fol. 21; "Padre Francesco Torres di anni 65 et forse più,

entrò in Roma del 67 è Dottor Teologo, Professo di 4 voti doppo 2 anni della sua entrata sano et mediocremente gagliardo per gli anni suoi"; ARSI, *Rom.* 78c, fol. 21: "Padre Lodovico Corbinelli di anni 52 entrò in Roma del 66 ha tre voti solenni, Confessore, mal sano et fiacco molto. ("aged 52, entered the Society in Rome in 1566; he has three solemn vows, is a confessor, with poor health and very weak").

35. ARSI, *Rom.* 78c, fol. 24: "è falegname et ha habilità per ogni officio, sano et gagliardo"; ARSI, *Rom.* 78c, fol. 29: "non ha ancora fatti i voti di coadiutore temporale semplici fa la dispensa et è buono per ogni officio, sano et forte"; ARSI, *Rom.* 78c, fol. 30: "sta alla cucina ... ha buona mano da scrivere perche fu notaro."

36. ARSI, *Rom.* 57 ("Romana Catal. Triennal. 1636–1639"): Giovanni Raffaele de Ferraris is mentioned in the 1639 first catalogue of the Collegio Romano at fol. 155v; then in the first catalogue of the "House of Probation" at S. Andrea, at fol. 168v; in the respective second catalogues, at fol. 213r ("Est satis boni ingenii, iudicii, prudentiae, atque experientiae: bene profecit in litteris: complexionis est sanguineae, atque cholericae: talentum habere videtur ad gubernandum"), and fol. 224v.

37. ARSI, *Ven.* 36, fol. 42r, "Giovanni Battista Viola Parmigiano d'anni 56, entrò nella Compagnia in Roma sono anni 32, fece professione di 4 voti in Parigi l'anno 1550 ... è maestro in Arti, et ha studiato Theologia alcuni anni, in Francia è stato Rettor del Collegio di Parigi, et de Biglione, in Italia ha havuto cura d'alcuni Collegii. Ha talento di governare, adesso attende alle confessioni."

38. ARSI, *Ven.* 36, fol. 43r (quoting the full relevant passage): "Padre Francesco Palmio Parmigiano d'anni 54 entrò in Bologna nella Compagnia sono anni 23 fece professione di 3 voti l'anno 1568 il primo di gennaio in Mano dell'Illustrissimo Cardinal Paleotti, ha governato il Collegio di Bologna 20 anni con satisfattione, ha predicato confessato, et aiutato molti Vescovi di quella città in molte opere per riforma della città et Diocesi." Francesco Palmio was connected to Gabriele Paleotti (1522–1597; cardinal, 1565; bishop of Bologna, 1567; archbishop from 1582), who requested him as visitor of his diocese in Bologna.

39. Catalogue information from ARSI, *Ven.* 36: (fol. 44r, and quoted passage at fol. 45v) "è di cervello gagliardo"; (fol. 46r) "è poco sano, et di poco talento" (this is one of the few criticisms in these catalogues of the Jesuit priests); (fol. 49v) "è stato da tre anni fuori dalla Compagnia, et si fece sacerdote, fu riaccettato dal Padre Leonetto"; see fols. 50v–51v for information about the sixteen priests who entered the Society from another congregation; (fol. 50v) "Padre Agostino Mutio Bergamasco d'anni 34 ... è dottor di Filosofia, et di legge, studiato Theologia, è d'acuto ingegno, per predicare, leggere, et essortare ha bisogno di freno."

40. ARSI, *Ven.* 36, fol. 53r: "Giovanni Botero dal Bene di Piedmonte ... d'anni 29 entrò nella Compagnia in Roma sono 14 anni, ha studiato il corso et

letto in Francia, et in Italia in diversi Collegii Rettorica, è buon Poeta, et ha buon Ingegno, studia Theologia, et legge ultima lectione di Rettorica, per legger et predicare." In the margin next to this entry, "sacerdote" is indicated.
41. ARSI, *Ven.* 36 (fol. 55r, about Giovanni Parodi from Genoa): "legge grammatica circa due anni poco talento, et Ingegno per altro"; (fol. 55r) "intende poco, per casi di conscientia, et confessare"; (fol. 55v) "Lutio de' Lorenzi Parmigiano... ha buon ingegno ma per esser troppo timido non riesce in leggere"; (fol. 56r, about Antonio Marzaro) "è duro di cervello et è stato inconstante nella Vocatione"; (fol. 54r, about Marcantonio del Bose) "è inquieto, et duro di cervello, si tiene in offitii bassi per aiutarlo"; (fol. 55v) "buon talento per predicar et governar" (fol. 55v).
42. ARSI, *Ven.* 36, fol. 59r: "Per ogni offitio poco sano"; "Alesso d'Argento Spoletino d'anni 34 entrò in Roma nella compagnia sono 18 anni patisce dolore di testa et d'humori malinconici"; "Clemente Persico... per ogni sorte di fatica è buono."
43. Claudio Acquaviva to Cesare de Vico, February 18, 1592, ARSI, *F.G.* 286 ("Lettere Dal 1585 al 1602"), unpaginated, quoting the complete relevant passage: "Ho veduto la lettera de Vostra Reverenza per conto de conti et però che mi è gran confusione per la moltiplicationi di tante partite sarà bene fuggir questo inconveniente con lasciar detta prattica per [illeg.]." Lamalle, "L'Archivio di un grande Ordine religioso," 97–98.
44. Togni, "Novices in the Early Society," 231.
45. Benedetto Palmio to Diego Laínez, Padua [n.d., but a margin annotation states "late 1558"], ARSI, *Ital.* 111 ("Epist. Italiae 1558 I"), fol. 381v: "bonissimo, ma non tanto per questo... quanto al governo Provinciale."
46. Ottaviano Cesari to Ignatius of Loyola, Naples, March 21, 1556: "come havevo ordine da V.R.P.... per essermi allhora levato da letto"; "molto fiacco" (*Epistolae mixtae,* 5:263); Francesco Palmio to Juan Alfonso de Polanco, Bologna, August 13, 1551: "Del resto tutti in casa stiamo bene, e se attende a studiare con diligentia. Occupationi al solito haviamo, e molto più, e speramo molto frutto.... Post scripta. V.R. me perdoni se questa è male scritta. L'occupationi ne sono state caggione" (*Epistolae mixtae,* 5:727–728).
47. Niccolò Lancillotto to Ignatius of Loyola, Quilón, January 11, 1551: "L'anno passato, scrissi a V.R. come stavano partiti et divisi, in questa vigna del Signor, li Padri della Compagnia, et come tutti facevan gra[n] frutto. Non vi è, al presente, alcuna cosa mutata, si non che tutti si affatigano nelli medesimi luochi quanto possono.... Intrare nelle cose particulare di lui [Paolo Battista da Camerino] et de li altri Padri saria mai finire," quoted in *Monumenta Missionum Societatis Iesu,* [vol. 5,] *Missiones Orientales: Documenta Indica,* [vol. 2,] *1550–1553,* ed. Josef Wicki,

MHSI 72 (Rome: IHSI, 1950), 150-153. For the Venice catalogue, see ARSI, *Ven.* 37 ("Catalogi Breves et triennales 1590-1602").

48. These passages are from *Const.*, part 8: "Helps towards uniting the distant members with their head and among themselves." It is introduced as follows: "The present treatise will deal first with what can aid the union of hearts and later with helps towards the union of persons in congregations and chapters" [655]. The passages quoted here belong to the latter aim, pertaining specifically to the use of letters in maintaining a virtual "union of persons," *Const.* [673-675].

49. Alessandro Valignano to Antonio Possevino[?], Mozambique, August 4, 1574 (with a fuller segment from the letter quoted here, about de Ribera): "mi par buono in substantialibus et figliuolo della Compagnia.... Movome a creder questo dalle infrascritte ragioni: La prima, per la pianezza et facilità con la quale mi ha discoperta et dato conto di tutta la sua vita, dalla quale ho cavato non essere in lui mancamento di buona volontà, ma solamente in alcune cose alcuna imprudentia et indiscretione ... per me credo ch'egli sia fidele et figliuolo alla Compagnia"; (about Vallareggio, quoting the full relevant section) "del quale né io, né gl'altri teniamo quanto al suo modo di procedere alcuna sodisfattione"; "Parmi che il P. Battista Rybera sarebbe per questo offitio molto più atto," in *Monumenta Missionum Societatis Iesu*, [vol. 21,] *Missiones Orientales: Documenta Indica*, [vol. 9,] *1573-1575*, ed. Josef Wicki, MHSI 94 (Rome: IHSI, 1966), 376-379. For Juan Bautista de Ribera, see *DHCJ* 4:3348 (J. Ruiz-de-Medina): He entered the Society in 1554 and in 1557 moved to Rome where, between 1560 and 1564, he was procurator general of the Society under Diego Laínez. In 1563 he asked Superior General Laínez for a post to the "Indies," where he spent ten years in several of the main locations of the Society's missions, as well as unsuccessfully seeking entry to its biggest prizes—Japan and mainland China. On his return journey to Europe in 1574, he met Alessandro Valignano in Mozambique. In 1582, no doubt following the repeated recommendations of Valignano, Ribera was appointed by Acquaviva as procurator general of the Society. For the colorful life and multiple journeys of Alessandro Vallareggio (or Valla, c. 1529-1580), see *DHCJ* 4: 3879 (J. Ruiz-de-Medina); see also Maria Iris Gramazio, "Gesuiti italiani missionari in Oriente nel XVI secolo," *AHSI* 66, no. 132 (1997): 275-300 (295); Dauril Alden, *The Making of an Enterprise: The Society of Jesus in Portugal, Its Empire and Beyond, 1540-1750* (Stanford, CA: Stanford University Press, 1996), 299. He had joined the Society in 1560 and was chosen by Superior General Borja to go to the Japan mission. After some digressions as military chaplain for Spain, when he was captured by Muslim fighters during the battle of Alcácer Quibir (present-day Morocco), he left Lisbon in 1565, was in Cochin in September of the same year, and was in Macao two years later, from where he traveled

on to Japan. He traveled and worked extensively there, assisting with the Society's governance and evangelization. In 1572 he returned to Europe and was in Lisbon when Valignano arrived there. Despite his experience in the East, his work in Lisbon from 1574 as procurator for the Indies was not considered a success; he left the role in 1576 and died in Cadíz, Spain.

50. ARSI, *Neap.* 81 ("Neapol. Catalogi Triennales, 1603-1625"), fols. 2r-4v (about Pietr'Antonio Minadois: the "Relatione" is identified with just the year of its composition, 1611).

51. Francesco Palmio to Juan Alfonso de Polanco, Bologna, August 13, 1551: "Del Padre don Silvestro puotria avisar' [a] V.R. de molte cose, ma le confessioni di questa solennità della Madonna non mel permettono. Solo le dirò in brevità.... Parla puoco, mangia meno, assai s'affatica, talmenti, che mi fa maravegliare"; "con li fratelli di casa et molto populo genuflessi, espettando la predica.... Finalmente, pregato da me, senza haver' studiato, andò in pulpito, et fece una predica tanto fruttuosa, et con tanto spirito et zelo, che quanti v'erano si vedeano e sentivano pianger' di modo, che molti, mossi da quella predica, deliberarno servir a Dio; e nanzi di partirti di chiesa, si confessorno più de dieci" (*Epistolae mixtae,* 5:726-727).

52. Ignatius of Loyola to Peter Canisius, Rome, November 22, 1554: ARSI, *Ital.* 105 I ("Germania, Hispania 1553-1554"), fol. 6v: "Chi vedesse la lettera di Vostra Reverenza et il modo che tiene in lamentarsi perché non si finiscono quelli libri, potrà pensare che non si ricorda Vostra Reverenza che habbiamo altro da fare in Roma. Voglio che sappia che di pochi mesi in qua sta occupato il Padre Frussio in questa opera, et di tal modo che essendo lettor pubblico del nostro Collegio, non può leggere, et può pensare se patirà nostro Collegio, o no." The *Spiritual Exercises* were first published in Latin in 1548; the *Constitutions* were first printed in Latin in 1558-1559. André des Freux was the translator; he was also one of those consulted in 1550-1551 over the completed Spanish text of the *Constitutions* of 1547-1550. The task of circulating the completed text throughout the Society was delegated to Nadal in the first half of the 1550s. The translation of the work into Latin got underway in 1555: see Ganss commentary in his introduction, *Const.,* 38-39. André des Freux was appointed rector of the Roman College in 1552. See also O'Malley, *The First Jesuits,* 7-9. André des Freux also produced a Latin grammar and a slightly reworked version of a text on pedagogy by Erasmus, published in Rome in 1556 and Cologne in 1558: Karl A. E. Enenkel, "Enargeia Fireworks: Jesuit Image Theory in Neumayr's Works," in *Jesuit Image Theory,* ed., Wietse de Boer, Karl A. E. Enenkel, Walter Melion (Leiden: Brill, 2016), 150-151. For Peter Canisius, see *DHCJ* 1:633-635 (P. Begheyn).

53. Ignatius of Loyola to Peter Canisius, Rome, November 22, 1554, ARSI, *Ital.* 105 I, fol. 6v: "Il disegno di Vostra Reverenza di non moltiplicare

collegii ma fondar bene questi di Vienna, Praga, et Ingolstario pare molto bene.... Del pigliar assunto delle Università, non c'è dubbio che bisognaria procedere con destrezza, et soavamente, et havendo pian pian l'assunto de tutte le lettioni di lingue, philosophia, et theologia, al resto si potrebbe pervenire facilmente."

54. Pontius Cogordanus (Ponce Cogordan) to Ignatius of Loyola, Avignon, March 17, 1556: "Per grande bisogno ch'io ho havuto, ho pigliato trenta scuti d'oro, quali, per una lettera ch'io ho scritto di mia propria mano a V.P., ho pregato V.P. fusse contenta fargli pagare a M. Melchior Valerio, sollecitatore di monsignor Illmo. Farnese. V.P., se gli pare, li potrà fare pagare. Sono tre gentilhuomini, che loro gli vogliono pagare per me, due ferentini et un bolognese, et li faranno pagare in Roma, essendo io arrivato. Noi andaremo pian piano. Siamo sani tutti duoi, se non ch'io mi sento gran catarro, et alcune sempre reliquie della malatia passata" (*Epistolae mixtae*, 5:262).

55. Pontius Cogordanus (Ponce Cogordan) to Ignatius of Loyola, Avignon, March 17, 1556: "tutta Provenza ne sta edificata veder' che una povera vecchia sia restituita nel suo primo bene" (*Epistolae mixtae*, 5:262). On this theme, see A. Lynn Martin, "Jesuits and Their Families: The Experience in Sixteenth Century France," *The Sixteenth Century Journal* 13, no. 1 (1982), 3-24; Miriam Turrini, "La vita scelta? Appunti per una storia della vocazione in età moderna," *Dai cantieri della storia: Liber amicorum per Paolo Prodi* (Bologna: CLUEB, 2007), 145-159. The theme runs throughout Adriano Prosperi, *La vocazione: storie di gesuiti tra Cinquecento e Seicento* (Turin: Einaudi, 2016).

56. Ottavio Cesari to Ignatius of Loyola, Naples, March 21, 1556: "Per gratia del Signor adesso sto meglio et senza febre, et di tal dispositione, che hoggi voglio descender dalla croce, nella quale un mese in circa sono stato, dico del star' nella casa paterna, et mi anderò col Signor nostro al colleggio, dove spero che mi ritroverò più meglio" (*Epistolae mixtae*, 5:263).

57. Giorgio Passiu to Diego Laínez, Cagliari, March 2, 1558: "la necessità tanto grande è in questa città, di sorte che, essendo chiamato per confessare una povereta, la trovai moreva di fame; son stato forzato andare a cerchare per tale persona et visitarla spesso" (Scaduto, *Storia della Compagnia*, 4:635n; the original letter is at ARSI, *Ital.* 111, fol. 270v); Pietro Spiga to Diego Laínez, Cagliari, January 13, 1558: "A los encarcelados digo la missa cada domingo, hóygolos de confessión, hágoles algunos razonamientos, consuélolos, hablo con los juezes y con otros por la despedición dellos; a la hambre, sed, frío y nudez que padescen les doy remedio con las lymosnas quel es pido por la tierra.... Quando los encarcelados me veen, alégranse como si vieren su ángel, y ruéganme que no los desampare, y antes me oluidaría de mí mesmo que dellos." *Litterae quadrimestres ex universis praeter Indiam et Brasiliam locis in quibus aliqui de Societate Jesu versabantur Romam misase*...

tomus quintus (1557–1558)... (Madrid: A. Avrial, 1921), 5:509–510; quoted in Italian in Scaduto, *Storia della Compagnia*, 4:636. For the early Jesuits on Sardegna, see Antonello Elias, "Il Collegio Gesuitico di Santa Croce nel Castello di Cagliari: Documenti inediti," *ArcheoArte* 1 (2010): 197–214. Laínez was elected in July 1558; from the time of the death of Ignatius in 1556, he held the role of vicar general of the Society, when these letters were written.

58. ARSI, *Ital.* 163 ("Epist. Italiae 1605–1626"), fols. 89v–90r (report about Narni, May 8, 1607, quoting a more complete section from the report than in the translation): "alcuni giovani principali, de' quali cene sono assai in questa città senza molte occupationi... Hor io son certo che sarebbe superflua tanto longa dimora, tuttavia mi resta qualche dubio se potremo noi da soli compire quel tanto, che s'è in cominciato in questo tempo che resta sin alli caldi"; (Giuseppe Alamanni, report about Venice from Turin, May 10, 1607, fol. 91r) "Andai a visitare l'Illustrissimo Ambasciatore di Venetia per gli antichi obblighi che ha la Compagnia all'Illustrissima sua casa, con occasione di portargli la narrativa dei sei martiri Giapponesi; e doppo i primi saluti, forse non come semplice privato, ma come ministro pubblico di quella Serenissima Repubblica uscì fuora meco in un ragionamento pieno di lamenti."

59. Francesco Pavone to Muzio Vitelleschi, Naples, July 16, 1616, ARSI, *Neap.* 194 II ("Neapol. Epist. 1615–1620"), fol. 353r: "Alle occupationi di leggere la Scrittura, di consultore, di ammonitore, di essaminatore, di confessore... di Prefetto delle prediche, di Padre della Congregatione de Preti... la Santa Obbedienza mi aggionge il leggere l'etica. Vostra Paternità può pensare se ho tempo di respirare"; Mario Beringucci to Claudio Acquaviva, Venice, March 5, 1583, ARSI, *Ital.* 157 ("Epist. Italiae 1583–1585"), fol. 23r: "Io havrei fatto volentieri almanco per qualche tempo un poco di vacanza da governi, ma poiché è parso a Vostra Illustrissima Paternità di raccomandarmi il governo di questa casa, io lo pigliarò come cosa commandatami da Iddio Nostro."

60. Giovanni Dionisi to Claudio Acquaviva, Venice, March 23, 1607, ARSI, *Ital.* 163 ("Epist. Italiae 1605–1626"), fol. 108r (quoting the full passage): "Molti mesi prima d'adesso desideravo scrivere la presente a Vostra Paternità ma come che disegnavo accompagnarla con l'Istoria della vita del fratello Carlo Casario di buona memoria... la qual fatica per diverse mie occupationi, et impedimenti è andata, et andrà più in longo di quello ch'io havrei creduto..."

61. Ignazio della Casa to Claudio Acquaviva, Venice, March 16, 1583, ARSI, *Ital.* 157, fol. 37r: "questa sera doppo cena andaremo alla nave laquale si partirà a 4 over cinco hore di notte vo animato a patire confidato grandemente nella santa obedientia et maxime intendendo che non ho autto né ho altro in questa missione dal canto mio che pura obedienza... con i travagli che sopraverranno i quali credo saranno molti et vari et forse con periculo de vita."

62. Letter of Alessandro Petrucci to Claudio Acquaviva, Siena, January 3, 1583, ARSI, *Ital.* 157, fols. 2r–3r: "della mia continua malinconia ... delle mie lunghe notti ... Ho in seno un fuoco ... Non vi è al mondo né luogo né porto di quiete per me ... Ho nella mia imaginatione un S. Andrea ... la mia casa mi sembra il collegio, la famiglia i Padri. ... Il mancamento del piede mi è dato, credo, per farmi provare che cosa sia indispositione di corpo ... il padre Ignatio ... un pochetto zoppeggiava ... et quanto grande sia a Senesi la memoria del Padre Girolamo Rubiola che fu un de primi che qua venessero et pure zoppicava ... questa imperfetione in uno della Compagnia che richiede gente scelta et compita di tutto punto, per l'occhi dei secolari, sopportabile sarà nell'occhi della carità domestica ... prego mi accetti per li servitii di casa, non per coagiutore ma per servo di un minimo coagiutore."
63. Scaduto, *Storia della Compagnia,* 3:240.
64. Juan Alfonso de Polanco to the rector of Perugia, Rome, August 18, 1564: "perché su quello pigli la forma delle informationi che si hanno da mandare"; "la moltitudine di lettere prolisse, che davano molto da fare già nel leggerle e molto più nell'esaminarle," quoted in Scaduto, *Storia della Compagnia,* 5:142 (the original is at ARSI, *Ital.* 65 ("Epist. Italiae 1564–1565"), fol. 145r).
65. Lamalle, "L'Archivio di un grande Ordine religioso," 115.
66. For Muzio Vitelleschi's letter to Giovanni Battista Picciolo, Rome, December 7, 1619, see ARSI, *Ven.* 35 I ("Ven. Epist. Gen. 1602–1626 Soli"), fol. 31v. For his letter to Marco Benavere, sent February 1620, see ARSI, *Ven.* 35 I, fol. 35r: "Ho ricevuta la vostra degli xi del corrente. In risposta vi dico che desidero molto la vostra consolatione: e che la vera strada di trovarla non è di mutar luogo, ma il porsi in tutto e per tutto nelle mani di Dio benedetto ... Pertanto fratello mio lasciatevi allegramente essere governato dal Padre Provinciale."
67. ARSI, *Ven.* 35 I, fols. 35v–36r (Vitelleschi to Benavere, February 1620): "Ho ricevuto la quarta lettera vostra et in risposta vi dico ... bisogna prima d'ogni altra cosa fare che il cuore stia quieto dentro di noi, che allora in ogni luogo esteriore troveremo quella tranquillità, che si può havere in questo essilio, dove sempre ci sarà insieme occasione di patire"; "che vegga se può trovarli qualche ricapito nella Provincia di Milano: e son certo che non mancherà di consolarvi per quanto potrà"; "e pregare per me."
68. Muzio Vitelleschi to the provincial of Parma, April 4, 1620, ARSI, *Ven.* 35 I, fol. 36v: "non se n'è fatto niente"; "ma per ricordarle che quanto piú soave rimedio si potrà trovare tanto sarà meglio."
69. ARSI, *Ital.* 76 II ("Epist. Secr. 1557–1573") (January 28, 1557, to the college rector in Loreto), fol. 48r (quoting a slightly longer passage here): "Vostra Reverenza avverta che Paulo si chiamava prima Urbano, et perché persone del suo paese gli davano fastidio si manda fuori di Roma, et seglie mutato il nome"; see also fol. 48r concerning a Jesuit allegedly sleep-talking about

the Devil at night; and for the difficult nature of one Jesuit (June 8, 1560), fol. 59r: "Baldassar Melo ha bisogno di esser tenuto basso per la sua natura... sarebbe soggetto atto a molte cose. Ma per adesso non conviene darli cura o superiorità di altro alcuno. Ma che curi se stesso."
70. Claudio Acquaviva to Alberto Laerzio, Rome, January 14, 1595, ARSI, *Gal.* 44 ("Epist. Secr. 1583–1602, Gall. Germ. Hisp. Lusit."), fol. 25r: "si vede bene il santo zelo che Nostro Signore le dà del suo santo servitio, e bene della Compagnia"; Claudio Acquaviva to Gnecchi-Soldo, Rome, January 14, 1595, ARSI, *Gal.* 44, fol. 26r: "Ho ricevuto quella di Vostra Reverenza delli 4 d'ottobre delle '92, et ho in essa visto con mia consolatione il santo zelo che tiene del servitio divino, e bene della compagnia che così me lo dimostrano gl'avvisi che mi dà intorno alla persona del padre Alessandro." For the circulation of religious material culture in the early modern world, see Luke Clossey, "The Early Modern Jesuit Missions as a Global Movement," University of California World History Workshop, October 31, 2005, http://repositories.cdlib.org/ucwhw/wp/3.
71. Both of the following quotations include the relevant passages in full. ARSI, *Gal.* 44, fol. 25r (Acquaviva to Laerzio, 1595): "del poco che s'attende alla conversione de Gentili, veramente m'ha dato gran dolore, come cosa tanto importante, e tanto propria del nostro instituto, et vocatione, ma voglio sperare che colli avvisi che ne diamo al Padre Provinciale vi si porrà efficace rimedio"; ARSI, *Gal.* 44, fol. 26r (Acquaviva to Gnecchi-Soldo, 1595): "Noi non manchiamo avvisarlo di quel che conviene, massime nelle cose delle spese, e prestiti, acciò per l'avvenire si ponga la moderatione che conviene"; for Acquaviva's letter to Alessandro Valignano, dated November 16, 1595, see fol. 27v. For Organtino Gnecchi-Soldo, see Gramazio, "Gesuiti italiani," 284.
72. ARSI, *Gal.* 44, fol. 25r (Acquaviva to Laerzio, 1595): "molte anime... ch'hora se ne stanno sepolte nelle tenebre della infedeltà, sibene secondo mi scrivono, quei padri hanno assegnato per ragion del loro ritorno, la poca speranza ch'haveano di poter fare quel frutto che si pretendeva." For Rodolofo Acquaviva (1550–1583), see *DBI* 1 (Pietro Pirri); *DHCJ* 1:12–13 (J. Correia-Afonso).

5. DEATHS AND DEPARTURES

1. "The dismissal of those who were admitted but did not prove themselves fit." *Const.* [204–242]; quoted passage at [204].
2. *Const.* [210, 212, 216]; quoted passage at [216].
3. For this further cause for dismissal, see *Const.* [217]; for the method of dismissal, see *Const.* [225, 226].
4. Useful analysis of the relevant section, *Const.* [602], and more generally of Jesuit attitudes to deviance within the Society is in Antonio M. de Al-

dama, *The Constitutions of the Society of Jesus: An Introductory Commentary on the Constitutions;* trans. Aloysius J. Owen (1979; repr., Rome and St. Louis: Centrum Ignatianum Spiritualitatis/Institute of Jesuit Sources, 1989), 241-242. See also John W. O'Malley, *The First Jesuits* (Cambridge, MA: Harvard University Press, 1993), 57.
5. *Const.* [235-237].
6. ARSI, *Ital.* 103 ("Assistentia Italiae, 1622" [although the date range of the documents is larger than the date given in the title]), fols. 2r-4v.
7. ARSI, *Hist. Soc.* 54 ("Dimissi, 1573-1640"). These records dedicate roughly one paragraph to each person, some giving details in Latin and others in Italian. The source includes an excellent recent typewritten index of names.
8. ARSI, *Hist. Soc.* 54, fol. 21v (Salvatore Castelano and Giovanni Pietro Massario); fol. 2v (Enea Ferrarese): "nondimeno secondo il debito della carità per consiglio di medici l'habbiamo licentiato per havere principio di una infermità pericolosa di fisico sperando essi che con questo mezzo potrà meglio, o ricuperare la sanità o vivere più lungamente"; fol. 3v (Luca Micalopoli): "non havere forze corporali bastanti per le fatiche che seco porta il nostro Instituto et la qualità degli essercitii ne' quali sarebbe convenuto che si impiegasse, habbiamo giudicato che meglio potrà servire a' Dio Signore Nostro fuori della nostra Compagnia"; fol. 3r (Giovanni Giorgio Sacalpiccia): "per entrar in religione di S. Francesco"; fol. 5r (Giovanni Andrea Monfellino): "habbia vissuto per alcuni anni nella nostra Compagnia, nondimeno ... in essa non ha fatto profession nessuna, et che per giusti rispetti per la facoltà della Santa Sede Apostolica a noi concessa l'habbiamo lasciato andare libero d'ogni obligazione della nostra Compagnia, et in fede."
9. For the quoted figures, see O'Malley, *The First Jesuits,* 55-59; A. Lynn Martin, "Vocational Crises and the Crisis in Vocations among Jesuits in France during the Sixteenth-Century," *The Catholic Historical Review* 72, no. 2 (1986): 201-221 (209-210). Useful points of contrast and continuity over time and regions can be observed in D. Gillian Thompson, "The Jesuit Province of France on the Eve of Its Destruction in 1762," *AHSI* 87, no. 173 (2018): 3-74 (33-44), which analyzes the reasons, grade levels, and possible policies that informed dismissals and departures in the Province of France prior to its suppression in 1762 (and including useful outlines of *dimissi* in the Society more broadly). Martin's article, "Vocational Crises and the Crisis in Vocations," presents five case studies from France as examples of the Society's general "crisis of vocation" and as evidence that *dimissi* very often in reality were voluntary departures. He also provides a useful discussion of litigious departures (213-216). For this theme in the early Society, see also Sabina Pavone, "I dimessi della Compagnia negli anni del generalato di Francesco Borgia: Una nuova questione storiografica," in *Francisco de Borja y su tiempo: Política, religión y cultura en la Edad*

Moderna, ed. Enrique García Hernán and María del Pilar Ryan (Valencia and Rome: Albatros Ediciones / IHSI, 2012), 465-479. For Jesuit attitudes to the problem of departures, see Mario Scaduto, "Il 'Libretto consolatorio' di Bobadilla a Domènech sulle vocazioni mancate (1570)," *AHSI* 43, no. 85 (1974): 85-102. Another treatment of Jesuits leaving the Society is in Adriano Prosperi, *La vocazione: Storie di gesuiti tra Cinquecento e Seicento* (Turin: Einaudi, 2016), chapter 15.

10. These data are provided in Mario Scaduto, *Catalogo dei Gesuiti d'Italia 1540-1565* (Rome: IHSI, 1968) and are collated and discussed in Martin, "Vocational Crises," 205-206.

11. Dauril Alden, *The Making of an Enterprise: The Society of Jesus in Portugal, Its Empire and Beyond, 1540-1750* (Stanford, CA: Stanford University Press, 1996), 46 (table 3.1), 291-293 (including table 11.10): Alden's analysis of dismissals and departures in the Portuguese Assistancy is at 287-297; Thompson, "The Jesuit Province of France," 35.

12. For relevant discussion of this subject, see Ganss commentary in *Const.,* 107n22. See also Martin, "Vocational Crises," and A. Lynn Martin, *The Jesuit Mind: The Mentality of an Elite in Early Modern France* (Ithaca, NY: Cornell University Press, 1988), 22-42, esp. 25-26, "The Burden of the Society": here Martin discusses why many wanted to leave, or did leave, and why many who stayed found the Society's demands difficult to live up to. For possible increasing awareness among applicants to the Society about its apostolic character rather than as a haven from the pressures of an active life, see Miriam Turrini, "La vocazione esaminata: Narrazioni autobiografiche di novizi gesuiti a metà Seicento," *Archivio italiano per la storia della pietà* 28 (2015): 311-388.

13. ARSI, *Rom.* 208 ("Notitiae de Sociis S.I. advenientibus, abeuntibus etc"), fols. 27r-28r (titled "Usciti dalla Compagnia 1588"); five departures discussed, with quotations about four (Giovanni d'Ama) "per povertà de suoi. Siciliano"; (Alessandro Fioravanti) "al principio di Aprile avanti Pasqua fu licentiato havendo domandato d'uscire dalla Compagnia"; (Giovanni Dolf) "partì senza licenza"; (Leonardo Catania) "fu licentiato in Bivona de Sicilia a il 12 de Maio 1588, essendo tentato . . . havendo sparlato et fatto romore."

14. ARSI, *Sic.* 4 ("Sicula Epist. Gener. 1595-1604"), fol. 198r (about Father Salvarezza, April 1601): "che pur è opera pia, non però da permettersi ad uno che stia nella Compagnia."

15. Claudio Acquaviva to Giacomo Domenichi, Rome, October 4, 1604, ARSI, *Sic.* 58 ("Sicula Epist. Gener. 1600-1773 Soli"), fol. 35v: (case 1) "mi par necessario che Vostra Reverenza ne faccia qualche dimostratione, se gli è publico per essempio d'altri, et edificatione a chi lo sa, e per correttione anche di quel Padre, il quale se bene egli meriterebbe di esser mandato via dalla Compagnia per la gravezza della colpa, il che se gli dovrà dire,

nondimeno per questa volta basterà dargli quel castigo a correttione, che a Vostra Reverenza parerà se gli convenga secondo le circostanze"; (case 2) fols. 35v-36r: "che è più fastidioso, et a che difficilmente vi si può metter il rimedio, dico che essendo questo caso d'inquisitione né Vostra Reverenza né io dubito potiamo metterci la mano, et il rimoverlo di Sicilia, o licentiarlo, oltre che non lo possiamo fare per esser questa inquisitione soggetta a quella di Spagna, e sarebbe esposto a pericolo"; "perché miglior mezo a me per hora non occore. In tanto lodo Vostra Reverenza di quel che ha fatto di haverlo rimosso del quel luogo et occasione, e tenghi gli occhi sopra."

16. Claudio Acquaviva to Giacomo Domenichi, January 28, 1606, ARSI, *Sic.* 58: fol. 41r-v (about Paolo Giuliani): "come si è scritto aspetteremo la verità delle cose che le gli imputano, e secondo quella delibereremo di lui, il quale ben si vede che non è per noi e se egli dice di voler venire a Roma non lo permetta in modo veruno."

17. ARSI, *Ital.* 76 I ("Epist. Gener. 1601-1646 Soli"), fol. 38r: "che se vole saper la causa della sua dimissione legga le constitutioni, dove troverà che né a lui sta bene, né alla Compagnia il stare in questa religione; che se egli medesimo Padre sa le cause oltre alle sue indispositione di malinconie e mal di cuore; per la Compagnia le sappiamo noi e che si ricordi de voti, con quali si obligò alla Compagnia."

18. ARSI, *Ital.* 76 II, fol. 84r ("Epist. Secr.").

19. ARSI, *Ital.* 76 II, fol. 59r: "modesto et virtuoso, et anche d'ingegno"; "per seduttione d'un'altro (che s'è mandato fuora) fece certo dissordine"; "lagrime"; "compassione"; "speranza"; "potrà col tempo accetarlo et darli un'altro nome."

20. Ignatius of Loyola, *Autobiography*, in *Spiritual Exercises and Selected Works*, ed. George E. Ganss (New York: Paulist Press, 1991), 65-111.

21. This source is the main focus of Prosperi, *La vocazione*. The first monograph study dedicated to Giovanni Battista Eliano is Robert Clines, *A Jewish Jesuit in the Eastern Mediterranean: Early Modern Conversion, Mission, and the Construction of Identity* (Cambridge: Cambridge University Press, 2019).

22. *Monumenta Missionum Societatis Iesu*, [vol. 51,] *Missiones Orientales Monumenta Proximi Orientis I. Palestine, Liban, Syrie, Mésopotame, 1523–1583*, ed. Sami Kuri (Rome: IHSI, 1989). Eliano is discussed in Prosperi, *La vocazione*, chapter 12 (with a focus on the responses of Eliano's mother to his conversion reported in the autobiography discussed here). See also an important dicussion about Eliano as part of a wider analysis of the relationship between the early Jesuits, the Jews, and Jesuits with Jewish ancestry in Robert Maryks, *Jesuit Order as a Synagogue of Jews: Jesuits of Jewish Ancestry and Purity-of-Blood Laws in the Early Society of Jesus* (Boston: Brill, 2009), 66-67. For Eliano, see also Gabriel Lance Lazar, *Working in the Vineyard of*

the Lord: Jesuit Confraternities in Early Modern Italy (Toronto: University of Toronto Press, 2005), 118–125; Shlomo Simonsohn, *The Jews in the Duchy of Milan: A Documentary History of the Jews of Italy* (Jerusalem: Israel Academy of Sciences and Humanities, 1982), 1324–1354; Mario Scaduto, "La missione di Cristoforo Rodríguez al Cairo (1561–1563), *AHSI* 27, no. 54 (1958): 233–253. Biographical overviews are at *DBI* 42 (Cesare Ioly Zorattini); *DHCJ* 2:1233–1234 (Ch. Libois).

23. *Hist. Soc.* 176 ("Vocationes Illustres I"), fols. 119–145, 146–160 (no recto or verso). The first text, which is complete and from which the following quotations are drawn, is reproduced in José C. Sola, "El p. Juan Bautista Eliano: Un documento autobiográfico inédito," *AHSI* 4, no. 8 (1935): 291–321. Quotations are from this published transcription. "Il desiderio, che V.R. sempre ha mostrato di voler, ch'io le scrivessi *la mia vocatione* alla Fede, et alla santa Religione" (emphasis added). For an analysis of the Eliano autobiography, see Robert Clines, "How to Become a Jesuit Crypto-Jew: The Self-Confessionalization of Giovanni Battista Eliano through the Textual Artifice of Conversion," *Sixteenth Century Journal* 48, no. 1 (2017): 3–26.

24. These narratives were not limited to the Christian sphere and perhaps may bear testament to an increasing awareness of the need to identify and distinguish oneself from the "other," as the world became "smaller" due to the breakup of Western Christendom and increased contacts that for the first time in human history had reached global dimensions. For the Mediterranean context of this literary phenomenon, see Tijana Krstic, *Contested Conversions to Islam: Narratives of Religious Change in the Early Modern Ottoman Empire* (Stanford, CA: Stanford University Press, 2011), 90–91. For a discussion of conversion narratives in the Catholic sphere, including a critical edition of a text that doubled as travel writing with a spiritual purpose, produced in the fraught religious context of the British Isles and continental Europe in the sixteenth century, see Brian Mac Cuarta, *Henry Piers's Continental Travels, 1595–1598* (Cambridge: Cambridge University Press for the Royal Historical Society, 2018).

25. Eliano, "Vocatione": "in questo l'ubedirò" (Sola, "El p. Juan Baptista Eliano," 295).

26. ARSI, *Hist. Soc.* 176 ("Vocationes Illustres I"), fols. 183r–195r (Antonio Possevino).

27. Eliano, "Vocatione": "al nostro partire mio fratello . . . non si lasciò trovare" (297); "et perche tra Giudei quella casa, che hà alcuno della famiglia christiano resta infame, convenemmo tutti di non volere manifestar questa infamia nostra presso gli Giudei del Cairo" (297); "io temendo di non essere infame presso li Giudei cercai di fuggir la pratica di mio fratello" (299) (Sola, "El p. Juan Baptista Eliano").

28. Eliano, "Vocatione": "et mi riprese grandemente ch'io così giovane ricercasse queste cose, aggiongendo, vuoi tu forsi andarti a precepitare, et rovinarti, come ha fatto tuo fratello...?" (Sola, "El p. Juan Baptista Eliano," 299).
29. Eliano, "Vocatione": "altri gentil'huomini... altri huomini letterati"; "m'intravano nel cuore"; "vedendoli tutti tanto modesti, et devoti, et reverenti, che mai prima havevo veduto, né tra Giudei, né tra Christiani" (Sola, "El p. Juan Baptista Eliano," 300-301). For André des Freux, see *DHCJ* 2:1537 (L. Lukás); translator of the *Spiritual Exercises,* and Paris trained like the original companions, he was cofounder of the College in Messina. Eliano's conversion coincided with a period in Venice for des Freux to found the college there, although he soon returned to Rome to help establish the Collegio Romano. He died shortly after Ignatius.
30. Eliano, "Vocatione": "et stando così sospeso, già non praticavo di spesso nella sinagoga de' Giudei"; "et perché in settembre vi sono molti feste de Giudei, alle volte mi veniva tentatione di partirmi et andare alla sinagoga, et buttarmi a piedi di tutti i Giudei per dimandargli perdono dello scandolo datogli in non essere venuto alla sinagoga in quelli tempi santi, et come ero stato troppo curioso in cercar le cose di altra legge, che quella, nella quale ero nato, et allevato"; "All'hora io mi trovavo in gran confusione, vedendomi in uno stato, che non ero né Giudeo, né Christiano" (Sola, "El p. Juan Baptista Eliano," 301-302).
31. Andreas Frusius [des Freux] to Ignatius of Loyola, Venice, September 26, 1551: "Quello hebreo, del quale fu già scritto, giovane di venti anni, di molto buono ingenio et giudicio, et assai versato nelle scritture hebraiche, essendo stato con noi, come uno delli nostri fratelli, più di un mese, finalmente per gratia d'Iddio, con la oratione, studio, dispute et bona conversatione ha cognosciuto la verità e ricevuto il Sto. Battesimo con gran solemnidate; et adesso che se gli proponeva elegger alcun partito per il suo star et viver, dice che gli pareria esser perso, uscendo di casa, et fa grande instantia che lo riteniamo per star alla obedientia della Compagnia." Quoted in *Litterae quadrimestres ex universis praeter Indiam et Brasiliam locis in quibus aliqui de Societate Jesu versabantur Romam missae, tomus primus (1546-1552)* (Madrid: A. Avrial, 1894), 1:441.
32. Eliano, "Vocatione": "havendone havuto nuova la mia madre che ancora era viva, la quale non mi haveva veduto, ne havuto nuova alcuna di me in xiij anni, fece grandissima istanza di volermi parlare, sperando che con la sua vista et parole mi haveria fatto restar' in Cairo, per ritornare al vomito" (Sola, "El p. Juan Baptista Eliano," 308-309).
33. Giovanni Battista Eliano to Claudio Acquaviva, Cairo, March 18, 1583, ARSI, *Gall.* 98 I ("Missio Constantinopolit. IV Aegypt. Aethiop. 1561-1763"), fols. 103r-104v: "L'andai a visitar; et essa... stette un pezzo senza

poter parlar, piangendo ... mi ha detto che non mi ritiri dalli Judei quali tutti sanno di me, et non sono mai per darmi fastidio alcuno. ... Et così l'ho visto in effetto che mi fanno molto onore."

34. Robert Clines posits that Eliano's conversion never could be complete, either for Eliano himself or for those around him. The instability and questionable permanence of religious conversions of minorities in this period—in terms of motivations, conviction, and the patronage, security, and benefits that came fitfully from the dominant Christian sphere—is one of the themes of Tamar Herzig, *A Convert's Tale: Art, Crime, and Jewish Apostasy in Renaissance Italy* (Cambridge, MA: Harvard University Press, 2019), which focuses on the famous goldsmith to Italy's northern courts, Salomone da Sesso, a Jewish convert to Catholicism (to escape criminal charges) who assumed the new name Ercole de' Fedeli (c. 1452/1457–after 1521).
35. See Martin, *The Jesuit Mind*, chapter 10.
36. Alden, *The Making of an Enterprise*, 581, 279–282.
37. *Sp. Ex.* [53], [1], [166].
38. Ignatius of Loyola, "Selected Letters," in Ganss, *Spiritual Exercises and Selected Works*, 326.
39. Ignatius of Loyola, "Selected Letters" (to Magdalena de Loyola y Aaroz), in Ganss, *Spiritual Exercises and Selected Works*, 339; (to Teresa Rejadell), 340.
40. *Const.* [595–601] (part 6, chapter 4), quotations from *Const.* [595–598].
41. *Const.* [676].
42. ARSI, *Hist. Soc.* 42 ("Defunti, 1557–1623"), fol. 4r: "A dì 15 di Agosto fu raccomandata l'anima del fratello Stanislao Kostka, polono, defunto in Santo Andrea di Roma a dì sudetto '68."
43. ARSI, *Rom.* 170 ("Novitii in Dom. Prof. admissi 1556–1569"), fol. 5v: "Venne in casa a dì sei di settembre 1556 fu essaminato per indifferenti, non havendo alcuno delli impedimenti proposti nello examen, si mostrò prompto a tutto quello che li fu proposto. Portò seco una berreta, un tabarro guernito di velluto ... un paro di calze al modo di soldato, quatro Camiscie, un capello per viaggio ... portò ancora di più una spada un paro di stivali da cavaliere con le speroni." For the record of Pietro della Torre's death, see ARSI, *Hist. Soc.* 42, fol. 2r. Famous Jesuits of course are listed side-by-side with unknown ones; on the same folio that recorded Pietro della Torre's death, the celebrated dramatist Stefano Tuccio is listed as having died in the Collegio Romano on January 27, 1597.
44. *Const.* [601]; ARSI *Hist. Soc.* 43 ("Defunti 1595–1642"), fol. 243r: "A dì 25 di novembre s'ordinò a tutte le Province d'Italia che ogni sacerdote dica 3 messe et ogni fratello 3 corone per l'anima del Padre Benedetto Palmio defonto in Ferrara li 14 detto come per Assistente che fu d'Italia et anco alle Province fuor d'Italia si ordinò ch'ogni sacerdote dicesse una messa et ogni fratello una corona." Prayers in Italy were intended for those in

need beyond its shores, both Jesuit and those among whom they worked, like the request for prayers in 1599 for situations outside Italy. The first page of these records carries the title "Libro secondo de' Defonti della Compagnia et de' Fondatori e Benefatori di essa: et degli ordini della medesima Compagnia cominciato l'anno del 1595."

45. ARSI, *Hist. Soc.* 43, fol. 1r: "23 di marzo Nostra Paternità ordinò che per li nostri di Scotia, defonti in quella missione, si debbano dire in questa Provincia di Roma due messe dai sacerdoti per ciascuno defonto; e 2 corone da ogni fratello, e tre da quei di questa Casa Professa, come per soggetti di questa Casa e Provincia. E due messe, e due corone per quei che morono in Hibernia."

46. ARSI *Hist. Soc.* 43, fol. 243r. "A dì di 4 febraro si ordinò per li nostri luoghi di Roma che si raccomandasse a Dio Nostro Signore nelle messe et orationi la città di Lisbona, hora oppressa dalla peste"; ARSI *Hist. Soc.*, 43, fols. 241r-243r (1595-1598), titled "Diversi ordini che per commissione del Reverendissimo Nostro Padre Generale si sogliono pubblicare o a' tutta la Compagnia o qualche provincia parlare."

47. ARSI, *F.G.* 685 ("Miscellanea 10. De Disertoribus"), unfoliated: "'Altri Giesuiti andati dicendo, che chi esce dalla compagnia, capita male. Io sono capitato molto bene.' In quell'anno medesimo successe la rivoluzione di Napoli." I wish to thank archivist Mauro Brunello at ARSI for directing me to this source.

48. ARSI, *F.G.* 685, unfoliated: "... comparse in Loreto dove, o forse altrove, prese moglie, esercitò ivi l'arte sua di Barbiere ... venne in sì estrema miseria che per vivere privo d'ogn'altera sostanza faceva il pane di cennere di scarti di vite, e mangiandolo si gonfiò in corpo in maniera che crepò e morse. L'uscita sua della compagnia si è nel 1616 al collegio Montepulciano."

49. ARSI, *Vitae* 5 ("Collectio Vitarum"), fols. 156r-163v ("Essempi di quelli che essendo usciti dalla Compagnia hanno fatto cattivo fine, o si son molto pentiti"): "et essendo stato mal sepellito fu da cani divorato" (fols. 156r-v); "altri diano per pazzia"; "alto quattro solari nella piazza che chiamano la pietra del pesce a Napoli" (fol. 156v); fol. 162r.

50. ARSI, *Vitae* 129 ("Esiti di alcuni usciti della compagnia"), fols. 14-308 (no recto or verso) (concerning the years 1540-1669): "Avvenimenti Funesti d'alcuni che o sono usciti dalla Compagnia, o chiamati da Dio alla Compagnia non vi sono entrati, o hanno procurato che quelli che v'erano chiamati Non v'entrassero, o ne uscissero. Parte I." There are two versions of these accounts, of different lengths.

51. ARSI, *Vitae* 129, fol. 16.

52. ARSI, *Vitae* 129, fols. 19-21 (1541): "Un certo Giacomo nato in Roma"; "di mutar stato, e entrar in altra religione più aspra, dove potesse darsi in tutto all'ozio della contemplazione"; "la mano di Dio"; "ospedale di S. Giovanni Laterano."

53. ARSI, *Vitae* 129, fol. 155; ARSI, *Vitae* 129, fol. 111.
54. ARSI, *Vitae* 129, fols. 300–301: "Il fratello Cristiano Sassone uscito dalla Compagnia apostatò dalla fede, non credendo cosa alcuna, né che vi fosse providenza né che l'anima fosse immortale, né battesimo, né altri sagramenti. E venne a tanta cecità, che negava esservi nel mondo Iddio, e diventò affatto Ateo. Scrisse empiamente contro tutta la Religione Christiana. Venne per questo odiato da tutti: e per fin da gli Eretici fu cacciato dalle loro radunanze, ancorché dal principio fosse stato da loro ben trattato"; "ritornò al vomito, e . . . fu abrugiato."
55. Martin, "Vocational Crisis," 217.
56. Niccolò Lancillotto to Ignatius of Loyola, Quilón, January 11, 1551: "Di M. Paulo, quel che havemo qua per superiore, non si può dire quanto travaglia in servitio di Dio, nel quale spende tutto il giorno et gran parte della notte, continuamente, di molti anni in qua, che ne fa stupire la sua constantia. È homo di poche parole et di molte opere." Quoted in *Monumenta Missionum Societatis Iesu:* [vol. 5,] *Missiones Orientales: Documenta Indica,* [vol. 2,] *1550–1553,* ed. Josef Wicki, MHSI 72 (Rome: IHSI, 1950), 153. For Niccolò Lancillotto (or Lancillotti), who entered the Society in 1541 under Ignatius and studied at Coimbra with proto-martyr Antonio Criminale before departing for the East in 1545 (he died in Quilón in 1558), see *DHCJ* 3:2276 (J. Wicki); Maria Iris Gramazio, "Gesuiti italiani missionari in Oriente nel XVI secolo," *AHSI* 66, no. 132 (1997): 275–300 (285); Mario Scaduto, *Catalogo dei Gesuiti d'Italia 1540–1565* (Rome: IHSI, 1968), 81.
57. Luís Fróis to the Jesuits of Portugal, Goa, December 1, 1560: "nos levou Nosso Senhor para si a nosso bom velho e bendito Padre Miser Paulo, depois de sua prolungada emfermidade em que muito, com o odor de sua virtude e religiosa paciencia, a todos nos edificou. Foy seu transito tão cheo de tanta tranquilidade e quietação, quanta era a paz interior que com o mesmo Deus tinha dentro em sua alma." *Monumenta Missionum Societatis Iesu:* [vol. 9,] *Missiones Orientales: Documenta Indica,* [vol. 4,] *1557–1560,* ed. Josef Wicki, MHSI 78 (Rome: IHSI, 1956), 729. Mario Scaduto, *Storia della Compagnia di Gesù in Italia: L'Epoca di Giacomo Lainez, 1556–1565; L'azione* (Rome: La civiltà cattolica, 1974), 4:760–770, presents a very interesting (if excessively laudatory) discussion of end-of-life accounts, quotated in Italian, about some of these first-generation Italian missionaries in the East.
58. Niccolò Lancillotto to Juan Alfonso de Polanco, Goa, October 10, 1547: "Soy yo tan flaco de complexión corporal que no puedo hazer o que ell ànimo desea: tengo quebrantado una vena en los pechos de do eche sangre muchas vezes y en mucha cantidad; ni puedo studiar ni a otros enseñar ni puedo tomar los trabajos como conviene a uno que tiene cargo, y parece que yo nascy para siempre dar trabajo a otros." *Monumenta Missionum*

Societatis Iesu: [vol. 4,] *Missiones Orientales: Documenta Indica,* [vol. 1,] *1540–1549,* ed. Josef Wicki, MHSI 70 (Rome: IHSI, 1948), 186.

59. Niccolò Lancillotto to Ignatius of Loyola, Cochin, January 28, 1556: "Estive assi en Caulão mui gravemente enfermo, e, por me parecer que hestava mui vessinho à morte, me fui pera Guoa . . . Dessejava eu muito morir antre esses Padres e Irmã da Companhia." *Monumenta Missionum Societatis Iesu:* [vol. 6,] *Missiones Orientales: Documenta Indica,* [vol. 3,] *1553–1557,* ed. Josef Wicki, MHSI 74 (Rome: IHSI, 1954), 452; Jerónimo Fernandes to André de Carvalho, Goa, December 6, 1556: "Partio de Coulão trazendome consigo, vindo ainda mui doente, per o rio que vay a Cochim, em huma empalega . . . E quanto neste caminho padeceo, sabe-o Deus Nosso Senhor" (587); Niccolò Lancillotto to Ignatius of Loyola, Cochin, January 10, 1557: "cada ano moiro e numqua moiro, Deus seja louvado para sempre. Despois que amdo nesta agonia e trabalho, falecerão muitos rijos e valemtes e virtuosos, que faziam muito serviço a N.S. e eu, arvore inútil e sem nenhum fruto, fiquo ocupamdo a terra sem proveito na vinha do Senhor" (607).

60. Antonio da Costa to the Jesuits of Portugal, Goa, December 26, 1558: "à hora de seu passamento, deu claro testimunho de quam certo servo de Deus foy vivendo, porque a mesma patientia que tinha na vida com todos seus trabalhos e enfermidades, essa mesma teve naquela derradeira hora"; *Documenta Indica* 4:180.

AFTERWORD

1. ARSI, *Rom.* 170 ("Novitii in Dom. Prof. admissi 1556–1569"), fol. 191v: "perché questa Vita vedo che se ne fugge come Vento."

ACKNOWLEDGMENTS

This book has been on a long journey. It has accompanied me across three continents and four countries: Australia, England, Italy, and (for brief stints) the United States. The many years since I first visited the Jesuit archive in Rome and discovered the world inside it—including textual traces of journeys extending as close to my homeland of Australia as any Europeans managed to go in the period that I research—have felt like time spent acquiring knowledge of a musical instrument or a new language more than the length of a project. During this time, I was free to discover, read, process, and attempt to account for the Society of Jesus—with its almost five centuries of history—and for its vast documentary repository, second only to the Vatican among Rome's many ecclesiastical archives.

The Society of Jesus indeed has its own language—and a distinct way of seeing the world—and I, a non-Jesuit female historian, have tried to learn it in an effort to recreate what it was like to belong to it many centuries ago. The result, like the Italian Jesuit missionary to China mentioned in this study, Sabatino de Ursis—who sought to explain the sounds of the Chinese language to his confreres back home through a combination of the original Chinese characters, Latin transcriptions, Italian translations of the words, and musical notation for the tones—is my aim to convey to the reader something of what I have discovered.

I would like to thank the many individuals, groups, places, and institutions that have assisted in the process of developing this work into a book. Beginning with institutions: the Archivum Romanum Societatis Iesu (ARSI) and the General Curia of the Society of Jesus (Rome); Villa I Tatti, the Harvard University Center for Italian Renaissance Studies (Florence); Harvard University Press (Cambridge, Massachusetts); the University of Newcastle (Australia); the Collegeville (Minnesota) Institute for Ecumenical and Cultural Research; the Pontifical Gregorian

University, Roma Tre University, Sapienza University of Rome, and the Australian embassy to the Holy See (all in Rome); the Jesuit College of Spirituality and Divinity University (both in Melbourne); the Institute for Advanced Jesuit Studies at Boston College (Chestnut Hill, Massachusetts); and the Universities of Newcastle and London (United Kingdom, especially Royal Holloway, Queen Mary, the Institute of Historical Research, and the Warburg Institute).

Several places have been important inspirations in the development and completion of this project, many tied to the institutions above, and others connected to the individuals with whom I shared them. I am grateful for them: the library, gardens, and hills of I Tatti; Melbourne's Bay at Beaumaris; Bloomsbury and North London; the Church of the Gesù, Rome; the coastlines of North England and New South Wales; central Minnesota's winter landscape; Portland, Maine; the woods of Massachusetts, near Boston; Harlem, New York; the southern United States, from New Orleans, through Alabama, to Atlanta; in central Italy, Orvieto, Spoleto, and Gradoli; Venice; Baselga di Piné in Trentino; and finally, in my adoptive city of Rome, the neighborhoods of S. Giovanni, Monteverde Vecchio, Vatican City and its Borgo, and *il centro storico*.

True to this book's interest in communities that shape individuals and vice versa, I would like to thank the following groups of people who have sustained this project in a variety of ways: my colleagues at ARSI; the worldwide Society of Jesus, especially those who live and work in Rome; the I Tatti Fellows for the year 2008 / 2009 and I Tatti's wider community of scholars; the Monastère de la Visitation, Paris; the Caravita community in Rome; the many authors with whom I have worked toward publication with Institutum Historicum Societatis Iesu and *Archivum Historicum Societatis Iesu;* and my colleagues and students at the institutions mentioned above, who, from their four corners of the world, came together to share in the adventure of exploring human history.

I wish to extend my thanks to the dedicated editorial and production management team at Harvard University Press, especially Andrew Kinney, Emily Silk, Emeralde Jensen-Roberts, Stephanie Vyce, and John Donohue at Westchester Publishing Services. I am grateful to the two anonymous peer reviewers of the book for their very helpful feedback and suggestions. At I Tatti, I thank the entire staff and especially Director

Alina Payne, and Series General Editor of I Tatti Studies in Italian Renaissance History Kate Lowe.

I thank the following individuals for their help with this project on many different levels, both scholarly and personal: Francesca Alongi; Paul Begheyn, SJ; Francesco Borghesi; Paolo Broggio; Alison Brown; Mauro Brunello; Daniel Canaris; David Chambers; Barry Collett; Emanuele Colombo; Joseph Connors; Caroline Copeland; Pedro Lage Reis Correia; Elisabetta Corsi; David Cox; Aaron Culbertson; Trevor Dean; Simon Ditchfield; Philip Dwyer; Julie Edwards; Alison Edye; Anna Esposito; the "Etrurians" of Rome; Jaom Fisher; Felicity de Fombelle; Elisa Frei; Nuno da Silva Gonçalves, SJ; Raúl Gonzalez, SJ; Patrick Goujon, SJ; Jim Grummer, SJ; Jan Hayes; Philippa Hitchen; David Holdcroft, SJ; Carolyn James; Bill Kent[†]; Deborah Kent; Anne Leader; the "Londoners" David, Farokh, and Stephanie; Chiara Luzzati; Brian Mac Cuarta, SJ; Peter Matheson; Querciolo Mazzonis; Thomas McCoog, SJ; Sinead McEneaney; Seth Meehan; Valeria Méndez de Vigo Montojo; Emily Michelson; Silvia Mostaccio; Paul[†] and Maureen Mutimer; Michaeline O'Dwyer, RSHM; Fr. Frank O'Loughlin; John W. O'Malley, SJ; Adriano Prosperi; Valentina Prosperi; Andrea Rizzi; Michael Rocke; Massimo Rospocher; Mark Rotsaert, SJ; Miri Rubin; Arielle Saiber; Rosa Salzberg; Peter Sherlock; Uta Sievers; Nicholas Terpstra; Miriam Turrini; Andrea Vanni; Filippo de Vivo; and Cindy Wooden.

A particular word of thanks to all of the members of my family, located between the Antipodes and Italy—in the Russell sphere, Wendy, Michael, Tim, Rachael, Rebecca, and Ken; in the Casari one, Christa, Ettore[†], Giorgio, Ute, and Paolo—and to the special members of the next generation: Marco, Bianca, Emily, Jude, Luke, Pietro, Paola, Fleur, Joshua, Iggy, Millie, and Hannah. Thanks to each of you for your unique accompaniment.

This book is dedicated to my husband, Mario Casari, with gratitude, esteem, and love.

INDEX

academies, 77
Academy of Nobles, 28
accommodation, 58, 59–60, 80, 94, 204n19, 207n30. See also *soave, soavamente* (sweet or kind)
Acquaviva, Claudio, superior general, 34, 55, 58–60, 67, 69–74, 77, 80–81, 82, 87, 89, 91–93, 101–105, 116, 125, 132, 134, 144–145, 152–153, 157, 161–162, 202n10, 204n20
Acquaviva, Rodolfo, 145
Ad maiorem Dei gloriam. See God
Africa. See Alexandria; Cairo; Egypt; Mozambique
age, 1, 22, 43–45, 46, 47–48, 63, 66, 75, 77, 124–125
agency, 14, 18, 50, 68, 72, 84, 94, 119–125, 170, 175, 235n23
Alamanni, Giuseppe, 140
Albertino, Francesco, 77, 79
Aldama, Antonio M. de, 148
Alden, Dauril, 163
Aleni, Giulio, 75, 83, 87–89, 106
Alexandria, 156
Álvares, João, 107–110
Ama, Giovanni d', 152
Anatomia ingegnorum, 122
Anderson, Benedict, 16
anti-Jesuitism, 2, 12, 47, 140, 184n20
apostate, 110, 169
apostolate, apostolic, 8, 117–118, 145, 151, 186n28, 196n69, 200n2, 207n30, 232n5, 232–233n6, 233n7
Aquinas, Thomas, 148
Arabic, 156; tradition, 121

archives, 9, 12. See also Archivum Romanum Societatis Iesu (ARSI)
Archivum Romanum Societatis Iesu (ARSI), 2, 9, 11, 60, 116–117, 137, 153, 158, 167, 174, 204–205n22
Argentina, 49
Argento, Alessio d', 132
artists, 27, 34, 64, 110, 121, 127; artisans, 30
Asia, 33, 34, 53–60, 62–63, 70, 76, 83, 86, 87, 89, 91–92, 95, 100, 102, 110–111, 114, 135, 144, 163, 201nn4–5, 201–202n8, 202nn9–10, 204nn19–20; attitudes toward, 56, 62–63, 94, 110–114, 204n19. See also China; Colombo; India; Indies; Japan; Malacca; missions
Assistancies, 5, 61, 67, 142, 205n24; German, 203n16; Italian, 5–6, 67, 74, 116–117, 205n24, 233n7; Portuguese, 53–60, 61, 75, 82–83, 107, 110, 112, 163, 201–202n8, 202n9, 204n20, 205–206n24, 246n11; Spanish, 54–60, 142, 201n5, 202n8, 205n24, 218–219n3
atheism, 169
Augustine of Hippo, St., 24
Augustinians (Order of St. Augustine), 168
Autobiography, 16, 19, 46, 155, 157–158, 183–184n18, 231n2, 235n23, 248n23
Autobiography (Ignatius of Loyola), 15, 155, 157, 158, 187n33

INDEX

autonomy, 14–15, 54, 68; organizational, 102, 205
Avignon, 138, 241nn54–55

"Barbarian" peoples, 62
Barberino, Francesco de, 24
Beijing, 88, 101, 102, 106, 107
Belgium, 19, 60, 127, 180n3, 205n24. *See also* Flanders
Bellarmine, Robert, 29, 192n34
Benavere, Marco, 143
Benedictines (Order of St. Benedict), 30, 148, 195n61
Beringucci, Mario, 140
Bernardo of Kagoshima, 19
biographical documents: characteristics, 2, 5–12, 15–17, 49–50, 53, 60, 100, 114, 115–119, 125, 132, 137, 141, 147, 163, 167, 168; chronology, 11, 116; criticism in, 129, 132, 135; as distinct genre, 5, 113; for evaluation of members, 89–94, 95–97, 102–103, 118, 126–137, 143; first-person (self-narrative or ego-documents), 7, 16–17, 19, 42–51, 60–67, 88–89, 116, 137–145, 155–163, 187n35; and governance, 9, 117–118, 129, 132, 149–150, 151–155; guidelines and origins, 7, 40, 100–101, 126; historical, 12, 113, 155–157, 163–171; and Jesuit foundational texts, 2–6, 26, 40, 49, 145, 146, 155, 174–175; second-person, 116, 125–137; spiritual features, 86, 115, 117, 125, 127, 137, 142, 145, 157. *See also* catalogues; *Constitutions*; correspondence; missions
biography, 5, 155–157, 183–184n18
Bobadilla, Nicolás, 25, 124–125, 133, 179–180n2
body, 49, 141, 163, 168, 171, 183–184n18, 190n10, 233n7
Bologna, 124, 129, 132, 133, 136, 142
Bonamici, Vespasiano, 63

books, 9, 24, 25, 26, 27, 28, 30, 34, 36, 65, 83, 122, 137, 140; in China, 103–104
Borgia, Francis (Francisco de Borja), St., superior general, 38, 154
Bose, Marcantonio del, 132
Botero, Giovanni, 129
Brazil, 53, 151, 201n5, 201–202n8, 206n25, 212n64
Brescia, 25, 28, 129. *See also* Academy of Nobles
British Isles, 19, 42, 53, 167, 248n24
Broët, Paschase, 179–180n2
Buzomi, Francesco, 62, 71–72, 207n29, 221–222n18

Cafiero, Giovanni Vincenzo, 92
Cagliari, 139
Cairo, 156–157, 159, 161
Calabria, 77, 95
Camerino, Paolo Battista da, 133–134, 170, 201n6, 238n47
Canisius, Peter, 137–138, 240n52
Caravita, Pietro, Congregation of (Oratory of San Francesco Saverio "del Caravita"), 47, 198n88
Carminata, Giovanni Battista, 74
Carthusians, Order of, 35, 151. *See also* Denis the Carthusian
Carvajal y Mendoza, Luisa de, 123, 235n23
Casa, Ignazio della, 141
Casario, Carlo, 141
Castelano, Salvatore, 149
catalogues, 2, 64, 67, 75, 76, 82, 118, 125, 126–134, 136, 165
Catania, Leonardo, 152
catechism, catechize, 58, 109, 156; in Chinese language, 88; for illiterates, 156
Catholic Church, 15, 23, 24, 41, 43, 49, 71, 92, 99, 119–120, 122, 162, 170, 232n6
Cattaneo, Lazzaro, 107

Cattani, Giovanni Battista, 44
centenary, first (1640), 2, 180n3
Cesari, Ottavio, 133, 139
character, 17, 24, 54, 75, 77, 84, 96, 111, 121, 124, 127, 132, 134, 214nn77–79
Chieti, 9, 72, 134
Chile, 28, 49
China, 55; mission, missionaries, 62–65, 69, 82, 87–94, 100–105, 163, 202n9, 218nn2–3, 219n4, 229n60; views about, 103–113. *See also* Beijing; Fujian; Nanjing
Christianity, 54, 63, 71, 86, 103, 109, 112, 117, 158, 162
Christmas, 99, 110
Chronicon Societatis Iesu, 17
Cicala, Antonio, 78
Clavius, Christopher, 110
clergy, secular (diocesan), 44, 47, 54, 232n6
Cleynaerts, Nicolas, 35
clothing, 1, 24, 28–38, 65, 194–195n55, 195n56
coadjutors: occupations, 127–128; spiritual, 21–22, 96, 103, 149; temporal, 20, 21–22, 27, 29, 30, 35, 73, 75–76, 78–79, 106, 120, 127–128, 132, 141, 149, 152, 168
Cochin, 55, 56, 171, 207n29
Cochinchina, 72, 92
Codure, Jean, 179–180n2
Cogordan, Ponce, 138–139
Cohen, Thomas V., 19, 41–42, 151
Coimbra, 94, 169, 229n62, 252n56
Cola (or Nicolao), Giovanni, 110, 229n61
Colacino, Giacomo Antonio, 62
college, colleges, 20, 21, 59, 70, 81, 97, 118, 124, 128, 129, 133, 138, 139, 142, 150, 154, 161, 165; in Bologna, 129; in Cagliari, 139; in Coimbra, 169; in Loreto, 143, 154, 169; in Messina, 152; in Montepulciano, 168; in Naples, 75; in Padua, 133; in Paris, 128; in Venice, 161. *See also* Collegio Romano
Collegio Germanico, 45
Collegio Romano, 28, 47, 50, 66, 69, 91, 96, 101, 110, 112, 128, 137, 156
Cologne, 45, 47
Colombo, 55, 217n93
Comitolo, Flaminio, 129
Confalonieri, Giovanni Luigi, 110
confession, 26, 28, 56, 117, 128, 132, 135, 137, 139, 232n6
confessor, 14, 18, 32, 40, 42, 45, 72, 117, 127, 128, 129, 136, 139, 159, 196n70
congregations, Marian, 47, 77
conscience, 13, 18, 25, 26, 40, 41, 42, 50, 61, 132, 174, 196n70
consolation, 113, 115, 117, 143, 144, 164–165
Constantinople, 156
Constitutions, 5, 7, 21–22, 26, 118, 125, 174; on admission and formation, 21–27, 29, 117–118, 120–121; on departures and dismissals, 147–150, 153; and life in the Society, 118; on missions, 100, 118; on organization and governance, 100, 118, 134, 137, 147–148, 165–167; on poverty, 31–32; "union of hearts," 7, 8, 100, 134; on vocation, 39–40, 147. *See also* correspondence; *General Examen*; Ignatius of Loyola
consultation. *See* dialogue, dialogic
Contarini, Giovanni Battista, 159
Conti, Pietro, 44, 50, 65
conversion, 15, 23, 35, 38, 54, 56, 59, 63, 78, 80, 81, 93, 106, 109, 143, 155–163, 175
Coptic Church, 156, 157, 161
Corbinelli, Ludovico, 127
Cornaro, Pietro, 70–71
correspondence, 6–8, 132–145; administrative, 116–117, 132–138, 142, 144, 145; to appeal a decision, 142–143; burden of writing,

correspondence (*continued*)
101–102, 132–133, 140–142; and the *Constitutions,* 134, 145; contents, 101–105, 112–114, 134–138; to govern, 102, 132–138, 142–145; between individuals, 134–137, 139–140, 164–165, 171–172; limitations, 101–103; method, 100–101, 132–134, 137–139, 142; from the missions, 71, 95–100, 101–114, 133–136, 140, 156; as news, 110, 112–113, 134, 137; published, 113–114, 139–140; purpose, 106–114, 116–117, 134–137; value, 105, 109–114, 116–117, 134, 144. *See also* biographical documents; paper; Society of Jesus; *soli*
Corsi, Francesco, 61
Corsica, 42
Corto, Cesare, 152
Costa, Antonio da, 171
Cotta, Ottavio, 129
Counter-Reformation, 12, 14, 34–35, 157
criticism, 42, 91, 129
Croce, Giacomo, 124
Cruz, Anne J., 123
culture, material, 110, 112
Cuncolim, 145
Curione, Giulio Cesare, 80, 92
Cyprus, 156

De Angelis, Girolamo, 92
death, 11, 12, 31, 36, 100, 146–147, 149, 155, 157, 163–172; age at, 163, 166; bad, 99, 167–170; in the *Constitutions,* 165; good, 99, 170–172; in letters of Ignatius, 164–165; painful, 171–172; in the *Spiritual Exercises,* 163, 165, 172; unity of members in, 166, 172; violent, 28, 49, 88, 97, 99. *See also* martyr, martyrdom
De cultura ingeniorum. See Possevino, Antonio
De Marini, Filippo, 110–112

Denis the Carthusian, 35, 194n52. *See also* Carthusians, Order of
departure, voluntary, 23, 25, 31, 146, 148–152, 154, 170; desertions, 168–170
De Schuldthaus, Giovanni Battista, 47
désenclavement, 13
devotional literature, 34–35. *See also* books
devil, demon, 70, 122, 123, 143, 164, 165, 169
dialogue, dialogic, 8, 13, 49, 66, 69, 72, 74, 94, 100, 119–121, 125, 137, 174–175, 182n10, 183–184n18; and consultation, 60, 74, 94, 174; and negotiation, 60, 72, 74, 84–85, 94, 119–121, 123, 125, 233–234n10
discernment, 40, 61, 67, 70, 88, 93, 119, 122, 137, 155, 174
discipline, 25, 37, 199n98
dismissal, 25, 31, 73, 75, 147–155, 168–170
Ditchfield, Simon, 13
Dolf, Giovanni, 152
Doménech, Jerónimo, 25, 59, 133
Domenichi, Giacomo, 152
Dominicans (Order of Preachers), 148
dreams, 110
Dubuisson, Valentin, 31

Eck, Johann, 35
education, 11, 20, 23, 42, 43–45, 50, 64, 117, 129, 138, 150. *See also* academies; college, colleges
ego-documents. *See* biographical documents
Egypt, 156. *See also* Alexandria; Cairo
Eliano, Giovanni Battista (Elia), 155–163; letters, 156; life, 155–156; his "Vocatione," 156–163
Eliano, Vittorio (Yosef), 156, 158
emotions, history of, 185–186n27, 186–187n32

England. *See* British Isles
Erasmus, Desiderius, 35, 121, 240n52
Erma, Barnaba d', 76
Epistulae Generalium, 68-69, 74
Eschinardi, Francesco, 47
Estado da Índia (Portugal), 55, 59, 82, 99, 103. *See also* Assistancies; Indies; Portugal
Este, Ippolito II d', cardinal, 25
Eugenio, Francesco, 92
Euskirchen, Guglielmo, 45, 47
evangelization, 2, 61-63, 76, 81, 109, 117. *See also* conversion; missions
Examen de ingenios para las ciencias (Examination of Men's Wits). *See* Huarte de San Juan, Juan
execution, 63, 113

Fabii, Fabio de, 34, 90-93, 102-103, 108, 152, 193n48, 193-194n49, 221n16
Fabre, Pierre-Antoine, 12
family, Jesuits and, 18, 33, 39, 45-46, 48, 50, 64, 78, 90-91, 97-100, 112, 135, 138-139, 152, 155-163, 169, 175; circumstances of, 14, 32, 39-40, 43-45, 47, 65, 71, 78-80, 84, 90, 93, 138, 152, 169; Society of Jesus as, 72, 79, 139, 172
Favre, Pierre, St., 179-180n2
fear, 96, 98, 99, 108, 120, 148, 222n23
female. *See* gender
Fernandes, Jerónimo, 171
Ferra, Antonio della, 43, 49
Ferrarese, Enea, 149
Ferraris, Giovanni Raphael de, 1-2, 66, 128
Ferreira, Cristóvão, 110-111, 230n63
finances, 24, 126, 132, 138, 145, 150, 193n42, 201n5, 209n38; of families, 32, 40-44, 65, 78-79, 90
Fioravanti, Alessandro, 152
first companions, 2, 7, 25, 53, 59, 124, 150, 169, 179-180n2, 187n34, 190n19, 249n29

Fishery Coast (India), 133, 170-171, 216n88, 217n93
Flanders, 43, 60, 180n3, 203n16, 205n24. *See also* Belgium
Florence, Jesuit college, 64, 70, 142
Florida, 53, 201n5
Forlì, 124, 142, 154
Formula of the Institute of the Society of Jesus, 21-22, 117
Formula scribendi, 8, 126; use on the missions, 100
fourth vow, 21. *See also* grades of membership; professed members
France, 19, 41, 128-129, 151, 169-170, 181n4, 188n4, 197n82, 205n24, 213n71, 245n9. *See also* Avignon; Montmartre; Paris
Francis, pope (Jorge Mario Bergoglio), 176
Franciscans (Order of Friars Minor), 148, 150, 205n23, 217-218n1
free will, 13. *See also* agency; conscience
Freux, André des, 137, 140, 159, 161, 240n52, 249n29
Friedrich, Markus, 119
friendship, 34, 91, 108, 111-112, 134
Fróis, Luís, 113, 170
Fujian, 87

Galen, 121
Galletti, Antonio Maria, 48
Galletti, Francesco, 31
Galletti, Vincente, 82
gender, 13-14, 122-125; female, 14, 16, 123; male, 24, 27, 39, 50, 122-125
General Congregation, 118, 126, 204n20
General Examen, 22, 26-27, 30-31, 36, 40, 42-43, 47, 52, 120, 166; on missions, 52; questions for candidates, 40-41
"gentiles," 62, 104-106, 144
geography, 5, 8, 44, 53, 55, 66, 109, 114

Germany, 19, 42–43, 49, 52, 56, 156, 169, 203n16, 211n57. *See also* Collegio Germanico; Holy Roman Empire
Gerson, Jean, 35
Giannone, Antonio, 92
Giard, Luce, 12
Giuliani, Paolo, 153
Gnecchi-Soldo, Organtino, 144–145
Goa, 55–57, 61, 63–64, 75, 81, 83, 91–92, 97, 99, 105–106, 113, 134, 144–145, 150, 170–171, 195n57, 201n6. *See also* provinces
God, 15, 48, 50, 63–64, 70–71, 89, 95, 110, 115, 148, 163–164, 169; debates over Chinese terms for, 88; for the greater glory of (*Ad maiorem Dei gloriam*), 22–24, 27, 43, 47, 51, 54, 56, 61, 111, 119–122, 155, 164–165, 174; see God in all things, 13, 52, 94, 111
Gomez, Antonio, 170
Gonzaga, Francesco Maria, 29, 35–36
Goujon, Patrick, 23
grades of membership, 20–22, 29–30, 96, 103, 120, 127, 150–151, 163, 188n2. *See also* coadjutors; professed members
Gratiani, Gioan Maria, 35–36
Greco-Roman world and tradition, 62, 121, 180n3, 218n1; books from, 34–35; languages, 30, 88, 111
Guasto, Pietro Antonio del, 79–80
Gubernali, Costanzo (Costantino), 44

health: corporate, 155; physical, 2, 22–23, 43, 76–77, 90–94, 122, 132–133, 138–139, 141, 142, 149; spiritual, 77, 147, 155
Heaven, 61, 98, 112, 115
Hebrew, 77, 88, 111, 155–156
Hell, 61
heresy, 16, 35, 167, 169, 232n6
heterodoxy, 16, 187n34
hierarchy, hierarchical, 5, 9, 14–15, 23, 28, 72, 74, 81, 94, 102, 105, 119, 120, 142–143, 174–175

Hippocrates, 121
historiography, 12–17, 19, 61, 69, 87, 111, 116, 151, 156
history, 11, 12, 155, 157, 169. *See also* biographical documents
Holland, 44, 111
Holy Office, Tribunal of (Inquisition), 103, 153, 157, 215n80, 232n6
Holy Roman Empire, 53. *See also* Germany
Holy Spirit, 148. *See also* Trinity
Homer, 35
homosexuality, 154
hospital, 117, 169–170
Huarte de San Juan, Juan, 121; *Examen de ingenios para las ciencias* (*Examination of Men's Wits*), 121–122
humanism, 34, 121, 204n19, 207n30
humoral theory, 121, 132

identity: collective, 49, 61, 67, 114, 125, 151, 155, 158, 166–167; divided, 160–163; individual, 17, 37–39, 49, 50, 54, 61, 67, 114, 121–125, 128, 155–163
Ignatius of Loyola, St., 2, 6, 27, 38, 65, 118, 127, 141, 157, 171–172, 179–180n2; correspondence, 7–8, 128, 133, 137–139, 161, 164–165, 170; early life as Iñigo Lopez de Loyola, 15, 38; and governance, 14, 22–27, 31–32, 58, 118–119, 148, 151; Ignatian thought, 13, 117–125, 148, 162, 165; Ignatian Tree, 2–3, 6, 172, 176; and missions, 54, 59; and spirituality, 15, 62, 80; writings, 15, 21–23, 155, 157–158. *See also Constitutions; Spiritual Exercises*
illiteracy, 29, 76, 156, 175
incorporation. *See* Society of Jesus
India, 53, 56, 133. *See also* Cochin; Cuncolim; Fishery Coast (India); Goa; Malabar; Mughal lands; Quilón

INDEX

indiano, indiani, 52–53, 63–64, 66, 71, 73, 86–87, 97. *See also* missions
Indies, 1, 53, 60, 70, 72, 83, 85, 92, 99, 134, 149; attitudes toward, 61–63. *See also* missions
indifference, 25, 29–30, 43, 61, 65, 115, 120, 166
individual. *See* identity
Inglese, Tommaso, 127
"Ingressus Novitiorum." *See* novitiate
initiative. *See* agency
Innocenzii, Innocenzo, 46
Inquisition. *See* Holy Office
interdict, papal, of Venice, 140
interviews, 29, 39, 42, 44, 47, 49–50, 154. See also *General Examen;* novitiate; questionnaires; surveys; vocation
Ireland. *See* British Isles
Islam, 55
Italy, Italian lands, 2, 5, 6, 9, 11, 12, 19, 21, 23, 25, 34, 41, 54, 59, 65, 77, 86, 88, 91–92, 94, 105, 116, 128, 149, 151; territories ruled by Spain, 59. *See also* Assistancies; provinces; vocation
itinerant (itinerancy), 8, 52–53, 115–118, 145, 173

Japan, 19, 29, 50, 55, 61–64, 66, 67, 69, 71, 75, 80, 88, 90–92, 96, 101–103, 106, 110–111, 113, 140, 144–145, 150, 163
Jay, Claude, 179–180n2
Jerusalem, 35, 53
Jews, Jewish, 35, 43, 47, 155, 157–162, 250n34; barred from entry to the Society, 157; books against, 35; *conversos,* 121; culture, 121; Jewish background and religion, 54, 156, 158–159; New Christians, 40, 43, 54; tradition, 161. *See also* Eliano, Giovanni Battista (Elia)

Keppler, Lorenz, 169
Kircher, Athanasius, 28, 180n3

Knox, Dilwyn, 24
Kormann, Eva, 16
Kostka, Stanislaus, St., 46, 166

Laccio, Francesco, 78
Laerzio, Alberto, 81, 83, 91–92, 144–145, 216n89
Laínez, Diego, superior general, 41, 124, 133, 139, 154, 179–180n2, 242n57
Lamalle, Edmond, 116, 132
Lana Terzi, Francesco, 28
Lancillotto, Niccolò, 133, 170–172
languages, foreign, 63–64, 86–88, 94–95, 102, 105–109, 111, 138, 156
Laverna, Giovanni Battista, 80
Lazarini, Ludovico, 45–46
Lebanon, 156
letters. *See* correspondence
Levanto, Niccolò, 80, 83
Levita, Elìa, 155–158
Lisbon, 53, 57, 76, 83, 88, 92, 94–99, 105, 112, 135, 167
Litterae annuae, 113
Litterae indipetae, 32; authors, 61–67, 111; characteristics, 60–61, 67; contents, 61–67; functions, 60–61; historiography, 61, 69; and provincial reports, 74–83; replies from the superior general, 68–74. *See also* martyr, martyrdom; missionaries; missions
Lombardo, Ottavio, 83
Lombardy, 5, 25, 124, 128–129, 133, 142, 154. *See also* Milan
Longobardo, Niccolò, 75, 87, 89, 90, 93, 100–107
Lorenzi, Lutio de', 132
Loreto, 35, 127–128, 142–143, 154, 168–169, 232n6
Loyola, Martín García de, 164
Loyola y Aaroz, Magdalena de, 164
Low Countries, Netherlands. *See* Holland
Lucari, Pietro, 64–65
Lukás, Ladislaus, 23

Macao, 55, 72, 88, 92, 101–107, 111
Majo, Stefano di, 79, 84
Malabar, 81–82, 92, 144–145
Malacca, 55
Maldavsky, Aliocha, 19
male. *See* gender
Manareo, Oliviero, 169
mandarin, 88; Mandarin language, 105
Marcellus II Cervini, pope, 29
Maronites, 156
Martin, A. Lynn, 19, 151, 170
martyr, martyrdom, 15, 50, 61, 63, 64, 77, 80, 92, 97–99, 111, 123, 140, 145, 151; in the *Litterae indipetae*, 63, 66, 69
Marzaro, Antonio, 132
Mascardi, Nicolò, 27, 48
Maselli, Ludovico, 101, 109
Massario, Giovanni Pietro, 149
Mastrilli, Marcello, 64, 77
Mastrilli, Nicola, 63–64, 66, 77
mathematics, 106, 110, 127
Mazancourt, Joseph de, 35
Medaglia, Giovanni, 75
meditation, 7–8, 62, 70, 164, 174
Mediterranean, region, 155–163, 248n24. *See also* Eliano, Giovanni Battista (Elia)
Mercurian, Everard, superior general, 55, 57–59, 95, 134
Messina, 9, 20, 48, 150, 152. *See also* college, colleges
Micalopoli, Luca, 150
Micheli, Antonio, 24
Milan, 59, 75, 80, 82, 83, 88, 90, 92, 101, 111–112, 129, 143
Minadois, Giulio, 135
Minadois, Pietro Antonio, 135
ministry, ministries. *See* Society of Jesus
misogyny, 123
missionaries: attributes of, 54–60, 70, 89–94; ideal, 80, 83–84; impediments to selection, 70–71, 73–80, 95–97, 141; Italian, 57–60, 82, 106; numbers, 53, 58–59, 67, 75–76, 82, 84–85, 87, 92, 106, 150–151; petitions to become, 53, 60–67, 68, 70–72, 88–89, 111; provenance, 54–60, 82; selection, 61, 63–64, 67, 71–73, 78, 80–83, 87–94; tensions between, 57, 88, 103
missions: in the Americas, 54, 72; arrival in, 99–100; in Asia, 33, 53–60; in Europe, 65; governance of, 66, 101–105; journey to, 58; methods, 57–60, 109–110; organization, 54–60, 69, 73, 84; popular, 77; reports about candidates for, 74–83, 85, 89–94; spiritual understanding of, 61–63, 66, 69, 73, 78, 84–85, 86, 99, 109, 111–114; vocations to, 43, 61, 73, 84, 92, 141; works, 56, 106–113, 116
modernity, 16, 121–122
Mogorr. *See* Mughal lands
Moleti, Benedetto, 76
Monclaro, Francesco (Francisco de Monclaro), 83
Monfellino, Giovanni Andrea, 150
Montmartre, 53
Monumenta Missionum Societatis Iesu, 156
Moraga, Giovanni di, 27, 31, 34
Mostaccio, Silvia, 119
Mozambique, 97, 113, 134–135, 170
Mughal lands, mission to, 71, 145
music, 45, 108–109
Mutio, Agostino, 129
mystic, mystical, 15, 62–63, 120

Nadal, Jerónimo, 26, 41, 151, 179–180n2
Nanjing, 88, 103
Naples, 5, 35, 59, 62–64, 69, 73–75, 77, 79–80, 83, 89–91, 93, 97, 132, 134–136, 140, 142, 152, 168. *See also* provinces
Nappi, Filippo, 139–140

Narni, 140
necrologies ("Defuncti"), 165–166
negotiation. *See* dialogue, dialogic
neighbor, help of, 43, 51–52, 62, 65, 81, 90, 115, 122, 165. *See also* souls, help of
New Society, 12, 60. *See also* Restoration
Nobili, Roberto de', 75, 92
Novellara, 25
novice masters, 75, 80–81, 91, 108
novices, 20; attributes, 22–25; and families, 32–33, 42; former Jesuit college students, 150; possessions on entry, 28–31, 33–38, 166; already priests, 29, 46; provenance, 19, 35, 42; social and family background, 33–34, 35, 38, 40, 43–48, 64; widowers, 44. See also *Constitutions; General Examen;* novitiate; S. Andrea al Quirinale; vocation
novitiate, 1, 20–21, 24–25, 60; admission to ("Ingressus Novitiorum"), 18–19, 27–39; age on entry, 23, 27, 28, 43; candidates to, 22–27, 64–65, 166; criteria for admittance and exclusion, 22–27, 150; departures and dismissals, 25, 27, 30–31, 150; education on entry, 22, 27, 43–50, 150; numbers, 23; occupation on entry, 40, 43–44, 64, 78; renunciation of goods and property, 26, 30–33, 38; and the *Spiritual Exercises,* 26, 27. See also *Constitutions; General Examen;* novices; S. Andrea al Quirinale; vocation

obedience, 12, 49, 84, 118–121, 140, 157, 162; negotiated, 119–121
Oliva, Giovanni Paolo, superior general, 112
O'Malley, John W., 19
Orientalism, 62–63, 111; "Catholic orientalism," 62–63; "spiritual orientalism," 62

Orsi, Giovanni Battista d', 73–74
Orsino, Giulio, 69, 70
Ory, Matthieu, 35
Ottolini, Paolo, 44, 48
Ottoman lands, 60, 62, 65. *See also* Turkey
"ours" (or "we Jesuits"), 81, 100, 103, 167

Padroado. See Portugal
Padua, 124, 133
painting, painters, 27, 30, 34, 62, 64, 110, 127, 147
Paleotti, Gabriele, cardinal, 129
Palermo, 75, 78, 80–81, 92, 152
Palermo, Giovanni, 77
Palestine, 156
Palliola, Francesco, 97–100
Palmio, Bendetto, 124, 133, 142, 154, 166
Palmio, Francesco, 124, 129, 136
Pantoja, Diego, 103, 108
papacy, 23, 58, 82, 129
Papal States, 140
paper, 174; walls metaphor, 6, 113, 116–117, 145, 174
Paraguay, 64, 83, 89
Paris, 52, 128, 179–180n2. *See also* Montmartre
Parma, 9, 70, 89, 128, 143
Pascual, Inés, 164
Passiu, Giorgio, 139
Paul, St., 13, 156
Pavone, Francesco, 63–64, 75–77, 140
Persico, Clemente, 132
Peru, 19, 64, 77, 88, 106, 201n5
Perugia, 142
petitions. *See* biographical documents; correspondence; missions
Petrucci, Alessandro, 141
Philippines, 54, 72, 97–98, 201n5
physical attributes, 1, 22–24, 50, 55, 76–77, 122–123, 141, 150, 165. *See also* health

physiology, 122. *See also* physical attributes
Picciolo, Giovanni Battista, 142
Piccolomini, Francesco, superior general, 48
Pichi, Girolamo, 48
Piedmont, 1, 129
Plato, 35
Polanco, Juan Alfonso de, 8, 17, 21, 127, 133, 136-137, 142, 171, 179-180n2
Poretta, Antonio, 33
Portugal, 19, 41, 53-55, 57-58, 61, 94, 96, 106, 170; criticism of, 103; missionaries, 102-103; its overseas missions, 53-60, 92, 99, 102-103, 106, 134, 149, 170-171, 201nn4-6. *See also* Assistancies; Coimbra; Lisbon
Possevino, Antonio, 97, 134-135, 158; and his *De cultura ingeniorum,* 122
prayer, 7, 13, 15, 23, 25, 56, 65, 71, 78, 80, 98-99, 120, 143, 166-167, 174
preachers, preaching, 48, 62, 76-77, 80, 117, 121, 124, 129, 132, 136-137
Presser, Jacob, 16
prison, prisoners, 117, 139, 167-168
probation, 1, 23, 26-27, 30, 32, 40-41, 102, 118, 128
procurators, 65, 67, 72, 83, 91-92, 96, 135; role in missionary appointments, 72, 83, 89-91
professed house (*casa professa*), 20, 78, 118, 127, 167
professed members, 20-21, 72, 76, 79, 103, 106, 120, 123, 127, 149, 167
property, 37; renunciation of, 26, 30-33, 38
prosopography, 5, 181n5
Prosperi, Adriano, 19
Protestant lands, Protestantism, 12, 14, 35, 43-44, 49, 157
provinces, 68, 69, 73, 75, 81-82, 84; in Italy, 5-6, 8-9, 54, 59, 68, 74-82, 84, 87, 91, 116-118

provincials, 124, 126, 133, 137, 140-143, 144, 152, 154, 165; and catalogues, 118, 125-133; office of, 21, 118; resistance to mission appointments, 66, 81-82; role in mission appointments, 56, 73-83. *See also* correspondence; Society of Jesus
psychology, 21, 24, 50, 121, 145, 165
Puccio, Cosimo, 25
Puerio, Girolamo, 72-73
punishment, 148, 152-153

quadrimestri letters, 139
questionnaires, 1, 11, 40-48, 52, 64-65, 84, 151. See also *General Examen;* interviews; surveys; vocation
Quilón, 170-171

Ragusa (Dubrovnik), 64
rectors, 24, 46, 64, 72-75, 89, 91, 118, 128, 133, 139, 142-143, 152, 154, 169
Reformation, 12, 14, 35, 43-44, 49, 153, 157; books on, 34-35
Rejadell, Teresa, 164
relatives. *See* family, Jesuits and
religious orders, compared with the Society of Jesus, 20, 54, 116-117, 148, 149, 169, 205n23, 232n6
Renaissance: Christian humanism, 24; culture and tradition, 34-35, 105, 172; in Italy, 5, 167, 176; in Spain, 121, 234n17. *See also* humanism
Restoration, 12, 60, 180-181n3
Retava, Agostino, 78
Rho, Giacomo, 207n30
Rho, Giovanni, 62, 207n30
Ribadeneira, Pedro de, 169
Ribera, Juan Bautista de, 113, 134-135, 239n49
Ricci, Bartolomeo, 71, 76, 80, 89, 93
Ricci, Matteo, 87-88, 101-110
Richardson, Catherine, 37

Rodrigues, Simão, 179-180n2
Romano, Antonella, 12, 119
Rome, 1-2, 5-6, 9, 18-20, 28, 34, 35, 38, 46-48, 50, 59, 65, 70, 75, 82-83, 91-92, 105, 109, 114, 126, 128, 135, 149, 153-154, 167, 169; and missions, 56-60. *See also* Archivum Romanum Societatis Iesu (ARSI); Assistancies; catalogues; Collegio Germanico; Collegio Romano; correspondence; Italy, Italian lands; novitiate; provinces; S. Andrea al Quirinale; Society of Jesus; superior general
Rossi, Angelo, 208n33
Rossi, Giovanni Cola, 168
Rossignoli, Bernardo, 75
Rubiola, Girolamo, 141
Ruggieri, Michele, 64, 83, 87
Rustici, Tommaso, 46

Sacco, Giovanni Alfonso, 79
Said, Edward W., 111
Salmeròn, Alfonso, 59, 150, 179-180n2
Salter, Elisabeth, 36-37
Saluzzo, Giovanni Luigi, 27, 44
salvation, 47, 62, 86, 98, 115, 164, 178
Sambiasi, Francesco, 75, 87-89, 95, 105-106
Sambiasi, Giovanni Andrea, 88
S. Andrea al Quirinale, 6, 18-21, 28, 34-35, 39-40, 42, 45-46, 52, 64, 91, 108, 128, 141, 166. *See also* novices; novitiate; vocation
Sardegna, 139
Sassone, Cristiano, 169
Savonarola, Girolamo, 35
Scalpiccia, Giovanni Giorgio, 150
Scaravellini, Giacomo Antonio, 45
Scharp, William (Guglielmo), 35
Schulze, Winfried, 16
schools. *See* academies; college, colleges; education
Scotland. *See* British Isles
Scriptures, 159, 161; books on, 34-35

secretary (of the superior general and of the Society), 8, 17, 21, 97, 134, 137, 142, 171
self-narrative documents. *See* biographical documents
Sementi, Donato, 68
Senas, Giovanni Bruneo de, 35
shipwrecks, 65, 98, 156, 158
Sicily, 5, 25, 59, 76, 81, 89, 93, 96, 124, 152-153, 168. *See also* Messina; Palermo; provinces; provincials
Siena, 141
Silvestro, don (preacher in Bologna), 136
sin, 24, 42, 46-47, 148, 163-164
Sirino, Girolamo, 35
soave, soavemente (sweet or kind), 138, 143, 148. *See also* accommodation
social background or rank, 23-24, 38, 41, 43, 64, 68, 78-80, 122-125, 140, 159-160. *See also* family; novices; vocation
Society of Jesus: appeal, 17, 21, 38, 39, 50, 67-68, 141, 160; common life, 2, 11, 49; departure from, 147-155; dispersal, 7-8, 53, 117; embodied, 94, 145; failures and problems, 140, 142-145, 146-149, 152-155, 172; formation, 20-21; foundational texts, 2, 5, 40, 49, 137, 146, 174; global, 8, 53, 122; government, 2, 7, 9, 25, 34, 55-60, 102, 118, 124-125, 133, 140, 137-145; identity, 13, 52-53, 151, 158; incorporation into, 20-21, 117-118, 121, 136, 147, 165, 176, 233n7; individual members, 9, 11, 22-24, 118, 122, 125-137, 145; as institute of clerks regular, 7, 36; itinerant, 8, 115-118; life expectancy, 163; life outside of, 19-20, 44-49, 68, 72, 123-124, 151-152, 168-170; life writings, 155-156; literary writings, 122; lived experience, 6, 50, 87, 118, 137-145, 155;

Society of Jesus (*continued*)
local, 9; members' provenance, 19, 127, 132, 151, 156–163; ministries, 117, 126–138, 140, 150–151; national identity in, 102, 151; numbers, 6, 17, 21, 126, 149, 150–151; organization, 2, 7, 53, 116–118, 132, 145; overwork, 132–133, 137, 140–141; papal ratification, 5, 7, 21, 53; and politics, 12, 103, 106, 129, 140, 158; progress in, 118–122; retention and changing of birth name, 37, 143, 154; structure, 7, 9, 117–118; unity, 7–8, 53, 67, 100, 105, 146–147, 154–155, 167, 172; universal, 9, 55

soli, 81, 102, 142–145, 153–154, 231–232n4, 226n45; from Asia, 144

souls, help of, 43–44, 51–52, 62, 78, 88, 115, 117, 139, 147, 155, 173. *See also* neighbor, help of

Spain, 19, 41, 54–55, 57–59, 77, 96, 153, 169; dissent from, 55, 59; its empire, 55; and overseas missions, 57–60, 145. *See also* Assistancies; Italy, Italian lands; Renaissance

Spiga, Pietro, 139

Spinelli, Luca, 168

Spinello, Antonio, 83

Spinola, Carlo, 80

Spinola, Uberto, 44, 45

Spira, Pietro, 106

spiritual attributes of members, 15–16, 21–24, 41, 43, 46–47, 68, 71–73, 75–81, 84, 87–90, 93–94, 97, 99, 111, 115–120, 123, 137, 144, 148, 150, 160, 164–165, 172, 175. *See also* biographical documents; correspondence; health; Ignatius of Loyola; missions; *Spiritual Exercises*; spirituality

Spiritual Diary, 15, 187n33. *See also* Ignatius of Loyola

Spiritual Exercises, 6–8, 13–15, 26–27, 49, 61–62, 70, 80, 94, 99, 111, 114–115, 119, 122–123, 125, 137, 145, 155, 163, 165, 167, 172, 174, 181–182n9. *See also* Ignatius of Loyola; Society of Jesus; spirituality

spirituality, 13, 115, 117, 118; apostolic, 117, 151; embodied, 86, 115, 117, 145; in the world, 151. *See also* biographical documents; correspondence; Orientalism; spiritual attributes of members; *Spiritual Exercises*

Spoleto, 132

Squadrini, Mario, 36, 64, 78, 93

Stock, Brian, 16, 174

Sulyok, Francesco, 35

superior general, 1, 5, 38, 41, 46, 48, 116, 118, 124–126, 132–133; correspondence from and to, 6, 8, 52–53, 60–74, 101–105, 107–108, 118–119, 124, 132–134, 136–145, 169; as father figure, 72, 139, 144; oversight of missions, 34, 54–60, 61, 66, 68–74, 80–84, 88–95. *See also* biographical documents; *Constitutions*; correspondence; Ignatius of Loyola; Society of Jesus

superiors, 8, 12, 26, 29, 41, 46, 66–67, 71–73, 82, 84, 94, 97, 103, 107, 109, 111, 120, 123–124, 126, 134, 168–169, 196n71, 198n95. *See also* biographical documents; *Constitutions*; correspondence; Ignatius of Loyola; missions; Society of Jesus

Suppression, 2, 6, 9, 55–56, 60, 176, 180–181n3, 245n9

surveys, 41–43, 47, 65, 151. *See also* interviews; questionnaires

talent and ability, 22–24, 51, 89–90, 121–125

Taraninfa, Gasparo, 80

temptation, 25, 45–47, 49, 70, 119, 149, 152, 164, 168–169

Tezzoni, Francesco, 75

theology, 77, 122, 127; studies in, 21, 75, 82, 92, 128–129, 138, 206n26

Tonkin. *See* Vietnam, northern (Tonkin)
Torniello, Carlo, 101, 111–112
Torres, Diego de, 89
Torres, Francesco, 127
transgression, 152–155, 167–170. *See also* sin; temptation
Transylvania, 35
travel, 65, 94–100, 141, 155–156; Jesuit ministry during, 95; literature about, 56–57
tree, 2–4, 99, 172; Ignatian (*see* Ignatius of Loyola)
Trinity, 13, 110
Turin, 140
Turkey, 65, 69
Turri, Benedetto, 68, 82–83
Turrini, Miriam, 16, 19, 49, 151
Tyrol, 47

Ursis, Sabatino de, 87–93, 106–111

Vagnone, Alfonso, 80, 82, 87–92, 101–103, 107, 111–112
Valignano, Alessandro, 33–34, 56–58, 62–63, 66, 77, 88, 91–102, 107, 112–113, 125, 134–135, 144–145
Vallareggio, Alessandro, 135
Vallone, Bartolomeo, 96–97
Vannuzo, Camillo, 34
Venice, 126, 140, 154–156, 159–161
Vergilio, Ignatio, 168
Vico, Cesare de, 132
Vieira, Francisco, 91
Vienna, 137
Vietnam, northern (Tonkin), 110
Villa, Giovanni di Polo da, 34
"vineyard," 8, 53, 67, 109, 118, 133, 171
Viola, Giovanni Battista, 128
Vipera, Francesco, 95–96
visitor, 25, 33–34, 56, 59, 66, 77, 88, 91, 95, 97, 100, 102–103, 125, 134, 145

Vitelleschi, Muzio, superior general, 34, 46, 60, 140, 143
Vitae, 155–163, 168
vocation, 18–19, 115–116; family protests against, 48–50, 67, 135–136, 158–163; genuineness of, 33, 136; from Italy, 6, 19; motivations and origins, 24, 43, 45, 47–50, 73, 84, 150, 151; obstacles to, 43–50, 65, 142, 147–150; outside the Society, 41, 48–49, 154; prose statements ("Vocationi"), 47–51; questionnaires ("Vocationi"), 18–19, 42–47, 49–51, 84; to the Society, 38; in the *Vitae,* 155. See also *Constitutions; General Examen;* missions; novices; novitiate; questionnaires; S. Andrea al Quirinale
"Vocatione" (Giovanni Battista Eliano), 156–163
Vocationes Illustres, 156–158
"Vocationi." *See* novices; novitiate; questionnaires; S. Andrea al Quirinale; vocation
vows. *See* coadjutors; fourth vow; grades of membership; professed members

"way of proceeding," 7, 57–58, 74, 80, 148
Weibel, Domenico, 44, 49
wills (last testaments), 36–37
Wisenbach, Franz (Francesco), 35
women, 13–14, 96, 122–124, 163–164. *See also* gender
writing, 6, 167; ability among candidates, 29, 35

Xavier, Francis, St., 46–47, 54–56, 62, 70, 76–77, 134, 170, 179–180n2

Zara, Antonio, *Anatomia ingegnorum,* 122
Zumbo, Antonio, 81–82, 92